CW01081349

DESERTED WIVES AND ECONOMIC DIVORCE IN 19TH-CENTURY ENGLAND AND WALES

This book considers Section 21 of the Divorce and Matrimonial Causes Act 1857 and their significant impact on previously invisible married women in the 19th Century.

Tens of thousands of women used this little-known section of the Act to apply for orders from local magistrates' courts to reclaim their rights of testation, inheritance, property ownership, and (dependent on local franchise qualifications) ability to vote. By examining the orders which were made and considering the women who applied for them, the book challenges the mistaken belief that Victorian England and Wales were nations of married, cohabiting couples.

The detailed statistical analysis and rich case studies presented here provide a totally new perspective on the legal status and experiences of married women in England and Wales. Although many thousands of orders were granted between 1858 and 1900, their details remain unknown and unexamined, primarily because census records did not consistently record dissolved marriages and there is no central index of applications made.

Using sources including court records, parliamentary papers, newspaper reports, census returns, probate records and trade directories, this book reconstructs the successful – and unsuccessful – experiences of women applying to magistrates' courts and the Court for Divorce and Matrimonial Causes to protect their assets across regions and decades.

Deserted Wives and Economic Divorce in 19th-Century England and Wales

'For Wives Alone'

Jennifer Aston
and
Olive Anderson

·HART·

OXFORD · LONDON · NEW YORK · NEW DELHI · SYDNEY

HART PUBLISHING

Bloomsbury Publishing Plc

Kemp House, Chawley Park, Cumnor Hill, Oxford, OX2 9PH, UK

1385 Broadway, New York, NY 10018, USA

29 Earlsfort Terrace, Dublin 2, Ireland

HART PUBLISHING, the Hart/Stag logo, BLOOMSBURY and the Diana logo are
trademarks of Bloomsbury Publishing Plc

First published in Great Britain 2024

Copyright © Jennifer Aston and Olive Anderson, 2024

Jennifer Aston and Olive Anderson have asserted their right under the Copyright, Designs and Patents
Act 1988 to be identified as Authors of this work.

All rights reserved. No part of this publication may be reproduced or transmitted in any form or by any
means, electronic or mechanical, including photocopying, recording, or any information storage
or retrieval system, without prior permission in writing from the publishers.

While every care has been taken to ensure the accuracy of this work, no responsibility for
loss or damage occasioned to any person acting or refraining from action as a result of any
statement in it can be accepted by the authors, editors or publishers.

All UK Government legislation and other public sector information used in the work is
Crown Copyright ©. All House of Lords and House of Commons information used in
the work is Parliamentary Copyright ©. This information is reused under the terms
of the Open Government Licence v3.0 (http://www.nationalarchives.gov.uk/doc/
open-government-licence/version/3) except where otherwise stated.

All Eur-lex material used in the work is © European Union,
http://eur-lex.europa.eu/, 1998–2024.

A catalogue record for this book is available from the British Library.

A catalogue record for this book is available from the Library of Congress.

Library of Congress Control Number: 2024944198

ISBN: HB: 978-1-50997-060-5
       ePDF: 978-1-50997-062-9
       ePub: 978-1-50997-061-2

Typeset by Compuscript Ltd, Shannon

To find out more about our authors and books visit www.hartpublishing.co.uk.
Here you will find extracts, author information, details of forthcoming events
and the option to sign up for our newsletters.

FOREWORD: *FOR WIVES ALONE* –
OUR UNUSUAL MOTHER
AND THE ORIGINS OF THIS BOOK

Figure F.1 Professor Olive Anderson
Image courtesy of the Anderson family.

When we think of our mother Olive Anderson, we see her in her study. This was a large, bay-windowed room at the front of the house, which was flooded with light in the mornings. There colourful birds of paradise swooped across the wallpaper, books balanced on rickety bookshelves, and two huge Chinese bergère chairs invited a small child to snuggle down and feel warm and safe. Above all, though, there was the magnificent bespoke desk which ran the whole length of one wall. Every inch was covered with files and documents which cascaded down to balance on the wastepaper basket. Only a tiny patch, the size of a laptop, was free and it was there that Olive wrote, as if she were fighting against the overwhelming encroachments of paper. And it was in that room, after Olive's death on New Year's Eve 2015, that we found three rather tatty ring binders labelled Part One, Part Two, Part Three full of typescript. We knew that she had been working on a book in the 1990s but had abandoned it when caring for our father made increasing demands on her time and above all emotional energy. It is this typescript which forms the core of *For Wives Alone*.

Who was our mother? A conventional *Who's Who* entry would read something like:

> Olive was born in 1926. In 1944 she was awarded a scholarship by St Hugh's College, Oxford to study History, graduated in 1947 and completed her BLitt in 1949. In 1950 she was appointed to an assistant lectureship at London University's Westfield College (now Queen Mary University of London) where she rose to become Professor of History and Honorary Research Fellow before her retirement in 1991. In 1954 she married Matthew Anderson, later Professor of International History at the London School of Economics. She had two daughters, Rachel and Harriet.

This we knew when she was alive. However, Olive rarely talked about her work, her difficult childhood, and the many challenges she faced to create the life she wanted. We knew these were key to understanding her, but they were private, mysterious. We didn't know how to probe but at the same time we wanted to know more. We sensed she was an unusual mother even while we took the way we lived for granted, as children do.

How did she come to write *For Wives Alone*? Although unfinished, this final book completely fits into Olive's body of work and development as a scholar. What links all her research interests is not the subject matter but her approach. She always sought to explore new ways of thinking about history and often trespassed into other disciplines such as the social sciences. Most of all, her interests lay with studying groups of people not then part of the historical mainstream.

As she herself said in a note written in 1995, when referring to her previous research interests and her work in the 1960s on the adoption of the New Ways of History at Westfield, 'Above all the "New Ways" fitted in with my own research. My old habit of occupying patches of terra incognita rather than the main historical highways was now increasingly seen as leading to fresh vistas and useful trespassing …'. Highly unusually for a woman in the late 1940s she first chose to focus on military history, at that time firmly a male preserve. Unlike most of her colleagues, she chose not to understand war in terms of campaigns. Instead, she looked at the significance for British politics of the treatment of prisoners of war captured during the American War of Independence.

Following on from this, her interests widened out into how fighting abroad impacts on government and above all economics at home. This led to research into England during the Crimean War and the publication of her first book *A Liberal State at War: English Politics and Economics during the Crimean War* (Macmillan, 1967). There she challenged the prevailing view of that war as a 'petty and futile episode, memorable chiefly as a field-day for eccentric aristocrats and incompetent officials' (as the dust jacket has it) and instead revealed the Crimean War to be Europe's first object lesson in the challenge war presents to a state committed to political and economic liberalism. This early work led to her often being referred to as a military historian, but she never understood herself to be one.

Her next areas of research had nothing to do with the military: the development of joint stock companies; the role of women preachers; the incidence of civil marriage; emigration and marriage break-up; correlations (or not) between suicide and industrialisation, to name just a few. As her research interests ranged widely, she published in a wide range of academic journals, and was happy to find platforms outside the historical mainstream. Olive was a researcher through and through. She was happiest when in an archive. All this meant we never knew what to say – as children or adults – when people asked us what our mother's 'special-ism' was. We would often say 'Victorian England' but knew this wasn't quite right, it was just the simplest way to end the discussion.

Olive's second book, *Suicide in Victorian and Edwardian England* (Oxford University Press, 1987), highlights the impossibility of pigeon-holing her work. The book is devoted to 'retrieving in depth the personal experiences of suicide of completely ordinary people'. She allows those ordinary people to express in their own words something of the texture of this aspect of Victorian and Edwardian life and gives the reader moving insight into how they thought and felt. She then investigates changing attitudes to suicide and closes with how Victorians and Edwardians sought to prevent it.

This is an immensely wide-ranging book. It offered new perspectives on the significance of time, place, age, gender; on law, literature, medicine, and collective mentalities; and on the police, philanthropy, and public policy. Unlike *A Liberal State at War*, this was a book she felt was appreciated and understood; we always felt this was her 'real book', the one she was proud of. Olive was particularly pleased, as a champion of porous boundaries between the disciplines, to address the Psychiatric Section of the Royal Society of Medicine in 1988 on 'Prevention of suicide and para-suicide: what can we learn from history?'.

From there it was a small step to research into the legal world. Olive herself described it in her note of 1995 as:

> Currently my forays into the legal world are revealing geological strata even more complex and tantalising than those I reported on in November 1992 in my James Ford Special Lecture on the Victorian origins of modern English family law – but this piece of rescue archaeology is being kept firmly within bounds.

These forays are the origin of *For Wives Alone*. But nothing was kept within bounds when Olive got really interested. Hence 10 years later she had managed to fill the three ring-binders of typescript we found in her study.

What shines out in all her work is the immensely humane way she wrote about the people who were the subjects of her studies. In many cases she gave a voice to those long forgotten, those who had never had a voice while they lived: the poor, the mad, the desperate, the misfits. Olive was interested in people who led quietly unconventional lives and how society perceived and treated them. She felt a special affinity to women on the fringes, those who managed to go their own way despite the odds: women preachers, deserted women, women who wanted to marry outside the church. For this was Olive's own story. She, too, led a quietly unconventional life.

Immersing herself in archives was her means of escape from a world where she often felt a misfit. It is as if she could connect with the dead with an ease which eluded her with the living. She was also driven by a quasi-religious belief in history and a furious passion for her subject. These three aspects – feeling to be a misfit, needing to escape, and a deep belief in history – have their roots in Olive's unusual childhood.

As we cleared the magnificent bespoke desk in her study, we found three pages of rough handwritten notes dated 25 January 2010 with Olive's observations on her life between 27 March 1926 (her date of birth) to January 1933 when her father became Principal of the Women's Missionary Training College associated with the Assemblies of God (an international Pentecostal denomination) based in Louth, Lincolnshire. She starts by posing the question:

> How far does OA's early childhood in Edinburgh bear out the belief that the years before a child's seventh birthday settle its fundamental characteristics – i.e. mould its personality (cf the Jesuit adage, give us a child for its first 7 yrs)?

The note is distressing for us to read (she stopped after only three pages as it was so upsetting for her to write) but it's clear she felt the answer is 'a very great deal'. The trauma of her first years was a critical factor in determining who she became.

Her father, Donald Gee, was a revered Pentecostal minister who, with Olive's mother Ruth, spent long periods away in China, southern Africa, the Congo, Australia, the United States, and the Pacific to preach and support Pentecostal missions. Their three children stayed in the United Kingdom. Before 1933, there was no settled place the children could stay. With great pain Olive would describe to us how she was 'dumped' (Olive's word) with different believers, charged to look after her. Her much older siblings were 'dumped' elsewhere. An excerpt (underlining is hers):

> More significant, though – the inner compulsion to <u>escape from strange people and surroundings</u>. This, I think, was the really important trait instilled by what happened to me, aged 2 to 5, when I was taken at least 3 times to an unfamiliar household and left there for some months, 'to be collected' later, when my parents returned from some foreign trip.

After 1933 (at which point she is seven years old and her short note ends) Olive lived with her mother at the Women's Missionary Training College; her father began a second stage of continual international travel. Though no longer 'dumped', Olive was growing up in a spiritual community which separated itself off from the world outside Pentecostalism. Despite being surrounded by her father's followers, it was an immensely lonely childhood. Her brother and sister found a way to leave as soon as possible. Due to a combination of ill health, parental disinterest (Olive writes 'I didn't see much of my mother until 1940–42') and Olive's resistance, Olive had almost no contact with other children and no formal schooling until her teens. Books were her great comfort. A voracious reader from a very early age and abandoned to her own devices, she could follow her own intellectual impulses without regard to others' sensibilities or interference.

King Edward VI Girls School in Louth gave Olive her first formal schooling and recognised her immense intellectual talent. The school arranged Latin tuition specially for her so she could apply to Oxford and in 1944 she won a place to read Modern History at St Hugh's College, Oxford. She often told us with glee how the school gave everyone a day's holiday to mark the first pupil to go from the school to Oxford.

But how to finance her studies? The family was not well-off. An excerpt from a note written by Olive in the 1990s when commenting on a biography of her father:

> I knew only comparative family affluence; while she [Wendy, her sister] and David [her brother] in the early 20s knew real privation (my mother being obliged to share ONE boiled egg between her two children – something I have never forgotten), and literally sometimes not knowing where the next meal would come from. 'The Lord will provide', but sometimes did so only at the very last moment.

The way she financed her studies was to 'live off her wits', as she often told us with quiet pride. And by her wits she meant her academic brilliance in winning scholarships and prizes. The resulting fear of financial precarity and deep belief in the importance of financial independence never left her.

In the bottom drawer of her desk, we found a small manila envelope marked 'Scholarships & Awards 1944–49', another marked 'Examination Papers' (with every exam paper she sat from the School Certificate in 1942 to History Finals in 1947) and another marked 'Testimonial Originals'. Olive kept everything. The slips of paper confirming awards include a hugely valuable and competitive Ministry of Education State Scholarship for five years of her study (a scholarship she never mentioned to us though it must have been a source of pride for her), together with Local Education Authority and St Hugh's scholarships plus smaller scholarships and prizes along the way. She applied for everything going.

The testimonials are moving. Partly for the pride we feel in reading of our mother's academic abilities but more for the sadness in how, by their variety and number, they show the great difficulty she had in finding the sort of job she wanted on completing her BLitt in 1949. All she could get was a history teaching post at a grammar school in Coalville, a Midlands town. The stroke of luck that changed her life was in 1950 when May McKisack, Professor of History at London University's Westfield College, contacted her. (Olive never forgot this and as children, we knew that May McKisack was somehow wonderful and hugely important to Olive but never understood quite why.) May had first encountered Olive at Oxford and been deeply impressed by her. An assistant lectureship came up at Westfield in 1950, May thought of Olive and encouraged her to apply. Olive was offered the job. She had got her foothold in academia.

The second stroke of luck was to meet and marry our father, Matthew Anderson. Matthew was later Professor of International History at the London School of Economics and a serious collector of antiquarian books on pre-revolutionary Russia. (His collection is now housed in the Special Collections Department of the Senate House Library, University of London.) Although a historian of a very different kind, he always recognised and affirmed Olive's identity as an academic and understood how important the life of the mind was to her. When they married in July 1954, his wedding present to her was life membership of the London Library.

Olive always recognised her good fortune. But at the same time, she did feel the weight of the double burden: to manage family and domestic life, and to live her life as an academic. She liked to do well at anything she turned her hand to and applied her great intelligence to domestic matters. She taught herself to cook cordon bleu meals; she sewed dresses for her young daughters out of Liberty remnants and lined them with men's cotton handkerchiefs; she baked fluffy Victoria sponge cakes; she made Christmas tree decorations out of drinking straws. Once her children were at primary school there was no outside home help – Olive felt it would disturb her writing – so we all took part in a weekly Sunday morning house cleaning routine. At the same time, she was teaching, researching, and writing. She was very aware of how structures, familial and professional, were weighted against her and women like her. She was aware of how she did not and could not fit the norms of wife, mother, and academic, however hard she tried. That she could have young children and pursue a career raised a few eyebrows of fellow (also female) academics as well as of other mothers.

But she pulled it off. She managed to combine family life with being a leading researcher and inspiring university teacher. In 1992, she was invited by Oxford University to deliver a James Ford Special Lecture. She chose to lecture on the Victorian origins of modern English family law (unsurprisingly, as she was researching *For Wives Alone* at the time). She considered this to be one of the greatest honours the University could bestow on a historian and was something she occasionally referred to for the rest of her life.

After Matthew died in 2006, when it was possible for her to return to writing *For Wives Alone*, she chose not to. She no longer had the energy for a larger piece of research, was no longer able to reach the archives and libraries that she knew so well, and although she appreciated the great benefits that digitalisation could bring the researcher, it was a step too far to adjust to such a different way of working. In her final years, although her interest in the past remained undimmed, she instead chose to write small vignettes on local features that caught her interest. A walk down the street where she lived might well include impromptu musings on, for example, the use of the sunburst motif in 1930s suburban housing.

It was a wonderful moment when Jennifer contacted us. We are immensely grateful to her. Jennifer has always sought to 'keep faith' with Olive and – in this rather unusual way – be a joint-author with Olive. Thank you, Jennifer, for all you have done to bring *For Wives Alone* to publication, perhaps the work which connects most with Olive's own life.

Olive believed strongly that the ability of women, including married women, to achieve financial independence matters. It matters socially, it matters politically, and it mattered to her personally. Even at the end of her life it mattered to her that we acknowledged that she had earned every penny herself through her own efforts and talents, that we recognised her immense achievement of having created the life she had in the face of considerable obstacles. *For Wives Alone* is a testament to that belief as well as a testament to the women who, like Olive, despite all the difficulties put in their way, managed to find cracks in the existing order of things in which they could flourish.

Rachel & Harriet Anderson
Spring 2024

ACKNOWLEDGEMENTS

I have been fortunate to become indebted to a number of individuals and organisations over the past three years and although I can never repay these kindnesses, it is my enormous pleasure to at least be able to acknowledge them here. First, I would like to thank Kate Whetter and her team at Hart Publishing for receiving *For Wives Alone* so enthusiastically, and for supporting the project every step of the way. We couldn't have found a better publishing home for this book.

Perhaps unusually in academic writing, the journey from ring-binders of typescript to published book has been far from solitary. Receiving one of the first Royal Historical Society Funded Book Workshop Grants in 2023 allowed me to spend a day with six wonderful scholars from the worlds of feminist legal scholarship and economic, legal, and women's history: Rosemary Auchmuty, Amy Erickson, Maebh Harding, Jane Humphries, Rebecca Probert, and Sharon Thompson. The detailed feedback I received on the manuscript, together with our wide-ranging conversations about scholarship and our experiences as women in academia made the workshop a professional and personal joy. I am very grateful to the Royal Historical Society for making such provision for mid-career scholars; the process has improved this work immeasurably. Delegates at the World Economic History Congress XIX and the Economic History Society Annual Conference 2021, and members of Copenhagen Business School Seminar and Cambridge Cultural History Seminar, provided thought-provoking questions and generous interest in the project. Their comments helped me to frame both the importance of the section 21 orders, and my writing partnership with Olive Anderson. Thank you to Charlotte Alston, Kerri Armstrong, Jenny Anderton, Elsa Devienne, Rachael Durkin, Hilary Francis, Felicia Gottman, Nicola Grey, Abby Hammond, Katarzyna Kosior, Daniel Laqua, James McConnel, Neil Murphy, Helen Rutherford, Brian Ward, Leigh Wetherall-Dickson, Dominic Williams, Rebecca Wright, and members of the Conflict and Society Research Group at Northumbria University, who have listened to my ramblings and offered advice, encouragement, and fun distraction in equal measure. Particular thanks must go to Joan Heggie for reading the entire manuscript. Any mistakes are most definitely mine alone.

There have been times when this project has felt a little like being on a scavenger hunt and I had a great deal of help along the way from staff at the British Library, the British Newspaper Archive, the Parliamentary Archives, the Mary Evans Picture Library, and The National Archives. I would especially like to acknowledge the kindness and support shown by Mary Painter and her colleagues at the Community History Centre at Blackburn Central Library, who retrieved original newspapers from the stacks, searched for lost microfiche, and suggested materials on nineteenth century Blackburn, all while simultaneously giving tours to school children and dealing with myriad queries from other library users. Harry Smith demonstrated incredible collegiality and patience in providing me with census data and playing detective as we tried to make sense of court circuit districts that bore little relation to any other administrative boundaries. Thank you to John Wyatt Greenlee for his care and attention in producing the excellent maps featured in the book. Descendants of the Maginnes family have generously allowed me to share photographs of Caroline Maginnes, who was granted her section 21 order in 1877, and her husband Henry. It is a pleasure to tell Caroline's remarkable story alongside her image.

In the Foreword to this book, Olive Anderson's daughters describe how their mother 'always recognised her good fortune. But at the same time, she did feel the weight of the double burden: to manage family and domestic life, and to live her life as an academic'. These words resonated deeply as I finished the book alongside caring for my two young daughters, some 60 years after Olive had been in a similar position. I too recognise my good fortune in having a full-time and permanent academic post, but I also find managing the double burden an almost daily balancing act (and one that I don't always get right). The days where I do manage it are only possible because of the support around me. My parents, Frank and Fiona, have always been my biggest cheerleaders and, along with my parents-in-law, Sue and Terry, have provided the most valuable commodity in the world of working parents: the luxury of loving childcare. My husband Shaun was the first to encourage me to pursue this project, recognising the importance not only of recovering the stories of the thousands of named and unnamed women who appear in this book, but of bringing Olive's typescript to life. He has remained (remarkably) tolerant of the idiosyncrasies of academia (and my compulsion to gather projects like a magpie) and, most importantly, he and our two beautiful girls give me an excellent reason to step away from research and return to the twenty-first century. I am especially grateful to the three of them for their love, encouragement, and patience. And yes, girls – the book is finished!

Finally, I would like to thank Rachel and Harriet Anderson. From our very first communication, they have demonstrated an incredible generosity of spirit, sharing not only Olive's typescript and papers, but also detailed and honest memories of their mother, all of which have helped me to understand her as a person and as a scholar (if indeed these two things can be separated). I cannot thank them enough for trusting me with Olive's legacy and for making the past few years such a unique and special experience. I hope that they – and Olive – take deep satisfaction in seeing this final version of *For Wives Alone*.

Jennifer Aston
Spring 2024

TABLE OF CONTENTS

LIST OF FIGURES

LIST OF MAPS

LIST OF TABLES AND CHARTS

TABLE OF CASES

TABLE OF STATUTES

Introduction

I. Economic Divorce

On a crisp winter's morning in January 1858, a 'respectable looking woman' entered Lambeth Police Court and, in just a few short minutes, underwent a radical legal transformation.[1] Mrs Lucy Freeman arrived in court as a deserted wife who had been using her skills as a dressmaker to make ends meet. As a married woman she was subject to *coverture* – the legal doctrine whereby a wife's legal identity was subsumed by that of her husband upon marriage – and was therefore unable to contract, raise credit, or sue on her own account.[2] More pressingly for Lucy, under *coverture* she was also unable to hold any earnings or property in her own name; any assets she accrued belonged under law to her husband John Charles Freeman who had deserted her the previous year and crucially, he – or his creditors – could return at any moment to claim them. After answering a few short questions from the sitting magistrate Mr Elliott, Lucy left the police court with an order that gave her all the legal advantages of a *feme sole* or unmarried woman except the ability to remarry. On 19 January 1858, Lucy Freeman became economically divorced from her husband.

This was not the first time Lucy had appealed to Lambeth Police Court for help in dealing with her absent husband. The previous year, Lucy and her five children, Martha, John, Lucy, William, and Walter had been forced to enter Lambeth Workhouse where she was recorded as being an 'able-bodied woman'.[3] In the same month Lucy appeared before the magistrate to charge John with desertion after he had left her 12 months prior without making any provision for her upkeep. On that occasion, John was found guilty and sentenced to 21 days in prison but he did not return to live with Lucy on his release or make any provision for her.[4] Fortunately, perhaps with the help of family or friends, Lucy managed to establish herself in business as a dressmaker to support herself and her children and escape the workhouse. When Lucy appeared before Lambeth Police Court on 19 January 1858, she had a new legal remedy available to her: section 21 of the Divorce and

---

[1] Freeman: 'Police Intelligence' *Sun* (London, 20 January 1858) 4.

[2] W Blackstone, *Commentaries on the Laws of England*, Vol 1 (Oxford, 1765) 442–445.

[3] *Workhouse Admission and Discharge Records, 1764–1921* (1857) London Metropolitan Archives; CABG/173/3.

[4] Freeman (n 1) 4.

Matrimonial Causes Act 1857. The Matrimonial Causes Act 1857 is most famous
as the piece of legislation that made divorce a civil, rather than an ecclesiastical
matter, but it also contained the most radical (but largely forgotten and misunderstood) legal instrument of the nineteenth century: section 21. Under this section
of the 1857 Act, women like Lucy could apply for the protection of:

> her earnings and property acquired since the commencement of such desertion, from
> her husband and all creditors and persons claiming under him, and such earnings and
> property shall belong to the wife as if she were a feme sole … if the husband or any
> creditor of or any person claiming under the husband, shall seize or continue to hold
> any property of the wife after such notice of any order, he shall be liable at the suit of
> the wife, which she is hereby empowered to bring, to restore the specific property … if
> any such order of protection be made, the wife during the continuance thereof be and
> be deemed to have been, during such desertion of her, in the like position in all respects
> with regard to property and contracts, and suing and being sued, as she would have
> been under this Act if she obtained a decree of Judicial Separation.[5]

Section 21 gave economic protection to wives who had been deserted by their
husbands and who were supporting themselves through their own economic
endeavours. More importantly however, it did this by removing a successful
applicant entirely from the restrictions of *coverture*, nearly 80 years before the
Law Reform (Married Women and Tortfeasors) Act 1935 made it that all married
women should be treated as *feme sole* with regard to property.[6] A section 21 order
did not completely dissolve a marriage but it did totally separate financial affairs
and reverted the legal status of the wife to that of a *feme sole*, or single woman,
thus giving her the ability to raise credit, sue (and be sued) and, following the
Municipal Corporation (Elections) Act 1869, the right to vote in local elections,
subject to property qualifications. Crucially, wives who had been deserted by
their husbands could access the protection of section 21 not only through the
Court for Divorce and Matrimonial Causes (CDMC), but by applying directly to
their local magistrates court at a cost of approximately six shillings, or £32 today.[7]
This was significantly cheaper than petitioning for divorce, which would likely
cost between £50 and £100, or £5,973 to £11,950 today, but could be significantly
higher.[8]

---

[5] Matrimonial Causes Act 1857 (MCA 1857), s 21.
[6] *Coverture* caused a woman's legal identity to be subsumed (or 'covered') by that of her husband
upon marriage: the most immediate consequence of this was that she could not hold property in her
own name; Law Reform (Married Women and Tortfeasors) Act 1935.
[7] Return of Judicial Statistics of England And Wales 1896 (Part II Civil Statistics) (104, C.8838,
1898) 52. All conversions in this book are calculated using the 'Real Price' measure on www.measuring-
worth.com/calculators/ukcompare/relativevalue.php.
[8] DC Wright, 'Untying the Knot: An Analysis of the English Divorce and Matrimonial Causes Court
Records, 1858–1866' (2004) *University of Richmond Law Review* 38, 903, Table 24. See also: J Aston,
'Petitions to the Court for Divorce and Matrimonial Causes: A New Methodological Approach to the
History of Divorce, 1857–1923' (2022) *The Journal of Legal History* 43, 161, 13–14.

II. Section 21 in Scholarship

The most pressing question is why, given the surge of interest in nineteenth century women's history of recent decades, the significance and impact of section 21 has received so little academic or popular attention. It is certainly not the case that it was not eagerly anticipated, nor that it received a lukewarm response from some mid-Victorian legislators or wives. Indeed, on Friday 7 August 1857, Sir Erskine Perry MP underlined the widespread desire for reform, telling the House of Commons,

> … he had received a letter from a Liverpool magistrate to the effect that wretched women were daily coming before him stating that they could support themselves and children, if only protected from their husbands, who made a practice of seizing and selling whatever property they acquired.[9]

Yet the only work thus far to examine the Divorce and Matrimonial Causes Act 1857 in detail, Henry Kha's *A History of Divorce Law: Reform in England from the Victorian to Interwar Years* makes no mention of section 21 at all, and although Lawrence Stone's seminal *Road to Divorce: England 1530–1987* describes the inclusion of section 21 in the draft divorce bill, he termed it a 'modest proposal' and offered no further analysis as to its enactment or effect.[10] Similarly, in setting up her examination of the role of magistrates in matrimonial proceedings following the introduction of the Judicial Proceedings (Married Women) Act 1895, Gail Savage contended:

> Legislators who enacted the 1857 Divorce Act took special care to deny the poorer classes ready access to a legal avenue that would afford them an escape from their family obligations for fear that this would lead to a general dissolution of working-class family life. Accordingly, the newly-created Divorce Court sat only in London.[11]

This view ignores the provision of section 21, which could be acquired for a few shillings from any magistrate in England and Wales. It also misrepresents the extensive debates between politicians, feminist campaigners, and legal practitioners in the decade preceding 1858 as they sought to find a way to protect the interests of working-class women who, it was widely recognised, would likely not have the financial wherewithal to access a court which sat only in London.[12]

Looking instead then to women's history, where one of the first works to consider the relationship between married women and property law was Lee

---

[9] *Hansard*, HC Deb (series 3) 7 August 1857, vol 147, col 1230.

[10] H Kha, *A History of Divorce Law: Reform in England from the Victorian to Interwar Years* (Oxford, Routledge, 2021); L Stone, *Road to Divorce England 1530–1987* (Oxford, Oxford University Press, 1990).

[11] G Savage, '"The Magistrates are Men": Working-Class Marital Conflict and Appeals from the Magistrates' Court to the Divorce Court after 1895' in G Robb and N Erber (eds), *Disorder in the Court: Trials and Sexual Conflict at the Turn of the Century* (London, Palgrave Macmillan, 1999) 232.

[12] This argument is further contradicted by Savage's own research into the socio-economic status of men and women petitioning the newly formed Divorce Court who, she argued, were drawn from a

Holcombe's *Wives and Property: Reform of Married Women's Property Law in Nineteenth Century England.* In it, Holcombe dismisses section 21 orders, stating that 'very few protection orders were granted – only 100 in the first three years'.[13] The reason for this, she argues incorrectly, is because 'protection orders could be granted only to women whose husbands had deserted them for two years' and their usefulness was extremely limited as they only protected property acquired after desertion.[14] This is perhaps rooted in the fact that an order of protection under section 21 did nothing to protect married women from physical abuse, which was seen as the more pressing issue by leading female activists and groups campaigning for legal reform at the time.[15] Nevertheless, the influence of *Wives and Property* and its place as a cornerstone in the field of women's history led to other scholars also framing mid-nineteenth century developments in married women's property rights as either hijacked by a misogynistic male agenda, or as an ineffectual and irrelevant inclusion in the 1857 Divorce Act.[16] Indeed, in *Family Law in the Twentieth Century: A History*, Stephen Cretney describes section 21 orders as 'largely a dead letter'.[17]

Holcombe's widely accepted but mistaken belief that a wife seeking a protection order must have been deserted for two years or more and that very few wives ever applied for a protection order under section 21 can be traced back to two misleading primary sources. The first, a special report written by the Select Committee On Married Women's Property Bill was printed on 17 July 1868 and detailed the evidence given by a number of individuals to a Select Committee chaired by Liberal MP George Shaw Lefevre, including the barrister, Secretary of the Social Science Association and later disgraced Member of Parliament for East Worcestershire, Mr GW Hastings.[18] Hastings erroneously told the Member of Parliament for Manchester, Jacob Bright, that if a deserting husband returned within two years then he would be able to take his unfortunate wife's hard-earned money, but if – *after* two years – she 'knew the law and took the trouble to apply to a magistrate, she

---

much wider demographic than might be expected. See: G Savage, 'They Would if They Could: Class, Gender, and Popular Representation of English Divorce Litigation, 1858–1908' (2011) *Journal of Family History* 36, 173, 177.

[13] L Holcombe, *Wives and Property: Reform of Married Women's Property Law in Nineteenth Century England* (Oxford, University of Toronto Press, 1983) 173.

[14] ibid.

[15] ibid; SM Cretney, *Family Law in the Twentieth Century: A History* (Oxford, Oxford University Press, 2003) 95.

[16] For eg: M Poovey, *Uneven Developments: The Ideological Work of Gender in Mid-Victorian England* (Chicago, University of Chicago Press, 1988) Chapter 3, see specifically fn 37; ML Shanley, *Feminism, Marriage and the Law in Victorian England* (Princeton, Princeton University Press, 1989) 48; and E Foyster, *Marital Violence: An English Family History, 1660–1857* (Cambridge, Cambridge University Press, 2005) 252.

[17] Cretney (n 15) 95.

[18] Hastings was expelled from the House of Commons in 1892 'having been sentenced for fraudulent conversion on his own confession to a term of imprisonment'. GW Hastings, *Cambridge University Alumni, 1261–1900*, Cambridge University Alumni, 1261–1900 [database available online at www.ancestry.com].

would be protected'.[19] This was incorrect: the statute stated that any wife believing herself to be deserted 'may at any time after such desertion', apply for an order of protection.[20] Holcombe cited the evidence in this report and perhaps would have sought further clarification (for she includes the text of section 21 in an appendix of *Wives and Property*, so must have been aware of the full clause) but for a second governmental report: the *Return of Number of Causes Filed in Registry for Divorce and Matrimonial Causes*. This report was printed on 30 July 1861 and stated that only 100 applications for an order of protection under section 21 had been made between 1858 and 1861, with over half being made in 1858.[21] Holcombe does not seem to have realised that these figures only described applications granted by the CDMC, and they did not account for orders granted by the police or magistrates courts. The combination of these statistics and the evidence given by Hastings to the Married Women's Property Committee, caused Holcombe to conclude that section 21 was poorly designed and although the CDMC experienced a brief flurry of activity as soon as the law came into effect, it was relatively insignificant and any interest quickly waned. As the following chapters will show, however, neither of these conclusions could be further from the truth.

Legal scholar Danaya C Wright is the only other researcher to examine applications made for section 21 orders in any detail. She published a series of articles based on her meticulous research of 24 per cent of all cases heard before the CDMC between 1858 and 1866.[22] The Court sat in London and was the only venue that could hear and grant petitions for divorce, however it also heard applications for other matrimonial provisions including judicial separation, the restitution of conjugal rights, and orders of protection.[23] Wright correctly identified that applications for section 21 orders made to the CDMC seemed to be operating in a different way to petitions made for full divorce and judicial separation,[24] and she hypothesised that perhaps applicants did not behave rationally due to an intersection of social status, property, and the structure of the court system.[25] The women

---

[19] *Special Report From The Select Committee On Married Women's Property Bill; Together with the Proceedings of the Committee, Minutes of Evidence, Appendix, and Index*, HC 441 (1867–68), 25. Note: the original reports have hand written numbers on the top right-hand corner as well as the original printed page numbers. These are illegible on ProQuest digitisations and so all page numbers given here are the original printed numbers given on the report pages.

[20] MCA 1857, s 21.

[21] *Return of Number of Causes Filed in Registry for Divorce and Matrimonial Causes* HC 99 (1862) 13–14.

[22] DC Wright, 'The Crisis of Child Custody: A History of the Birth of Family Law in England' (2002) *Journal of Gender and Law* 11, 175; Wright (n 8); DC Wright, 'Well-Behaved Women Don't Make History: Rethinking Family, Law, and History' (2004) *Wisconsin Women's Law Journal* 19, 212.

[23] J 77 contains 'Files of papers arising from petitions for divorce, judicial separation, declarations of legitimacy, applications for protection of a wife's earnings, etc, in the Court for Divorce and Matrimonial Causes and Probate, Divorce and Admiralty Division of the High Court of Justice. Some later files also relate to appeals from decisions of magistrates' courts in matrimonial causes. See Catalogue Description for Court for Divorce and Matrimonial Causes, later Supreme Court of Judicature: Divorce and Matrimonial Causes Files', J 77 catalogue description, The National Archives, Kew, available at https://discovery.nationalarchives.gov.uk/details/r/C9685.

[24] Wright (n 8) 962.

[25] ibid 966–67.

applying under section 21 were, observed Wright, frequently recorded as owning small businesses, including 'dressmakers, milliners, shopkeepers, innkeepers, and boarding house keepers', suggesting that, like those submitting petitions for full divorce, the demographic of CDMC users was far broader than might be imagined.[26] Wright repeated the error of definition first made by Holcombe by assuming that wives must be deserted for two years or more before they could apply for economic protection.[27] More significantly though, because Wright's source base was the J 77 files submitted to the CDMC, she did not take into account the applications made to the police and magistrates' courts, which accounted for the vast majority of orders granted. As there was a drop off in the number of applications for protection under section 21 made to the CDMC toward the end of Wright's period of study, her research reinforced the pre-existing narrative of section 21 orders as a less useful (and less utilised) version of Judicial Separation.[28]

III. Rethinking Section 21

But where and how does Olive Anderson, this book, and my own research fit into the story of section 21? Well, somewhat embarrassingly, I have also under-estimated the full ramifications of section 21 orders in my previous work. My doctoral research, which took place between 2009 and 2012, examined female business owners operating in mid-to-late nineteenth century England.[29] One of the women I studied was named Mary (or Mary Ann) Wilcock who lived in Leeds. Mary's husband, George, had disappeared in 1848 when she was seven months pregnant with their fifth child. Left alone, Mary both raised their five children and established a highly successful business as a waste dealer, which allowed her to build a sizeable property and investment portfolio.[30] When a copy of Mary's probate records arrived on my desk they were unlike any others I had seen before. Attached to the front of Mary's last will and testament, written on 12 March 1873, was a document detailing a section 21 order of protection issued by Leeds Magistrates' Court in January 1858. It declared Mary's right to own and bequeath any property she had acquired since her husband deserted her in March 1848. Mary needed to establish this fact so she could make a legally binding last will and testament: in 1873, under *coverture*, she was unable to legally hold property in her own name or bequeath it without her husband's permission. A search of the digital newspaper archive revealed that Mary had in

---

[26] ibid 967, fn 321; Savage (n 12) 173.
[27] Wright, 'Well-Behaved Women' (n 22) 282.
[28] Wright (n 8).
[29] The research from this study was published as J Aston, *Female Entrepreneurship in Nineteenth-Century England: Engagement in the Urban Economy* (London, Palgrave Macmillan, 2016).
[30] Mary Wilcock, *England & Wales National Probate Calendar (Index of Wills and Administrations) 1858–1995* (1881) 306.

fact been the first woman in Leeds to secure the protection of section 21 though, as the *Leeds Mercury* noted, she would certainly not be the last.[31]

While I recognised in 2010 how important it was for Mary Wilcock to have a section 21 order that would allow her to contract as a business owner and protect her assets from a feckless husband, I did not make the connection between the legislation of section 21, Mary's section 21 order, and the structure of the magistrates' court system. A decade later, as I carried out research for a separate grant application, I returned to the original text of the Divorce and Matrimonial Causes Act 1857. Re-reading the legislation itself made me appreciate that a section 21 order did not only ring-fence the financial assets of deserted wives and allow women holding such an order to own and bequeath property, but they also actually reverted the wife to *feme sole* status. This directly addressed a question that I and many other historians of business had sought to answer in the years since completing my PhD: we knew that married women were 'doing' business, but *how* were they doing it?[32] Crucially, if, as the *Leeds Mercury* purported, Mary was only the first of many women to apply to the Leeds magistrates for such an order, was there a possibility that the same situation was being replicated in every magistrates' court in England and Wales?

Intending to survey applications for section 21 orders made to magistrates and police courts in England and Wales, I began searching for section 21 applications and orders in the archive. It quickly became apparent that the (lack of) survival of records was the likely reason for their absence and the confusion over their implementation in the existing scholarship. There were very few surviving copies of section 21 applications of the myriad cases heard before local magistrates' courts, and only brief entries in the magistrates' registers gave any indication that the cases had ever been heard. Enquiries with the Legal Records team at The National Archives confirmed that no central register of section 21 applications made to magistrates or police courts survived and so, a little frustrated, I instead turned to digitised newspaper collections as a way to collate information on women like Mary who had applied for orders. I set about gathering data on applicants, recording their geographic location, their business or occupation, and success of the application, with the intention of writing a journal article on the orders and their impact on the commercial world.

---

[31] 'First Case in Leeds Under the Divorce and Matrimonial Causes Act' *Leeds Mercury* (Leeds, 21 January 1858) 2.

[32] H Barker, *The Business of Women* (Oxford, Oxford University Press, 2006); N Phillips, *Women in Business, 1700–1850* (Woodbridge, Boydell and Brewer, 2006); AC Kay, *The Foundations of Female Entrepreneurship: Enterprise, Home and Household in London, c. 1800–1870* (Oxford, Routledge, 2009); E Gordon and G Nair, *Public Lives – Women, Family and Society in Victorian Britain* (Yale University Press, 2009); C van Lieshout, H Smith, P Montebruno and RJ Bennett, 'Female Entrepreneurship: Business, Marriage and Motherhood in England and Wales, 1851–1911' (2019) *Social History* 44, 440; J Aston and C Bishop (eds), *Female Entrepreneurs in the Long Nineteenth Century: A Global Perspective* (London, Palgrave Macmillan, 2020); X You, 'Working with Husband? "Occupation's Wife" and Married Women's Employment in the Censuses in England and Wales between 1851 and 1911' (2020) *Social Science History* 44, 585; J Aston, H Barker, G Durepos, S Garrett-Scott, PJ Hudson, A Kwolek-Folland, H Dean, L Perriton, S Taylor, and M Yeager, 'Take Nothing For Granted: Expanding the Conversation About Business, Gender, and Feminism' (2022) *Business History* 66, 93.

My initial conclusion was that the anonymous journalist in the *Leeds Mercury* had been correct; many, many more applications had been made to local magistrates and police courts following the Act's introduction in January 1858 and in just a few days I had gathered details of over 200 cases. However, more interestingly than the sheer number of applicants, it very quickly became apparent that there was an important story to tell about women's geographic location and their experience of the judicial system. Women located in the north-west of England appeared to be granted protection under section 21 with virtually every application, whereas women applying in London were routinely told that their case either did not meet the criteria, or they met the criteria too well and they should reapply for a full divorce at the CDMC. I was also beginning to suspect a link between the 'hot spots' of the section 21 applications, namely Lancashire in the north-west and London, in the mid-nineteenth century, and the high concentration of female suffrage societies toward the end of the nineteenth and beginning of the twentieth century. I began drafting an article based on this sample of section 21 applications made by deserted wives from across England and Wales between 1858 and 1885.

I knew however that the evidence gathered from my trawl of newspaper reports was limited by selective reporting in the newspapers. There was certainly no evidence to suggest that the press reported all applications, or even all those granted or rejected. Then, in a happy moment of serendipity, I was preparing an undergraduate seminar on emigration in the nineteenth century and came across a short article written by Olive Anderson, 'Emigration and Marriage Break-up in Mid-Victorian England' published in *The Economic History Review* in 1997. In it, she explored the experiences of women appearing in magistrates courts in the mid-1800s, particularly those who had recounted tales of desertion so they could apply for an order under section 21.[33] Unlike previous examinations of section 21 which relied almost entirely on one government report, or a small number of case files surviving in the J 77 archive, Anderson had analysed the annual judicial statistics reports which were returned by all magistrates court circuits each year, providing data on the activities of that circuit. These gave the number of all orders of protection issued under section 21, revealing that rather than section 21 orders issued in the first few years of the Matrimonial Causes Act being limited to 100 or so, there had been at least a further 2000 orders granted by magistrates across England and Wales.[34]

Anderson expanded upon the material covered in *The Economic History Review* in 'State, Civil Society and Separation in Victorian Marriage' published in *Past and Present* in 1999.[35] Understanding the role that magistrates and police courts played is the missing piece of the puzzle. As Danaya C Wright pointed out, the story borne out in

---

[33] O Anderson, 'Emigration and Marriage Break-up in Mid-Victorian England' (1997) *Economic History Review* 163, 104.

[34] Holcombe (n 13) 173; Wright (n 8) Table 2, 993. Figures of section 21 orders granted by magistrates are taken from *Return of Judicial Statistics of England and Wales, 1859–1861* (see Bibliography for a full list of reports). It is worth noting that no figures exist for the number of applications granted by magistrates in 1858 and if the pattern of high application rates for the first year seen in the CDMC was replicated in local courts then the number of orders granted between 1858 and 1862 may well be over 3000.

[35] O Anderson, 'State, Civil Society and Separation in Victorian Marriage' (1999) *Past & Present* 163, 161.

her examination of the applications in the J 77 files just did not make sense.[36] Yet if we consider those 100 applications heard in the CDMC in the broader context of those heard in the magistrate and police courts across England and Wales, the role of section 21 as a radical legal instrument utilised by deserted married women at a local level is suddenly thrown into sharp relief. Both Anderson's articles teased the reader that 'these figures [numbers of section 21 orders made] are fully analysed in a book I am currently completing on the mid-Victorian beginnings of magistrates' matrimonial jurisdiction' and, 'I discuss these orders fully in a book now nearing completion'.[37] Scouring library catalogues in 2021, no such book could be found, however an internet search did produce an obituary written by Anderson's daughter, Harriet, published in *The Guardian* in 2016.[38] Among Anderson's impressive range of achievements, Harriet wrote, 'at the time of her death, she [Anderson] left the typescript for her final book with the working title *For Wives Alone*.[39] I reached out to Harriet through the editor at *The Guardian*'s obituaries desk and, following a telephone conversation, visited Harriet and Rachel in October 2021 to examine the typescript.

IV. *For Wives Alone*: The Typescript

It actually feels as though the typescript would be more accurately written as THE TYPESCRIPT such is the importance it has come to have in my life since that initial meeting. It is itself worthy of historical research, and I will briefly describe its physical fabric here both because it is so remarkable and because I believe working with it as a tangible object rather than a computer file has shaped so much of what unfolds in the following chapters.[40] It consists of three ring binders, each repurposed from previous projects or acquired at some point from corporate firms. Each binder contains several drafted chapters, carefully typed on a word processor and covered in minute, pencil written annotations that corrected an occasional spelling mistake, added a missing reference, or strengthened an argument with a further example. The folders contain the sketched-out structure of a book with three parts; some chapters were more complete having gone through multiple revisions, others were rough drafts, accompanied with heavy annotations for future corrections and arguments. Neat notes of dates and versions in the top right-hand corner of most chapters served to remind Anderson that different versions were saved on floppy disks, though these had long since become obsolete and had been disposed of.

What is most remarkable about the typescript however, and what has occupied far too much of my attention in this writing process, is the paper the chapters are typed on. Olive Anderson was a true child of the early twentieth century.

---

[36] Wright (n 8) 966–67.
[37] Anderson (n 33) fn 5; Anderson (n 35) fn 32.
[38] 'Olive Anderson Obituary' *The Guardian* (London, 24 February 2016). Although her obituary was published in February 2016, Anderson died aged 89 on New Year's Eve, 2015.
[39] ibid.
[40] The rich material culture of Anderson's typescript will be dealt with in a separate publication.

Born in 1926 and the daughter of missionaries, she experienced the restrictions of the Second World War and was part of a generation where waste was shameful. Whether as a result of this, or perhaps simply due to her character, she was extremely thrifty, and every one of the more than 300 pages contained within the folders is written on the reverse of an existing document. The range of material is staggering, there are letters from accountants and financial advisors; minutes from Westfield College committee meetings; expenses receipts; admissions application letters (and decisions); staff references; student references; junk letters from garden furniture suppliers, and everything in between. The dates of the documents that were printed on – the earliest from 20 November 1986 (a letter from the Resident Director of the Tufts-in-London programme, posted just before I was born) and the latest (from an investment company, sent in November 2001) – anchor her research to a period of academic life before email and digitisation, and provides an incredible archive of academic ephemera at a time when Higher Education, in particular Westfield College where she had worked since 1949, was undergoing significant structural changes.

Although Olive Anderson and I never met, I had been aware of her work following the important 'London's Women Historians: a Celebration and a Conversation' event, organised by Laura Carter and Alana Harris, held at the Institute of Historical Research (IHR) in March 2017.[41] The event was intended to redress the gender balance within the IHR, introducing the portraits of 20 notable female historians (Anderson among them) to the main staircase which had previously only featured portraits of the (then all male) IHR directors.[42] Olive Anderson was one of the earliest female professors of history, a celebrated scholar, and a widely respected teacher and university administrator. Her arrival as a legal historian came about via war studies, medical humanities, and then finally, to the Victorian origins of English family law. My own journey to legal history and section 21 has been similarly circuitous and came by way of an accidental discovery while researching Board of Trade Bankruptcy records at The National Archives during my time as an Economic History Society Eileen Power Research Fellow at the IHR. Divorce petitions were frequently mentioned as a cause or consequence of bankruptcy and after reading a divorce file out of curiosity, I soon realised that so many of the questions I had initially had during my PhD research about how women were doing business and functioning in the so-called 'public sphere' could be explained by studying their interactions with official institutions and the law. Examining what the letter of the law *said* should happen, what cultural, economic, political, and societal influences *wanted* to happen, and then – most importantly – viewing what *did* happen through a gendered and feminist lens revealed radical new information about the interaction between state, judiciary, society, and gender, forcing a reassessment of long-held assumptions in multiple fields of scholarship.

---

[41] Anderson's daughters, Harriet and Rachel, were also at this event although we were unaware of each other's presence at the time.

[42] Professor Jo Fox was appointed as the first female Director of the IHR in 2017 and was succeeded by Professor Claire Langhamer in 2021.

Figure I.1 A Page from the Typescript of *For Wives Alone*

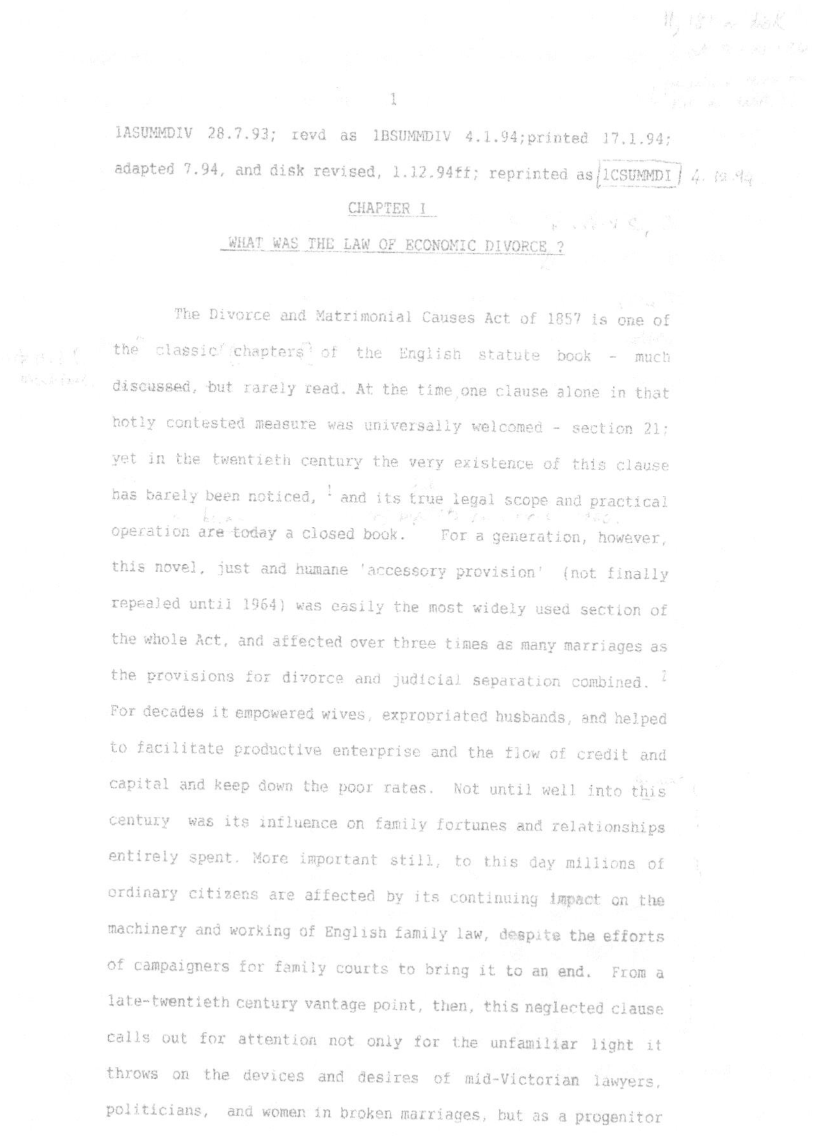

1

1ASUMMDIV 28.7.93; revd as 1BSUMMDIV 4.1.94;printed 17.1.94;
adapted 7.94, and disk revised, 1.12.94ff; reprinted as 1CSUMMDI 4.12.94

CHAPTER I

WHAT WAS THE LAW OF ECONOMIC DIVORCE ?

The Divorce and Matrimonial Causes Act of 1857 is one of
the classic chapters of the English statute book - much
discussed, but rarely read. At the time one clause alone in that
hotly contested measure was universally welcomed - section 21;
yet in the twentieth century the very existence of this clause
has barely been noticed, [1] and its true legal scope and practical
operation are today a closed book.   For a generation, however,
this novel, just and humane 'accessory provision' (not finally
repealed until 1964) was easily the most widely used section of
the whole Act, and affected over three times as many marriages as
the provisions for divorce and judicial separation combined. [2]
For decades it empowered wives, expropriated husbands, and helped
to facilitate productive enterprise and the flow of credit and
capital and keep down the poor rates. Not until well into this
century was its influence on family fortunes and relationships
entirely spent. More important still, to this day millions of
ordinary citizens are affected by its continuing impact on the
machinery and working of English family law, despite the efforts
of campaigners for family courts to bring it to an end. From a
late-twentieth century vantage point, then, this neglected clause
calls out for attention not only for the unfamiliar light it
throws on the devices and desires of mid-Victorian lawyers,
politicians, and women in broken marriages, but as a progenitor

Note the tracking of the different drafts and versions at the top of the page, and the shadow of minutes from a Queen Mary University of London Launch Task Force meeting held on 2 July 1990 shining through from the reverse. Image courtesy of the Anderson family.

Initially hoping that my visit to Harriet and Rachel would help me find some central statistics that had so far eluded me in my own research, as I scanned through the typescript, I quickly realised the significance and value of what Anderson had started. One line in particular jumped out from the pages before me: 'when mid-Victorian penny capitalism comes to be more fully explored, the survival strategies of lone married women and widows may become a great deal clearer'.[43] She made this observation circa 1995, more than a decade before the first works examining women's role in nineteenth century business were published and I began my undergraduate dissertation into female entrepreneurship in mid-nineteenth century Birmingham. I could not help but imagine how different the overlapping fields of business, economic, gender and legal history – and my own work – might have been had Anderson seen her typescript through to conclusion. With Harriet and Rachel's encouragement and support, I set about completing and expanding the project to write the first history of the largely forgotten and almost wholly misunderstood section 21 protection orders, which were available for wives alone.

V. Typescript to Manuscript

Beginning a new book project is always difficult, but stepping into a half-completed project, especially when it is not possible to ask the original author for clarification, brings its own unique set of challenges. Although some of the pages from the typescript date from the 1980s, most of the chapters appear to have been drafted between 1994 and 1996, with meticulous notes at the top of each draft detailing when the chapter was originally drafted, printed, revised, and reprinted. Some chapters underwent multiple revisions over a short period of time. There is also evidence that, after seemingly ceasing to work on the text after 1996,[44] Anderson returned to the project in early 2003, though she made no further annotations to this freshly printed material. As we sat in Rachel's kitchen in 2021 discussing how the manuscript might be updated and made ready for publication, the lack of secondary literature dealing directly with section 21 was striking given the enormous growth of scholarship on women's history in the intervening decades.

My first step was to take the original typescript and transcribe it to create a digital copy. I briefly considered outsourcing this work, but quickly realised that typing Anderson's words became a way to enter conversation with her and to sense her intentions. Even at this initial stage there were important editorial decisions to make, which began the process of shaping the original draft typescript into a jointly authored monograph. As I mentioned above, some chapters had undergone

---

[43] O Anderson, typescript of '*For Wives Alone: Economic Divorce*' binder 2, 22. The manuscript is held privately by the estate of Olive Anderson.

[44] I suspect she paused work on the book project at this point to write the research note published in *Economic History Review* and the article published in *Past and Present*, which appeared in 1997 and 1999 respectively. This would fit with the usual submission and revision timeline.

multiple revisions which were lost to us through now obsolete technologies and the passage of time. In many ways the fact that the typescript exists at all is a small miracle and I am eternally grateful to Rachel and Harriet for their foresight in preserving it when they prepared the family home for sale. Other chapters were outlined but never completed. Pencilled annotations, written in a tiny hand not designed to be read by anyone other than their author, pepper the ring-bound pages. Upon beginning the transcription process I was momentarily stumped about how to treat these later edits: should I type the original text and then add a comment box where I could write the suggested change or correction? Or should I type the original text and then make the amendments using track changes? After some (very unsatisfactory and frustrating) experimentation with both these methods, I made the decision to include the pencil edits in the version I typed, thereby creating an updated version of the drafts that Anderson had last worked on. At this stage I resisted making any changes myself, with the exception of correcting (very occasional) spelling mistakes but it was the first step in taking ownership of the project.

When I had created the digital version of the surviving typescript, I was then faced with questions about what to do with the material. It is clear from the typescript that by the end of 1996, Olive Anderson envisaged a book with three parts, though a series of heavily annotated draft contents pages reveal that the scope and titles of the chapters, focus of the parts, and title of the book itself, changed frequently. The parts of the original typescript can be broadly described as: (i) the law of 'economic divorce' and its workings; (ii) women's experiences of section 21 in Lancashire and London; and (iii) the creation of the magistrates' jurisdiction. The third part of the book (as she envisaged it) was largely incomplete, and I realised that her final chapter (the one last printed in 2003 mentioned above) actually consisted of detailed notes which had already been integrated into other chapters. The first part was the most complete, though it contained no reference to any scholarship published after 1997 – including her own *Past and Present* article – suggesting that she did not engage with the project in a meaningful way beyond this date.[45]

From the beginning of the project, we agreed that for the book to be a success it should be written as a whole book, rather than as separate, individually authored sections and it was important that the flavour of Anderson's distinct style be retained. It was equally as important however, that the book evolve to embrace all the possibilities and opportunities brought by the intervening decades to fulfil the project's potential. The immediate issue was therefore how to finish the second part and write the third, but this quickly evolved to a question of how to best marry Anderson's deep understanding of the technical aspect of the law and the male personalities that shaped its drafting and implementation, with my own research into the people (especially women) who were subject to the outcome of

---

[45] It was at this time that caring responsibilities absorbed much of her time.

the personality clashes, debates and compromises that occupied leading politi-cians in the summer of 1857. Underlying this silent discussion was the undeniable fact that Olive Anderson and I are both women of our time. Anderson went to libraries and archives where she accessed physical copies of newspapers, judicial reports, and solicitors' handbooks. In contrast, I had searched and read digit-ised newspapers online, used UK Parliamentary Papers to access papers from the House of Commons, and subscribed to genealogy websites to build detailed case studies of the lives of applicants and their families. We were historians born two generations apart, who could sadly never meet, but nevertheless, it felt like a genuine collaboration was possible.

After careful thought, spending time reading the chapters in different orders, and discussing the manuscript with Harriet and Rachel, and six participants at a Royal Historical Society Funded Book Workshop in January 2024, I made the deci-sion to maintain the original three-section arrangement but with some significant restructuring and additional content.[46] *Deserted Wives and Economic Divorce in Nineteenth Century England and Wales: 'For Wives Alone'* therefore no longer bears close resemblance to the original structure, but I believe still retains Anderson's determination to show this piece of legislation and its effects in its full colours for the first time. During the writing process there were a small number of instances where something she had typed did not make sense to me, or I could not read one of her tiny amendments. I occasionally found myself muttering aloud to myself 'what do you mean here, Olive?', and fortunately, without exception, it always became clear. There were also moments where I laughed out loud in my office – sometimes at her withering assessment of some politician or judge whose behaviour or argument she found lacking, but also upon realising that what I had fondly imagined to be my own original insights into section 21 had in fact been observed some 20 years earlier.

There were also a very small number of instances where I found myself disa-greeing with Anderson (thankfully not with her research which was impeccable), but with her opinion of certain individuals and her reading of their actions. Upon reflection, I concluded that this was entirely to be expected: we are women born over 50 years apart and it would be more unusual if we had agreed on everything. The majority of these instances were easily resolved by referring to subsequent scholarship which allowed for a fresh conclusion to be drawn, however, our biggest difference of opinion concerned Lambeth Police Magistrate George Chappel Norton, husband of Lady Caroline Sheridan Norton. Anderson viewed George as a much-maligned character who exhibited genuine care and compas-sion toward the inhabitants of his Lambeth jurisdiction and also as the victim of a

[46] I am deeply grateful to the Royal Historical Society for the generous funding they provided through a RHS Funded Book Workshop grant awarded in 2023, which paid for six leading scholars in legal history, family law, economic history, and women's history to come together and read the draft manuscript of this work.

smear campaign based on the considerable literary powers of his estranged wife.[47] There were complimentary reports of George's behaviour as a magistrate from users of Lambeth Police Court but, in my opinion, his abhorrent behaviour toward his wife and children from the 1830s onwards, which directly brought about the legislation he was then entrusted with implementing, cannot be dismissed. In this case I chose to retain the evidence presented in the original typescript, but to draw upon more recent scholarship to include full details about his conduct and his role in bringing about the Matrimonial Causes Act 1857, thus allowing readers to draw their own conclusions.

What you read in the following chapters is based on Anderson's original vision for the book, with careful editing and additional research. Part I consists of two chapters which explain how section 21 came to the English statute books, and describe the key individuals and politicians involved in its conception and introduction. It also explains what section 21 was, and how it was enacted by the Judge Ordinary, stipendiary, and lay magistrates. These chapters are drawn from the original typescript and they are predominantly Anderson's work. As one might expect, the language and style used may now seem slightly antiquated but both have been retained wherever possible as they demonstrate her deep attention to detail in her research and also her joy at sharing these observations in her writing. For example, when Anderson describes a parliamentary performance by Attorney-General Sir Richard Bethell as being 'no doubt delivered in his usual lisping, sharply articulated, supercilious-sounding drawl and provokingly suave, smiling manner', the reader can *hear* Bethell landing his political point across the baying House to the frustration of his opponents.[48] And when she explains that a debate in the House of Commons on 13 August 1857 was 'particularly bad-tempered, no doubt because that night a stiflingly hot spell in London ended with violent thunderstorms'… and Members found particularly offensive the 'noxious vapours; coming from the opposite side of the river, which the Lambeth Vestry refused to do anything about', we appreciate all the more how decisions of government are not made in isolation but are subject to pressures of seemingly mundane extraneous circumstances.[49] Part II has been written collaboratively and seeks to examine section 21 in the national context. It begins by exploring the practicalities of section 21's implementation and considers how exactly the judicial machinery was expected to work, both in terms of the courts and the individual officers who were responsible for putting the legislation into practice. Attention then turns to how section 21 operated in practice: as can be seen from Sir Erskine Perry MP's comments at the beginning of this Introduction, politicians were aware of the need for deserted wives to have legal recourse, but did the prescribed remedy work and how did uptake of this provision vary across the country?

---

[47] Olive Anderson described Lady Caroline Norton as 'histrionic': Anderson (n 35) fn 5.
[48] See Chapter One, text at n 92.
[49] See Chapter One, text at n 78.

Whereas the first two sections take a 'top down' view of section 21, Part III investigates economic divorce first and foremost through the lives of those deserted wives who appeared before their local magistrates' court. By exploring the lives of women from the two areas where the highest number of section 21 orders were awarded, London and Lancashire, analysis reveals not only the ways in which deserted wives attempted to access the protection of a section 21 order, but also how this interaction with the legal system fitted into their wider life story, highlighting important regional differences. The final chapter in this section is totally new research and extends analysis of women who applied to their local magistrate and police magistrate for protection under section 21 to those who made their application to the central CDMC between 1858 and 1914. Approximately 327 deserted wives applied to the CDMC during this period, however when Anderson was writing, these records were stored along with other petitions made to the CDMC at the Public Record Office and very poorly indexed, making them extremely difficult to use.[50] They were also under a 100-year rolling embargo. Since then however, the whole J 77 collection including petitions for divorce, judicial separation, restitution of conjugal rights, and applications for the protection of earnings made to the CDMC from 1858 to 1918 have been digitised as part of an ongoing partnership between The National Archives and Ancestry.[51] This digitisation project has enabled a systematic examination of how the CDMC treated applications made by deserted wives for a section 21 order, building upon the important work of Danaya C Wright and Olive Anderson's earlier articles to reveal new information about the functioning of the CDMC and its relationship to magistrate and police courts. Part III therefore compares and contrasts applications heard before lay magistrates who served voluntarily and had no formal legal education, police magistrates who were drawn from the legal professions but were at the bottom of the judicial ladder, and the President of the CDMC who was one of the most senior judges in the United Kingdom.

VI. The Legacy of Section 21

Understanding the full extent of these orders (and how they worked in practice) fundamentally shifts our perspective not only of Victorian family law, but of the geographic and institutional biases of the English legal system, and the legal, economic and social opportunities available to wives in mid-nineteenth century England and Wales. Historian Joanne Begiato has argued for the eighteenth century that 'focusing on the limitations placed upon married women

---

[50] For a discussion of the difficulties in using these records, see G Savage, 'The Operation of the 1857 Divorce Act, 1860–1910 a Research Note' (1983) *Journal of Social History* 16, 103; Aston (n 8); and Wright (n 8).

[51] The records do exist beyond 1918 but may be restricted by a rolling 100-year embargo. At the time of writing, post-1918 J 77 records are in the process of being digitised by Ancestry.com and The National Archives.

can mean that their significance as agents and actors in broader social, cultural, economic, and political forces is marginalised or exceptionalised'.[52] The same is true for the mid to late nineteenth century. Although the experiences of women as employees has been widely acknowledged and the role of women as business owners is receiving evermore attention, by ignoring the existence of the tens of thousands of women who did use section 21 to restore their *feme sole* status and secure protection for their economic assets, the historiographical discussion has remained focussed on the de facto position of a male breadwinner model, with the female contribution (where it is mentioned) being viewed as supplemental. One reason for this is the lack of relevant statistical data such as Integrated Census Microdata (I-CeM), the large-scale analysis of which has allowed many preconceptions of female economic activity to be reconsidered.[53] As later chapters will show, women who were awarded protection orders under section 21 can be identified and traced through census returns but crucially, as their legal marital status remained 'married', they do not reliably appear in this data as a discrete cohort. For example, of the 9,937,993 women recorded as living in England and Wales in the I-CeM 1861 dataset, 5,765,758 were single; 3,264,129 were married; 701,761 were widowed; 141,900 were married with spouse absent; 64,437 were not recorded/ unknown; and eight were divorced.[54] This figure highlights the significant minority of married women living apart from their husband (though of course, this could be due to reasons other than marital discord) but also underscores the difficulty of using census data to accurately trace marital status. With 440 divorces granted between 1858 and 1861, there were clearly more than eight divorced women living in England and Wales, however 'divorce' only became a census category in the 1921 census, meaning that particular marital status was not routinely recorded.[55]

Some economic historians, notably Sara Horrell, Jane Humphries, and Jacob Weisdorf, have made considerable efforts to counteract this. Rather than seeking answers using existing datasets, they have examined the economic activities of families through each stage of the lifecycle, for each decade between 1280 and 1850. This approach has allowed them to bring

> into focus historically common family types that have been crowded out by the fixation on the male breadwinner model: where fathers had died or abandoned their families; and, where fathers were present but unable or unwilling to earn at the levels assumed in the standard model.[56]

[52] J Begiato, 'A "Master-Mistress": Revisiting the History of Eighteenth-Century Wives' (2023) *Women's History Review* 32, 1, 3.

[53] van Lieshout, Smith and Bennett (n 32) 440. See outputs from The Cambridge Group for the History of Population & Social Structure, available at www.campop.geog.cam.ac.uk/ for examples of the largescale studies which can be carried out with I-CeM data.

[54] See: www.icem.data-archive.ac.uk/#step1.

[55] Office for National Statistics, 'Divorces in England and Wales' dataset (2022 edition), Table 1(a), available at www.ons.gov.uk/peoplepopulationandcommunity/birthsdeathsandmarriages/divorce/ datasets/divorcesinenglandandwales.

[56] S Horrell, J Humphries and J Weisdorf, 'Beyond the Male Breadwinner: Lifecycle Living Standards of Intact and Disrupted English Working Families, 1260–1850' (2022) *Economic History Review* 75,

It is also important to remember that subsistence was not sufficient: in an era with few public safety nets, squirrelling away savings for an almost inevitable rainy day was essential and a task which required everyone to contribute something, however small it might be. These are exactly the types of families that the majority of wives who appeared before the police court and petty sessions magistrates came from. They were neither rich, nor very poor, rather they were drawn from the masses. They came from economic groups and families who were frequently unable to rely on a 'competent' male breadwinner and were therefore used to combining forces with parents, siblings, spouses, children, and other extended kin, or even friends, to ensure economic stability.[57] The importance of a male or family wage might well have dominated popular rhetoric, but it certainly did not reflect the economic structure of the majority of homes.[58] Furthermore, in areas where a male breadwinner model did dominate, for example in the coalmining regions of the north-east of England and south Wales, the effect on married women was profoundly negative and gave them a poorer quality of life than those women living in areas where they were able to work.

The middling ordinariness of the married women who applied for an order under section 21 does not just provide important new contextual informa- tion about the day-to-day functioning of the nineteenth-century economy, but also illuminates our understanding of the relationship between women and the nineteenth century legal system. Women's engagement with the law in the early modern period has been particularly well explored, with Alexandra Shepard and Tim Stretton observing that 'in archive after archive, they [legal scholars and histo- rians] found evidence of women actively asserting and defending their rights and property interests in a range of legal contexts'.[59] Moreover, 'so great was the auton- omy exercised by certain knowledgeable and well-resourced women that recent scholars have begun to minimize the influence of coverture'.[60] Wealth has always carried the promise of legal privilege whether through the funds to pay for formal legal representation, or being positioned within a social and cultural milieu that carried the expectation of legally enforceable financial provision. Yet we should remember that the effects of *coverture* could only be minimised with the right legal mechanisms, namely a marriage settlement or trust and with a very small

---

530, 532. See also: S Horrell and J Humphries, 'Women's Labour Force Participation and the Transition to the Male Breadwinner Family, 1790–1865' (1992) *Economic History Review* 48, 89; S Horrell and J Humphries, 'The Origins and Expansion of the Male Breadwinner Family: the Case of Nineteenth Century Britain' (1997) *International Review of Social History* 42 (supplement 5) 26; S Horrell, J Humphries and J Weisdorf, 'Family Standards of Living Over the Long-Run, England 1280–1850' (2021) *Past and Present* 250, 87.

[57] Horrell, Humphries and Weisdorf, 'Beyond the Male Breadwinner', ibid, 547.

[58] J Humphries, 'The Lure of Aggregates and the Pitfalls of the Patriarchal Perspective: A Critique of the High Wage Economy Interpretation of the British Industrial Revolution' (2013) *The Economic History Review*, 66, 693.

[59] A Shepard and T Stretton, 'Women Negotiating the Boundaries of Justice in Britain, 1300–1700: An Introduction' (2019) *Journal of British Studies* 58, 677, 679.

[60] ibid 679.

number of exceptions, the women whose stories feature in these pages are not drawn from those classes: they accessed legal protection under section 21 in spite of their socio-economic status, rather than because of it. This opens up exciting new avenues of research into the legal knowledge of 'ordinary women': how did married women in mid-nineteenth century England and Wales become informed about the protections offered under section 21? How did they navigate the inherently gendered world of the legal system, where they could be absolutely confident that whatever else happened, it would be men deciding the validity of their case?

The individual circumstances of the many thousands of applications made under section 21 also shines new light on the experiences of wifehood in the mid-to-late nineteenth century. In explaining the circumstances that made them eligible for an order under section 21, a wife was forced to construct a detailed timeline of marriage, desertion, and economic self-sufficiency. Desertion might have occurred at any time following marriage, sometimes within just a few weeks, while other husbands, like George Wilcock, deserted after many years and left behind not only his wife, but his children too. Although these testimonies come with the caveat that we (nearly) only ever hear one side of events, the testimonies given by wives paint a world where safety and security, both economic and personal, could turn in an instant. Husbands, instilled with the confidence of belonging to a patriarchal society, made decisions about finances, jobs, and living conditions with little or no consultation with their wives who, almost without fail, were contributing in some way to the family economy. A wife's complaint about such a situation could be, and seemingly was, frequently met with physical violence before the subsequent economic violence of desertion. Descriptions of abuse, including beatings with fists, being dragged about, the transference of sexually transmitted infections, and beatings with implements such as fire pokers, situate much of the abuse within the domestic sphere and analysis of the applications therefore contributes important evidence to a growing literature examining the relationship between space, place, and domestic abuse.[61]

The following chapters will detail the experiences of the tens of thousands of married women in Victorian England and Wales who applied for protection under section 21 of the Matrimonial Causes Act 1857. Chapter One explores the drafting of section 21, examining how key groups and personalities managed to take the widely held conviction that any new divorce legislation must contain some provision to assist deserted wives and use this leverage to introduce the most radical clause concerning women and property of the nineteenth century into law. Chapter Two examines the law of section 21 itself, analysing how the brief guidance

[61] JC Wood, *Violence and Crime in Nineteenth Century England: The Shadow of our Refinement* (Abingdon, Routledge, 2004); Foyster (n 16); A-M Hughes, 'The 'Non-Criminal Class: Wife-Beating in Scotland (c.1800–1949) (2010) *Crime, Histoire & Sociétés / Crime, History & Societies* 14, 31; J Begiato, 'Beyond the Rule of Thumb' (2018) *Cultural and Social History* 15, 39, 55; GJ Fryar, *Suffering or Fallen Angels? Wife-Beating in Victorian Liverpool 1850–1889: Class, Cause and Community Response* (The Open University, Unpublished MA Thesis, 2022).

set out in the Act was interpreted by the CDMC and the way conflicts and uncertainties were resolved. Chapter Three studies the machinery of the magistrates courts and how section 21 was interpreted and enacted by these, the lowest ranking sections of the English justice system. Chapter Four moves on to examine the numbers of section 21 orders granted in England and Wales, revealing stark contrasts in experience across localities. The individual circumstances of these applications are then examined through the two detailed case studies of women who applied to the metropolitan police courts in London and the local magistrates courts of Blackburn, Lancashire for an order under section 21 in the first year of its operation. Chapter Five compares and contrasts the different ways wives in London and Blackburn experienced desertion and explores the ways they sought to establish their economic independence. Chapter Six analyses their experience of applying for protection under section 21, revealing the approaches of police and lay magistrates, and the ways that deserted wives used the legal system to their advantage. Chapter Seven then offers a different perspective, analysing all surviving petitions made to the CDMC between 1858 and 1914, to reveal important new information about family dynamics, the role of wives as economic agents, female knowledge of the legal system, and the often complicated reasons why deserted wives chose to apply directly to the CDMC rather than to avail themselves of the services of the local magistrate.

This book therefore draws together the work of two historians, working decades apart, with different source material and methodologies. It demonstrates that this largely forgotten legal device, which certainly does not enjoy the popular understanding of other key legislation affecting women in the nineteenth century such as the Married Women's Property Acts, was one of the most radical pieces of legislation to enter the statute books and forces a reappraisal of legal, economic, social and women's history. Ultimately, if *Deserted Wives and Economic Divorce in Nineteenth Century England and Wales: 'For Wives Alone'* had been solely authored by either of us, then it would likely have been a different book entirely. Yet, in our slightly unconventional collaboration, I believe that we have managed to marry our two approaches to the subject of section 21 to create a final work that is greater than the sum of its parts.

PART I

Creating 'Economic Divorce'

1

'That Useful Exotic from France': Mid-Victorian Personalities, Politics, Culture, and How the Matrimonial Causes Act 1857 Reached the English Statute Book

Obtaining an order of protection under section 21 in the first few months of 1858 certainly had a positive effect on the lives of Lucy Freeman and Mary Wilcock. The 1861 census return shows Lucy living at number 8 Broadway, Deptford, with two of her children and working as a milliner, while her estranged husband John was lodging at a house in Camberwell.[1] Sadly, Lucy died on 22 September 1863, but the protection offered to her under section 21 allowed her to make a last will and testament, which was duly proved by her executor brothers in 1865.[2] During the five years between the magistrate Mr Elliott granting Lucy's application under section 21 and her death, she had managed to acquire assets of £200, the equivalent of over £22,000 today.[3] Similarly, while Mary Wilcock moved with her family to a larger home on an elegant Georgian square and eventually left an estate worth £500 (£59,870 today),[4] her husband George disappeared from the records after he was released from York Castle debtors jail in June 1858.[5] These anecdotes suggest that the wives described in Sir Erskine Perry MP's speech to the House of Commons were correct; they could support themselves, if only they were protected from their husbands. But how did such a radical legal instrument enter the English statute book? This chapter explores the origins of section 21 of the Matrimonial Causes Act 1857 (MCA 1857) and analyses how the key characters who influenced its creation made use of the political culture of the early 1850s to fundamentally rewrite the legal relationship between married women and property.

[1] 'Lucy Freeman' *England Census* (1861) RG9/394/137/9/542629; 'John C Freeman' *England Census* (1861) RG9/381/45/21/542627.
[2] 'Lucy Freeman', *England & Wales National Probate Calendar (Index of Wills and Administrations) 1858–1995* (1865) 308.
[3] ibid.
[4] Mary Wilcock, *England & Wales National Probate Calendar (Index of Wills and Administrations) 1858–1995* (1881).
[5] 'Yorkshire Insolvent Debtors Court' *The Leeds Mercury* (Leeds, 15 June 1858) 3.

Divorce in England and Wales prior to 1857 was a complicated, expensive, and heavily gendered process reliant on proving the 'guilt' of one party and the 'innocence' of the other. Sybil Wolfram has identified 325 full divorces – that is the termination of an 'existing marriage to allow remarriage during the lifetime of a spouse' – between 1700 and 1857.[6] Of this extremely small number, only four cases brought by wives were successful and all were brought between 1801 and 1857.[7] This complicated 'tripartite' system was so called because it required those seeking divorce to first establish adultery by bringing a charge of *criminal conversation* (to prove adultery) in the Assize Courts, before then securing divorce *a mensa et thoro* (divorce of bed and board) in the Ecclesiastical Courts, and finally applying to the House of Lords for a private act of Parliament, which would formally dissolve the marriage by a divorce *a vinculo matrimonii* (divorce from the bonds of matrimony) and return the couple to an unmarried state.[8] Obtaining a full divorce was therefore beyond the means of the vast majority of married couples. As Stone notes, there had been growing consensus among leading lawyer-politicians that English matrimonial property law had some serious flaws and ought to be made less archaic, and 'by 1850 reform of the divorce law had at last become part of the official agenda'.[9] Yet much of the credit for establishing divorce reform as a priority of Parliament can be ascribed to the articulate and persuasive arguments of well-educated middle class women who campaigned relentlessly from the mid-nineteenth century onward for the rights of women to education, employment opportunities, property ownership and the franchise.

Perhaps most well-remembered of these individuals is Lady Caroline Sheridan Norton, who made a deeply unhappy marriage to George Chapple Norton, a Member of Parliament and (as we will see in future chapters) a stipendiary magistrate. Physical violence and emotional abuse had plagued the marriage from the start and culminated in George removing their children from Caroline, and then (unsuccessfully) suing Lord Melbourne, a close friend of Caroline's and the sitting Prime Minister, for *criminal conversation* in 1836.[10] As a wife subject to *coverture*, Caroline was unable to launch any legal suit to gain access to her sons and so she set about using her literary talents to campaign ferociously for mothers to have rights of access to their children. This resulted in the Custody of Infants Act of 1839, which allowed separated mothers the right to petition the courts for custody of their children up to the age of seven, and for access to older children.[11]

---

[6] S Wolfram, 'Divorce in England 1700–1857' (1985) *OJLS* 5, 155, 155–56, fn 3.

[7] L Stone, *Road to Divorce England 1530–1987* (Oxford, Oxford University Press, 1990) 360–62.

[8] For a history of the tripartite system see, Wolfram (n 6); Stone (n 7); H Kha, *A History of Divorce Law: Reform in England from the Victorian to Interwar Years* (Abingdon, Routledge, 2021).

[9] Stone (n 7) 367.

[10] For a detailed biography of Caroline Norton, see D Atkinson, *The Criminal Conversation of Mrs Norton* (London, Random House, 2012); and A Fraser, *The Case of the Married Woman: Caroline Norton and Her Fight for Women's Justice* (London, Pegasus Books, 2022).

[11] Custody of Infants 1839. It should be noted that a mother found guilty of adultery could not avail herself of this legislation, though no such condition was placed on a father found guilty of adultery.

To Caroline's dismay, following the *criminal conversation* trial, she realised that neither she nor George could establish grounds for divorce under the pre-1857 tripartite system. The verdict of the Melbourne trial proved that Caroline had not committed adultery, and George's behaviour, although appalling, was not sufficiently horrendous to constitute extreme cruelty. Despite agreeing a private separation, Caroline found that her financial affairs continued to tie her to George, even though they lived apart and she was earning her own income through her writing. She therefore turned her attention to the reform of divorce legislation, writing a pamphlet titled *English Laws for Women in the Nineteenth Century* where she gave an impassioned account of her own experiences as a wife.[12] This was followed by a public letter written to Queen Victoria, *A Letter to the Queen on Lord Chancellor Cranworth's Marriage and Divorce Bill*, which detailed a litany of legal afflictions suffered by married women:

> A married woman in England has no legal existence ... She has no possessions, unless by special settlement; her property is his property ... An English wife cannot make a will ... An English wife cannot legally claim her own earnings ... An English wife may not leave her husband's house ...[13]

The widespread newspaper coverage of her marital disharmony, coupled with her undoubted talents as an author, cemented Caroline Norton as a key voice advocating for reform of the law as it related to married women as wives and mothers.

In a less personal but no less effective way, Barbara Leigh Smith Bodichon also played a pivotal role in garnering public support around the intertwined issues of women's legal position with regard to education, marriage, employment, children, and property. Bodichon published *A Brief Summary in Plain Language of the Most Important Laws Concerning Women; Together with a Few Observations Thereon* in 1854, and in this brief 18-page pamphlet, she set out in easy-to-follow terms the stark difference in the legal position between unmarried and married women.[14] The pamphlet became an instant best-seller with further editions printed in 1856 and 1869.[15] As Joanna Conaghan observed, the way that Barbara Leigh Bodichon structured her work, and the language she used, were in sharp contrast to Norton's highly personal account, with Bodichon choosing to follow the convention of standard legal commentaries, making no mention of her own circumstances at all.[16] This is perhaps why she was so successful: although readers often felt intense sympathy for Norton and her situation, it was explicitly framed as a situation happening to someone else, whereas Bodichon made it clear that this

---

[12] CS Norton, *English Laws for Women in the Nineteenth Century* (London, 1854).

[13] CS Norton, *A Letter to the Queen on Lord Chancellor Cranworth's Marriage and Divorce Bill* (London, Longman, Brown, Green and Longmans, 1855) 8–14.

[14] BLB Smith, *A Brief Summary in Plain Language of the Most Important Laws Concerning Women; Together with a Few Observations Thereon* (London, 1854).

[15] J Conaghan, 'A Brief Summary of the Most Important Laws Concerning Women by Barbara Leigh Smith Bodichon, 1854' in E Rackley and R Auchmuty (eds), *Women's Legal Landmarks: Celebrating the History of Women and Law in the UK and Ireland* (London, Bloomsbury Publishing, 2018) 57.

[16] ibid 58.

was the legal reality for *all* married women, regardless of whether their husband was cruel, or loving and benevolent who shielded them from the full effects of *coverture*. It is important to note that Barbara Leigh Bodichon addressed more than just divorce reform in her pamphlet and in her wider activism. She was at the centre of the 'Ladies of Langham Place', a group that included Bessie Rayner Parkes, Emily Davies, Eliza Fox, Anna Murphy Jameson, Mary Howitt, Jessie Boucherett, Frances Power-Cobbe, Sophia Jex-Blake, and Louisa, Elizabeth, and Millicent Garrett. Together, under the auspices of various organisations including the Society for the Promotion of the Employment of Women and the Married Women's Property Committee, they sought to improve the situation of women through improving their access to education and employment opportunities, to bring about female enfranchisement, and to give married women the same property ownership rights as unmarried women.[17]

The widespread popular support generated by the writings of Bodichon and Norton were harnessed by the Married Women's Property Committee in a petition to Parliament signed by 26,000 women. It was presented on 14 March 1856, and in February 1857 Lord Brougham introduced the proposals made in the petition as a Married Women's Property Bill in the House of Lords, although nothing happened immediately as a General Election was called. In May 1857 Sir Erskine Perry introduced a further Married Women's Property Bill to the House of Commons, with some amendments from the Law Amendment Society, which would not change the legal status of marriage settlements but did propose that married women be treated as *feme soles* in all other ways relating to property. Holcombe argues that it was positioned as an alternative to the Divorce Bill, which was also winding its way through the parliamentary process. Although it passed its second reading, it was the Divorce Bill which held the attention of the House and the Married Women's Property Bill disappeared from view.[18] For women like Barbara Leigh Smith Bodichon, Bessie Rayner Parkes, and Helen Taylor, who campaigned under the Married Women's Property Committee and other banners, the MCA 1857 was not a success, nor did it mark an end to their campaigns. As Holcombe notes, the 1857 Act was 'very far from embodying the thoroughgoing reform of the married women's property law which feminists had been demanding – the right of married women to own and control their property as unmarried women did'.[19]

Bruised by the experience of coming so close to achieving their goals, key members of the Married Women's Property Committee reconfigured into groups agitating for the promotion of women's employment opportunities, for example the Society for Promoting the Employment of Women (SPEW), which was founded by Jessie Boucherett and other members of the Langham Place group in 1859.

---

[17] L Holcombe, *Wives and Property: Reform of Married Women's Property Law in Nineteenth Century England* (Oxford, University of Toronto Press, 1983) Chapter 4.
[18] ibid 93.
[19] ibid 108.

Other women, including Lydia Becker and Barbara Leigh Smith Bodichon, continued to campaign for married women's property rights by focussing on the key topic of female enfranchisement, which, by virtue of the law at the time, required voters to meet certain property qualifications. Despite their disappointment however, as Holcombe argues, a third resolution that had been introduced in Brougham's Divorce Bill, namely that 'until reform of the married women's property law could be carried through, a wife should be given easy and speedy access to a court in order to secure protection for her property', was a way of forcing the inclusion of some provision for married women's property even as the Married Women's Property Bill fell by the wayside.[20]

After prolonged and often furious debate on both sides, the Divorce Bill was finally passed on 28 August 1857. It removed divorce from the jurisdiction of the Ecclesiastical Courts and made it instead a matter for the newly formed Court for Divorce and Matrimonial Causes (CDMC), which sat only in London, and was initially presided over by Sir Cresswell Creswell. The Act set out five main matrimonial remedies, namely: nullity, restitution of conjugal rights, judicial separation, full divorce, and an order of protection.[21] The grounds for each of these treatments varied both by treatment and by the sex of the applicant. Applications for nullity, whereby a marriage was dissolved on the grounds that it should never have been made in the first place, and the restitution of conjugal rights, whereby a spouse could be compelled to return to the marital home, could both be made at the CDMC by a husband or by a wife. Applications for judicial separation could also be applied for only at the CDMC in London and was available to a husband or wife 'on the ground of adultery or cruelty, or desertion without cause for two years and upwards'.[22] It operated in much the same way as the previous divorce *a mensa et thoro* and separated the legal and financial affairs of husband and wife, making the wife a *feme sole* and the husband therefore no longer responsible for her debts.

Divorce, meaning the full dissolution of marriage, operated in a similar way to the old divorce *a vinculo*, and permitted both parties to remarry. It required a petitioning husband to prove his wife's adultery and he could also name his wife's alleged lover as a co-respondent. A petitioning wife, however, would have to prove that her husband:

> has been guilty of incestuous adultery, or of bigamy with adultery, or of rape, or of sodomy or beastiality (sic) or of adultery coupled with such cruelty as without adultery would have entitled her to a divorce *a mensa et thoro*, or of adultery coupled with desertion without reasonable excuse for two years or upwards.[23]

These stipulations made it more difficult for a wife to meet the required threshold to bring a petition for divorce. This is reflected in statistics from the Divorce Court,

---

[20] ibid 90.
[21] Matrimonial Causes Act 1857 (MCA 1857).
[22] ibid s 21.
[23] ibid s 27.

with approximately 40 per cent of petitions being made by wives compared to 60 per cent by husbands, although it should be noted that wives were slightly more successful in securing a full divorce.[24] Petitions had to be made to the CDMC in London, and although the process was more accessible and cheaper than it had been under the previous tripartite system, it was still expensive.[25] The additional burden of proof, together with the high cost of divorce, might suggest that judicial separation, where wives only had to prove adultery OR cruelty OR desertion without cause for two years, rather than a combination of the two, would have been a popular option for unhappily married wives, yet as Laurence Stone and Gail Savage have observed, that this was not the case and judicial separations remained a relatively underutilised provision.[26]

The final remedy – an order of protection – worked differently from any other provision made under the Act. An order of protection as described under section 21, enabled a deserted wife to 'at any time after such desertion', apply to either the police magistrate, justices in petty sessions, or to the CDMC for an order that would:

> protect any money or property which she may become possessed of after such desertion, against her husband or his creditors or any person claiming under him; and such magistrate or justices or court if satisfied of the fact of such desertion, and that the same was without reasonable cause, and that the wife is maintaining herself by her own industry or property, may make and give to the wife an order protecting her earnings and property acquired since the commencement of such desertion, from her husband and all creditors and persons claiming under him, and such earnings and property will belong to the wife as if she were a feme sole.[27]

This short clause therefore radically changed English law, making it possible for a married woman to earn, acquire, manage, and dispose of property as a *feme sole* for the first time, totally free of the strictures and limitations of marriage settlements or trust law. Moreover, section 21 of the MCA gave this power to the lowest courts, the majority of which were not presided over by individuals with any legal training.

Long before it had reached the statute book on 28 August 1857, the MCA was confidently expected to include a clause safeguarding a deserted wife's earnings from seizure by her husband or his creditors.[28] Yet the clause finally inserted for this purpose was produced only at the last minute and it proved so startlingly bold that even the lawyers in the Chamber were initially at a loss, and several

---

[24] G Savage, 'The Operation of the 1857 Divorce Act, 1860–1910 a Research Note' (1983) *Journal of Social History* 16, 103, 105.

[25] DC Wright, 'Untying the Knot: An Analysis of the English Divorce and Matrimonial Causes Court Records, 1858–1866' (2004) 38 *University of Richmond Law Review* Table 24, 1010.

[26] Stone (n 7) 386; Savage (n 24) 105.

[27] MCA 1857, s 21.

[28] Stone (n 7) 376; Holcombe (n 17) 91.

reporters in the Gallery turned in entirely mistaken reports to their newspapers.[29] Nor are these puzzled reactions surprising, for Palmerston's Attorney General, Bethell, had devised a clause as novel as it was drastic. A police magistrate or two Justices of the Peace were to be able to protect a self-supporting wrongfully deserted wife on the spot, at least so far as property, contracts, suing and being sued were concerned. Once she had such a 'protecting order', her husband would have no more right to her earnings or property (or liability for her debts) than a stranger; she could trade on her own account and sue in her own name; indeed, she could even sue her own husband for torts committed during marriage – and all this after no more than a summary and potentially *ex parte* hearing at her local magistrates' court. This was strong stuff. Hitherto no married woman had been able to do any of these things; now, the summary jurisdiction of a pair of country justices or a single metropolitan police magistrate was to extend transforming a self-supporting deserted wife into a statutory *feme sole* in every respect except with regard to remarriage.

Misunderstandings and confusion were all the more understandable since two quite different methods of protecting deserted wives' earnings had earlier been incorporated into the Government's divorce bills. Palmerston's Lord Chancellor, Cranworth, held that the English law of husband and wife meant that a husband's right to his deserted wife's earnings could not be removed while she retained her status as his wife. Accordingly, his quite adventurous third Divorce Bill of February 1857 allowed a wife to petition for a divorce *a mensa et thoro* after two years' wrongful desertion, which the ecclesiastical courts had allowed only for adultery or brutal cruelty. In the Government's opinion, this satisfactorily supplied the protection needed, since from July 1856 onwards successive divorce bills had provided that such a divorce would make a wife 'mistress of her own property' with 'all the rights and privileges of a single person'.[30] Ultra-Conservatives who opposed judicial divorce or any departure from the law and practice of the ecclesiastical courts, however, found it intolerable that a divorce *a mensa et thoro* should be given for mere desertion, and the floodgates thereby opened to easy divorce by collusive agreement. Meanwhile very many moderate and socially sensitive Conservative and Peelite peers who were not opposed to divorce in principle, could not accept

[29] Bethell's clause was taken to relate to judicially separated wives, and wives whose husbands were guilty of adultery and the like by the *Morning Advertiser*, *Daily News* and *Manchester Guardian*: while *Hansard* made Bethell refer to renewed cohabitation by a wife with an order as ending 'the judicial separation' (*Hansard* HC Deb (series 3) vol 147, col 1889). At this period, Hansard's reports were compiled from the morning newspapers and were thus very far from authoritative: see O Anderson, 'Hansard's Hazard's' (1997) *Economic History Review* 112.

[30] The Lord's Select Committee chaired by Lyndhurst that recommended that a wife with a minor divorce should thereby become a *feme sole* with regard to property, contracts, suing and being sued, proposed that a wife deserted for two years or more should be eligible for an order for alimony, payable direct to herself or her trustee. However, when the Cabinet considered its law Bills for the coming session in November and December, it agreed to 'considerable additions' to its next Divorce Bill: Brougham MSS, University College London, 13306, 13307, Lyndhurst to Brougham, 2 and 4 Dec, 1856.

that a wrongfully deserted wife should be driven to the Divorce Court as the only way of protecting her earnings and property.

In the second reading debate of 3 March 1857 the testy former Tory Lord Chancellor, St Leonards, declared that instead, he would simply 'take away the right of the husband to the wife's property after his desertion had continued a certain time'.[31] When the Lords went into Committee on 25 May 1857 on the Government's fourth (and final) Divorce Bill, he accordingly proposed two new clauses. The first was extremely badly drafted, but his ally Samuel Wilberforce, Bishop of Oxford, the High Church leader of opposition to divorce, removed its worst flaw. In its amended form, this first clause allowed a wife who had been wrongfully deserted for a year and was 'maintaining herself by her own lawful industry' to apply to any Justice of the Peace and 'show cause that she has reason to fear that her husband or her husband's creditors will interfere with her earnings'. Thereupon the Justice, if he thought fit, could give her an order restraining her husband (or any creditor or agent of his) for six months from interfering with her earnings or property acquired from her earnings during her desertion, on penalty of a fine of £20 or two months in prison. This order could be varied or discharged by any two justices in petty sessions.

The second and more straightforward clause allowed any wife who had been deserted without reasonable cause for a year or more, to petition the new 'Court of Marriage and Divorce' for an order that would have exactly the same effect as a divorce *a mensa et thoro* so far as concerned property, contracts, and suing and being sued.[32] In the debate that followed, all praised St Leonard's intentions, but Cranworth and the Government's supporters urged that the local machinery envisaged would not work satisfactorily, and persisted in maintaining that a wife's property could not be made secure against her husband's claims so long as her status as his wife remained unchanged. Conservative anti-divorce ultras and moderates nevertheless mustered 52 votes to the Government's 44 and thereby inflicted the Government's first defeat in the new Parliament.[33] From 25 May 1857, the Divorce Bill thus provided a second method of protecting a deserted wife's earnings against her husband – a method always seen as 'carried against the Government' by St Leonards benevolent efforts, and repeatedly praised for at last placing justice 'within the reach of the honest woman who lives by the labour of her hands and the sweat of her brow'. The Government had indeed offered a deserted wife the remedy of divorce *a mensa et thoro* from the expensive new central Court in London, but 'desertion is more frequent, self-support more common, among the

---

[31] *Hansard* HC Deb (series 3) 3 March 1857, vol 144, col 1702. This provision would turn Cranworth's 'impossible Divorce Bill' into 'a judicious and salutary law', readers of *The Times* were told on 18 March 1857: 'In the present state of affairs it needed not' *The Times* (London, 18 March 1857) 8–9.

[32] *Hansard* HC Deb (series 3) vol 145, col 799 and (as amended) 806807.

[33] The passing of these amendments has often been misrepresented as intended to prevent the passing of Perry's Married Women's Property Bill, introduced a few days earlier in the Commons. In reality they were a necessary first step towards St Leonards' prime object of removing from the Government's Divorce Bill the provision allowing divorce *a mensa et thoro* for two years' wrongful desertion.

poorer classes', and 'it is the poor sempstress, laundress, or domestic servant who most needs that her earnings should be secured to her'. Now, any self-supporting wife who had been deserted for a year or more and could show a local magistrate that she had reason to fear interference by her husband or his creditors with her earnings, or property bought with them, would be able to obtain an order forbidding any such interference for six months, 'this will cost her nothing, or next to nothing'; and it would 'meet the case'.[34]

The Commons, however, took a very different view of St Leonard's first clause (then clause 17 of the Bill). Notice of a motion to expunge clause 17 in Committee had been given by JW Henley, the Conservative frontbencher who handled his party's response to the Divorce Bill in the Commons and was also the front-bench voice for the county justices and when this clause was reached, all sides praised its humane intention, but agreed that its provisions were so unworkable that 'to amend it was simply impossible'.[35] One alternative after another was mooted and found unsatisfactory. In order to make progress, the Attorney General undertook to try to frame an entirely new clause that would provide 'a certain, ready and economical mode of giving wives in the humbler classes this description of protection', and since St Leonards' two clauses were connected, the second was negated as well as the first.[36] On 18 August Bethell duly brought up his single-clause replacement for St Leonards' two discarded clauses, and these were debated at the report stage two days later in a thinning House preoccupied with the critical events in India and the winding up of the session's business.[37] All the objections made earlier to St Leonards' proposal had been removed at a stroke by Bethell's novel approach. The discussion was a bi-partisan technical one, between Bethell, Henley, the leading Conservative Chancery silk Richard Malins, and a handful of common lawyers (Kenneth Macaulay, AS Ayrton, WH Adams, Erskine Perry, and William Bovill), of how Bethell's boldly simple (and therefore intentionally perplexing) clause would enable a wife to enforce her 'protecting order' against her own husband. The existing methods of protecting a married woman's property under the rules of equity were altogether different, Bethell explained. Under his new clause, as soon as the wife was granted an order protecting her property, she was to be considered a *feme sole* so far as her civil rights were concerned: the relation between husband and wife in these respects therefore became the same as that between 'Jane Thomas and John Brown'. He had removed the problem at its root,

---

[34] JW Kaye, 'The Marriage and Divorce Bill' (1857) *North British Review* 27 164, 167; 'Punches Essence of Parliament' *Punch*, 32 (London, 6 June 1857) 223.

[35] Sir Erskine Perry MP pointed out three obvious defects: protection was only available after a year, so that a parasitic husband could return every 364 days and mulct an industrious wife; a £20 fine was no deterrent if the property seized was worth more than £20; no definition was given of who would own the protected property, so that if a wife was trading alone, her creditors would be unable to get access to it. Henley emphasised that justices would be unwilling to implement it, since they would be 'liable to action after action and might be subjected to heavy penalties'.

[36] *Hansard* HC Deb (series 3) 7 August 1857, vol 147, cols 1227–36.

[37] *Hansard* HC Deb (series 3) 18 and 20 August 1857, vol 147, cols 1851, 1888–91. *Hansard's* compilation is poor for this discussion, which is more fully and intelligibly reported in the press.

by 'unmarrying' the wife with regard to her property – although not her person. When the Bill went back to the Lords, St Leonards predictably 'did not think the clause an improvement', but he contented himself with increasing the damages given to a wife against a husband who flouted an order, and on 28 August it duly reached the statute book as section 21 of the Divorce and Matrimonial Causes Act 1857.[38]

Not surprisingly, this drastic last-minute volte-face caused persistent misapprehensions and misunderstandings, as it still does among historians today. The change brought about in the common law position of husband and wife was so great that 'it seems almost impossible to appreciate it to its full extent', remarked the *Morning Advertiser*'s legal correspondent, all too correctly.[39] TW Saunders in updating his successful magistrates' handbook, explained that 'the new jurisdiction conferred upon magistrates by section 21 is so novel and important' that it required a separate chapter.[40] The concept of the statutory *feme sole* was even more strange than the placing of such large powers over property rights in the hands of a pair of country justices. Yet perhaps as potent a source of lay confusion was the publicity already given to St Leonards' earlier and far more easily understood proposals. His name had become indelibly associated with 'protection orders' for deserted wives' property, and then as now, his proposals were readily assumed to be in all essentials those that reached the statute book.[41]

In reality however, the clause that became part of the law of the land was widely different in both legal principles and administrative machinery. First and most important, the wife's property was to be protected not by a magistrates' order prohibiting her husband (or his creditor or agent) from interfering with it on pain of a fine or imprisonment, but indirectly, by giving the wife the status of an unmarried woman from the fate of her desertion with regard to the whole gamut of civil rights and liabilities.[42] No special protection was then needed for her property, since her husband had no more rights over it than a stranger. The ordinary law of the land would therefore protect it as satisfactorily as it protected the property of every man and unmarried woman in the country. Such a solution was too novel to be easily grasped and there were some indignant calls for this supposed oversight to be remedied and a husband's interference with his wife's protected earnings made punishable by summary fine or imprisonment bracket, as had been proposed by

---

[38] In addition to the power already given to the wife to recover double the value of the specific property seized, St Leonards added the power to recover the specific property itself: *Hansard* HC Deb (series 3) 24 August 1857, vol 147, col 2043.

[39] 'The New Divorce Bill – Protection to a Deserted Wife's Earnings' *Morning Advertiser* (London, 3 September 1857) 4.

[40] TW Saunders, *The Complete Practice of the Laws of England*, 2nd edn (London, 1858) 223.

[41] For example, *Punch* in its otherwise very accurate rhyming summary of the Act's provisions, described the effects of St Leonards' discarded clause, not those of clause 21 itself: 'The Divorce Bill Dissected' *Punch* 33 (5 September 1857) 95, 103, stanza 9. St Leonards is credited with the clause that replaced his own in (for example) Anonymous, *Solicitors' Journal* 8 (4 June 1864) 607; and Holcombe (n 17) 102 (followed by subsequent studies).

[42] See Appendix I for the text of s 21 of the MCA 1857.

one of St Leonards' discarded clauses.[43] More new ground was also broken by the provision that an order was to be available to any deserted wife 'maintaining herself or her own industry *or property*' (our italics) and that its protection extended to any 'property which she may be possessed of after such desertion' instead of only to her earnings and property bought from her earnings. It thus applied to gifts and inheritances as well as earnings and it was open to rich and poor alike. In the same socially comprehensive vein moreover, and very significantly for the future machinery of English family law, the two-tier system proposed by St Leonards that was familiarised by the County Courts was discarded. No matter how substantial the property involved might be, a single Metropolitan Police magistrate or two justices in petty sessions were to possess exactly the same power as the Divorce Court itself to bestow upon a self-supporting deserted wife all the civil rights of a single woman, and thus deprive her husband at a stroke of his marital rights over her earnings, property and legal capabilities, lock, stock, and barrel.

Three further new departures were of considerable practical importance. A wife did not need to wait for two years to be eligible for this far-reaching order; she only had to satisfy the magistrate of the fact that she was deserted and maintaining herself, and this might be clear enough in a matter of days. Furthermore, her order would remain permanently enforced unless the husband, his creditor, or any person claiming under him successfully applied for its discharge to the police magistrate or justices by whom it was made. If the couple lived together again, although the protection order would cease thenceforth, the property the wife had acquired during her desertion was to remain her separate property. Finally, although notice did not have to be given to the husband or his creditors and the hearing could be *ex-parte*, the wife was required to enter her order within 10 days with the registrar of her local County Court.

These were radical innovations, and immediately recognised as such by practitioners. 'In truth, there is subject matter in these few lines for a good size act of parliament' complained TW Saunders when confronted with the task of exposition.[44] Yet 'these few lines' were not the result of the usual long-drawn-out process of legislative compromise; they were on the statute book, virtually unchanged, only 10 days after they were first introduced. Bethell had settled the 'accessory provision' for protecting deserted wives' property, just as he had approached the rest of the Divorce Bill through the Commons – by instant resourcefulness and intense application. He had devised (at speed) a clause entirely free from the defects that had led members to reject St Leonards' suggestions, that was far more reaching than anything previously envisaged: a clause that authorised the lowest tier of courts in the land to summarily bestow upon a self-supporting deserted wife all the rights concerning property, contracts, and litigation that Lyndhurst had earlier secured for wives who extracted a decree of judicial separation from the Divorce

[43] See, eg, *Hansard* HC Deb (series 3) 20 August 1857, vol 147, cols 1889–91; 'The New Divorce Law' (May 1858) *English Woman's Journal* 186.
[44] Saunders (n 40) 224.

Court after a wait of two years. When he called it 'the most important clause in the bill', he was right in a way he could not have foreseen, for it proved even more significant in the history of domestic proceedings in English magistrates' courts than in the relations between English married women in civil society. Thousands of self-supporting mid-Victorian lone wives did indeed regain all their civil rights, but section 21 also marks the first step in the journey of magistrates being instilled with a quasi-matrimonial jurisdiction exercised on equal terms with the CDMC, which would, by the late twentieth century, eventually see them responsible for granting the vast majority of full divorces in England and Wales.[45]

Far reaching social and institutional consequences like these can only increase interest in how it came about that Palmerston's Attorney General drafted and successfully carried a new clause along these bold lines – lines unsanctioned by ecclesiastical matrimonial law and practice, and inconsistent with the Government's centralising and conservative policy for matrimonial proceedings. Above all, lines running counter to Chancery's development of the wife's 'separate property' and to the pattern of married women's property law reform that was to triumph in 1870. Indeed, once proposed, this last-minute clause, like others, might well be carried to the statute book by the momentum given by political pressures and personalities, by the shibboleths of mid-Victorian public culture, or by the urgent need to wind up the session in a passable way. But what was the initial source of the unorthodox idea that a pair of local justices should be empowered to give a deserted wife living on her own earnings or property not only absolute rights of possession, but also full powers to contract, sue, and be sued?

On the face of it the likely inspiration may seem to be the American-style economic feminism that attracted some English women's rights campaigners in the mid-1850s, and their well-publicised demand in 1856 that marriage should make no difference to women's property rights. Advocates for married women's property reform were well aware of the increasing number of US states passing laws to grant limited property rights to married women and newspapers reported the Law Amendment Society's intelligence-gathering trips to the United States. The Law Amendment Society described Perry's 1857 Married Women's Property Bill as aiming to establish

> the same state of the law as now prevails through the greater portion of the United States of America. It does not interfere in any way with marriage settlements, but enables a married women, in the absence of a settlement, to retain her own property and earnings, as if she were a femme (*sic*) sole, making her liable at the same time on her own debts and engagements.[46]

---

[45] The Administration of Justice Act 1920 gave 10 Assize Courts the power to hear divorce petitions and the decentralisation of divorce happened at pace through the 1920s and 1930s. See D Ranyard, *'Decree Nisi with Costs, my Lord?': A Study of Divorce in England and Wales, 1909–37* (University of Lincoln, unpublished PhD thesis, 2019) 99–118; Office for National Statistics, 'Divorces in England and Wales' dataset (2022 edition), available at www.ons.gov.uk/peoplepopulationandcommunity/birthsdeathsandmarriages/divorce/datasets/divorcesinenglandandwales.

[46] 'Law Amendment Society' *Sun* (London, 28 April 1857) 4.

Reform to the English law regarding married women's property rights was also framed in terms of the American model in the House of Commons, with the campaigners' spokesman in the Commons, Sir Erskine Perry, drawing on the work of the Law Amendment Society to draft his bill.[47]

Yet after Perry's Married Women's Property Bill had fallen by the wayside and the Divorce Bill became the sole opportunity for reform, the clause that gave local justices summary powers to deal with a wife's complaint of her husband's abuse of his legal control of her earnings, property, and powers of contract and litigation was borrowed from the French Civil Code – and specifically, from the process of judicial *autorisation* as practised in the *cours d'arrondissement* in the 1850s.[48] In so far as this clause was a foreign exotic, it came not from New York, but from Paris.[49] Certainly Perry welcomed Bethell's new clause warmly. It was 'an enormous concession', he enthused; for the first time, the law now gave a wife 'an absolute property in her earnings' – although regrettably only in very limited circumstances.[50] This limitation was, however, of the essence. In Bethell's clause, the basis of entitlement was not rights, but specific marital fault and the means of access were as important as what was given. A wife was to regain a single woman's powers of independent action only as a protective remedy for a dysfunctional marital relationship but that remedy was to be obtainable instantly, on her own doorstep.

The inner history of this story begins at the Hotel Imperial, Boulogne-Sur-Mer in August 1856, where one of the British holiday-makers was John Fraser Macqueen, a genial Scottish Chancery practitioner who was (remarkably enough) the protégé and intimate of both Lord Campbell and Brougham.[51] This hard

---

[47] *Hansard* HC Deb (series 3) 14 May 1857, vol 147, cols 266–75.

[48] In 1964 one of Sir Jocelyn Simon's five reasons for the nature of the 1870 Married Women's Property Act was (incorrectly) that 'comparative jurisprudence was virtually unstudied at this time; and there was in any event a tendency to regard French political and social institutions with a well-bred distaste': *With All My Worldly Goods* (1964) paper given to the Holdsworth Club of the University of Birmingham. These views were given wide circulation among students by their reproduction in B Hoggett and D Pearl, *The Family, Law and Society: Cases and Materials*, 3rd edn (London, Butterworths, 1991) 140.

[49] Although this inspiration may have taken some reformers by surprise, nineteenth century lawyers had looked to continental Europe for inspiration as they began to produce legal textbooks and also sought inspiration for legislation, see, eg, Catharine Macmillan on the European influences on contract law: C Macmillan, 'Rogues, Swindlers and Cheats: The Development of Mistake of Identity in English Contract Law' (2005) 64 *Cambridge Law Journal* 711–44.

[50] 'Parliamentary Report' *Morning Advertiser* (London, 21 August 1857) 4. Bethell had established the rights of the wife 'on a sound ground', said Perry: *Hansard* HC Deb (series 3) 20 August 1857, vol 147, col 1890.

[51] On Macqueen (1803–1881), see the Oxford Dictionary of National Biography, available at www.oxforddnb.com. Macqueen was a lively correspondent as well as an effective lecturer and writer. He succeeded in his declared object of making his works 'useful, clear and short' JF Macqueen, *The Rights and Liabilities of Husband and Wife at Law and in Equity* (London, 1848) vii – although his succinct, readable style of law was not to all Scottish tastes: *Journal of Jurisprudence and Scottish Law Magazine* 2 (19 July 1858) 330. An off-print of this review is among the collection of Law Tracts of the Institute of Advanced Legal Studies, London.

working, enterprising and knowledgeable barrister specialised in Scottish and divorce appeals in the House of Lords, had been secretary to the Royal Commission on Divorce, and in the manner of his ilk, he made his holiday reading in Boulogne the latest report of the French Minister of Justice. There he noted remarkably high numbers of separations and illegitimate births, which he suspected were the result of the French law of divorce. He decided to visit Paris to collect further information, and accordingly equipped himself with some introductions from Brougham, who prided himself on knowing the leading French lawyers. He made good use of these in Paris, but nothing might have come of his brief trip had he not been obliged to accompany his wife on a visit to her parents at Outwell Rectory, near Wisbech, Cambridgeshire at the end of September. As he had nothing else to do there, he applied himself vigorously to his new study of the French law of divorce and separation.[52] A few weeks later, Brougham announced enthusiastically in the *Law Magazine and Review* that

> a most valuable addition will be made to the information obtained in the Committee of last session (Lyndhurst's Select Committee) by the result of inquiries made in France by the able and learned Secretary of the Matrimonial Law Commission (Mr Macqueen) during the recess.

He went on: 'I have had access to his statements on the French law and practice as to separation and divorce and trust he may be induced to make them public before the commencement of the next session'.[53]

By December Macqueen had taken an important decision: to say 'something also of the rights of married women in France' – although, as he acknowledged to Brougham on 13 December 1856, 'this is dangerous ground. I fear your Lordship will hold me rash'. He sent his first proofs to Brougham and Campbell, and both advised him to continue. Brougham was then invited to mark 'on the margin things that may be wrong or unwise or unadvisable', and Campbell, as chairman of the Royal Commission on the Laws of Divorces, solved the problem of publication costs. Macqueen's work, he said, would come out as a communication to the Commissioners from their Secretary, printed by the Queen's Printer – this despite the fact that the Commission had reported as long ago as 1853.[54] Word of Macqueen's paper soon spread to those responsible for drafting the Government's next Divorce Bill, and he was invited to the last of Cranworth's December Bar Dinners, where he was sought out by Walter Coulson, Cranworth's assistant and parliamentary counsel to the Home Office.[55] Early in January all the

---

[52] Macqueen to Brougham, Brougham MSS, 3794 (16 August), 3795 (8 September), 3796 (28 September), 6087 (3 October 1856).

[53] 'Extract of a Letter from Lord Brougham to the Earl of Radnor' (November 1856) 2 *Law Magazine and Review* 112.

[54] Macqueen to Brougham, Brougham MSS, 3799 (13 December), 3798 (16 December), 3800 (18 December 1856).

[55] Spencer Walpole (a member of the Divorce Commission) and Lyndhurst were also invited, and Macqueen believed 'Divorce was one object of the convention': Macqueen to Brougham, Brougham MSS, 3801 (23 December 1856).

members of the Divorce Commission duly received off-prints of their Secretary's 'Communication', as did the Law Officers; and on 12 January 1857, Macqueen could report that two Commissions, Vice-Chancellor Wood and Dr Lushington, both liked it, as did the Attorney General, and 'I don't think the Chancellor is otherwise than pleased, for he wrote saying he would consider the paper'.[56]

As soon as the Lords reassembled in February 1857, Campbell declared that it was

> of great importance that they should all have the opportunity of reading the most valuable paper on French Laws on Divorce and Separation composed by the Secretary of his Commission during the recess, before the Chancellor introduced his Divorce Bill.

It was understood the new Bill

> would be more comprehensive than the two earlier Bills, which had simply been founded on the recommendations of his Commission and would consider what should be done with regard to the rights of women who had been separated from their husbands, and the various rights and liabilities arising from the relation of husband and wife.

His motion for this paper was seconded by Brougham in his usual highly-coloured style ('it was impossible to overestimate the importance of the information it contained'), and within a week Macqueen's 'Communication' had been printed as a Sessional Paper, under the title, *The Law of France as to Divorce and Separation, with comparative views of eleven other codes … Also the wife's rights and protective remedied under the Code Napoleon, more especially with reference to her earnings.*[57] This – a purely private paper – therefore achieved official circulation in the Lords, thanks to the author's two patrons' exploitation of parliamentary facilities for circulating Royal Commission papers.

This new Blue Book was soon pressed into use by two very different tacticians with very dissimilar objectives. The first was Brougham himself. Law reform had long been his acknowledged stamping ground. As President (and founder) of the Law Amendment Society, he had undertaken to introduce that Society's Bill to amend drastically the laws on the property of married women. Usually the introduction and first reading of a Bill was a formality; but Brougham was about to leave London for several months, and he was determined to put fully on record his personal views on the subject. In order to do this, he decided that

---

[56] Macqueen to Brougham, Brougham MSS, 6086 (12 January 1857).

[57] *Hansard* HC Deb (series 3) 6 February 1857, vol 144, cols 146–48; *Hansard* HL Deb (series 3) 6 February 1857, vol 133, cols 246–49. The House of Lords heard that JF Macqueen had 'composed a most valuable paper, which he had laid before the Commission, having reference to the whole laws on the subject of husband and wife; and divorce, which prevailed in France under the *ancien régime*, under the Code Napoleon … It was, he thought, of great importance that their Lordships should all have an opportunity of reading this valuable paper before the whole matter was brought before them, on the Bill being introduced by the Lord Chancellor; and what he proposed was, that a copy of it should be laid on the table, and should be printed and circulated for the use of the Members of the House'. The motion was granted.

before presenting the Society's controversial bill, he would move (and then with-draw without putting to the vote) three resolutions of his own. He therefore set about preparing one of his flights of eloquence on this topic.[58] Macqueen had often devilled[59] for him in the past, and he now marked for him the passages in his Blue Book on the property and protective remedies of married women under French law that were likely to be of use, 'beginning on page 20'. Since the long extract here from the great French civiliste Jean Charles Florent Demolombe was 'a little too rhetorical and somewhat metaphysical' on the question of earnings, he suggested he should 'look at a footnote or two of mine in which I endeavour to bring out this learned and now popular writer's meaning, on pages 23–25', for 'the barristers I spoke to in Paris spoke of him as *the man* of authority on questions of husband and wife'.[60] Brougham knew very well that by enlisting Macqueen's help he was priming himself with arguments against the official line of the Law Amendment Society. At an exciting public meeting the previous May that Society had resolved that England should adopt what was presented as an American-style separate matrimonial property regime, under which every woman who married without a pre-nuptial settlement would retain all the rights of a *feme sole*. Until this last-minute coup, however, opinion within the Society had been divided, and Macqueen had been one of the most outspoken and weightiest dissenters from the American solution.[61] That February, Brougham's intention was to use his speech in the Lords to outline a practical compromise which could be supported by reformers of all shades and would consequently have a chance of becoming law immediately through the Divorce Bill – unlike the Society's sweeping proposal.

He therefore began by acknowledging that the simplest and most complete remedy was indeed to give every wife the rights of a *feme sole*, as already happened in 'the greater part of the United States', but quickly went on: 'in France there is a different plan'. There, a married woman's legal rights were not very different from ours, 'but she has a great advantage through a difference of judicial procedure'. The French system, he explained, consists in not only giving the wife access to the Judge in the suit for *separation de biens* (separation of property) without *separation de corps* (separation of bodies), but also giving her 'an easier and more summary protection by the procedure of *autorisation*', by which she became as capable in the eyes of the law as if she were not married.[62] *Autorisation* he emphasised,

---

[58] Brougham's 'absurdly theatrical' speeches disgusted some peers, among them Lord Broughton: Diary, Broughton MSS 43761, f.6 (24 July 1857).

[59] '"Devilling" is the long-established practice among self-employed barristers by which one barrister obtains the assistance of another, usually a more junior, barrister to carry out work to help the first barrister discharge his instructions', The Bar Council Ethics Committee, 'Devilling' (2020), available at www.barcouncilethics.co.uk/wp-content/uploads/2017/10/Devilling-Feb-20.pdf.

[60] Macqueen to Brougham, Brougham MSS, 6090 (11 February 1857). Demolombe's declared object was to interpret the Code Napoleon '*comme loi vivante*': *Dictionnaire de biographie française*, 10 (1965). (The Code Civil was identical with the Code Napoleon decreed in 1803, apart from the provisions for divorce.).

[61] Macqueen to Brougham, Brougham MSS, 3790 (3 June) and 3799 (13 December) 1856.

[62] For the Articles in the Civil Code which enabled a French wife (who could otherwise neither give, lend, borrow, alienate, mortgage, contract, transact, nor acquire anything), to obtain an *autorisation*

'is expeditious and summary, and offers a most valuable remedy'. This could be seen from the illustration given 'by Mr Macqueen, in his admirable paper', of the washerwoman, called on to pay a debt of her husband's out of her earnings, who left her tub for half an hour to go to the court of her *arrondissement* and returned with full legal protection for her earnings; whereas a French milliner working in London was robbed by her husband with perfect impunity, and obliged to leave 'your barbarous country'.[63] No doubt the American system would ideally be the best solution, but it would be 'deemed by many too sudden and extensive'. For the time being, therefore, he concluded, wives who needed it should be enabled 'by application to court of easy access, to obtain protection for their earnings from the claims of their husbands or their husbands' creditors'. To all this 'Pussy' Granville, the Government's Leader in the Lords (who knew that Brougham's resolutions were not intended to be put to the vote), purred that 'it was universally admitted that there was great room for improvement in the law' on these matters and that he hoped that Brougham's exposition would enable lawyers on both sides of the House to concentrate on obtaining 'the best practical result', and so to arrive at some satisfactory solution 'during the present session'.[64]

After the next month's snap General Election and just before the new Parliament was sworn in, these arguments for 'following the French course' were repeated in an article in the *Law Magazine and Law Review* surely written by Brougham. 'Mr Macqueen's excellent and most instructive paper' was again cited, and emphasis laid on his description of the flexible and sympathetic way in which judges were currently interpreting the authority given them by the text of the Codes to override the husband's powers and make the wife as capable as if she had not been married. Readers were informed that 'the practice of the (French) courts has considerably extended the wife's protection, affording her a much more easy and expeditious remedy than the process of *separation de biens*, by extending the process of *autorisation* given in the Codes'. The real practical grievance in England was that of the ordinary working wife, and 'the importation of some such law, or some such judicial practice, would effect an extraordinary amendment in our system'. Even those who objected most strongly to 'the solution borrowed from certain American states' could have no objection to this less considerable but most beneficial improvement. The Society for the Amendment of the Law's American-style solution was too extreme to be practicable at present; whereas the French

---

which had the effect of making her as capable in law as if she had not been married, either from her husband, or failing him, and on showing cause, from the Court of her *Arrondissement*, see particularly Articles 217–19, 905, 934, 1029 *Code Civil Des Français: Éd. Originale Et Seule Officielle*. Many other Articles provide for *autorisation* by the husband, or family, the judge, in circumstances where this remedy was required by the wife.

[63] This telling story, originally told in a footnote in Macqueen's paper as happening 'in the course of a morning' in August 1856, was continually repeated with various embroideries: for example, she was 'pestered by an idle, drunken husband' according to *The Times* (18 March 1857). By 1864 'the washerwoman case' had been turned into 'the French leading case' by one legal journalist: 'Anonymous' *Solicitor's Journal*, vol 8 (4 June 1864) 607.

[64] *Hansard* HC Deb (series 3) 13 February 1857, vol 144, cols 605–18.

system of giving the wife a certificate of *autorisation* when needed was certain to be generally acceptable.[65]

By the time the Lords went into Committee on Cranworth's fourth and (as it proved) final Divorce Bill on 25 May, Macqueen's *Communication* and 'the French Plan' for protecting women's property against their husbands, when necessary, through a magistrate's certificate had been fairly well-publicised in leading legal and political circles, at least in general terms. In mid-March, *The Times*, after noting St Leonards' intention to provide that after a year's desertion a wife's earnings and property should become her separate estate, had commented encouragingly,

> Lord St. Leonards is in possession of Mr Macqueen's book (sic) upon the law of France, and he will find from the returns and the statements of French jurists that it is safe and profitable to deal largely and boldly with the husband's right to see his wife's good and to demand her earnings.

Macqueen's exemplary tale of the tub was then repeated.[66] Nevertheless there were no 'large and bold dealings' in St Leonards' proposals of 25 May; only after waiting a year would a deserted English washerwoman be able to apply to 'the lowest class of magistrate', and then all she could get would be a temporary injunction forbidding her husband or his agent from interfering with her earnings or property bought with her earnings, on pain of a £20 fine or imprisonment in lieu. Moreover, only from the Divorce Court itself would she be able to get anything resembling a certificate of *autorisation*, again after waiting a year.

Still, St Leonards' first clause did contain an echo of the French system of locally available protective remedies for wives, and was certainly believed to have been inspired by that system.[67] When Gladstone said 'No' to the Attorney General's remark in the Commons on 7 August that 'the Committee were doubtless aware of the manner in which this clause had got into the Bill in the House of Lords', Bethell explained that 'a noble and learned Lord, from motives of benevolence and humanity' (here the caustic 'Miss Fanny' surely used his most satirical tones)[68]

---

[65] 'The Married Woman Question' *Law Magazine and Review* 3 (May 1857) 89–95. (Brougham continued to feed material into the amalgamated journal, as he had into the *Law Review*). An editorial note observed that 'the Society entirely abide by the view taken in their report' and referred to the backing recently received from the American law reformer Dudley Field, stating flatly, 'we have given in the above article all that can be urged on the side of the lesser measure'. This stance is not surprising, for although the Society's loss-making *Law Review* had been amalgamated with the *Law Magazine* in May 1856 and articles in the combined journal were declared not necessarily to reflect the Society's views, nevertheless the authorised publication of its papers and reports was confined to its pages, and the connection was close.

[66] *The Times* (18 March 1857) 9.

[67] This may have been second hand. *The Times*' leader quoted above, which St Leonards will almost certainly have read, simply describes Macqueen's washerwoman as returning after 30 minutes 'with a certificate which protects her wages' *The Times* (18 March 1857) 9.

[68] Bethell's 'singularly affected style of address which he cultivated, termed by some namby-pamby pedantry, and which at one time earned him the offensive sobriquet of "Miss Fanny"': Anonymous, 'Recollections of Lord Westbury' *Macmillan's Magazine* 47 (April 1883) 469, 470.

was desirous of introducing into this county a practice which prevailed in France, where a wife who had been deserted or cruelly beaten by her husband could apply to a magistrate – even of the lowest class – and obtain an order to protect her earnings against her husband.[69]

Bethell's habitual contempt for St Leonards' draftsmanship was well known, and it can have been no surprise that in his opinion 'the clause, as it at present stood, if passed into law, would be most mischievous'. With this one Member after another agreed, and Bethell undertook to 'use all his resources' to devise 'a form of machinery' and 'course of procedure' better adapted to achieve the desired protections, 'although he really for the moment was at a loss to determine' how this should be done.[70]

On Friday 7 August, then, although there had been plenty of references to 'the French practice', the outlook for its adoption in England was hardly prom- ising. Nevertheless on Monday 10 August, Bethell gave notice of his proposed amendments,[71] and on 18 August brought up a new clause that made available to self-supporting deserted English wives, a machinery and procedure closely similar to that available in France, that made her forthwith '*aussi capable, ni plus ni moins, que si elle n'était pas mariée*'.[72] This clause would give a wife in need redress from 'the incapacity which fetters or paralyses her at every turn' by infor- mal personal application to the equivalent Court of her Arrondissement for an '*autorisation*': the English magistrates. The editor of the *Solicitors' Journal* was entirely correct when he explained in 1864 that the precedent for clause 21 of the Divorce Act was

> the beneficial 'authorisation' which under the civil code of France, the husband may give to the wife with the effect of making her capable as if she had not been married, and which by Article 218, if the husband refuses, the Court of the Arrondissement may give.[73]

---

[69] Gladstone had hardly gone near the House till mid-July: H Reeve (ed), *The Greville Memoirs* (8 vols, 1911 edn) (London, 3 June, 19 July, 1857).

[70] *Hansard* HC Deb (series 3) 7 August 1857, vol 147, cols 1231, 1235. St Leonards and Bethell were notoriously two of the least amiable of men: 'Punch's Essence of Parliament' *Punch*, 33 (29 August 1857) 83, 83.

[71] On 17 August, Bethell mentioned 'the clauses with respect to the local jurisdictions of which he had given notice' *Hansard* HC Deb (series 3) 17 August 1857, vol 147, col 1751, and on 21 August Sir George Grey said that notice of Bethell's proposal with regard to local jurisdiction for judicial separa- tions was 'placed on the paper on 10 August', which Sir William Heathcote explained why shortage of time had prevented Members from considering 'this important clause' in the last few days: *Hansard* HC Deb (series 3) 10 August 1857, vol 147, cols 1984, 1987. In all probability these clauses included the clause on local jurisdiction for deserted wives applying for property protection but not judicial separation.

[72] 'As capable, neither more nor less, as if she were not married' in C Demolombe, *Du Mariage et de la Separation de Corps* 2 (Paris, 1854) 364.

[73] 'Anonymous', *Solicitors' Journal* 8 (4 June 1864) 607. Very many other sections of the *Code Civil* as well as Article 218 provide for authorisation, eg Articles 219, 221–24, 905, 934, 1029, 1449, 1555. This writer was nevertheless misleading in saying that St Leonards had taken the Civil Code as a prec- edent 'when he introduced the clause now forming, with the alternations made in it by the Commons, section 21 of the Act'. As has just been shown, St Leonards' clause neither envisaged giving to *Justices*

The initial idea of the wife's protecting order was thus a 'useful exotic' brought over from France. But why was Bethell so quick to use this idea over the weekend of 8–9 August 1857? He can have spent little time on deliberation, hard worker though he was, for the Shrewsbury Peerage case opened before the Committee of Privileges of the Lords on Monday 10 August, and in this he had a heavy role.[74] He had close to hand the paper by his old Chancery friend and colleague, Macqueen, on the French system, which he had said he liked when sent an off-print in January,[75] and remembered its contents – as he demonstrated when his opponents suddenly exploited it as a storehouse of ammunition against the Bill.[76] On 13 August Lord John Manners claimed on its authority that 'adultery committed in the conjugal residence' was a ground for divorce under French law and persuaded the House to add this to the grounds already in the Bill; where upon Bethell correctly pointed out that Manners had entirely misunderstood both the French Code and Macqueen's account of it.[77] He then quoted the passage in question, and suavely but vainly proposed an amendment to Manners' amendment that adopted the language of the Code itself.[78] But in any case, Bethell's own stance as a long-standing law reformer made him disposed to admire the *Code Civil* in general, and likely to favour its procedure of *autorisation* in particular. He had often expounded his views: the study of the civil law, 'that is, Modern Roman law', should be the basis of English legal education; codification and legal argument by the application of simple principles rather than the exposition of precedents were

of the Peace the equivalent of the power of *autorisation*, nor was it the basis of section 21, except in the most remote sense.

[74] 'Sixteen hours a day for labour, and eight for meals and sleep, we imagine is something like the division of his time': W White, *The Inner Life of the House of Commons* (London, 1898) 37.

[75] The two had long shared a concern for issues of law reform; indeed it was after a discussion with Macqueen while they were both 'engaged in a heavy Corporation cause' that Bethell joined the Law Amendment Society in 1846: Macqueen to Brougham, Brougham MSS, 12104 (24 January 1846) and 3776 (25 May, no year but probably 1850). Bethell's 'valuable advice and important suggestions' were gratefully recorded in Macqueen (n 51) vii and xx. See specifically in Macqueen to Brougham, MSS, 23328 (n.d., 1849).

[76] 'Your Lordship will have seen that the "Twelve Foreign Codes" were abundantly cited in the Commons', wrote Macqueen to Brougham: Brougham MSS, 6091 (endorsed 1857, probably 23 August); and *Hansard* bears him out: *Hansard* HC Deb (series 3) 13 August, vol 147, cols 1534, 1560–61, 1590, 1602, 1630–32, 1636 (14 August), 1762 (17 August). The Government was loudly accused of high-handedness in failing to make Macqueen's Blue Book available to the Lower House.

[77] *Hansard* HC Deb (series 3) 13 August 1857, vol 147, col 1556–59 (13 August 1857). The *Code Civil* allowed a wife to divorce her husband 'when he has kept his concubine in the common residence', but excluded 'occasional and fugitive infidelities', as Macqueen correctly noted and Bethell pointed out. Manners' misunderstanding of Macqueen's account was thus responsible for much of the criticism of this well-known amendment and its ultimate rejection in the Lords, where both St Leonards and Monteagle emphasised that he had 'entirely misunderstood the enactment of the French law which he had attempted to copy': *Hansard* HC Deb (series 3) 24 August 1857, vol 147, col 2030, 2040.

[78] Bethell was accused of trying to evade the Committee's decision by his amendment, and there-fore withdrew it. That evening's debate was particularly bad-tempered, no doubt because that night a stiflingly hot spell in London ended with violent thunderstorms: *The Annual Register* (London, 1857) 154 and Members found particularly offensive the 'noxious vapours', coming from the opposite side of the river, which the Lambeth Vestry refused to do anything about: *Hansard* HC Deb (series 3) 13 August 1857, vol 147, col 1533.

highly desirable; the common law was archaic, and must be adapted to modern circumstances; and the comparative method should be applied to law revision, through the investigation of foreign codes.[79] As for English matrimonial property law, like many other leading lawyers and laymen of that decade he had no doubt that some reform was needed, and deplored that there was no way of enforcing the common law's 'true rule' – namely, that the husband's right to the wife's property depended on his fulfilling his obligation to protect and maintain her. Any husband who deserted his wife ought therefore to forfeit all his marital property rights. His own personal 'scheme of legislation on married women's property', outlined in the Commons on 14 May 1857, envisaged a legal matrimonial property regime adapted to harmonise with equity practice, and reflected not only his own long leadership of the Equity bar, but that ubiquitous progressive catchword of the day, 'fusion' (that is, of the jurisdictions of law and equity).[80] He would give the husband only a life interest in a wife's personal property and acquests, he said, as was already the case with regard to her real property; and this should revert immediately to the wife if he ill-treated or deserted her. The courts of Equity, he pointed out, were already in the habit of recognising the separate interests of the wife in property she acquired by any trade or business she carried on without her husband's assistance; and this should of course apply *a fortiori* to a deserted wife.[81] All this 'would undoubtedly go a great way', the Law Amendment Society's keen young Secretary George Hastings, enthused privately.[82]

Bethell's general outlook was thus broadly in harmony with the French matrimonial property regime as then interpreted in the French courts.[83] Indeed in 1870, when his political career was over, he told the Lords categorically that

---

[79] See his Presidential Addresses to the Juridical Society of March 1855 and 1856, summarised in TA Nash, *The Life of Richard Lord Westbury* I (London, 1888) 171–73 and 191–94; and for his role in setting up the Council of Legal Education, see *Report of the Commissioners Appointed to Inquire into the Arrangements in the Inns of Court and Inns of Chancery, for Promoting the Study of the Law Aad Jurisprudence; together with Appendices*' HC 18 (C (1st series) 1998) (1854–55), 160–61. While he was Solicitor General in 1855, Bethell was simultaneously Chairman of the Council of Legal Education (of which he had been the chief creator), President of the newly formed Juridical Society, and a Vice-President of the Law Amendment Society; Macqueen also served on the Council of each of the last two.

[80] In this debate, for example, fusion was aired by both Cockburn and Malins, and declared to be favoured by Cranworth: *Hansard* HC Deb (series 3) 10 June 1855, vol 142, cols 1277, 1279.

[81] In voluntary separations too separate property was increasingly regarded as right: *cf* the view of Malins, the leading Conservative Chancery lawyer, *Hansard* HC Deb (series 3) 14 May 1857, vol 145, col 281. Under a private deed of separation, the wife's trustees often covenanted with the husband to indemnify him against her debts, while the husband covenanted with them to allow her to live separately and enjoy her property as a *feme sole*, with some provision for her separate maintenance: the example given in Macqueen (n 51) 119–20.

[82] Hastings to Brougham, Brougham MSS, 13090 (23 May 1857).

[83] The wife's earnings in any trade or business carried on entirely on her own should be her own property, but her real and personal property should be invested, and the husband should have the management and administration of the income until he made a bad use of his power, while gifts after marriage should be settled for the benefit of the wife and children: *Hansard* HC Deb (series 3) 14 May 1857, vol 145, col 281.

what England needed was a regime 'similar to the regulations which applied to the community of goods in France'.[84] When appropriate or necessary, he was in favour of providing for the separation of a couple's property, but not otherwise. But how was this to be achieved? In June 1856, like some other distinguished Chancery silks, he expressed misgivings that the Courts of Equity had gone too far with the doctrine of separate uses.[85] An alternative route was to give a married woman the property rights of a *feme sole* strictly for specific purposes, or in case of manifest need. By 1857 there were some precedents for this: since 1833 the Court of Common Pleas had possessed a little-used statutory power to authorise a married woman to effect a real property transaction as a *feme sole* without her husband's concurrence;[86] and from June 1856 successive Divorce Bills gave a wife with a divorce *a mensa et thoro* the status of a *feme sole* with regard to property, contracts, and suing and being sued. Nevertheless in May 1857, it will be remembered, Cranworth could see no way of meeting the need of wives 'in the humbler ranks of life' for cheap and immediately accessible protection of their earnings and scraps of personal property bought with them: 'the real defect' he said (and the Commons proved to agree), 'was the want of some cheap tribunal' to provide them with a separation.[87]

Bethell was notoriously contemptuous of Cranworth's abilities both as a lawyer and a draftsman: that he would attempt to succeed where Cranworth had failed could be safely predicted. Bold solutions were his forte. His personal knowledge of Macqueen's work; his reputation as a 'scientific' law reformer who valued the civil code as a model and whose goals for English law were uniformity, simplicity, and utility; his support for the current nostrum of the 'fusion' of jurisdictions; and his sceptical insider's view of Equity's current approach to the rights and liabilities of husband and wife all make his swift solution less surprising. A supremely cheap tribunal would now bring 'to the doorstep' of all wives, and not only those 'in the humbler ranks of life', a novel mode of separation that gave them instant security for their earnings and belongings simply by ending their coverture in all matters of property, contracts, suing and being sued, so long as their wrongful desertion lasted. A pair of country justices was to do summarily and *ex parte* what had hitherto only been thinkable for the new Court of Divorce to do, by due process, and after a prescribed interval.

[84] *Hansard* HC Deb (series 3) 21 June 1870, vol 202, col 607.

[85] In the debate on Perry's motion of 10 June 1856, Bethell, Malins and JG Phillimore expressed misgivings that 'Equity had gone too far with the doctrine of separate uses': *Hansard* HC Deb (series 3) 10 June 1856, vol 142, cols 1279–82.

[86] Bethell was no doubt aware of this, given it was his extensive practice and the acknowledgement of his 'valuable advice and important suggestions' included in the treatise which particularly drew this power to practitioners' attention: Macqueen (n 51) vii, 113–15. The Court had to be satisfied that a woman had made a proper application to her husband and that the cause of his non-concurrence (for example, lunacy, imprisonment, transportation, or absence or inaccessibility for any reason) was such as to justify this authorisation to effect real property transactions as a *feme sole*: Fines and Recoveries Act 1833, s 91. It is worth noting that Malins' Act of 1857 enabling married women to dispose of reversionary interests and 'equities to a settlement' in *personal* property made no such provision.

[87] *Hansard* HC Deb (series 3) 25 May 1857, vol 145, cols 800, 803, 805.

Such boldness was completely in character. Both as a lawyer and a politician Bethell's self-confidence and independent mindedness were famous and his
indispensability to the Government at that juncture removed any remote chance
that he might opt for caution. His own acute, subtle, intensely logical mind – only
Gladstone was his match in dialectical skill – was matched only by his capacity for
pedantry and gross errors of judgement.[88] As the President of the Juridical Society
in 1856, he characteristically asked:

> Why is there not a body of men in this country whose duty it is to collect a body of
> judicial statistics, or, in more common phrase, make the necessary experiments to see
> how far the law is fitted to the exigencies of society, the necessities of the times, the
> growth of wealth, and the progress of mankind?[89]

In his persistent manoeuvres to get the Divorce Bill through the Commons,
he abundantly demonstrated what insiders euphemistically termed 'an aplomb
possessed certainly by no other man in the House', and won praise outdoors
for 'unflinching courage' and 'energy and resolution'.[90] That summer's debates
furnish continual examples of his ingenious twists and turns and ability to strike
the right note in the House, as well as his readiness to 'give a very good measure
of sarcasm and contumely for what he receives'[91] – always no doubt delivered in his usual lisping, sharply articulated, supercilious-sounding drawl and
provokingly suave, smiling manner.[92] As a lawyer he had an incomparable and
disconcerting 'power of reducing a case to a simple nude proposition'.[93] Many
(although not all) of his legal projects were too radical to come to much and in
1859 his opinions were 'too advanced' to make him acceptable as Chancellor
to the Whigs in Palmerston's new Cabinet.[94] It is altogether in character that

---

[88] JB Atlay, *Lives of the Lord Chancellors* (London, 1906) vol II, 240; Nash (n 79) vol I, 221 and 234.
'Gladstone never wants A word, but Bethell wants THE word' was William White's apt summary in
White (n 74) 37. Testimonies to Bethell's supreme cleverness abound: for example, his performances
in Parliament made John Duke Coleridge in 1861 sit 'absolutely wondering at the possibilities of the
human mind': EH Coleridge, *Life and Correspondence of John Duke Lord Coleridge, Lord Chief Justice of
England* (London, 1904) vol I, 265.

[89] Nash (n 79) vol I, 191.

[90] *Hansard* HC Deb (series 3) 13 August 1857, vol 147, col 1541; 'Sketches in Parliament' *Illustrated
London News* (8 August 1857) 130; *Law Times* (15 May 1858) 106; and similarly *Law Times* (29 May
1858) 130. Jowett of Balliol, who both knew Bethell well and liked him, later emphasised his 'uncom-
mon courage and self-reliance': Bethell papers, Bodleian, MS Don.c.150 f.103 dorso, Jowett to RBD
Morier (16 June 1873).

[91] 'Sketches in Parliament' (n 90).

[92] Abundant examples of Bethell's caustic wit survive. 'Miss Fanny's' intonation and manner are
described in Nash (n 79) vol I, 75–76. 'His diction lent an especial quality to those bitter sayings which
rendered him more dreaded that any man of his generation': Atlay (n 88) vol II, 223.

[93] 'Recollections of Lord Westbury' (n 68) 476. This is a useful sketch, though occasionally too sharp.
The historian of twentieth century Lord Chancellors singles him out as a major legislative reformer and
also a considerable jurist with a 'flair for writing an authoritative judgement based on general principles and without the cumbrous citation of precedents': RVF Heuston, *Lives of the Lord Chancellors,
1940–1970* (Oxford, Clarendon Press, 1987) 127.

[94] Nash (n 79) 273. 'Bethell as a law reformer was somewhat in advance of his time', concluded Nash
in 1888: Nash (n 79) vol II, 304.

he had the temerity to 'dismiss Hell with costs' in the celebrated *Essays and Reviews* case in 1864;[95] and equally so that in 1865 he became the only modern Lord Chancellor hounded to resign in disgrace.[96] In short, probably no other Victorian Attorney General would have been so ready as this brilliant, arrogant man to ignore precedent over two such sensitive matters as matrimonial property and magistrates' powers, and borrow from the *Code Civil* the procedure and machinery which to his lucid mind exactly met the exigences of the case.

In terms of the final upshot, however, what matters most is not how the French system of *autorisation* came to the attention of influential London circles, nor even how it came to commend itself to Palmerston's Attorney General, but why the Government's proposal to introduce a similar system in England was swiftly carried through Parliament and warmly welcomed with open doors. That summer no plausible measure to protect hard working deserted wives from being plundered by their shameless absentee husbands could have been sagely rejected, given the public indignation that had been roused on that score. What ensured the ready and even enthusiastic acceptive of Bethell's radically novel way of providing this protection, however, was the sudden emergence of a pressing political need for a substantial package of local facilities for matrimonial relief.

In origin the Divorce Bill was simply another measure for modernising court machinery and procedure; and like other measures for remodelling England's legal institutions in the age of reform (and beyond), it was bedevilled by pressures for thoroughly expert and impartial metropolitan courts conflicting with those for thoroughly expert and impartial local tribunals. Advocates of centralisation urged that the highly technical business of the ecclesiastical courts could only be properly dealt with by secular courts which possessed an experienced, able, and impartial bar and bench – especially initially, when judicial decisions would be establishing a body of case law. To campaigners for cheap, accessible justice suitable to the needs of modern life, on the other hand, the new County Courts were the obvious replacement for the consistory courts which operated locally.[97] 'We see no good ground whatever for removing the administration of justice in any instance from the immediate locality where the parties who it most

---

[95] 'He told me that until then he had always accepted the orthodox views of religion', but when he had to consider his judgment, 'he saw how untenable the orthodox views were': Jowett to Dean Stanley, 23 July 1873, Bodleian, MS Don. c.150, f.103.

[96] 'Well, Cranny', the Queen is somewhat improbably said to have remarked on receiving his replacement, the plodding, conscientious Cranworth, 'Kingsley is right, it *is* better to be good than clever': Atlay (n 88) vol II, 75. Jowett was not far wrong, however, in telling Dean Stanley that Bethell 'fell quite as much from his virtues' as his faults: Bethell Papers, Bodleian, MS Don. c. 150 f. 103 (23 July 1870). Sir John Rolt, who predicably never liked him, privately summed him up in 1867 as 'wonderfully clever and unwise ... No one could have drawn from the imagination such a character ... He was truly an original': Sir J Rolt, *Memoirs of the Right Hon. Sir John Rolt* (privately printed, 1939) 328.

[97] In fact, by limiting the power to grant judicial separations to a single court in London, the law under these proposed reforms would actually become less accessible.

concerns are residing', declared a contributor to the *Law Review* (the journal of the Law Amendment Society and a favourite vehicle for such views); centralisation was 'practically a virtual violation of the royal pledge not to "sell, delay, or deny justice"'.[98] Behind these conflicting ideals of legal administration lay the conflicting professional and financial interests of metropolitan versus provincial practitioners, as well as barristers versus solicitors. 'The present system of centralising (business) in London might be convenient to a few judges, a few agency houses, and a few barristers whom they specially patronise', but to other practitioners it could seem 'an absolute denial of justice', not to mention how it would appear to barristers convinced that attorneys were 'absorbing all the local business of the country'.[99] All extensions of the jurisdiction of County Courts (where attorney had rights of audience) or further reductions in the civil business of the Assizes (where their own right of audience was exclusive) were to be firmly opposed.

Within Parliament itself the scales were weighted in favour of judicial centralisation and the interests of the Bar. Around an eighth of MPs were barristers,[100] and the vital committee stages of law reform measures were always dominated in the Commons by leading barristers, and in the Lords by the handful of Law Lords.[101] Yet in the newspaper press as well as among populist orators the Bar had few friends while that octogenarian loose cannon, Brougham, was still firing salvoes against the legal status quo (Chancery and Chancery lawyers were especially vulnerable: *Bleak House* had done its work well). For centralisers, caution was particularly wise in the 1850s, when the cry of 'local liberties' was as powerful a political shibboleth in legal administration as it was in local government and could bring strange allies into the same division lobby. Paternalists and defenders of 'our territorial constitution', country gentlemen and Members for distant towns as well as the Shires; Liberal-radical populists and advanced law reformers, with their gospel of cheap law, and justice at every man's door; Russellite Whigs, always ready to pay homage to 'the people's liberties' (and all the more so that summer, when Lord John was in factious mood and set on turning out Palmerston)[102] – this troika's support could easily win partial or temporary parliamentary victory for an anti-centralisation issue, even if in the end the flow of business to the superior Courts and the fees of the Bar were usually little harmed.

---

[98] Without decentralisation, the courts would continue to present 'all the offensive features of an oppressive class monopoly': 'Legal and Judicial Administration' (1856) *Law Review* 23, 328.

[99] 'Today, they have most of the business in courts of bankruptcy, they exclude the bar from County Courts, petty sessions are now taking over much Quarter Sessions business, at judicial inquiries under Acts of Parliament the advocates are almost always attorneys': 'The Etiquette of the Bar' (August 1857) *Law Magazine and Law Review*, vol III, 242, 253.

[100] In the 1852–57 Parliament, there were approximately 100 lawyers: see AS Rosser, 'Businessmen in the Parliament of 1852–7: Players or Spectators?' (2013) 32 *Parliamentary History* 477, 503.

[101] In 1857 there were only five law lords apart from Cranworth, the Lord Chancellor; but of these Lyndhurst, Brougham, Campbell, and St Leonards were formidable operators: only the newcomer, Wensleydale, was an inaudible, pedantic, lightweight.

[102] *Broughton Diary* 43, 760, f. 119 (7 June 1857).

The tussle to prevent total centralisation of matrimonial relief was thus part of a long-running conflict between supporters of centralisation and the interests of the London legal elite and superior courts on the one hand, and champions of local jurisdictions and the lower reaches of the legal profession on the other: in effect, between quality and accessibility. Above all, it was inseparable from the almost simultaneous battle to stop centralisation of the ecclesiastical courts' testamentary jurisdiction. The Probate and the Divorce Bills both had as their object the withdrawal of secular business from the ecclesiastical courts and raised similar issue of legal machinery and institutions. Between 6 and 20 July the Commons were in committee on the Probate Bill, and between 4 and 19 August on the Divorce Bill. The struggle over provincial probate facilities thus provided a practice round of the struggle over provincial facilities for matrimonial causes. Wills mattered far more than divorce to Palmerston and Bethell, to bankers and solicitors, and indeed to all but devout High Churchmen for death was certain, but divorce very unlikely indeed.[103] Throughout, the Government's proposed limitations on local probate registrars were stubbornly resisted. Bethell's uninhibited warning that local registrars would be incompetent and great frauds would follow was met by the retort that 'No doubt, if they took the opinion of the London professional gentlemen, every mother's son of them would say that the country Courts were not equal to the duty'.[104] Despite Palmerston's personal efforts and Bethell's insistence that probate required 'great critical nicety, great care and a knowledge of the law', the Government's proposal to centralise wills business in London had to be abandoned.[105]

Could this victory for the local testamentary jurisdiction be repeated for local matrimonial jurisdiction? On 7 August this was finally put to the test. Newly in the forefront were those eloquent *devots* and 'fanatics', Lord John Manners, Henry Drummond, and Gladstone, and the Irish lawyer-leader, Isaac Butt, busily making himself useful to the Conservatives. Many of the cast, however, were the same as before. Leading roles were again played by certain veteran knights of the shire (Graham, Henley, Buller) and University Members (Wigram, Heathcote); by notable

---

[103] Ordinary readers of *Punch* as well as the likes of Lord Granville thought what should be done over divorce was a fairly minor matter of common sense. The political correspondence of these months is almost barren of reference to the Divorce Bill; whereas (for example) Palmerston urgently sought assurances from both Cranworth and Bethell that the Probate Bill would not extend probate duty to real property: British Library (BL), Add. MSS. 48580, f.334 (10 December 1856); Cranworth to Palmerston, MS62/PP/GC/CR48, Broadlands Archive (10 December 1856); Bethell to Palmerston, BL, Add. MSS. 48580 f.335 (11 December 1856). Bethell had long taken a particular interest in probate reform.

[104] JW Henley, *Hansard* HC Deb (series 3) 20 July 1857, vol 147, col 82.

[105] Palmerston to Bethell, BL, Add 48580, f.200 (7 July 1857); Cranworth to Palmerston MS62/PP/GC/CR/56 Broadlands Archives (17 July 1857); *Hansard* HC Deb 6 July 1857, vol 146, cols 1019–20, Viscount Palmerston, *Hansard* HC Deb 10 July 1857, vol 146, cols 1302–22. District registrars had to be allowed to grant probate with no property limits whatever and only two safeguards: that the validity of the will was not contested, and the testator died within the district. In that case, the County Court's jurisdiction was limited to personalty under £200 and real property under £300, Court of Probate Act 1857, s 54.

members of the Law Amendment Society (Napier, Perry, Goderich) and leading Chancery lawyers (Malins, Kelly); by Lord John Russell, that factious arch-Whig and friend of the People and by AS Ayrton, the loquacious new radical Member for Tower Hamlets, and the usually silent Thomas Collins of the Northern Circuit and West Riding Sessions and MP for Knaresborough. (Opposition to centralisation of every kind was inevitably strong in the north.) One speaker after another, while agreeing the St Leonards' clause was unworkable and must be expunged, rubbed home the point that his was the only clause in the bill to provide local facilities of any sort. Whatever replacement was devised 'must be given to the people gener- ally', Ayrton warned Bethell, 'for it was impossible the Liberal Members could allow a bill to pass which constituted a Court that afforded a remedy to the rich alone'. The same message came from the leading Irish Conservative lawyer, Joseph Napier, and the Peelite heavy weight Sir James Graham: what was needed was 'a domestic tribunal on the spot'.[106] But where could such a tribunal be found? There were objections not only to a single justice, but to two justices in petty sessions, a County Court judge, and the Chairman or Vice-Chairman of quarter sessions. The Committee therefore accepted Bethell's promise that as soon as the remaining clauses of the Bill had been dealt with, he would 'endeavour to use all his resources' to find some machinery that they could consider appropriate,[107] and moved on to the next clause: that after two years' desertion, a judicial separation should be obtainable from the new Divorce Court.

Immediately a sharp attack was mounted on what was politically much the Bill's weakest point: that far from giving the poor access to divorce, as repeatedly promised, it deprived them of the local facilities they already had by requiring them to go to an expensive metropolitan Divorce Court for divorce *a mensa et thoro*, hitherto available from the 50 or so provincial consistory courts. The issue of local tribunals, declaimed Isaac Butt, would settle whether the Bill was to be 'an injury or a boon', and he called on Members 'to preserve to the people of England that great principle of local administration which … had established their liberties in the days of Alfred, and which preserved them in the days of Queen Victoria'. With only one great central Court, could anyone believe that the Government really desired 'to extend a boon to the middle and lower classes', asked Drummond; and one Member after another won cheers with variations on the theme that 'it was of importance in the case of the poor to bring remedies for grievances to the doors of the poor'.[108]

In 1857 such rhetoric warned of danger ahead: centralisation and robbing the poor of justice were two of the gravest sins in the mid-Victorian

---

[106] 'It would be a reproach to the Committee if, after floundering through a number of clauses to erect an unapproachable tribunal, it could not, on arriving at a clause giving a domestic tribunal on the spot for the protection of the earnings of the poor wife deserted by her husband, make that clause perfect for its purpose': *Hansard* HC Deb (series 3) 7 August 1857, vol 147, cols 1232–34.

[107] ibid, col 1235.

[108] ibid, cols 1237–38 (Butt), 1249 (Drummond), 1242 (Perry).

political canon. Practical men, moreover, urged that experience showed that most wives in a broken marriage wanted only separation with maintenance rather than full divorce, and joined those opposed to divorce on religious grounds in insisting that facilities for separation must not be thus restricted. On the previous night the attack on the Bill's centralisation of all divorce facilities in London had been foiled by a rare personal intervention from Palmerston; but that day the Prime Minister had left for Osborne House by the one o'clock train, and his Attorney General now declared himself 'extremely desirous' of making judicial separation 'as inexpensive and facile' as was compatible with 'the interests of morality'.[109] He would accept Butt's proposal to give County Courts the power of adjudicating judicial separations, he said, 'whenever they depended on grounds insufficient to warrant divorce' – weasel words which allowed him to claim as the attack developed that he had been poorly rewarded for having shown 'the greatest readiness to meet that proposal fairly and openly', yet deny he had given a qualified promise to incorporate local jurisdiction into the Bill.[110] Despite the sensible suggestion by two Conservative Chancery silks (Malins and Wigram) that the clause should be taken later so that provision for the judicial separation and protection of the property of deserted wives could be 'brought into one harmonious system', he insisted on putting to the vote Butt's proposal that judicial separation should be entrusted to the County Court judges, taking care to emphasise the haste and disorderliness of County Court proceedings and imply that his new clause for protecting deserted wives' property would provide what humbler wives usually wanted – namely, protection against the husband 'extending to her property and to her support'.[111] Clearly he hoped in this way to split the anti-Government vote. He was decisively outmanoeuvred, however, when that life-long Young Englander, Lord John Manners, devised an amendment which left unspecified which local court was to be given a matrimonial jurisdiction, and (with Butt's backing) challenged Members to vote against it if they believed that the jurisdiction ought to be centralised in London, and that the remedy proposed to be given should only be available to persons of rank, wealth, and social position.

Amid increasing excitement other opposition frontbenchers rammed home the point. 'One great palace would not suit the people throughout the country', said Henly, 'and therefore they asked the Government, in whatever way they pleased, whether by moveable tents or otherwise, to give the people some opportunity of

---

[109] As Gladstone reminded the Committee, Palmerston had interposed that local facilities for judicial separation were undesirable because divorce was better than separation: ibid, col1243, referring to *Hansard* HC Deb (series 3) 6 August 1857, vol 147, col 1194. This was probably an impromptu expression of his personal opinion: he was in the House only because Clarendon had mislaid his invitation to go to Osborne on the occasion of the visit of the French Emperor and Empress. It is notable that the only reference to the Divorce Bill in Palmerston's very scanty Diary is under 6 August: 'Hs of Cs Divorce Bill', MS62/PP/v/D/17, Broadlands Archive (6 August 1857).

[110] *Hansard* HC Deb (series 3) 7 August 1857, vol 147, cols 1240, 252 ('No! No!'), 1256.

[111] ibid, cols 1245–49.

getting at those remedies which they now possessed'. Even Disraeli was moved by the prospect of defeating the Government on a popular issue to utter his first and last words in the long Divorce Bill debates 'the real issue is whether there should be a local jurisdiction or not', he told his troops; they had an opportunity now to assert a principle which he believed to be 'sound, just and politic, and to which the people of this country were devoted'. Lord John Russell had only to declare in Whiggish vein that 'the destruction of the local tribunals would be a great injury to the people', and amid triumphant laughter and loud cheers Manners' amendment was carried by 98 votes to 87: judicial separation was now available from the Divorce Court '*or any other Court hereinafter authorised by the Act*'.[112] To thus 'engraft a local jurisdiction upon the highly centralised machinery of the Government Bill' far outweighed in practical importance any of the 'nice distinctions' in the grounds of divorce so lengthily and heatedly debated, as was widely appreciated outdoors.[113]

This was the Government's first defeat in the Commons on the Divorce Bill. The combination of Conservatives, Peelites, Whigs, advanced Radicals and Irish that had driven Palmerston to hold a General Election in March had won another victory; and an outcry over centralisation and robbing the poor might well prove more dangerous that the earlier one over Canton. Plainly Bethell's new clauses must be drafted to remove any protection for further righteous indignation, by providing undeniably cheap and accessible local facilities for deserted wives to secure judicial separation and protection for their earnings. This was not easy: England still notoriously lacked an adequate local court structure,[114] despite the efforts of the previous decade.[115] For judicial separation there were four possibilities: Assizes, County Courts, Quarter Sessions, and peripatetic special Commissioners; and of these only Assizes would undeniably provide the dignity and discretion combined with judicial and forensic expertise thought necessary by some even for mere separation.[116] Assize judges, however,

---

[112] ibid, cols 1252–57.

[113] 'Curiosities of Local Courts' (15 August 1857) *Solicitors' Journal* 1, 721. Similarly a very different weekly: 'the Government were beaten on a proposal which, though made by the Tories, is really more for the benefit of the humbler orders than anything in the Bill. This was to create a local jurisdiction in divorce cases, so that a poor man or woman in Northumberland or Cornwall may not be compelled to come to London, and live there while seeking redress': 'Punch's Essence of Parliament' *Punch* 33 (15 August 1857) 61.

[114] Erskine Perry had recently treated it as a conclusive argument against introducing a continental-style communal matrimonial property regime, that 'England, with its centralised establishments, and very important development of local tribunals', could not provide the wife with the necessary legal protection against a dissolute, profligate or heedless husband: 'A Review of the Divorce Bill of 1856, with Propositions for an Amendment of the Laws Affecting Married Persons' (January 1857) *Edinburgh Law Review* 203, and similarly in his report to the Law Amendment Society, printed in 'Report of the Personal Laws Committee on the Law Relating to the Property of Married Women' (August 1856) 1 *Law Magazine and Law Review* 404–405.

[115] Notably in the County Courts Act 1846, Indictable Offences Act 1848, Summary Jurisdiction Act 1848, and the Justices Protection Act 1848. The latter three were known as 'Jervis's Acts of 1848–9'.

[116] A persistent legacy from the old regime of the ecclesiastical courts was the mystique clinging to what had hitherto been called 'divorce', though in reality it was merely separation, and a matter of

were already overburdened in the populous areas likely to produce most matrimonial work, and moreover came only twice a year, so that there might be a
delay of six or seven months in getting a decree. Bethell therefore proposed to
use Quarter Sessions as well as Assizes; then substituted Borough Recorders for
the plainly unsuitable Quarter Sessions.[117] He next swung obligingly backwards
and forwards to meet views expressed in Committee on 18 and 19 August, and
finally settled on 20 August that 'Judges of Assize and any person named in the
Commission of Assize, and also Quarter Sessions', should deal with petitions
for restitution of conjugal rights as well as judicial separation.[118] After vacilla-
tion like this it can have been no surprise that the Lords swiftly deleted 'Quarter
Sessions' from the clause on 24 August, nor that the Commons readily agreed
to their amendment.[119] Certainly this in no way lessened the praise lavished
upon Bethell by the local jurisdiction lobby for 'the great pains' he had taken to
meet the wishes of the House: he had 'not only fulfilled his promise, but done so
in a way which gave every reason to believe their intentions would be properly
carried into effect'.[120]

Bethell's promise, however, had been a two-fold one, and in the set of inter-
connected clauses he drafted during the weekend of 8–9 August he also provided
new local machinery for protecting the property of deserted wives.[121] These
clauses completely ended the monopoly of the new Divorce Court over the granting of *feme sole* status – a monopoly still intact when the Bill left the Lords at the
end of June. For the first time, a wronged wife was to be equally able to regain
her *feme sole* status from local tribunals or from the Divorce Court, whether with
regard to her person and property, or with regard to her property alone; and in
the case of the latter, that *feme sole* status was to be instantly available from the
very lowest tier of neighbourhood tribunals – as in France, under the practice of
autorisation.[122] Magistrates' summary powers, although only recently put on a

---

purely private not social concern, usually sought to secure a financial settlement: this topic was covered
extensively in the *Solicitors' Journal* of 15 May 1858: *Solicitors' Journal* (London, 15 May 1858).

[117] Quarter sessions were open to all local justices, and County quarter sessions had a lay Chairman
and Vice-Chairman and were still heavily concerned with county administration.

[118] This was in response to a suggestion from Henley: *Hansard* HC Deb (series 3) 18 August 1857,
vol 147, col 1850.

[119] The many Chairmen of Quarter Sessions in Parliament expressed unease about using these Courts,
and in the Lords, feeling was so strong that Granville, the Government's Leader, 'at once told Fortescue
and Somerset (two leading objecting Liberal peers), that if they would suggest the change, I would agree
to it': Granville to Brougham, Brougham MSS. 7070 (25 August 1857); *cf Hansard* HC Deb (series 3)
24 August 1857, vol 147, col 2041. That morning Palmerston had scribbled to him, 'I think the Hse of
Cns will make they minds up to sacrifice the Quarter Sessions': Granville Papers The National Archives
PRO30/29/19/22 (24 August 1857).

[120] *Hansard* HC Deb (series 3) 18 August 1857, vol 147, cols 1847 (Henley), 1850 (Manners);
21 August 1857, col 1974 (Henley).

[121] Clauses 17 to 26 of the MCA 1857.

[122] Doubts about the fitness of justices in petty sessions to decide whether a wife had established
desertion 'without reasonable cause' survived among lawyers but were stifled in Parliament by the fact
that they alone could provide instant property protection for every deserted wife, wherever she lived,
and however humble.

footing for growth, now included in effect partial judicial separation. They could not end the duty to cohabit, nor order alimony. These limitations, however, might well seem unimportant to a wife whose husband had disappeared, especially if she believed he had emigrated (as was often the case in those peak emigration years); and even if she intended to apply in due course for a judicial separation or divorce, an order from her local magistrates would always be useful, since it would instantly end her *coverture* from the date of her desertion, instead of only from the date of any decree she ultimately obtained.[123] Undeniably, every self-supporting deserted wife would henceforth be able to gain immediate release from that barbarous 'relic of the savage character' of the ancient law of marital relations that the current public mood made intolerable, whether she was rich or poor.[124]

At the Commons' insistence Palmerston's Attorney General had thus provided provincial facilities which were expected to make it rarely necessary for those living at a distance from London to apply to the high powered and no doubt expensive metropolitan Divorce Court. Dissolution of Marriage remained available only in London (as it did until the 1920s); but in 1857 the primary demand was expected to be for separation, not full divorce.[125] True, there might be a delay of six or seven months in getting a decree of judicial separation or restitution of conjugal rights at the local Assizes; but the instant availability of a property protection order as an interim measure made delay in getting a full judicial separation less important. By the end of the session not even the most factious critic could accuse the Government of 'robbing the poor' of local access to matrimonial justice; and it was wholly undeniable that for deserted wives the law had been 'greatly improved both in point of actual justice and in point of humanity – with respect both to the condition of women and the protection of the weak against the tyranny of the strong'.[126]

---

[123] See O Anderson, 'Emigration and Marriage Break-up in Mid-Victorian England' (1997) 1 *Economic History Review* 104–109.

[124] This universalism was a notable departure from current practice. A two-tier system always operated in the County Courts and had been accepted for the new district probate registries; it had been incorporated into St Leonards' proposals and was mooted for both protection orders and judicial separation in the debates of 7 August, even by Bethell himself: *Hansard* HC Deb (series 3) 7 August 1857, vol 147, cols, 1232, 1250. Nevertheless, where considerable property was at stake, it was wise for a woman to apply to the Divorce Court, since then an appeal would be possible if her application was refused: JF Macqueen, *A Practical Treatise on Divorce and Matrimonial Jurisdiction Under the Act of 1857 and New Orders* (London, W Maxwell, 1858) 98.

[125] All the arrangements for the new Court were based upon the expectation that it would not be a busy Court, and that petitions for full divorce would make up only a small part of what little business it had. Despite the mockery prompted by hindsight, this was not an unreasonable guess. Separations by private deed – as famously tried by George and Caroline Norton – were certainly increasing; and on 18 August 1857 an MP who wanted to maximise the likely workload predicted from Scottish experience 200 separations and 100 divorces a year: *Hansard* HC Deb (series 3) 18 August 1857, vol 147, col 1848 (McMahon).

[126] *Hansard* HC Deb (series 3) 30 July 1857, vol 147, col 734 (Bethell).

This liberal response to political necessity was rewarded by widespread approval of the Act as genuinely giving more equal access to matrimonial relief, reflected in Punch's rhyming summary:

> On one point it affirms let us chiefly lay stress,
>
> That wrong and not Gold, gives the right of redress;
>
> And that HELEN, the Countess, no longer can buy
>
> What to NELLY, the Laundress, tribunals deny.[127]

Local facilities for judicial separation and the new protection orders were singled out for praise. The mass-market Weekly Times enthused:

> The women of the humbler classes will be protected against the tyranny or the rapacity of idle and drunken husbands, and enabled to place themselves, by a simple and inexpensive proceeding, in a position to carry on any lawful industry.[128]

At the other end of the social spectrum the temperamentally captious *Saturday Review* acknowledged that, 'In conferring local powers on the Judges of Assize, and in providing a summary remedy for the protection of deserted wives, the act promises to some extent an equitable succour to the poor'. The *Morning Post* too, praised the willingness to 'bring speedy and cheap justice home to every man's door' that had led the Commons to provide judicial separation at Assizes or Quarter Sessions, and condemned the Lords' elimination of the latter.[129] In their last-ditch debate, die-hard Conversative peers had indeed rousingly abused the Government for conceding local matrimonial jurisdiction to 'a mere abstract vote' of the Commons inspired by a claptrap desire 'to bring divorce home to the poor man's door'.[130] Yet it was precisely that pliant Government populism that won a measure of unqualified approval for the new Act. And rightly so; for as the

---

[127] *Punch* 33 (5 September 1857) 96.

[128] *Weekly Times* (20 September 1857). Not surprisingly there was some confusion between those two newly coined terms, a 'judicial separation' and a 'protection order'. For example in the *Spectator* – which also thought this part of the Act might be used as an auxiliary to 'Mr Fitzroy's Act' (against wife-beating): 'The New Marriage Law' (29 August 1857) vol 29, 904, and a 'Police Order' was all too often assumed to work in the way proposed by St Leonards, and not in the way actually introduced by Bethell: *Illustrated London News* (29 August 1857) 211; See also, 'The Divorce Bill Dissected' *Punch* 33 (5 September 1857) 103:

> 'And while she's deserted, if DARBY (the Beast)
> Interferes with her poor little goods in the least,
> She may go to a Beak, whose proceedings are quick,
> And Policemen Z 1 will administer Stick'.

[129] 'The Divorce Act' *Saturday Review* (London, 19 September 1857) 262–63; 'The House of Lords Last Night' *Morning Post* (London, 25 August 1857) 4.

[130] *Hansard* HC Deb (series 3) 24 August 1857, vol 147, cols 2015, 2026 (Redesdale and St Leonards). In a speech often greeted by 'Hear, hear', and far more colourful than *Hansard's* report suggests, St Leonards had told the Lords, 'As to the jurisdiction given to what were called local courts, it was a thing to laugh at': 'The Debate of Friday on the Divorce Bill – Explanations' *London Evening Standard* (London, 25 August 1857) 3.

Solicitors' Journal had pointed out after the decisive votes of 7 August, in reality what would make a difference was not making the law of separation and divorce laxer but giving a cheap and accessible local remedy. Without local tribunals, 'the poor man's divorce bill, as it has been called, would *increase* the average cost of all proceedings except those for divorce *a vinculo*.[131] Bethell's last-minute package of clauses fully deserved their welcome: for they alone had rescued the Bill and the Government from this damning outcome.

As a result of a train of events beginning with a Scots barrister's summer holiday in Boulogne, then, the French system of *autorisation* and its practical success across the Channel became known for the first time in leading legal and political circles in England. Following directly from that, the idea came into circulation that some version of that system might be introduced into the Divorce Bill then going through Parliament, to meet the well-publicised and widely supported need for 'protective remedies against the legal right of an English husband to seize the earnings of the wife he had deserted'. An urgent last-minute political need to incorporate local facilities into the Bill prompted the boldly logical Attorney General of the day to give the lowest tier of English magistrates, instead of the new Divorce Court alone, a discretionary power similar to that entrusted to a French *juge d'arrondissement*. In England, as in France, a deserted wife was to be able to apply to her local magistrate for an order giving back to her certain civil rights and powers (and liabilities) surrendered at marriage to her husband, just as if she were not married. '*La femme autorisée devient donc aussi capable, ni plus ni moins, que si elle n'était pas mariée*', in the words of the great *civiliste* Demolombe quoted by Macqueen, and an English magistrates' order was now to have the same effect, although only if the wife could show she had been wrongfully deserted and was maintaining herself.[132] Political circumstances ensured, too, that a matter of days after this 'exotic from France' was implanted in the Divorce Bill, it was accepted by both Houses and became part of the law of the land: but how well did it take root in English soil?

---

[131] 'Local Divorce Courts' *Solicitors' Journal* (London, 15 August 1857) 721.

[132] '*L'effet général de l'autorisation accordée a la femme, soit par son mari, soit par la justice, est de lever l'incapacité qui résultait pour elle de l'état de mariage*': Demolombe (n 72) 364. Parliamentary provision had also been made for the publicity declared by Demolombe to be vitally in the interests of third parties and implied by the Code.

2

What was the Law
of 'Economic Divorce'?

The Matrimonial Causes Act 1857 is one of the classic sections of the English statute book – often mentioned but rarely read. At the time, one clause alone in that hotly contested measure was universally welcomed – section 21; yet as the Introduction has shown, in the twentieth and twenty-first century, the very existence of this clause has barely been noticed.[1] For a generation, however, this novel, just, and humane accessory provision was easily the most widely used section of the whole Act, and affected over three times as many marriages as the provisions for divorce and judicial separation combined.[2] For decades it empowered wives, expropriated husbands, helped to facilitate productive enterprise and the flow of credit and capital, and to keep down the poor rates. Not until well into the twentieth century was its influence on family fortunes and relationships entirely spent. More important still, until relatively recently, millions of ordinary citizens were affected by its continuing impact on the machinery and workings of English family law. From a twenty-first century vantage point then, this neglected clause calls out for attention not only for the unfamiliar light it throws on the devices and desires of (male) mid-Victorian lawyers and politicians, and women in broken marriages, but also its role as a progenitor of two prominent features of English life today: the widespread use of magistrates' courts for domestic proceedings, and the possession by married women of the same civil rights and responsibilities as men and single women.

What were the provisions of this almost forgotten clause which served as a gateway to complete legal autonomy for thousands of self-supporting mid-Victorian wives, and set what proved to be momentous precedents? To appreciate their significance it is necessary to keep in mind that under English common law a woman lost her separate civil identity on marriage. Immediately and automatically

---

[1] See Introduction. Textbooks of legal history rarely mention section 21, with the importance of the legislation eclipsed in mid-twentieth century works by study of the Married Women's Property Acts, eg, RH Graveson and FR Crane (eds), *A Century of Family Law, 1857–1957* (London, Sweet and Maxwell, 1957) 122. ME Doggett, *Marriage, Wife-Beating and the Law in Victorian England* (South Carolina University Press, 1993).

[2] For typical approving comments on the humanity and wisdom of this clause, see 'The Divorce Act' *Saturday Review* (19 September, 1857) 262–63. For data on the numbers of matrimonial cases heard, see subsequent chapters.

she became a *feme covert* existing only under the wing (and theoretically, protection) of her husband, instead of a *feme sole* with all the rights and powers of a person who is *sui juris* (of age and independent). Even when property was settled upon her under the rules of equity for her separate use, this had to be vested in a trustee, and was subject to restraints on anticipation and alienation; it was never strictly accurate to say that a married woman was made in equity a *feme sole* in respect of her 'separate property'. In effect, no married woman could own money or property,[3] make contracts or a will, or sue or be sued in her own name alone, freely and without any restraint.[4]

Section 21 of the Matrimonial Causes Act enabled a wife quickly, cheaply, and easily to recover the capacity to do all these things exactly as though she were once more a single woman; provided she could show that she had been deserted without reasonable cause and was maintaining herself by her own lawful industry or property. In these circumstances she could apply to her local police magistrate if she lived in the metropolitan district; or to two justices at petty sessions if she lived in the country; or to the new Court for Divorce and Matrimonial Causes wherever she lived, for an order whose immediate effect was to give her the status of a *feme sole* with regard to all her earnings and property acquired since her desertion. She was directed to enter this order within 10 days with the Registrar of her local County Court (unless it was granted by the Divorce Court itself, which had its own Registrars). Her husband or any creditor or other person claiming under him could apply for its discharge, but while this order continued, she was to be, and be deemed to have been, from the date of her desertion, 'in the like position in all respects, with regard to property and contract and suing and being sued, as she would be under this Act if she obtained a decree of judicial separation.'[5] And what was this position? Sections 25 and 26 of the Act provided in some detail that

---

[3] There are, of course, different types of property. Any chattels and money that a wife brought to the marriage became her husband's. A husband also acquired the right upon marriage to manage any freehold property belonging to his wife and to take the income during their joint lives. Leasehold property remained the wife's, however, the husband acquired not only the right to rents and profits, but the right to sell the lease during their joint lives.

[4] This is a rough summary of a complicated subject. For a near contemporary account with helpful clarity, particularly in regard to the limitations of married women's property rights under equity, see AV Dicey, *Lectures on the Relation between Law and Public Opinion in England* (London, 1905) 371–95. For a historian's examination of wives and property, see E Spring, *Law, Land and Family: Aristocratic Inheritance in England, 1300 to 1800* (University of North Carolina Press, Chapel Hill, 1993); AL Erickson, *Women and Property in Early Modern England* (Abingdon, Routledge, 1993); and J Heggie, 'Women's Involvement in Property in the North Riding of Yorkshire in the Eighteenth and Nineteenth Centuries' in A Capern, B McDonagh and J Aston (eds), *Women and the Land 1500–1900* (Woodbridge, Boydell and Brewer, 2019). For an examination of trusts and their complexities see C Stebbings, *The Private Trustee in Victorian England* (Cambridge, Cambridge University Press, 2002). Opposing interpretations of the common law doctrine and its consequences can be found in G Williams, 'The Legal Unity of Husband and Wife' (1947) 10 *MLR* 16–31.

[5] Matrimonial Causes Act (MCA) 1857, s 21. For the full text of section 21 see Appendix I. Section 21's direction with regard to registration is another way in which it marks the beginning of the twentieth-century English system of matrimonial justice, for today County Court Registrars deal with practically all the ancillary work in divorce.

a judicially separated wife was to be considered a *feme sole* not only with respect to her property of every description however acquired, but also for purposes of contract, matters of the civil courts and matters of probate; her husband was also not to be liable for her contracts, torts, or costs. Metropolitan police magistrates or justices in petty sessions were thus empowered to restore to a self-supporting deserted wife all the rights, powers and liabilities of an independent person so far as earning and property were concerned. In short, they were given a power best described as 'economic divorce'.[6]

As Chapter One explained, this startlingly bold final formulation of section 21, 'embrac(ing) high and low', was the last-minute handiwork of Sir Richard Bethell, Palmerston's clever, self-confident, 'half-Radical' and disconcertingly flexible Attorney General. It was 'the most important clause in the Bill', he told the Commons, and his appraisal soon proved correct in terms of legal innovation and also practical usefulness.[7] The other clauses of the Act saw to it that the old ecclesiastical law of divorce and matrimonial causes survived substantially intact until after the First World War;[8] and applications to the new Divorce Court were scanty and often unsuccessful for the next 70 years or more.[9] In contrast, section 21 was

---

[6] The less accurate and thoroughly confusing term 'protection order' will be avoided here despite its long usage, in favour of 'economic divorce'. The habit of referring to both section 21 orders and the very different orders made under section 4 of the Matrimonial Causes Acts Amendment Act 1878 as 'protection orders' has been a constant source of error and misunderstanding among hopeful applicants, legal luminaries, and academic writers alike. In 1890, for example, Montagu Williams was driven to distraction as a police magistrate by the stream of working-class women who came to his East End court asking for 'protection orders' against some alleged ill-treatment. Williams himself, a successful defence counsel who had in effect been invalided out to a police court, continually rebutted all such requests, insisting (quite incorrectly) that 'there is no such thing as a protection order': see, M Williams, *Later Leaves: Being the Further Reminiscences of Montagu Williams, Q.C.* (London, 1891) 308; J Davis, 'A Poor Man's System of Justice: the London Police Courts in the Second Half of the Nineteenth Century' (1984) 27 *Historical Journal* 309–35.

[7] *Hansard* HC Deb (series 3) 20 August 1857, vol 147, col 1889. Bethell (1800–1873) was the first President of the Juridical Society formed in 1855, as well as a Vice-President of the Law Amendment Society, and believed strongly that the law should be 'fitted to the exigencies of society': TA Nash, *The Life of Richard, Lord Westbury* (London, 1888) vol I, 171, 191. See also Chapter One. His political and personal reputation was probably at its peak at this juncture, when his resourcefulness in piloting the Divorce Bill through the Commons against High Church obstruction won much praise. Jowett of Balliol, who knew him well, instanced his protection of the earnings of married women through section 21 as typical of this 'half-radical': Jowett to Stanley, Bodleian Library, MS Don C.150, f.103 (23 July 1873).

[8] Although the MCA 1857 changed the terminology, the principle behind divorce *a mensa et thoro* (the new 'judicial separation') and divorce *a vinculo* (total dissolution of the marriage) whereby adultery was an essential component of any petition and establishing the 'guilt' of one party and the 'innocence' of the other, remained. The misogynistic double standard which made securing a divorce much more difficult for wives than for husbands also remained and was not removed until the Matrimonial Causes Act 1923. Grounds for divorce were expanded by the Matrimonial Causes Act 1937 and the Divorce Reform Act 1969, but it was not until the Divorce, Dissolution and Separation Act 2020 (which came into force in 2022 following a delay caused by the COVID-19 pandemic) that divorce no longer relied on fault or separation.

[9] As late as 1891 the rate of divorce was only 3.75 and that of judicial separation 0.33 per 10,000 of the married population, *Royal Commission of Divorce and Matrimonial Causes*, HC 20 (C 6482) (1912–13) App.III, Tables V, IX, 29–31. In the English Divorce Court there was 'a much lower average of successful

immediately much used ('its name is now a household word', one lawyer enthused in June 1860), and was moreover altogether free from the legal conservatism that permeated not only the law of divorce, but the Married Women's Property Acts of 1870–93.[10]

The scope and practical usefulness of this clause were further increased by some provisions in the short statute passed in 1858 to correct some of the errors and omissions in the Act which had been pitchforked together the previous summer.[11] A 'protection order', that is, an order given to a wife under section 21 of that Act, was now specifically declared to include 'property to which she has become entitled as Executrix, Administratrix, or Trustee since the … commencement of the desertion', and also property to which she was 'entitled from an estate in remainder or reversion at the date of the desertion'.[12] More important still, the interests of third parties dealing with a wife in reliance on such an order were secured by a clause providing that every protection order must state the time of desertion and that this statement was to be conclusive, and another indemnifying third parties against loss through the reversal or discharge of an order.

In this legislation of 1857–58, Parliament had pioneered an approach to the legal capacities and financial rights and liabilities of husband and wife thoroughly familiar in England today, but utterly foreign to the established workings of equity as well as the common law at the time. As Bethell emphasised in introducing the newly drafted section 21 to the Commons on 20 August 1857, 'here the legislature for the first time gave her (the married woman), by positive enactment, the same right of property as if she were a *feme sole*'.[13] Not surprisingly, the parliamentary

---

suits than in some countries', pointed out J Macdonell, the outstandingly able jurist responsible for the remodelling of the Civil Judicial Statistics from 1894: *Judicial Statistics, England and Wales 1894 Part II (Civil Judicial Statistics)*, Introduction, HC 94 (C 8263) (1896) 56; L Stone, *Road to Divorce England 1530–1987* (Oxford, Oxford University Press, 1990) 387. Barely two-thirds of petitions for divorce and one-third for judicial separation were successful.

[10] JF Macqueen, *A Practical Treatise on Divorce and Matrimonial Jurisdiction Under the Act of 1857 and New Orders* (London, W Maxwell, 1858) 379. On Macqueen's central role in the making of section 21, see Chapter One.

[11] Matrimonial Causes Acts Amendment Act 1858, ss 7–10. 'Divorce and Matrimonial Amendment Bill' *The Times* (24 July 1858) 8.

[12] This provision (s 7) is a good illustration of the judicial momentum behind successive amendments of the legislation of 1857. It was prompted by the case brought against the Bank of England by Mrs Bathe, who had been deserted in New Zealand in 1845, obtained a section 21 order, and registered it at Clerkenwell County Court, London in February 1858. In November 1857 she had been appointed sole executrix (and residuary legatee) under the will of one Jane Howroyd. On Howroyd's death she took out probate and applied to the Bank to be allowed to sell the consols standing in her testatrix's name and receive the dividends due on them. This the Bank refused, because of a doubt whether section 21 was intended to apply to a wife's fiduciary property. In a typically rambling judgment on 4 June 1858, Wood VC (later Lord Chancellor in Gladstone's first government) concluded that if as executrix she had the liabilities of a *feme sole*, she ought also to have the rights of a *feme sole* in that capacity, *Bathe v Bank of England* (1858) 70 E.R. 235 ChD. Wood's oral judgments were well described as 'in the main undoubtedly right, but often of inordinate length, diffuse, wandering and in great part unintelligible', see: Sir J Rolt, *Memoirs of the Right Hon. Sir John Rolt* (privately printed, 1939) 119.

[13] *Hansard* HC Deb (series 3) 20 August 1857, vol, 147, col 1889.

spokesman of the radical feminist Married Women's Property Committee warmly welcomed the new clause as establishing 'the rights of the wife on a sound ground'.[14] This drastically simple method of dealing with the problem of matrimonial property automatically gave effect to that Committee's three basic principles: separation of property, separation of liabilities, and equality of legal status and capacity for husband and wife. Yet for nearly 80 years this approach remained available only to a wife whose marriage was legally declared to have broken down. Despite all efforts to secure otherwise, the Married Women's Property legislation of 1870–1893 adopted instead equity's roundabout, artificial, complex, and incomplete device of making every married woman's property her 'separate property' – a term whose highly technical and limited meaning has been too little appreciated. There has also been some confusion that the protection offered by a 'protection order' under section 21 was personal protection of the body, rather than protection of property, which has further muddied understanding of the clause, its uptake and its importance. This misapprehension is most likely because following the Matrimonial Causes Act 1878, a wife could apply for an order of *physical* protection if her husband:

> shall be convicted summarily or otherwise of an aggravated assault within the meaning of the Offences against the Person Act, 1861, section forty-three, upon his wife, the court or magistrate before whom he shall be so convicted may, if satisfied that the future safety of the wife is in peril, order that the wife shall be no longer bound to cohabit with her husband; and such order shall have the force and effect in all respects of a decree of judicial separation on the ground of cruelty.[15]

In some ways then, these orders were similar as both reverted a subset of married women to *feme sole* status. Crucially though, wives who applied under section 21 for *economic* protection did not have to rely on having convinced magistrates that their physical maltreatment was serious enough to warrant a conviction under Offences against the Person Act, nor did she have to convince the magistrate that her future safety was 'in peril'. Perhaps even more importantly, unlike a section 21 order where the wife was deemed a *feme sole* from the (precise) date desertion occurred, a physically abused wife who managed to secure an order under section 4 would be a *feme sole* only following that judgment. Not until 1935 did Parliament return to the radical and direct approach accepted in 1857 and embark upon the process of giving every wife that straightforward equality of status and capacity with a man or unmarried women with regard to property, torts and contracts possessed since 1858 by (the many) wives who secured an order under section 21 – but otherwise only by those granted a separation by the Divorce Court or (after 1878) by a magistrate.[16]

---

[14] ibid, col 1880 (Sir Erskine Perry).

[15] Matrimonial Causes Act 1878, s 4.

[16] By extending the equitable conception of the wife's 'separate estate' to the earnings and property of all wives subsequently married, the Married Women's Property Act gave all wives equality with the well-off wives who had long had marriage settlements, but not with men or unmarried or widowed

The whole of the statute law on summary economic divorce under section 21 is contained in these few brief clauses passed in 1857–58.[17] Thereafter, the development of this branch of the law was the work of the judges. The repercussions of an order whose effect was to unmarry a married woman with regard to property and contract, suing and being sued, went far beyond the simple safeguarding of a deserted wife's earnings and possessions from her worthless husband which alone is usually attributed to these misleadingly named 'protection orders'. Conflicts of interest and legal uncertainties and disputes were the inevitable result. Over the next 40 years the higher courts (and particularly successive Masters of the Rolls) were repeatedly called upon to clarify the far-reaching legal ramifications of magistrates' startling new statutory power summarily to alter the effects of marriage on the spouses' economic rights and liabilities and a wife's legal capacity, thus establishing a judge-made law.

At the outset what was required from the Divorce Court was simple guidance for magistrates in the exercise of their new matrimonial jurisdiction.[18] Applications began to come in as soon as the Act came into force on 11 January 1858, well before the first meeting of the new Divorce Court itself, and magistrates inevitably made some odd initial decisions.[19] By July 1858 permanent guidelines had been provided for them by a handful of cases dealt with by Sir Cresswell Cresswell, the very capable common law judge who after some hesitation had agreed to leave the Common Pleas and become the first Judge Ordinary of the new Court.[20] Thereafter, successive editions of justices' handbooks included a detailed

women (as demanded by feminist campaigners including the Married Women's Property Committee, see Introduction). The consequent special disabilities and privileges of married women with regard to property, torts and contract were not fully removed until the radical Law Reform (Married women and Tortfeasors) Act 1935 and subsequent legislation, notably the Married Women (Restraint upon Anticipation) Act 1949 and Law Reform (Husband and Wife) Act 1962. See O Kahn-Freund, 'Recent Legislation on Matrimonial Property' (1970) *MLR* 33, 601, 604, fn 12.

[17] With one exception: in 1864, 27 & 28 Vict. C.44 s 1 gave the power to discharge a section 21 order to any magistrate, instead of only to the magistrate of justices who had granted it or the Judge Ordinary of the Divorce Court, as provided in 1857. This amendment was prompted by the proceedings *ex parte* Sharp, which came to the Queen's Bench when Wilde, the Judge Ordinary of the Divorce Court at the time, decided that section 21 did not authorise him to rescind an order made by a deceased magistrate of the Westminster Police Court: 33 LJ QB 214 (5 May 1864).

[18] 'Magistrates' and 'justices' are used as interchangeable terms in this section.

[19] This was the comment made at the end of the first month by JF Macqueen, who added, 'as the rulings of the Court are to instruct the inferior magistrates, it is to be hoped that these rulings will not be in chambers', Macqueen (n 10) 100. Some of the magistrates' blunders, inconsistencies and laxities are discussed in later chapters.

[20] Palmerston felt obliged to offer the post initially to Bethell, who predictably declined, Nash (n 7) vol I, 235. The first thought of the Lord Chancellor, Cranworth, was the aged Lushington; failing him, he felt 'a common lawyer out to be selected, though there is little to induce any of the Judges of Westminster Hall to accept the post': Cranworth to Brougham, Brougham MSS, 33, 399 (18 September 1857). Cresswell was 'not at first very willing to accept the post', which would oblige him to learn some new law and bring no additional salary, but it was generally expected (quite wrongly) that it would 'give him a fair share of leisure': Cranworth to Brougham, Brougham MSS, 33, 399 and 35, 222 (18 September and 26 October 1857). Thus the Divorce Court acquired a sound common law judge to oversee the fusion there of ecclesiastical law and procedure with the oral evidence and jury trial of the common law.

section describing their new statutory power of 'Divorce' (sic) under section 21, together with the leading judicial rulings on its proper use. Here they learnt that they could grant an order on the wife's affidavit alone and without the service of a citation on the husband, provided the information she supplied was sufficiently full and precise to satisfy them of the fact of desertion.[21] A husband's absence in his ordinary occupation was not desertion, and they should not take into account an earlier desertion terminated by a return to cohabitation.[22] Most important of all, they were told that the meaning of desertion was different in different sections of the Act, and in section 21 it meant not only that the husband had left his wife, but that he had left her unprovided for and had made no *bona fide* offer to return.[23] If in doubt, they should remember that 'in general it will be safer to make the Protecting Order rather than refuse it, because it is always open to the husband or his creditors to have it discharged'.[24] An order must always be in general terms, however, and leave open the question of title to specific property.[25]

Once a wife had been granted an order, it became vital for third parties dealing with her in reliance on her new status of *feme sole* that there should be no grey areas. The supplementary legislation of 1858 had settled that the term 'property' in section 21 was to include fiduciary property[26] to which she became entitled after her desertion, and also property to which she was entitled from an estate 'in remainder or reversion at the date of her desertion' and importantly, in May 1864 Vice-Chancellor Wood ruled that it was *ultra vires* (beyond their powers) for magistrates to word an order so as to exclude any class of property statutorily declared to come within its scope.[27] The same supplementary legislation, it will be remembered, required every order to state the time at which her desertion began,

---

[21] *Ex parte* Hall (1858) 27 LJ 19 and *ex parte* Sewel (1858) 28 LJ 8. Later editions of handbooks recommended the service of notice on the husband if his whereabouts were known, in view of the practice of the Divorce Court under Creswell's successor, JP Wilde (later Lord Penzance), as reported in *Matthew v Matthew* (1869) 19 LT 662.

[22] *Ex parte* Aldridge (1858) 31 LT 40.

[23] *Cargill v Cargill* (1858) 27 LJ 69. Justices' manuals never ceased to cite this case, although as counsel pointed out in 1891, Mary Cargill was applying for a judicial separation, not an order, and Cresswell's remark was 'only a dictum ... given very shortly after the passing of the Act and not supported by any subsequent case': *Mahoney v McCarthy* (1892) P 21-4. Counsel might have added that Cresswell's successor Wilde, had delivered a contrary opinion in 1868.

[24] Macqueen (n 10) 99, following Creswell in *ex parte* Hall. This quickly became enshrined orthodoxy. At the turn of the century, for example, justices were still being routinely recommended to 'leave the man to take steps to get the order discharged if he can' and informed moreover that 'on appeal the Probate and Divorce Division, the wife's evidence where it conflicts with the husband's will be taken as correct', eg, GB Kennett (ed), *Stone's Justices' Manual for 1899* (London, 1899) 968–70. This last instruction was a continuation of the practice in the ecclesiastical courts.

[25] *Ex parte* Mullineux (1858) 27 LJ, P&M 19.

[26] That is, property which is managed or held by a third party for their benefit.

[27] *Re Whittingham's Trust* (1864) 12 WR 775 ChD. This ruling prevented magistrates from allowing Mrs Catherine Evans' dividends to go to her bankrupt husband's creditors. Forty years later the *Justice of the Peace* still had to assure a correspondent that a section 21 order covered a share of residuary estate bequeathed before desertion which did not become payable until after desertion: 'Husband and Wife – Protection Order – Effect Of' *Justice of the Peace* (5 April 1902) 223. This, however, was probably a reflection of lawyers' increasing unfamiliarity by then with this type of business.

and declared that this statement was to be conclusive. This provision was crucial, since the severe restraints and incapacity imposed on the property dealings of a married woman were removed only from property which came into the wife's possession *after* her desertion. An 'economic divorce' thus operated retrospectively from whatever date of desertion was accepted at the magistrates hearing.

Plenty of room remained, however, for disputes about whether or not some particular property or 'chose in action' was reduced into the wife's possession after the certified date of desertion, and therefore at a time when she must be deemed to have been a *feme sole*. This was a vital issue for creditors, executors, trustees, vendors, and purchasers, and one which could sometimes be settled only by the higher courts. For example, was the wife or the husband the owner of money refunded after the date of desertion by a company liquidator in respect of shares which were the wife's' property, but had necessarily been registered prior to the desertion in the joint names or herself and her husband? In November 1877 Sir Edward Fry, as a newly appointed additional judge in the Chancery Division (where he did much to adapt law and practice to change conditions), established in *Nicholson v Drury Buildings Co* that such money was the property of the wife. Although the right to the shares in question had been vested in Eleanor Nicholson of Kendal as one of her intestate uncle's next-of-kin *before* her desertion, the money due in respect of these shares only became payable to her when the company went into voluntary liquidation *after* the desertion.[28]

Far more notable, however, was the ruling of Sir John Romilly MR in August 1858 that a section 21 removed all restraints on a wife's freedom to dispose as she wished of any capital it covered. In July 1858 Mrs Sophia Anne Cooke obtained such an order, and thereupon instructed her trustees to pay to her only daughter the trust fund of £10,000 her father had bequeathed to her with the usual restraint on anticipation after her desertion in 1826. Her trustees refused. After studying the terms of section 21, however, Romilly was clearly of the opinion that where a trust fund was bequeathed to a wife subsequent to her desertion, an order obtained under that section removed any restraint on anticipation. He therefore ordered Mrs Cooke's trustees to comply with her instructions.[29] Thereafter this case was to be regularly cited to show that 'the restraint on anticipation only lasts during an effectual coverture; when the coverture is suspended, it ceases'.[30] A section 21

---

[28] *Nicholson v Drury Buildings Estate Co* (1876) 7 Ch D 49–55. Fry, a strong Quaker and a man of many interests who had begun in the family cocoa business, had made his early reputation with a *Treatise on the Specific Performance of Contracts* (London, 1858) and specialised in company work. After his retirement he was much in demand as an arbitrator and conciliator: AWB Simpson, *A Biographical Dictionary of Common Law* (London, Butterworths, 1984) 195. For an earlier decision on a pecuniary legacy not actually paid until after desertion and therefore declared to be covered by a section 21 order, see below: R Coward and Adam's Purchase LR 20 Eq 17, fn 44.

[29] *Cooke v Fuller* (1858) 53 ER 834, reprinting 26 Beav. 99. Romilly had been a distinguished Liberal Law Officer, and Mrs Cooke's counsel, Roundell Palmer (later Earl of Selbourne), was to become an even more distinguished Liberal Law Officer and Lord Chancellor.

[30] *Waite v Morland* (1888) LR 38 Ch D 13.

order (which suspended coverture) could thus give a married woman control of her trust capital, as well as the income accruing from it. This was a very rare state of affairs indeed, since it was standard practice for a trust to include such a restraint, in order to secure a wife's capital from her own folly or a foolish, needy or unscrupulous husband, attorney or agent.[31] Indeed, the restraint on anticipation was a common feature of trusts created for unmarried women too, probably also to safeguard against any future misfortune, meaning that a wife with a section 21 order and a trust, might well enjoy greater legal freedom than her unmarried counterpart.

Some hazards still remained in dealing with a wife on the strength of a section 21 order. The chronology of possession was all important, as one mortgagee learnt to his cost 35 years later, first from a judge in chambers, then from the Queen's Bench Division, and finally from the Court of Appeal itself. For in October 1893 the then (very different) Master of the Rolls, Lord Esher (alias the former Conservative Law Officer William Brett, a 'very peppery', domineering, impatient and undistinguished judge),[32] sitting with HC Lopes (another former Conservative politician, but by contrast 'a slow, steady, careful advocate')[33] and AL Smith (later Master of the Rolls and the most capable of the three), agreed that the rents received by one Mrs Cooper from leasehold property bequeathed by her father with a restraint on anticipation *before* her desertion, could not be regarded as property received *after* her desertion. Since an order applied only to property received *after* desertion, it followed that she had no power to mortgage her life interest in these rents. Accordingly, her mortgagee, who had relied on the *feme sole* status given by her order when he accepted these rents as security in 1889, had no redress when she broke her contract to repay him, and the courts refused to allow the income of her life interest to be transferred to him. Perhaps in the less rigid, narrow, and formalist judicial atmosphere of the 1860s and 70s, these payments accruing from time to time might have been deemed property coming into Mrs Cooper's hands *after* her desertion, as indeed was argued by counsel in the court below and thought there (at first) by Alfred Wills Jr (a Nonconformist alumnus of University College London).[34]

In the Court of Appeal, however, Mrs Cooper's creditor briefed the Liberal HH Cozens-Hardy QC (an even more able alumnus of University College London, and another future Master of the Rolls), and he put forward a very different argument, hardly calculated to win over a judge of Esher's highly conservative temperament.

---

[31] See: J Aston, *Female Entrepreneurship in Nineteenth-Century England: Engagement in the Urban Economy* (London, Palgrave Macmillan, 2016) Chapter 6; Erickson (n 4); and Stebbings (n 4) chapters 2 and 3.

[32] Simpson (n 28) 75. Esher's irascibility was apt to have a bad effect on the Court of Appeal: JA Strahan, *The Bench and Bar of England* (Edinburgh, 1919) 26–29.

[33] AGC Liddell, *Notes from the Life of an Ordinary Mortal* (London, 1911) 128.

[34] Wills characteristically disapproved publicly of the practice of yielding to the jury's application for payment by the day, which greatly prolonged trials: Sir J Hollams, *Jottings of an Old Solicitor* (London, 1906) 60.

A protection order under section 21 changed the status of a married woman and 'for this purpose has the same effect as divorce', claimed Cozens-Hardy, and 'it is a necessary consequence of acquiring the right to contract and sue and be sued as a *feme sole* that the restraint on anticipation is removed for the purposed of those contracts'.[35] The Appeal Court gave this argument short shrift: a woman was either covert or non-covert, and that was the end of the matter.[36] Esher's account of the intentions and meaning of this distinctive mid-Victorian development in matrimonial property law was as dogmatic as it was inaccurate and confused – and thoroughly typical not only of his own hasty judicial style, but of many other late Victorian lawyers' increasingly hazy grasp of this branch of matrimonial property law, by then rapidly sinking into obsolescence.[37]

For third parties such questions of possession were always vital; but to the families of the two spouses and to any children of the marriage it was usually the testamentary consequences of a wife's acquisition of *feme sole* status which mattered most. These were dramatic. A *feme covert* could bequeath her personal property by will only with her husband's consent, which could be withdrawn at any time before the will was proved; but a wife with a section 21 order was statutorily given precisely the same freedom of testation as a judicially separated wife, namely that of a *feme sole*. She could dispose of everything she had acquired since the date of her desertion exactly as she liked, and appoint her own relations or friends as her executors; and since the effect of an order was retrospective, this would hold good for a will made at any time after her desertion, even if she did not obtain an order until some years later.[38] Given so powerful an incentive, it can be no surprise that the imminent approach of death sometimes prompted a wife or her relatives to secure an order forthwith and thereby oust her absent husband from his marital right to all her personal property. Thus Betty Faraday of Bury in Lancashire, who

---

[35] *Hill v Cooper* (1893) 69 n.s. LT 216–219. Cozens-Hardy was one of the bi-partisan group of MPs who prepared and brought in the 1895 Summary Jurisdiction (Married Women) Act, a landmark in the development of magistrates' matrimonial jurisdiction.

[36] It is probably not irrelevant that on an earlier occasion Smith had agreed with Hawkins J in rejecting counsel's argument that a wife's status was changed by a magistrate's order under section 4 of the Matrimonial Causes Acts Amendment Act 1878: *Haddon v Haddon* (1887) 18 QBD 778.

[37] Esher was apparently confusing magistrates' orders under section 21 with those under section 4 of the Matrimonial Causes Acts Amendment Act 1878 – not unsurprisingly, since both were often referred to as 'protection orders', eg, *Re Emery's Trusts* (1884) 50 LT 197. The bafflement expressed by Cotton LJ in 1888 at Romilly's decision 30 years before in *Cooke v Fuller* (n 29) provides a further illustration of late-Victorian judges' growing incomprehension of this increasingly unimportant area of matrimonial property law. Even Lindley LJ, yet another alumnus of University College London, future Master of the Rolls, and 'remarkable for impartiality and versatility', apparently did not fully grasp the basic point that unlike a decree of judicial separation or a section 4 order, a section 21 order was statutorily declared to operate retrospectively from the date of desertion, and not from the date of the decree or order: *Waite v Morland* (n 30) 135. Indeed, even the best of the many textbooks on matrimonial property law stimulated by the 'revolution' brought about by the notoriously obscure Married Women's Property Act 1882, could sometimes mislead on this point: eg, R Thicknesse, *A Digest of the Law of Husband and Wife as it Affects Property* (London, 1884) 172; WP Eversley, *The Law of Domestic Relations* (London, 1885) 322.

[38] MCA 1858, ss 21, 25; *In the goods of Ann Elliot* (1871) LR 2 P&D 274-5 (per Penzance JO).

had supported herself since her husband left her in 1832, applied for an order in 1861 just 12 days before her death, promptly made a will appointing as her executors her three sons (who may well have been the moving spirits in disinheriting their scrounging absent father), and had her order registered only a few hours before she died.[39]

The moment a wife secured an order, her husband was automatically disinherited for he thereby lost his *jus mariti* (rights of the husband) from the date of his desertion, and his relation to her became almost that of a stranger.[40] If she died intestate, all the property she had acquired since her desertion went exactly as if he were dead, and her own next-of-kin, moreover, not her widower, would be granted administration of her estate.[41] If she left minor children, her husband's right to their guardianship *ad litem* was ousted, and a maternal uncle or grandmother or other kin elected by the children would be made their guardian for the purpose of taking out letters of administration of her personal estate and effects for their use and benefit until they reached the age of 21, even if their father was willing and able to act.[42]

Testamentary consequences like these naturally provoked challenges and family feuds. It was in such dispute in 1881 that the notably calm and fair-minded Judge of Probate and Divorce, Sir James Hannen, ruled that the validity of an order could be questioned even after the wife's death, and even when the husband had knowingly acquiesced in its existence during her lifetime for 20 years, although the difficulties of proof must necessarily be much greater.[43] Still, 10 years later Michael McCarthy, a former worker in the shell factory at the Arsenal who had failed to make good in America, but whose wife Mary had done so well from her registered lodging-house at Woolwich that she had left £3,000 to her own relations on the strength of her stealthily-acquired section 21 order, succeeded in convincing Hannen's successor, Sir Francis Jeune, that her order had been obtained in 1876 by fraudulent concealment of material facts, and must therefore be set aside. The Court accordingly pronounced against her will and gave

---

[39] *In the Goods of Betty Faraday wife of Martin Faraday (deceased), on Motion* (1861) 164 ER 1039. Her order was registered two days later than section 21 prescribed; this case settled that an order would not be invalidated by a delay in registration.

[40] The justice of this was pointed out in a leading textbook: 'as the husband has been in fault and obliged his wife to have recourse to the protection of the court, he ought not on her death to seize upon the property which she may have become entitled to or earned during the separation': Eversley (n 37) 237.

[41] MCA 1857, ss 21, 25; *In the goods of Maria Worman* (1859) 29 LJR, ns, 164 (per Cresswell JO).

[42] The guardian however had to give justifying security to meet the contingency of the child dying during its minority, in which event the father became entitled to the property: *In the goods of Mary Weir* (1862) 164 ER 1071, reprinting 2 Sw. & Tr 450 (per Cresswell JO); *In the goods of Naomi Stephenson* (1866) LR 1 P & D 287 (per Wilde JO).

[43] *Mudge v Adams* (1881) 6 PD 54–59. As Hannen remarked, he could settle both aspects of such a suit, since fortunately his division of the High Court had jurisdiction in both matrimonial and testamentary causes. Interestingly, Hannen had already decided that an order could be challenged after the wife's death when he heard the application for discharge of Myers Abrahams, husband of Shenck Mackleh Abrahams, in 1877: see Chapter Seven, page 223.

letters of administration to McCarthy, who thus retrieved from his in-laws what amounted to a small fortune.[44] As early as 1865, moreover, it had been established in the Court of the Exchequer by Sir Charles Edward Pollock CB that a section 21 order only protected earnings or goods which were 'the lawful fruits of lawful industry'.[45] Consequently, proof that a deceased wife's property was the result of 'vice and profligacy' (common brothel-keeping) invalidated her order, and therefore her will, as effectively as proof that she had obtained her order by fraud or concealment of facts. In either case her husband thereupon obtained the whole of her property by his revived marital right.

Clearly, therefore, the posthumous impact of a wife's order on family fortunes could be considerable, for good and ill. Nor is this all. The only way in which a wife living apart from her husband could herself achieve possession of a legacy was by acquiring the *feme sole* status given by a section 21 order, since a legacy left to a married woman must be paid to her husband; only he could give the executors a valid receipt. True, under the Trustees Relief Act 1847 they could pay her legacy into the Court of Chancery, which would then pay her the dividends; but her capital remained in limbo unless and until Chancery concluded that her husband had been absent long enough for his death to be safely assumed. No such delays and difficulties confronted a wife with a magistrates' order, as Anne Woolley, a well-advised cousin of academic, social reformer, and author Charles Kingsley, found in July 1858. Such a wife could petition the Court of Chancery in her own name and without a next friend, declared Romilly MR, and the Court would order the bequest to be paid out to her against her receipt alone as if she were a *feme sole*, provided it was satisfied that the legacy was part of her protected property; and Anne Woolley's executors were instructed accordingly.[46] A few months

---

[44] *Mahoney v McCarthy*, LR (1892) P. 21–27. Rather surprisingly, the self-declared illiterate and impecunious McCarthy was represented by William Willis QC (1835–1911) (see Oxford Dictionary of National Biography (ODBN), available at www.oxforddnb.com), a 'fervid and voluble' alumnus of University College London, former radical/Liberal MP, and future President of the Baptist Conference – perhaps an instance of denominational networking between solicitors and the Bar.

[45] In this case the widower simply employed an auctioneer to realise the contents of the brothel that his adulterous 'protected' wife, Mary Wild, was running when she died, and then left the administrators of her will to bring an action against the auctioneer – an action which they won at Liverpool Assize (the judge having ruled that an order was good until discharged), but then lost in the Court of Exchequer: *Mason v Mitchell* (1865) 34 LJ Ex 68 (Pollock CB with Channel and Piggott BB). Mary Wild's paramour had astutely paid the expenses of obtaining her order in 1860, three years after she left her husband.

[46] *Re Kingsley's Trusts* (1858) 53 ER 828. Anne Woolley had been left £400 in three per cent reduced annuities under the will of Jane Kingsley, who died on 11 March 1853. She was the widow of a stockbroker cousin of Charles Kingsley's father, who bequeathed her late husband's fortune (very unevenly) to his two first cousins and their children. Charles and Henry Kingsley's windfalls of £500 paid off their debts, and enabled Henry to go to Australia: B Colloms, *Charles Kingsley: The Lion of Eversley* (London, Constable, 1975) 167; SM Ellis, *Henry Kingsley 1830–1876: Towards a Vindication* (London, 1931) 38, fn 1. Their cousin Anne, however, had great difficulty in getting the £400 she had been left, because of her husband's absence in Turee, New South Wales since 1845. She got him to send her a power of attorney, dated 21 February 1855, authorising the executors, Charles Kingsley Snr and Robert Wills, to pay the legacy to a 'person named in the power' but they refused to accept her signature. On 19 April 1858 she secured a section 21 order from the Somerset Justices and registered it at Taunton County Court,

later another wife, Mary Crew, obtained a section 21 order and thereupon success-fully petitioned Chancery in her own name for the payment of a legacy payable on the death of a tenant for life which had fallen into her possession *after* her deser-tion in 1845, and which the Court had hitherto refused to pay to her.[47]

It was thus quickly established that a married woman with a section 21 order could give a valid receipt for any property which fell into her possession after her desertion. This was a boon for every lone wife who was left a legacy, large or small (and for their would-be benefactors, often anxious to ensure that their gift would not be diverted to an errant husband or be left in limbo). It could also be of the first importance in enabling vendors and purchasers to establish a valid title, and therefore a good sale. This was made very clear in April 1875 by the then Master of the Rolls and a former Liberal Law Officer, Sir George Jessell (yet another alum-nus of University College London), when he assured the purchaser of a copyhold estate which had been charged with a legacy of £400 to one Mrs Leggatt that his title to the property was good, since the vendor had paid Mrs Leggatt's legacy *after* her desertion, and the receipt she gave under her section 21 order was therefore valid.[48]

The judges' interpretation of the legislation of 1857–1858 had thus established that a valid order made under section 21 gave a wife compete possession and control over every kind of property she acquired after the date of her desertion. These rights, however, carried with them heavy corresponding liabilities. With full contractual capacity came full liability for her contracts, damages, and debts, for which she could now be imprisoned – unlike all other married women, even those with separate property.[49] Henceforward her husband ceased to be liable for necessaries supplied to her by tradesmen, unless she petitioned for divorce or a judicial separation and he failed to pay the alimony *pendente lite* granted to her by the Court.[50] Only his liability under the Poor Law remained, for if she became chargeable to the poor rates and he was able to maintain her, the Court of Common Pleas ruled in 1875 that he must still do so.[51] Once assumed, moreover,

---

but the executors refused to do more than pay her legacy into Court under the Trustees' Relief Act – hence her petition to Chancery. Thus while her brother and male cousins got their legacies at once from the executors (who were their respective fathers), Anne Woolley's wait of five years was ended only by her determination in taking advantage of section 21.

[47] *Re Rainson's Trust* (1859) 28 LJ Ch 334 (per Kindersley V-C).

[48] *Re Coward and Adam's Purchase* LR 20 Eq 179. This was an application for a ruling from a judge in chambers under the Vendor and Purchaser Act 1874, s 9. It was in the areas of equity, real property and contract that Jessel's contribution as MR was outstanding: Simpson (n 28) 281.

[49] Unlike a wife with a protection order, a married woman with separate property had no true contractual capacity. Since a contract made by her bound not herself but her separate property, a married woman without a s 21 order could not be imprisoned – an immunity which was not removed by the Married Women's Property Act 1882: Dicey (n 4) 392 and fn 1. For a detailed examination of imprisonment for debt in the eighteenth century, see A Wakelam, *Credit and Debt in Eighteenth-Century England: An Economic History of Debtors' Prisons* (Abingdon, Routledge, 2020).

[50] MCA 1857 ss 21, 26; *Tempany v Hakewill* (1858) 175 ER 799–800 (1 F&F 439); *Hakewill v Hakewill* (1860) 30 LJP & M 254 (per Cresswell JO).

[51] A year after she secured a section 21 order, Mrs Harriet Barton was sent as a 'pauper lunatic' to Littlemore asylum, where the charge was 10s 3d per week. The Oxford City Guardians applied to the

she could lay down neither her new powers nor her duties; for although an order could be granted only on the wife's own application, it could be revoked solely on the application of her husband or his creditors. Rightly or wrongly, the *Law Times's* prediction was that when section 21 came into force the chief gainer would probably be the husband, since his freedom from liability for her debts or damages 'will in the majority of cases and probably especially in the case of the middle and lower classes, be more than an equivalent to her self-acquired property'.[52]

Plainly the capacity to sue and be sued given to a wife by an order was a very necessary accompaniment of such onerous new responsibilities. A desire to embark upon litigation, however, was sometimes in itself enough to prompt a wife who was not living with her husband to secure such an order, since only by becoming a statutory *feme sole* could a married woman bring an action without being non-suited. As early as April 1858 one of the Commissioners in Bankruptcy laid down firmly that a married woman with a section 21 order was entitled to take steps herself to recover money she had lent after her desertion to a man who went bankrupt.[53]

More strikingly, in 1860 a wife with an order successfully maintained an action against a shopkeeper for recovery of the savings from her earnings for looking after his shop she claimed to have deposited with him for safe-keeping; for although cross-examination indicated that she had gone to live with her lover before the certified date of her 'desertion', an order remained in force until discharged.[54] In 1880, a Manchester woman who had been deserted for 21 years and was living with a man not her husband, was still obliged to get a section 21 order to enable her to sue the railway company for compensation when she was injured in an accident.[55] In a lengthy Chancery suit a little earlier, a wife suing as a *feme sole* by virtue of her section 21 order was twice required to satisfy the Court that her separation from her husband continued, and that her order was therefore still in force.[56]

But did an order give a wife retrospective right of action, in the same way that it gave her retrospective property rights? That efficient and supremely practical,

Justices for an order on her husband for maintenance of his wife. The Justices submitted the case to the Queen's Bench, who held that section 21 did not affect the husband's liability to maintain a destitute wife: 'Guardians of Oxford City v. Barton' (1875) *Justice of the Peace* 39, 725–26 (per Cockburn LCJ and Mellor and Quain, JJ, 13 November 1875). It was later surmised that equally, a section 21 order would not remove a married woman's liability under the Married Women's Property Act 1882, s 20 to maintain her husband out of her separate property if he became chargeable to any union or parish: 'Practical Points' (1886) *Justice of the Peace* 50, 493.

[52] 30 *Law Times* 298 (20 February 1858).

[53] *Ex parte* Cartwright, *re* Ince (1858) 31 LTR 91 (per Mr Commissioner Evans). However, if after litigation had begun, the husband was able to convince the magistrate that he had never deserted his wife and the order was accordingly discharged, this was ruled by Chancery to mean that the wife had no time in reality been a *feme sole*, and therefore her husband had always been a necessary party to the suit, since his rights had never been altered: *Rudge v Weedon* (1859) 28 LJ, Ch 889 (per Kindersley V-C).

[54] *Thomas v Head*, 175 ER 9710972 (2 F&F 87, coram Hill J).

[55] That dedicated campaigner, Lydia Becker, used this woman's case to illustrate the defects of the law with regard to the rights of married women: 'On the Progress of the Movement for the Enfranchisement of Women' (1880) *The National Association for the Promotion of Social Science* (1879).

[56] *Ewart v Chubb* (1875) LR 20 Eq 454 (Hall VC).

Sir William Earle (an expert in commercial law who overtly considered wider social bearings of his decisions)[57] soon settled that it did not. In May 1861, sitting as Chief Justice of the Court of Common Pleas with Sir James Shaw Willes, Sir John Barnard Byles, and Sir Henry Singer Keating JJ, he overruled a decision in Westminster County Court awarding damages to Mrs Annie Pye against the Midland Railway Company, on the ground that Mrs Pye secured her protection order *after* she had begun her action for compensation for loss and damage to her chandeliers, carpets, apparel and household goods while in transit from Nottingham to Pimlico. Her counsel had argued that under section 21 'the married woman is a statutory *feme sole* from the date of the desertion, not the protection order, as regards not only property but the right of action itself'. Erle, however, although he acknowledged that the section might be thus construed, insisted that the intention of the legislature must be considered. He could 'well understand' that Parliament intended to give the wife's property retrospective protection, but he could not accept that the section's retrospective effect was intended also to include her right of action, since 'incalculable mischief must be the result'. His colleague, Keating, who had been Solicitor-General when section 21 was before the Commons, fully agreed, declaring roundly that its 'retroactive operation … does not extend to the length of enabling a woman who has commenced her action as a wife, and afterwards clothed herself with a protection order, to maintain that action as a *feme sole*.'[58]

Still, the courts were prepared to construe broadly the power to sue of a wife already equipped with an order of protection, particularly after 1875, when it was established that such an order entitled a wife to sue in respect of a tort as well as the breach of contract specifically mentioned in section 21. In that year, Mrs Ramsden brough an action for libel against one Brearley, with whom she had been trying to establish a boarding-house but who had ceased to 'know or to deal further with her', thus injuring her trade. The rising QC Farrer Herschell (the future Liberal Lord Chancellor and yet another alumnus of University College London) argued on her behalf that since the Act of 1857 requested sections 21 and 26 of that Act to be read together, it was evidently Parliament's intention that a wife with an order under section 21 should be able to sue in respect of a tort, despite the fact that 'wrongs and injustices' were mentioned in so many words only in section 26, which dealt with a judicially separated wife. All the rights of action of a *feme sole* were plainly equally essential for both categories of lone wives. The four Queen's Bench judges who heard the case proved very willing to agree, although for different reasons. That polished relic of an earlier period and long-standing supporter

---

[57] Simpson (n 28) 166. 'For no judge of the past had I greater admiration than for Sir William Erle … He knew how and when to make up his mind', commented a knowledgeable old hand: Hollams (n 34) 142, 241. Erle's later concern with trade union law was entirely in character.

[58] *Midland Railway Company v Pye* (1861) 4 *Law Times*, n.s. 510 (Erle CJ, with Willes, Byles and Keating JJ). Willes agreed on the ground that 'the general rule is, that a person cannot sue who has not the right to do so with the action commences' – a typical judgment from this reclusive, solitary man, whose greatest pleasure was conversing on legal principles: Hollams (n 34) 175, 241.

of married women's property law reform, the ageing Sir Alexander Cockburn CJ (who had been Attorney-General during the early debates on the divorce legislation), doubted whether Parliament ever envisaged section 21 being applied to an action for libel, but eloquently declared that to put a narrow interpretation on its words would not be justice: 'justice requires that a deserted wife, abandoned by her lawful protector, shall be entitled to protect herself, her property, her character and reputation, as though she were a *feme sole*'. It was left to his brother judges, Mellor J (who had been a Member of the House when section 21 was passed), Lush J (another veteran) and Archibald J (a lawyer from Nova Scotia) to eschew this well-worn rhetoric of the 1850s and agree with the matter-of-fact young Herschell that since section 21 had to be construed with sections 25 and 26, Parliament clearly intended to give 'the power of protecting herself as well against strangers as against her husband ... as fully to the woman who obtained a protecting order as to one who had obtained a judicial separation'.[59]

'Divorce before magistrates' always had at its core a symbiotic, indeed a parasitic, relationship with judicial separation. Section 21 of the 1857 Act explicitly declared that a wife with one of the new magistrates' orders 'shall ... be ... in the like position in all respects, with regard to property and contracts, and suing and being sued, as she would be under this Act if she obtained a decree of judicial separation'. From the beginning the overlapping identity thus statutorily created between section 21 orders and decrees of judicial separation meant that decisions on either of these were employed interchangeable in legal argument. For example, Romilly's important decision of 1858 that a section 21 order removed a restraint on anticipation was cited in 1872 by counsel for a judicially separated wife; and conversely, in 1877 counsel for a wife with a section 21 order, Mrs Nicholson, relied on two cases involving judicially separated wives. In 1893, one of the two cases on which the argument turned in *Hill v Cooper* concerned a judicially separated wife, and the other a wife with a section 21 order. Many other examples could be cited. Such cross-argument by bar and bench makes it clear that practising lawyers were accustomed to handle the two as matrimonial orders of the same kind in many important respects. At the heart of this interdependent relationship was their common involvement in a paradoxical legal novelty: the creation of the statutory *feme sole*. In 1857 this enigmatic status was given alike to every wife with a decree of judicial separation, and to every wife with a

---

[59] *Ramsden v Brearley* (1875) 10 QB 147. When Palmerston's Attorney-General, Cockburn had immediately 'cordially concurred' with Perry's proposed motion, 'That the rules of common law (with regard to married women's property) are unjust in principle and injurious in their operation': *Hansard* HC Deb 10 June 1856, vol 142, col 1273. Although sometimes 'authoritative and impetuous' as CJ of the Common Pleas, he retained his easy eloquence and 'liberal disposition and remained a ladies' man, although he seemingly moderated his 'loose habits' (he had been prone to take 'a different Lady Cockburn' with him every time he left town): H Reeve (ed) *The Greville Memoirs* (London, 1911) 66–68; Hollams (n 34) 141. In contrast, Lush was noted for his clarity and logic, as was the prim workaholic Herschell, who fastened at once on the real point in a case: Hollams (n 34) 193; JB Atlay, *The Victorian Chancellors* (London, Smith, Elder & Co, 1906) 450, 455.

section 21 order but to them alone. In every such case, Parliament had declared, the wife shall, whilst so separated, be considered a *feme sole* with regard to property and contracts, and wrongs and injuries, and suing and being sued in any civil proceeding. Accordingly, each such wife became a married woman whose *coverture* was suspended with regard to this whole range of civil rights, liabilities, and capacities.

This simple method of reforming the law of husband and wife by changing the wife's *personal* status and capacities was thereafter eschewed altogether by general legislation until the mid-twentieth century. In sharp contrast, the Married Women's Property Acts of 1870–1893 operated primarily through altering the nature of her *property* – a very different matter. Even the full contractual powers given to a married woman by the Act of 1882 were only full powers as to her equitable and legal interest *in her separate property*. That legislation, having made all a wife's property her statutory separate estate, adhered to the equitable fiction that the *feme covert* put not herself but her separate property forward as the contracting party.[60] Her husband, moreover, continued to be liable for her torts.[61] In short, under the Married Women's Property Acts a married woman continued to be a *feme covert*. The only wife who could be deemed a *feme sole* with regard to property, contracts, and litigation was still a wife with an order under section 21 or a judicial separation.

The consequences of this basic difference of approach could be considerable for women and their families. This chapter has shown the multitude of economic incapacities, obligations, liabilities, and privileges arising out of coverture which were removed from a statutory *feme sole*. As successful text, *The Law of Domestic Relations* warned in 1885, 'the interest in and powers over her property' conferred upon a wife by the Court of Chancery with regard to her 'separate property' whether statutory or otherwise, were not the same as those possessed by a statutory *feme sole*.[62] For example, although the property of a statutory *feme sole* who died intestate went to her own next of kin, the property of other intestate wives still automatically went to the husband, since the equitable separate estate ceased upon a wife's death, and the husband's right over her property therefore revived. Many such differences were removed by the Married Women's Property Act of 1893; but some remained. Above all, a statutory *feme sole* was released from the 'restraint upon anticipation' imposed by equity upon a married woman's use of her separate property since this restraint was only applicable to the property of a

---

[60] *Cooke v Fuller* (n 29) was cited by counsel for the plaintiff, a judicially separated wife, in *Munt v Glynes* (1872) 41 LJ Ch 639; counsel for Mrs Nicholson (see above n 28), cited *Johnson v Lander* (1869) LR 7 Eq 228 and *re Insole* (1865) LR 1 Eq 470, both of which involved judicially separated wives. (In the latter, counsel had cited inter alia, *re Whittingham's Trust* (n 27), which concerned a section 21 order). In *Hill v Cooper* (n 35), counsel argued from both *Waite v Morland* (n 30) 135, relating to a judicially separated wife, and *Ramsden v Brearley* (n 59).

[61] Indeed, by the end of the century some eminent lawyers were no longer accurately distinguishing between the two: see n 36.

[62] Eversley (n 37) 213–15.

woman under coverture: this was a freedom not enjoyed by other married women until 1949.[63]

Strikingly, 'DIVORCE' was from the beginning, and long remained, the heading given to the pages dealing with magistrates' section 21 orders in the two handbooks in almost universal use: *The Magisterial Synopsis: a Practical Guide for Magistrates, their Clerks, Attorneys and Constables*, compiled annually by GC Oke, Chief Clerk to the Lord Mayor of London, and *The Magisterial Formulist*.[64] Less remarkably, many local and national newspapers headed their regular column on applications for these orders: 'DIVORCE BEFORE MAGISTRATES', and numbers of ordinary men and women remained convinced for years that magistrates had been given divorce powers and told magistrates that they 'wanted a divorce'.[65] To some extent, the lawyers and laymen who used this language were doubtless simply clinging to familiar ways of speaking and thinking, instead of adopting overnight the narrower, more precise, new-fangled terminology suddenly prescribed by Parliament. After all, until the new legislation of 1857 the most familiar meaning of the word 'divorce' to everyone – lawyers, clergy and lay public alike – was separation from bed and board (the ecclesiastical lawyers' divorce *a mensa et thoro*) rather than that great rarity, dissolution of marriage (divorce *a vinculo*), and it was not to be expected that the traditional broader usage would be quickly discarded.[66] Yet it was also the case that this use of the term 'divorce' had both practical and legal logic. When magistrates made an order under section 21 of the Divorce Act, they broke the economic and civil ties between husband and wife far more thoroughly than the ecclesiastical courts had ever done by a divorce *a mensa et thoro*, and moreover with an immediate retrospective effect not possessed by the new decrees of divorces and judicial separation granted by the Divorce Court.[67] As long

---

[63] For this and many other persistent survivals in the law of husband and wife, see O Kahn-Freund, 'Inconsistencies and Injustices in the Law of Husband and Wife' (1952) *MLR* 15, 133–54 and ibid, 'Recent Legislation on Matrimonial Property' (1970) *MLR* 30, 601–33.

[64] GC Oke (1821–74) (see ODNB), GC Oke, *Oke's Magisterial Synopsis*, 14th edn (edited by SH Lushington) (London, Butterworths, 1893) 956–58 and GC Oke, *The Magisterial Formulist: Being a Complete Collection of Forms and Precedents for Practical Use by Magistrates, their Clerks, Attorneys and Constables*, 4th edn (London, 1868) 745–47.

[65] For examples of press and popular talk of 'divorce before magistrates' in 1858, see Chapters Five, Six and Seven. For discussion of the persistent belief that magistrates could save a trip to the divorce courts, see J Davis, 'A Poor Man's System' (1984) *Historical Journal* 27, 309, 322.

[66] The first debate on the proposal which led in the end to the passing of section 21 also saw the first suggestion from Cranworth, then Lord Chancellor, that divorce *a mensa et thoro* should instead be called a 'separation', so that a married woman could be given that altered status which he insisted would alone make it possible to protect her earnings against her husband: *Hansard* HC Deb (series 3) 25 May 1857, vol 145, cols 803, 805. Two law lords, Campbell, and St Leonards disagreed and resisted this proposal. Several lay peers however, supported it, since there was 'an ambiguity in the word divorce, which would lead to confusion in common minds, and ought to be removed'; the 'general public did not understand the legal distinction between a divorce *a vinculo* and a divorce *a mensa et thoro*', and Latin should always be got rid of where possible: ibid, cols 1405–1407 (Fitzwilliam Grey, Wicklow, 9 June 1857).

[67] An ecclesiastical divorce did not make the wife a *feme sole* with regard to her after-acquired property. Judicial separation was in fact 'a great improvement on divorce *a mensa et thoro*': Macqueen (n 10) 61.

as marriage continued to transfer to the husband a woman's property rights, legal capacities and liabilities, any order which legally deprived him of these marital rights and duties did in truth dissolve some of the closest and most meaningful bonds of matrimony.

Contemporary parlance thus offers some endorsement of the use of the term 'economic divorce' in this study of section 21 orders. Neologism though it is, this term has been preferred to 'protection order' in the interests not only of clarity and descriptive accuracy, but also increased historical understanding. In 1857 Parliament entrusted magistrates with a true minor matrimonial jurisdiction shared only with the Divorce Court; yet this has seldom been fully appreciated. No doubt the intrinsic reason for this is the incongruity within section 21 itself to which the *Solicitors' Journal* drew attention in 1864: 'the terms of the order are not co-extensive with the significance of its effect'.[68] The terms of these orders have always been indicated accurately enough, but their effect has never been spelt out. This curtailment of the truth has arguably hampered understanding of those intertwined later developments in married women's autonomy, the law of married relationships, and magistrates' domestic jurisdiction which shaped the relationship of millions of husbands and wives in England and Wales throughout the twentieth century. But has it also lessened our larger understanding of law-making in mid-Victorian England itself? In countries influenced by civil law traditions with a regime of community of matrimonial property and the transfer of legal capacity to the husband, provisions protecting the wife by enabling her to apply for judicial dissolution of the joint economic relationship and authorisation of her independent legal acts have been familiar enough.[69] That mid-Victorian England was also such a country has been forgotten. This hardly matters if economic divorce was never more than an esoteric rarity among mid-Victorian wives, but as the following chapters will show, this could not be further from the truth.

---

[68] 'There is an incongruity in the Act': 8 *Solicitors Journal* 607 (4 June 1864).

[69] For example, the Civil Code of the province of Quebec of 1866 did not recognise divorce but allowed a wife to bring an action for separation as to bed and board or for separation of property: W Friedman (ed), *Matrimonial Property Law* II (London, Stevens, 1955) 147. Other legal systems where judicial action could dissolve the spouses' economic relationship alone, as opposed to the marriage, include France, Louisiana, Sweden and South Africa: ibid, 67, 197, 423. For the French system (the model for section 21), see Chapter One.

PART II

Enacting 'Economic Divorce'

3

What was the Machinery for 'Divorce Before Magistrates'?

How any new legislation actually works depends very largely on the machinery and (before 1919) the men used to implement it, and this was particularly true of section 21 of the Matrimonial Causes Act 1857.[1] That hasty piece of last-minute drafting was full of 'vagueness, looseness and uncertainty'[2] and left much room for judicial discretion; yet its interpretation and implementation fell almost entirely into the hands of the country's hotch-potch of local tribunals. As will be shown, very few applications indeed were made to the Divorce Court itself, though those that were submitted there are explored further in Chapter Seven. In the months before the Act came into force the intention behind section 21 was much praised, but the machinery and procedure for granting the new orders attracted a good deal of criticism. What was this machinery and procedure? Did it deserve so much criticism? And how was the working of section 21 affected by the ways and means provided for getting an order granted or discharged?

By the time the Matrimonial Causes Act was passed in 1858 the campaign to replace the country's lay justices by a network of stipendiaries had clearly failed. Instead, the existing dual system of amateurs and professionals was being fitfully rationalised and provided with a code of practice. In January 1858, when the Divorce Act first came into force, there were only 33 professional magistrates – 23 in the metropolis, appointed by the Home Secretary and paid handsome salaries 'as Her Majesty shall direct',[3] and 10 in the provinces, most of them considerably less handsomely paid.[4] (Urban radicals campaigning for a stipendiary were always

---

[1] The first female magistrate was Ada Jane Summers who was appointed to the Stalybridge Police Court in December 1919 following the passing of the Sex Disqualification (Removal) Act 1919: 'First Woman on the Bench' *The Times* (1 January 1920) 9.

[2] TW Saunders, *The Practice of Magistrates' Courts*, 2nd edn (London, 1858) 224.

[3] George Chapple Norton was paid £1,000 (the modern-day equivalent of £107,800) per annum when he became a stipendiary magistrate at Whitechapel Police Court in 1831 (he moved to the Lambeth Police Court in 1845): www.historyofparliamentonline.org/volume/1820-1832/member/norton-hon-george-1800-1875.

[4] The salaries of the Stipendiary Magistrates outside of London in 1855 ranged from £300 to £1,000 per annum. In 1855, Charles Sidebottom, the Stipendiary Magistrate for Worcester, wrote a rather petulant letter complaining that he was paid a 'scanty salary' which was the same as his 1833 salary as a Town Clerk. His submitted return for 1855 shows that even though he sat 'generally every legal day', the number of cases coming before his court that year was 467. This might be contrasted with the Liverpool

likely to be defeated by economisers.) Each of these men could do alone everything that two lay justices could do in petty sessions – including granting or discharging an economic divorce.[5] The acknowledged elite of the band were the 23 metropolitan 'police' magistrates, who were often men of some personal distinction, and enjoyed increasing public esteem as well as great professional independence; the term 'police' was already a misleading survival. A pair of these magistrates manned each of London's 11 police courts (Bow Street needed three) and each sat for three days a week from 10am to 5pm, where they began by distributing advice, alms and summonses to the people who came to ask for them, before rapidly dispatching the usual flow of charges of assault, drunk and disorderly and the like.[6] Many stipendiary magistrates had previous experience as Recorders, Commissioners of Bankruptcy, or provincial stipendiaries and all were required to have practised at the bar for at least seven years before their appointment. It was not until 1858 that the Home Secretary was allowed to waive this statutory requirement, and then only when the appointee had served as a provincial stipendiary.[7] In 1859–60, John Smith Mansfield of Liverpool, Daniel Maude of Manchester and John Leigh of Wolverhampton were all given metropolitan vacancies, and such promotions were both natural and useful, for although a provincial stipendiary's position was linked with local politics and brought less status and prestige, his day-to-day work might be a good preparation for the metropolitan courts. This was certainly true of the Liverpool and Manchester stipendiaries, who handled about 20,000 cases each year,[8] and to a lesser extent those at Salford, Hull, Newcastle, Stoke, and Wolverhampton, with their 5,000 or more cases a year; only those at Merthyr Tydfil, and above all Brighton and Worcester, with their insignificant workloads, were unlikely to progress through this *cursus honorum* of stipendiary ranks.[9] The officials of the metropolitan police courts formed another subordinate professional elite. Two full-time professional clerks were attached to each court, as well as other staff (often from well-entrenched legal dynasties), all again appointed by the Home Office and generously paid. In 1866, Henry Hayle of Blackburn was paid £330 per annum, while Robert Winder of Bolton was paid £400, and the Clerk to Sunderland and Wolverhampton borough courts drew a salary of £500 per annum.[10]

Police Court, where John Smith Mansfield oversaw 24,907 cases in 1855. See: *Return of Stipendiary Magistrates in England and Wales, 1855*, HC 50 371 (1856), 1–6.

[5] Stipendiary Magistrates Act 1858, ss 1–2.

[6] J Davis, 'A Poor Man's System of Justice: The London Police Courts in the Second Half of the Nineteenth Century' (1984) 27 *Historical Journal* 309–35.

[7] Stipendiary Magistrates Act 1858, s 14.

[8] Liverpool stipendiaries regularly progressed to the metropolis, as had TJ Hall, the Chief Metropolitan Magistrate in 1858, in 1839.

[9] *Return of Stipendiary Magistrates in England and Wales* HC 371 (1856).

[10] *Return of Number of Justices' Clerks Paid by Salary instead of Fees in England and Wales* HC 276 (1866).

In the metropolis and a few of the largest provincial towns then, the apparatus which was to put into force section 21 of the Matrimonial Causes Act was a thoroughly professional one, staffed by a small band of experienced and often able and humane judicial functionaries. But how many wives lived within their jurisdiction? In 1858, only about a fifth of the population of England and Wales resided within the districts served by these 33 professional magistrates and their 22 courts.[11] For the remaining four-fifths of the population, economic divorce, like most other kinds of civil and criminal summary justice, was to be sought at the petty sessions held for the place where they lived by two (or more) of the country's thousands of lay justices.

The contrast between these two sorts of tribunal – professional and lay – could hardly have been sharper. Lay justices had only one thing in common: they were all local notables of some sort. Every county bench was filled with local landowners and a sprinkling of clergy (lawyers were not eligible),[12] except in Lancashire and the Black Country, where manufacturers and coal and iron masters already predominated.[13] 'Dignity' and 'respectability' were secured by confining appointments to those recommended by the County's Lord Lieutenant – a far higher hurdle than the statutory property qualification then in force. A county's justices were truly a local oligarchy. By 1857, however, 200 towns had escaped from the 'thraldom' to their county bench[14] by acquiring a bench of their own under the provisions of the 1835 Municipal Corporations Act, these included 18 newly incorporated industrial downs in the north and midlands.[15] These borough justices (who needed no property qualification and might be solicitors) were a different breed. They were appointed by the Home Secretary on the nomination of the Town Council and after consultation with the local MPs, and their chairman was *ex officio* the Mayor of the day. Political services and social, business, family, and religious networks could thus be even more important in securing a place on a municipal than on a county bench. It follows that the very places in the provinces where economic divorce was most likely to be in demand – that is, urbanised, industrialised countries and large municipal boroughs – were also

---

[11] Taking the figures of the 1851 Census, the population covered by the 10 provincial stipendiaries in post in 1855 was 1.6 million: *Return of Stipendiary Magistrates in England and Wales* HC 371 (1856). A further two million or so lived within the metropolitan magistrates' district. This was smaller than the metropolitan police district, which contained 2.5 million people in 1851: *Return of Number of Police Force employed in Metropolitan District, and City of London, 1841, 1851, 1861 and 1866* HC 89-1 (1867–68). The total population of England and Wales in 1851 was just under 18 million.

[12] Solicitors' Act 1843, s 33.

[13] In 1863, according to the Conservative MP for Lancashire J Wilson-Patten, only 200 of Lancashire's 600 Justices of the Peace were 'connected exclusively with land': *Hansard* HC Deb 19 June 1863, vol 171, col 1171. Just over half of the Staffordshire Bench were coal and iron masters by 1860: D Philips, 'The Black Country Magistracy, 1835-60' (1975–76) *Midland History* 3 161, Table 1, 163. Similar developments in Yorkshire and Cheshire came more slowly.

[14] The attraction of incorporation for Manchester were so described by Cobden: quoted D Fraser, *Urban Politics in Victorian England* (Leicester University Press, 1976) 150.

[15] They are listed in D Fraser, *Power and Authority in the Victorian City* (Oxford, Basil Blackwell, 1979) 150.

the places where justices' involvement with local political, sectarian, and business networks was likely to be closest.

Any and every tribunal made up of local notables was bound to reflect a powerful web of local interests and prejudices, political groupings, and clans. To such a body, fairness was likely to mean not so much impartiality, as turn and turnabout. 'The very circumstances that elevate a country gentleman or a prosperous tradesman to the bench', expostulated the maverick Sir George Stephenson in 1854, 'are such as to disqualify him for an impartial discharge of its duties'. He had been put in the commission because of his 'local consequence'; inevitably, therefore, it was 'difficult to bring any party before him with whom he is not more or less acquainted, or towards whom he does not stand, directly or indirectly, on some definite relation'. Even worse, most country justices were 'ignorant not only of law but of legal principles' and therefore relied heavily on the whispers in their ear of their clerks who were usually incompetent as well as irresponsible, since no really able man would be content with 'this ill-paid and humble office'.[16] These charges were not without some foundation. The attorney who serviced a local petty session part-time was indeed usually remunerated not by salary but by fees from the parties,[17] and was unlikely to be a standard-bearer for the wider interests of his emergent profession; very few, for example, were members of the Law Association.[18] The most successful among them were specialists in local government work and had acquired a string of appointments as clerk to the burial board or local board of health, County Court registrar and the like. Family dynasties of attorneys abounded, and magistrates' clerks were as much part of local political culture as the justices themselves, and as closely tied into networks of friends (and opponents) who inevitably included some of the many local solicitors establishing or expanding their practice on the basis of petty sessions work like economic divorce.

The working of section 21 was thus entrusted to this very disparate machinery, which provided a set of courts manned by full-time professional experts for one-fifth of the population, and another very different set manned by laymen and part-timers for the rest. The adoption of this extensive disparate machinery had been very much *faute de mieux*; several Members of Parliament, for example, had considered the County Courts better suited for the new task. In August 1857, however, the political priority was to give every wife in the land immediate as well as cheap and easy access to a tribunal with exactly the same powers of economic divorce as the Divorce Court itself, and this could only be achieved by using the very lowest tier of the courts, imperfect patchwork though it was.

---

[16] Sir G Stephenson, *Magisterial Reform Suggested in a Letter to Viscount Palmerston* (London, 1854) 5, 12–18. Stephenson was making a highly coloured case for the replacement of lay Justices by a network of stipendiaries.

[17] In 1859 only two Lancashire Justices' Clerks were paid by salary: *Return of Sessions at which Clerks to Justices are paid by Salaries* HC 24 (1859).

[18] In Blackburn, for example, out of 26 certificated attorneys only three were members of an association in 1858: *Law List 1859*, 279.

The price of bringing justice to every woman's door was bound to be some local variation in the justice dispensed to her there. Arguably, however, the result of a woman's application depended on where she happened to live to a quite unnecessary extent. The deficiencies of justices in petty sessions were well known, and the London legal world had long considered it important to limit their capacity for damage by defining as precisely as possible any new statutory duties and powers entrusted to them. This, section 21 signally failed to do. Indeed, its wording was so loose that the author of one successful practitioners' handbook felt obliged to provide a separate chapter on it immediately, with the comment that

> in truth, there is a subject-matter in these few lines for a good-sized act of parliament; and if grave difficulties shall hereafter arise in carrying out the provisions of the section or in giving interpretation to its language, the fault will undoubtedly rest with the legislature.[19]

JS Macqueen's verdict that 'Section 21 would have puzzled Lord Mansfield himself', was pithier.[20]

In the first place, Parliament could undoubtedly very fairly be accused of having left the procedure to be followed in granting or rescinding an economic divorce too much to the discretion of individual magistrates and justices. A statutory obligation to follow a more than usually cautious procedure was what was needed, since every order granted under section 21 had an effect far graver and more far-reaching than the terms of the order itself – a fact by no means always appreciated, then or later. As the *Solicitors' Journal* pointed out in 1864, there was 'an incongruity in the Act' between the terms of the order, which simply protected the wife's earnings and property acquired since her desertion against her husband and all persons claiming under him, and its drastic effect – which was to make her a *feme sole* with regard to property, contract, wrongs and injuries.[21] Every order granted under section 21 automatically unmarried the couple in these respects from the declared date of desertion, and no attempt by the magistrates to restrict its terms or alter its effect could succeed. This was established in *Re Whittingham's Trust* in 1864,[22] where Vice-Chancellor Wood ruled a reversionary interest of property that came into the wife's possession after her desertion was covered under the Act, even though the magistrate in the case had only specified the 'money and property acquired by the wife by her lawful industry since the date of her desertion' in the

---

[19] Saunders (n 2) 223.

[20] JS Macqueen, *A Practical Treatise on Divorce and Matrimonial Jurisdiction Under the Act of 1857 and New Orders* (London, W Maxwell, 1858) 99. See Chapter Two for how Macqueen inspired section 21.

[21] *Solicitors' Journal* (4 June 1864) 607. If a deserted wife's earnings and property had been protected against her husband and his creditors through the familiar device of a simple magistrates' injunction, as St Leonards originally proposed and as has too often been assumed ever since, the consequences would have been far less momentous for both the couple concerned and the long-term development of English family law.

[22] *Re Whittingham's Trust* (1864) 12 WR 775 ChD.

initial section 21 order hearing.[23] The implementation of section 21 thus entailed the expropriation of husbands, summarily, usually in their absence, and with effect from an earlier date than either a decree of divorce or a judicial separation from the Divorce Court. It followed that an order wrongly given might inflict a very grave denial of justice upon the husband and his creditors, or others interested in the maintenance of his marital right to his wife's property.

Yet almost no procedural safeguards were included in the Act. First, although in the nature of things the deserted wife's application would usually be heard without her husband's knowledge and in his absence, there was no statutory requirement for her to be sworn, nor for a written deposition, nor for witnesses to be called. Less surprisingly, there was also no provision for her to be asked if she knew where her husband was, so that notice of her application could be served on him where possible. One metropolitan police magistrate who elicited from the first wife who applied to him that she knew her husband's whereabouts said he would prefer him to be present, but then it bethought him that 'perhaps it was intended that the order should be made first, and then for the husband to appeal if he thought proper'.[24] These thoughts proved correct. 'The service of a citation on the husband is not necessary', ruled Cresswell in the Divorce Court a month later, remarking, 'he may come to the court at any time and apply for a discharge of the order'.[25]

The right to apply for the order to be rescinded was thus the husband's or the creditor's only safeguard. But how was such a discharge to be secured? Section 21 provided simply that 'it shall be lawful for the husband and any creditor or other person claiming under him' to apply for the discharge of an order, and that the application must be 'to the magistrate or justices by whom such order was made'. No provision was made for summoning the wife to show cause why the discharge should not be granted, nor even for giving her notice of the application; and no indication was given of the grounds on which magistrates might properly discharge their order. Creditors' claims initially raised particularly awkward issues. Ought an order be revoked when the wife's property was wanted to pay the husband's debts? 'That can scarcely be a reasonable ground after an order has been made for any length of time', considered the *Justice of the Peace*, 'even if it would be right to discharge it on such a ground at the outset'.[26] This difficulty disappeared only when it became clear that an order only protected property the wife had acquired after her desertion and without the use of stock or equipment left behind by her husband;

---

[23] 'Married Women's Protection Order' *Sheffield Independent* (11 June 1864) 3.

[24] 'Protection of Deserted Wives Property' *Lloyds Weekly* (24 January 1858) 4.

[25] *Ex parte Hall*, 17 LJ P&M 19 (27 February 1858, per Cresswell, JO). Later, however, the Divorce Court's rules required a wife applying to that Court to state in her application whether she had any knowledge of her husband's residence; if so, notice was to be served on him (Rule 197: GA Browne, *A Treatise on the Principles and Practice of the Court for Divorce and Matrimonial Causes*, 3rd edn (London, 1876) 194.

[26] 'Justices' Authority to Protect Wife's Property in Case of Desertion' *Justice of the Peace* (23 January 1858) 50.

everything else was still his, and should go to his creditors.[27] A more lasting flaw was the requirement that the application must be 'to the magistrate or Justices by whom such order was made'. This was bound to lead to serious delay if the magistrate who had made the order was ill or away, and to the denial of justice altogether if he was dead or no longer in post. In August 1858, for example, a Liverpool husband returning from Ireland found himself locked out of his own house by his triumphant wife, yet powerless to get the discharge of the order she had secured from the Liverpool stipendiary, JS Mansfield, because Mansfield was away.[28] Not until 1864, when complete deadlock was reached over John Sharpe's application for the discharge of an order granted in 1858 by a Westminster magistrate, Thomas Paynter, who had died in 1863, was a short amending act at last passed to remedy this careless piece of drafting.[29] The gravest omission of all, however, was perhaps the failure to make any provision for a wife to appeal if her application was refused. True, magistrates and justices were officially recommended to give her the benefit of any doubt and grant an order, leaving the husband and creditors to lodge an appeal if they saw fit. When a great deal of property was at stake, however, a well-advised woman would apply to the Divorce Court, there she would always have an appeal, since every decision of the Judge Ordinary was subject to appeal at the full court.[30]

It is worth noting that a section 21 order could also be discharged by the 'mutual consent and renewed cohabitation of the parties'.[31] Crucially, just as a formal discharge from the magistrate or justice who had granted the order would reinstate the husband's *jus mariti* over his wife's property only from the date of discharge, so too the informal dissolution of a section 21 order maintained the wife's *feme sole* status for any property acquired in the period between the date of desertion as established in her application and the date of their resumed cohabitation.[32] The phrase by 'mutual consent' is also important as it suggests that legislators had little appetite to force women into potentially unpleasant and economically precarious domestic conditions. If a wife refused to resume cohabitation, the husband's only recourse was to show cause why magistrates should annul her order as obtained by false allegations and perjury. If his motive seemed to be to get possession of her protected property, he might well fail in this, as happened at Clerkenwell Police Court in 1869, when a Mr Jones tried to have his wife's protection order set aside four years after it was granted, 24 years after he had deserted her, and less than a year since she had inherited a house worth £4,000

[27] A wife who applied for an order when threatened with County Court proceedings by his creditors might therefore be granted an order, provided she convinced the bench that all the property left her by her husband had already gone to pay them off.
[28] 'The Matrimonial Causes Act: Caution to Husbands' 31 *Law Times* 237 (14 August 1858).
[29] Matrimonial Causes Act 1864; *ex parte Sharpe* (1864) 33 LJ QB 214. This difficulty did not arise with orders given by justices in petty sessions. See also, Chapter Seven.
[30] Matrimonial Causes Act (MCA) 1857, s 55.
[31] ibid s 25.
[32] The number of discharged section 21 orders is examined in Chapter Four.

from her late father.[33] The Clerkenwell justices told Mr Jones that they would not rescind the order, and if he wanted to pursue the case, he would have to enter proceedings in the Divorce Court for the restitution of conjugal rights. Rather surprisingly, the question of whether a husband's mere offer to resume cohabitation and support ended his desertion and thus terminated a wife's protection under section 21 was not argued in the higher courts until 1891, when counsel dismissed Cresswell's dictum in *Cargill v Cargill* (much cited in justices' handbooks) as 'not a binding decision' and claimed, 'If a man deserts his wife and she afterwards becomes possessed of means, she has a right to get a protection order and refuse to take him back'.[34]

The lack of clarification and definition within section 21 thus allowed courtroom procedure to vary very widely indeed. The Divorce Court issued a first set of rules for its own proceedings early in 1858; but the procedure of each magistrate's court of petty sessions remained a matter for itself alone. On the face of it the risk of wrong was as great to husbands as to wives. 'Want of due consideration' in granting an order, warned the *Justice of the Peace*, could lead to an act of great injustice to the husband by depriving him of property to which he would have been clearly entitled; yet for the sake of the wife, 'caution is certainly quite as requisite in discharging the order as in making it'. In either case, however, opined this leader with pious optimism, 'the Justices will, no doubt, be more than ordinarily circumspect in carrying the Act into operation, and will endeavour, by their own care, to supply the shortcomings of the legislature'.[35] Clearly the legal press had good reason to rebuke Parliament for the 'offhanded' way in which the Act allowed magistrates to deal with applications from deserted wives.

What doubts and difficulties arose from these statutory shortcomings, and how were they dealt with? One successful *'Practical Guide for Magistrates, their Clerks, Attornies, and Constables'*, promptly provided detailed advice on what was good and proper. It would be 'as well', they were told, that the wife's deposition and those of her witnesses be taken in writing upon oath and signed; and 'it is conceived' that a husband or creditor who applied for a discharge should be allowed to try to controvert the facts upon which the order was originally made, or show that 'the condition of things which rendered the former order justifiable no longer exists' or that the wife herself wished its discharge.[36] Another manual recommended clerks

---

[33] 'Proceedings to upset a Protection Order', 33 *Justice of the Peace* (11 December 1869) 793.

[34] *Mahoney v McCarthy* (1892) P.21 and see Chapter Two, n 23 on *Cargill v Cargill* (1858) 27 LJ 69.

[35] 'Justices' Authority' (n 26) 50.

[36] GC Oke, *The Magisterial Synopsis: A Practical Guide for Magistrates, Their Clerks, Attornies, and Constables, in All Matters Out of Quarter Sessions; Containing Summary Convictions and Indictable Offences, With Their Penalties, Punishment, Procedure, &C,* 8th edn (London, 1862) 957, fn 5; GC Oke, *The Magisterial Formulist: Being A Complete Collection Of Forms And Precedents For Practical Use In All Matters Out Of Quarter Sessions,* 3rd edn (London, 1861) 684–86. It has not been possible to trace copies of the 6th and 7th editions of Oke's *Magisterial Synopsis,* published in May 1858 and November 1860 respectively. The *Formulist* printed model forms covering an application, order and discharge of order. These were modelled on the forms prescribed early in 1858 by the Divorce Court for use

to make the order in duplicate, 'one for the registrar, one for the wife' and offered appropriate Forms of Application, Order and Discharge to add to the piles of other forms they kept to hand on their tables.[37] Such guidance, based at first simply upon general practice, naturally became fuller and more exact in successive editions, as decisions in the Divorce Court multiplied.[38]

Practitioners' handbooks, however, are always a poor guide to the realities of daily practice. The problems confronted by the justices' clerks who largely settled procedure and decisions at petty sessions can be better gauged from the weekly column of readers' 'Queries and Answers' printed by the *Justice of the Peace* under the heading 'Practical Points'. This was evidently a service much appreciated by conscientious clerks. At the outset, two questions were repeatedly asked: was the wife a competent witness to prove her marriage? (Yes, this was not a criminal proceeding against the husband, and therefore not within the prohibition in the Evidence Act 1851, s 3 and Evidence Amendment Act 1853, s 2.) The second question, must her marriage certificate be produced? (No, the wife's testimony would be enough.) Many other doubts and difficulties were aired. For example, who should enter the order with the County Court Registrar? (The wife.) Should a duplicate of the order be made? (One could be made if the justices thought fit, but since it was not required by the Act, fees could not be charged for it unless it had been applied for by the wife.) Was it necessary to give a written notice to a husband or creditor who seized property covered by an order? (No, any notice was sufficient, verbal or written.) A correspondent who raised four points not satisfactorily covered by 'the accompanying form of order settled by Mr Archbold' (that all too prolific legal pundit), was wisely told to include nothing in an order not expressly authorised by the Act – advice shortly borne out by a ruling of the Judge Ordinary.[39]

Uncertainties over the scope of an order gave trouble from the beginning. Occasionally a question simply showed that the Act had not been read sufficiently carefully. The clerk dealing with an application from a woman deserted 10 years before, for example, should not have needed to ask whether he could make out the order to protect all the property acquired since then, 'or for what period'.[40] Some of the issues raised by these punctilious clerks, however, were of the sort which soon occupied the wisdom of the higher courts. For example, if a wife was given an order and then got a thousand-pound legacy, would the order protect the

there: *cf Return of Rules and Regulations Concerning Practice and Procedure of Court for Divorce and Matrimonial Causes* HC 106 (1859) 8–9.

[37] Saunders (n 19) 226–29. A specimen form on the order was included in the new chapter.

[38] See Appendix II for suggested templates for an application under section 21 and a petition for the discharge of an order.

[39] 'Practical Points' 22 *Justice of the Peace*, 103, 119–21 (13 and 20 February 1858); *ex parte Mullineux* (1858) 30 LTR 352 (per Cresswell, JO). On JF Archbold (1785–1870), see the Oxford Dictionary of National Biography (ODNB), available at www.oxforddnb.com.

[40] 'Practical Points' 22 *Justice of the Peace* (6 March 1858) 153. Perhaps he can be excused, for the unlimited retrospective effect of an order was novel enough to be difficult to credit.

money? When the wife had enjoyed an annuity before marriage, would the order cover that? Can a trustee pay out a legacy to a wife with an order? Yes, yes, and yes, provided the legacy was given to her separate use and she was deserted before the death of the testator, they were told.[41]

What troubled the lay public far more than such uncertainties over procedure and the exact consequences of an order, however, was the conundrum Parliament had left unresolved at the heart of section 21: what constituted 'desertion without reasonable cause'? When former Tory Lord Chancellor St Leonards' clauses were replaced by section 21, he touchily pointed out that although 'the main objection was that magistrates would not know what desertion was, yet the word was kept',[42] and this was true, although there had been many more objections than this to his handiwork. Yet it is entirely understandable that Bethell's new clause kept the word 'desertion' without providing any statutory definition: to this day such a definition has been resisted.[43] Although in 1858 constructive desertion did not amount to legal 'desertion' in the opinion of the *Justice of the Peace*, it certainly did by the end of 1886, when a doubtful reader was assured that certain justices were entirely correct in treating a wife driven out by her husband's ill-treatment as deserted.[44] What were the legal landmarks in the acceptance of constructive desertion as orthodoxy? In 1864 Wilde, Cresswell's successor as Judge Ordinary and a very different judge, had ruled in *Graves v Graves* that the husband's bad behaviour to his wife amounted to desertion, and that she was therefore entitled to a judicial separation.[45] In 1868 in *Yeatman v Yeatman*, a decision with important implications for section 21, Wilde had disregarded Cresswell's early and always much-cited obiter dictum of 1858 in *Cargill v Cargill*, by holding (unlike Cresswell) that 'a permanent abandonment of cohabitation on the husband's part, without and against the consent of the wife, will constitute desertion, even though the husband should continue to support the wife'.[46] After all, that section required the wife to show *in addition* to desertion that she was maintaining herself by her own industry or property: to be abandoned without pecuniary means was thus not a necessary part of desertion, but an additional requirement for a section 21 protection order. Thus in the Divorce Court itself, by the end of the 1860s 'desertion' could be established not only by showing that the husband's absence was neither involuntary nor exonerated by the wife's consent, her bad conduct, or her refusal of his genuine distinct offer to return; but also by showing that his conduct had been so bad that she was justified in refusing even such an offer to resume cohabitation.

---

[41] 'Practical Points' 22 *Justice of the Peace* 119, 328, 359 (20 February, 22 May and 5 June 1858).

[42] *Hansard* HC (series three) 24 August 1857, vol 147, col 2043.

[43] In the closing stages of the Divorce Bill's progress through Parliament, the radical AS Ayrton tried to get a definition of desertion inserted, but failed: ibid, 14 August 1857, col 1634.

[44] *Justice of the Peace* (18 December 1886) *Graves v Graves* was cited: see below.

[45] *Graves v Graves* (1864) 164 ER 1310; 'Interesting Law Cases: The Divorce Court' *Leeds Evening Express* (13 February 1864) 3.

[46] 'In the Law Court' *Birmingham Journal* (30 May 1868) 4. *Yeatman v Yeatman* (1864) 164 ER 1315.

From the point of view of providing a remedy for desertion under the poor law and not under the divorce and matrimonial causes legislation, ie, not a matrimonial decree but a matrimonial order, the crucial case was *Thomas v Alsop* in 1870.[47] This case judgment laid down that section 33 of the Poor Law Amendment Act of 1868 'provided expressly for cases to which that decision (i.e. the harsh ruling on appeal in R. v. Flanagan, 1857)[48] has previously been applicable', that is, cases when 'the wife would have to return to her husband or starve', because she would not be entitled to poor relief if her husband offered to take her home and maintain her, however brutal the behaviour which had caused her to leave him.[49] The decision in the Flanagan case, though correct in law, was rightly regarded by the *Justice of the Peace* as sure to be seen as 'uncomfortable' and unreasonable by both parish officers and the public; it made brutality a sure way for a husband to rid himself of all criminal liability for his wife's maintenance. 'It would certainly be desirable that some remedy should be devised' for this situation;[50] but with the slowness typical of legislative remedies for acknowledged wrongs, this remedy was not on the statute book until 1868. In *Thomas v Alsop*, the Queen's Bench justices declared that the law under the Divorce Act 1857 was 'altogether different in scope and effect' from the Vagrancy Act 1824, and that the new legislation seemed designed to deal with exactly the problematic situation highlighted in the Flanagan case, whereby a wife had to choose between physical harm and destitution.[51]

The passing of the Married Women (Maintenance in Case of Desertion) Act in June 1886 confronted justices with frequent private claims from wives (not from the Poor Law authorities, as hitherto), for a maintenance order against the husband, often on grounds of his constructive desertion. Thereafter until 1895 – when the doctrine of constructive desertion was spelt out in legislation – the *Justice of the Peace* constantly explained that the decisions in 1858 in *Cargill*

---

[47] *Thomas v Alsop* (1870) LR 5 QB 154.

[48] In *Flannagan v The Overseers of the Poor of the Parish of Bishop Wearmouth* (1857) 120 ER 168, the Queen's Bench heard that Mrs Flanagan had been ill-treated by her husband and so left the marital home. Mr Flanagan had first offered to provide payment for her but did not and later said that he would support her only if she returned to live with him (despite him not actually having a home). Mrs Flanagan refused on account of his previous ill-treatment and she appealed to the Parish for Poor Relief, which was paid and the Parish then sought to recover costs from Mr Flanagan under The Vagrancy Act 1824. The Queen's Bench heard Mr Flanagan's appeal where he argued that he had offered to support his wife if she returned home and therefore, he had not 'wilfully refused and neglected to maintain his wife'. The Justices agreed stating that the 'magistrates consider that the wife, on account of the apprehended ill usage, is not bound to go and live with the husband: but that is very different from a refusal by him to maintain her', and Mr Flanagan's conviction was quashed. Mrs Flanagan could choose to be financially supported and return to live with Mr Flanagan, or she could continue to live separately to him without his financial support, but local magistrates did not hold (in November 1857) the power to allow her to live separately and be maintained.

[49] *Thomas v Alsop* (n 47).

[50] 'Husband's Liability to Conviction for not Maintaining Wife' *Justice of the Peace* (14 November 1857) 721.

[51] *Thomas v Alsop* (n 47).

and *Cudlipp*[52] (still being reproduced in justices' manuals and then lay matter) had been superseded, and that if the justices concluded that the husband by his conduct drove the wife to leave, he was guilty of desertion. Thus the 1860s were the crucial decade for this development: the problem was, to spread awareness of the new thinking to justices and their clerks – something only achieved by the passing of legislation in 1895, legislation which was in reality novel in form, rather than substance.[53]

Continual difficulties arose for justices because the question, 'what is desertion?' might be differently answered for purposes of criminal liability to maintenance, entitlement to settlement, civil liability for debt to a tradesman or to the Guardian of the Poor, and a matrimonial order or decree. As Field J put it in *R v Cookham Union* in 1882, 'desertion in an Act of Parliament relative to separation and divorce is not necessarily applicable to Desertion in an Act relative to the management of the poor'. The same circumstances might be desertion for the purposes of one remedy, but not desertion for the purposes of another.[54] Whether or not a woman had been deserted had deliberately been left as a question of fact, not law, and therefore a matter for magistrates and justices to decide on the evidence before them in each individual case. The result was bound to be as Macqueen predicted: 'constant questions as to the meaning of the word desertion, respecting which different, and opposite, and singular, and inexplicable conclusions will be come to every day'.[55] The idea of constructive desertion and its incorporation into magistrates' matrimonial jurisdiction did not begin to become a practical idea among justices, however, until after *Thomas v Alsop* in 1870, and in 1880, as for long afterwards, it was necessary for the *Justices of the Peace* to explain to its readers that 'desertion may be by leaving for good cause as well as dismissing the other for good cause'.[56]

The same was true of the vital proviso, 'deserted *without reasonable cause*'. As *Punch* explained a few days after the Divorce Act reached the statute book:

> What the law calls 'excuse' must remain to be seen,
> It may be much nagging, or much crinoline,
> Or a constant piano, a parrot's vile shriek,
> Or your mother his guest more than three times a week.[57]

Precedents and practice soon accumulated. Magistrates and justices remained statutorily required to use their subjective discretion in each individual case,

---

[52] The case of *Cudlipp v Cudlipp* (1858) 164 ER 705 saw Sir Cresswell Cresswell uphold that a wife whose husband had initially left the marital home in 1843 but then briefly returned to his wife the following year before finally writing in 1848 to inform her that he would never return, could be held to have deserted in 1843 'because he never made any definite or distinct proposal or offer of another home'.

[53] Summary Jurisdiction (Married Women) Act 1895.

[54] *R v Cookham Union* 9 QBD 522 (per Field J) 528; *Justice of the Peace* (31 July 1880) 485.

[55] Macqueen (n 20)381.

[56] *Thomas v Alsop* (n 47).

[57] 'The Divorce Bill Dissected' *Punch* (5 September 1857) 103.

however since they were empowered to make an order only 'if satisfied of the fact of such desertion, and that the same was without reasonable cause'. Their discretion extended, moreover, to the length of absence required to establish desertion. Few people were as clear as Macqueen on this point. Briskly he pointed out that since section 21 required magistrates and justices to 'be satisfied that the wife is maintaining herself by her own industry or property', the test must be whether the husband's absence had been 'long enough to put the woman on her resources, whether of body or mind' – something which was purely a matter of individual circumstances.[58] Yet even among those who should have known better, misconceptions persisted – partly no doubt because an absence of 'two years and upwards' was specified for a full divorce or judicial separation.

Willy-nilly, then, discretion was bound to play a large part in the implementation of economic divorce; and magistrates and justices were accordingly bound to be accused of whims and caprice, however they handled applications. As the *Law Times* remarked at the outset, an order under section 21 was 'a very uncertain remedy'.[59] Still, each court (and its clerk) naturally tended to possess its own working definition of 'desertion without reasonable cause'. What influences shaped these working definitions? On such matters, as on points of procedure, a conscientious justices' clerk anxious not to be at a loss when an application came before his bench might seek guidance beforehand from the editor of the *Justice of the Peace*. Such help was particularly sought in the months before the handbooks began to cover this new magisterial jurisdiction and distil for practitioners the upshot of the Divorce Court's decisions. In March 1858, for example, 'A.B.C.', having read a disturbing newspaper report that a London police magistrate had refused a wife an order because she had been deserted in Australia, which to his mind was 'not in accordance with the spirit or letter of the Act', sought that paper's advice 'on how to act in case a similar application (a not by any means unlikely one) should be made to the bench for which I act as Clerk'. 'We should certainly make the order', he was assured, provided there was satisfactory evidence that the husband was not about to live with her again in England.[60] Another correspondent asked whether a wife separated by consent was eligible for an order, and was firmly told she was not. But what if the husband had gone abroad ostensibly for three years with the wife's concurrence and leaving her what money he could spare, yet six years later had not communicated with her and had written to other persons saying he intended not to return? In this case, he was told, 'the proof of desertion seems enough'.[61]

In most of the country, however, both the working definition of 'desertion without reasonable cause' and procedure adopted by a bench and its clerk owed little to expert advice in the legal press from London lawyers, and far more to

---

[58] Macqueen (n 20) 98.
[59] *Law Times* 298 (20 February 1858).
[60] 'Practical Points' 22 *Justice of the Peace* (6 March 1858) 152.
[61] 'Practical Points' 22 *Justice of the Peace* (3 July and 22 May 1858) 423, 328.

local circumstances, values, and personalities, and the well-established habits of their own sittings.[62] Lay justices did not see themselves as either agents or partners of Parliament or the Courts,[63] and were rarely legally-minded; rather, they were men of affairs who hurried through this new business along their usual lines, applying to it their accustomed priorities. Only in the stipendiaries' courts, above all in London, were the influences for making continuity and local adaptation comparatively weak. Since desertion had not been an offence in the ecclesiastical courts, they were weakest of all in the new Divorce Court; but that Court's working is not under discussion here. A new stipendiary could change the style of a court overnight and turn a vigorously used statutory summary power into a local dead-letter.[64] Metropolitan police magistrates in particular, with their social and professional contacts with the world of Parliament, the superior courts, and the Inns of Court, and their staff of well-qualified full-time clerks, were always likely to be influenced far more by the written and far less by the unwritten local law than country justices. Often, they paid careful attention to the precise terms of section 21 and interpreted doubtful points cautiously pending clarification from Parliament or the Courts; and although they too heard these new applications in accordance with their established routines, they were usually far more disciplined and coherent than those prevailing in most petty sessions.

Neither stipendiaries nor lay justices, however, started with a *tabula rasa* in implementing this novel addition to their summary jurisdiction. There was never any question of their being 'left entirely in the dark' by the absence of textbooks or judicial decisions on matrimonial desertion, as that ultra-conscientious Conservative country gentleman, JW Henley, had predicted.[65] Long before the Divorce Act made desertion for the first time a specific matrimonial offence with specific remedies in matrimonial law, magistrates and justices everywhere had had abundant experience of dealing under the Poor Law with the public consequences of desertion in the everyday sense of that word. Since the end of the wars against France, a single justice had often been applied to by Overseers or Guardians to summon an absent husband whose dependents had become chargeable to the poor rate to show why he should not be ordered to repay the cost of the civil debt thus incurred, on pain of imprisonment; and if the absentee could not be reached, the parish officers could apply to two justices for a warrant to

---

[62] The same point has recently been made of the working of the criminal law in mid-Victorian Kent, which was 'still primarily determined by the values and priorities of the local community': CA Conley, *The Unwritten Law, Criminal Justice in Victorian Kent* (Oxford, Oxford University Press, 1991) 7.

[63] This point is well made in C Bellamy, *Administering Central-Local Relations, 1871–1919* (New York, Manchester University Press, 1988) 2–6.

[64] As it happened, there was an exceptionally high turnover of metropolitan magistrates in the early years of economic divorce. Shortly after 1858, six retired, four moved to a different court, and six new appointments were made, so that by 1861 only four of the 11 metropolitan police courts had the same magistrates, namely, Lambeth, Southwark, Westminster, and Hammersmith: see *Law Lists*. Whether these changes had any discernible effect on the handling of applications remains to be investigated.

[65] *Hansard* HC Deb (series three) 7 August 1858, vol 147, col 1232.

seize his goods.[66] Moreover, since 1824, a single justice had been able summarily to convict as a rogue and vagabond 'every person running away and leaving his wife or his or her children chargeable'.[67] Lay justices and stipendiaries alike were thoroughly familiar with the task of deciding whether a particular man's absence amounted to desertion in the sense of wilful neglect to keep his family off the parish.[68] Habits thus learnt were not readily discarded, inappropriate though they were to the task of deciding whether to accept a financially independent wife's claim that she had been 'deserted without reasonable cause' and that her husband and his creditors should therefore lose all right to her subsequently acquired money or property. When requests for economic divorce began to be heard, three familiar guiding principles thus often continued to do service:

- keeping down local expenditure (which could mean ensuring that a wife who was successfully keeping herself off the rates did not have her means of livelihood seized by her husband or creditors);

- dealing severely with rogues and vagabonds (and therefore readily depriving a chronic absconder, wife-beater, and womaniser of all rights over his wife's property); and

- protecting local property interests (which could prompt care that substantial creditors were not deprived of any property to which they were entitled).

One other form of matrimonial misbehaviour that had long been handled by magistrates and justices everywhere was marital violence. To them, the brutal husband was as familiar as the runaway. Urban magistrates in particular had abundant experience of binding over wife-beaters (and occasionally husband-beaters) to keep the peace, or sentencing them to one, two or even six months' hard labour. Sometimes they waived the prison sentence on condition the couple agreed to separate, with the husband making the wife an agreed weekly allowance – a practice which led a *Times* reviewer to assert in January 1857 that 'the police magistrates already exercise an imperfect power of granting separation and alimony'.[69]

---

[66] Poor Relief Act 1819, ss 29, 31; Poor Law Amendment Act 1834, ss 56, 58, 59; Summary Jurisdiction Act 1848, s 23. the goods of a deserter still in the parish could not be seized: R Burn, *The Justice of the Peace and Parish Officer*, 28th edn six vols (London, 1837) iv, 85.

[67] The Vagrancy Act 1824, s 4. After 1861 magistrates could also be required to decide whether a wife had been deserted, in order to determine whether she could become exempt from removal in the same way as a widow.

[68] This was frequently pointed out in the debates on the feasibility of St Leonards' original proposal, *Hansard* HC Deb (series three) 25 May 1857, vol 145, cols 802, 804 (Powis and St Leonards) and ibid 7 August 1857, vol 147, cols 1233, 1235 (Napier and Henley).

[69] To this a correspondent retorted, 'imperfect indeed, in committing a husband to prison for brutal ill-treatment of his wife, or for non-payment of a wretched scanty allowance to prevent her from "cumbering the parish in which she resides"': *The Times* (27 January 1857) 4; *The Times* (20 January 1857) 10. The legal status of wives after they had appealed to magistrates for help and been granted separation or alimony was not always fully understood and this confusion is highlighted in bigamy prosecutions: 'A Singular Bigamy Case' *The People* (1 February 1885) 13.

For generations the ecclesiastical courts had considered that brutality could justify a wife in leaving her husband;[70] and there was a growing feeling that a destitute wife should not be compelled to return to a brutal husband, but that he should be compelled to make her a maintenance allowance.[71] Could section 21 be held to apply to a wife who had left her husband 'in consequence of his adultery, cruelty or other gross misconduct, and gone to reside at a distance, where she has maintained herself by her own industry?', enquired a correspondent of the progressive new *Solicitors' Journal* in May 1858. He himself thought not, although 'I have heard that opinion disputed, and am inclined to think that some of the magistrates are disposed to extend the operation of the Act to include such cases'.[72] No evidence has been found that section 21 was deliberately extended in this way,[73] although constructive desertion was certainly being mooted as a ground for 'divorce before magistrates' many years before Parliament made it so, and well before the Divorce Court began to accept it as a ground for judicial separation and dissolution of marriage.[74] Clearly, however, failure to enquire into the circumstances of the couple's separation may not always have been the result of mere carelessness, haste or impressionability. Orders were certainly sometimes granted to wives who, by their own account, had left their husbands and refused to return,[75] as well as to some (perhaps many) liars on this point.[76]

In the broadest practical sense, then, section 21 simply empowered magistrates and justices to deal in a new way with a sort of misbehaviour long brought before them: the disregard of conjugal duties. In law, however, it was this 'new way' that was all-important. TW Saunders was altogether correct in claiming that

[70] As Joanna Miles, Daniel Monk and Rebecca Probert point out, 'although it is often claimed that only "life-threatening" cruelty would suffice, this is a misleading contraction of Sir William Scott's exposition in *Evans v Evans*. What Scott actually said was that it was necessary to establish that there was a "danger to life, limb, or health", and that in assessing the threat there must be a 'reasonable apprehension of bodily hurt': J Miles, D Monk and R Probert (eds), *Fifty Years of the Divorce Reform Act 1969* (Oxford Hart Publishing, 2019) Introduction, 13.

[71] That there was already some acceptance of the concept of constructive desertion for poor law purposes is illustrated by the comment that the overturning of *R v Flanagan* (n 48) would seem to parish officers to be putting 'a premium on brutality': 'Practical Points' *Justice of the Peace* (14 November 1857) 721.

[72] 'Protection of Wife's Earnings' 2 *Solicitors' Journal* (29 May 1858) 625. This new journal's founders included William Shaen, that very active proponent of women's rights.

[73] That favourite recourse of doubtful justices' clerks, the *Justice of the Peace*, insisted at the outset that a wife who had left a cruel husband was not eligible for an order, even when she had not had a farthing from him, and had given him money to get rid of him: 'R.R.' 22 *Justice of the Peace* 121 (20 February 1858).

[74] In August 1857, Gladstone and his temporary ally AS Ayrton, who were attempting to widen the ground of divorce available to wives, had tried to induce the Commons to agree that a man could be guilty of 'the animus and substance of desertion' even if he did not actually leave his wife: *Hansard* HC Deb (series three) 13 and 14 August 1857, vol 147, cols 1540.

[75] For example, the Darwen weaver Betty Richardson, who had left her husband in Liverpool: 'Protection under the Divorce Act' *Blackburn Weekly Times* (2 April 1859).

[76] Litigation in 1860 revealed that the Bow Street magistrate David Jardine (1794–1860) (on whom see ODNB) had given an order in March 1858 to a woman who in reality had left her husband to live with her lover: *Thomas v Head* (1860) 175 ER 971–972, reprinting 2 F&F 87.

section 21 conferred upon magistrates 'an entirely new jurisdiction'.[77] For the first time they were empowered to change the relations of husband and wife *under matrimonial law*. A wife's application for a property protection order might seem essentially a civil dispute over property rights in which one party would usually be absent – and justices had long adjudicated upon civil disputes, for example between master and servant, or officers and members of friendly societies. In reality however, there was a very essential difference, for the *ex parte* claim to be heard was that the husband had committed a certain statutory matrimonial offence, and that the wife's conduct and circumstances were such that she was entitled to the matrimonial remedy statutorily attached to that offence.[78] Once they were satisfied that the applicant had been deserted without reasonable cause and was maintaining herself by her own earnings or property, magistrates and justices were forthwith to give her the prescribed remedy. And what was that remedy? Because the Commons' had rejected St Leonards' clauses, it was not the already established remedy of a temporary injunction forbidding the husband to mistreat his wife (in this case, by seizing her earnings and property), on pain of a £20 fine or two months' imprisonment. Instead, he was to be deprived indefinitely of his civil rights and liabilities as a husband, and the wife made a *feme sole* with regard to her earnings, property, and contracts. Thus the radical novelty lay not in empowering a deserted wife to seek from her local magistrate or justices protection from her husband's misbehaviour or a declaration that she was entitled to the possession of her earnings or property, but in the nature of the remedy they were statutorily required to give her.

When that 'useful exotic' from France, section 21, came into force in January 1858, then, it provided the country with a new and very local matrimonial jurisdiction, albeit a limited one, and the legal press repeatedly warned justices of the gravity of their new responsibility. Yet from their own point of view and that of those directly involved in their courtroom proceedings, they easily seemed to be undertaking little more than a variant of their familiar task of punishing a husband for ill-treating or neglecting his wife, and past experience of dealings with bad husbands seems to have shaped the behaviour in court of all concerned – wives and their legal advisers, as well as justices and their clerks. Thus the wife usually concentrated on emphasising that her husband had not given her 'a farthing' during whatever period of time was consistent with her story, and often recounted his ill-treatment and cruelty, sometimes also detailing goings-on with 'another woman', and occasionally drinking. Her solicitor (if she had one), would not fail to mention any convictions anywhere, for any offence whatever, and his task would be easy if he could tell the bench that the husband had already been charged in the same court with assaulting his wife, or with desertion within the meaning of the poor law, that is, neglecting to maintain his family.

---

[77] Saunders (n 19) 1.
[78] Oke, *Magisterial Synopsis* (n 37) 4–5.

Information like this convinced justices that they were dealing with a bad husband, and disposed them to be 'satisfied' that the wife had been 'deserted without reasonable cause' within the meaning of the Matrimonial Causes Act 1857 without hearing specific evidence on that issue, or enquiring whether the husband's absence was exonerated by the wife's bad conduct, consent, or refusal of his genuine offer to return.[79] Few knew enough law to appreciate clearly that the legal meaning of the term desertion might not only be different from its ordinary meaning, but different for different legal purposes.[80] These few – stipendiaries, some justices active in national as well as local affairs, the most conscientious or professionally distinguished justices' clerks – tended to be cautious in implementing the new law and attentive to the legal press and the continually up-dated practitioners' manuals (often compiled by one of their number).[81] The many justices who were 'ignorant not only of law but of legal principles', however, and whose part-time clerk had 'familiarity with the routine of business' but no more,[82] easily interpreted their new power of protecting wives under the Matrimonial Causes Act in the light of their accustomed dealings with runaways and wife-beaters under the poor law and the ordinary criminal law; and so did the humbler wives who applied to them. Rarely were the issues given prominence in Divorce Court hearings and rehearsed in practitioners' manuals investigated: whether she was being supported by herself and not her family or friends, whether the husband's absence was unlawful, unjustifiable, and permanent, whether it was without her consent, and whether he had left her unprovided for and never made a bona fide offer to return and provide for her. Instead, their hearings usually focused on one familiar question: was he maintaining her?

Nevertheless it would be wrong to suppose that this was solely the result of transferring old habits to new tasks. The husband's side of the story was necessarily unlikely to emerge in his absence; and in any case, given that what was at stake was his common-law right to the wife's money and property, there is nothing surprising about the focus upon his failure to fulfil his corresponding

---

[79] The Commons expressed some scepticism about this novel penalty and hankered after the addition of a fine or imprisonment. In the Lords, St Leonards' last-minute amendment making a husband who seized a wife's protected property liable to restore both the property and double its value was accepted: *Hansard* HC Deb (series 3) 20 and 24 August 1857, vol 147, cols 188–1891, 2043. It is even more surprising, given its great practical significance that the date of desertion given by the wife seems never to have been questioned.

[80] This was a lesson many justices and practitioners were slow to learn. As early as July 1858 the first Judge Ordinary of the Divorce Court, Cresswell, said that 'desertion' did not mean the same thing in every clause of the Matrimonial Causes Act. This *obiter dictum* on section 21 was always quoted in magistrates' manuals, but never his successor's contrary opinion delivered 10 years later: *Cargill v Cargill* (n 34); *Yeatman v Yeatman* (n 46).

[81] TW Saunders produced four editions of his *The Practice of Magistrates' Courts* (n 19) before becoming a magistrate at the Thames police court in 1878. In later years a series of prominent justices' clerks were responsible for the annual revision of *Stone's Justices' Manual* (JR Roberts (ed), *Stone's Justices' Manual* (London, Butterworths, 1907)).

[82] Stephenson (n 16) 7, 12.

common-law duty to protect and provide for her. That duty lay not only at the core of matrimonial property law, moreover, but of Church teaching, early Victorian romantic ideals of marriage, and a deeply ingrained popular understanding of what made a good husband. The provision for economic divorce in section 21 found immediate favour in Parliament and the press, with lawyers and laymen, and with wives of many descriptions, because it expressed the logic of common justice, common sense, and the common law, and the gendered imperatives of the romantics as well as traditional, gentlemanly, and plebeian concepts of conjugal duty: a husband must maintain and protect his wife, and should therefore have the disposal of her earnings and property – but if he failed in the one, he lost his right to the other.[83]

In 1857 Parliament had empowered the very lowest tier of local tribunals to give a wife an economic divorce, and had left to their discretion not only the procedure to be followed in hearing applications, but the upshot itself of those hearings. The grant of an order was dependent solely upon the magistrate or justices concerned being subjectively 'satisfied of the fact' that the wife had been deserted 'without reasonable cause' and was 'maintaining herself by her own industry or property'. Accordingly, all over the country section 21 was applied in ways broadly in accordance with local habits and expectations, if not always to local satisfaction.[84] From the beginning the localism and flexibility of this machinery provided a sharp contrast with the single, central Divorce Court at Westminster and its strict rules – a contrast which goes far to explain why barely two per cent of applications for these orders were made to that Court and was a prime cause of the mistrust and lack of understanding between these two matrimonial jurisdictions so conspicuous 50 years later. From its very first months, magistrates were practical, ad hoc, and intensely local, and matrimonial jurisdiction was set to develop along lines which paid scant regard to consistency or adherence to legal principle.

The machinery and procedure of 'divorce before magistrates' ensured not only that it would be speedily accessible to every deserted wife in the country, but that it would be administered in near-total independence of the Divorce Court, and most likely by men who had no legal training, and potentially, little understanding of the letter of the law. Much remains to be discovered about the relationship between the rapidly expanding summary powers and duties under the criminal and civil law magistrates' and mid-Victorian Town Councils or Boards of Guardians, but

---

[83] Most Victorian weddings still took place in Church, where the husband made the centuries-old vow, 'with all my worldly goods I thee endow'. Among the London poor in the later nineteenth-century, a husband's refusal to provide an income was a cause for leaving him and gave the wife freedom to take up with another man: E Ross, '"Fierce Questions and Taunts" Married Life in Working-Class London, 1870–1914' in D Feldman and G Stedman Jones (eds), *Metropolis: London, Histories and Representations since 1800* (Abingdon, Routledge, 1989) 223, 234.
[84] See Chapter Six.

the potential impact of it is plain.[85] Only detailed investigations of what went on in some individual courtrooms can begin to establish how this novel machinery for helping wives in broken marriages actually worked in practice, and bring to light the interactions between an applicant, her 'legal advisor', the court officials, and those important but very different social administrators – a professional magistrate sitting alone or lay justices in petty sessions.

[85] The workings of magistrates courts and their officers in the nineteenth century have historically received less academic attention than other areas of the judiciary and court system. This has impacted understanding of legal provision available to men and women, as well as analysis of English entrepreneurial performance. Fortunately this situation has changed in recent years, though more work remains to be done. See: H Berghoff and R Moller, 'Tired Pioneers and Dynamic Newcomers? A Comparative Essay on English and German Entrepreneurial History, 1870–1914' (1994) *Economic History Review* 47, 262; SM Cretney, *Family Law in the Twentieth Century: A History* (Oxford, Oxford University Press, 2003) chapter 11. L Ryland-Epton, 'Parliament and the English County Magistrate: The Parliamentary Aspirations of Sir George Onesiphorus Paul 1780–1810' (2022) *Parliamentary History* 42, 213; and FC Boorman, 'Developments in the History of Arbitration: A Past for the Present' (2022) *Amicus Curiae* 109.

4

How Widespread was the Use of 'Economic Divorce' Through Section 21 Orders in Victorian England and Wales?

Section 21 of the Matrimonial Causes Act 1857 was clearly innovative in terms of legal principles and jurisdictions. It was also innovatory in a way which would significantly shape the mould of twentieth-century English family law; but was it a practical success? Was it much used? As previous chapters have shown, the only historians to give the matter even passing attention have been quite clear that section 21 was neither of these things. Yet, as has already been discussed, this is a serious (though understandable, given the scarcity and scattered nature of the source material) misapprehension, and in fact, there were over 2,000 section 21 orders granted during the first three years of the Act, rather than the c.100 which had previously been stated. Moreover, this flow continued apace for the following four decades, only tailing off following the passing of the Married Women's Property Act 1882. But how did such a fundamental contemporary misapprehension of scale arise – a misapprehension which originated among the contemporary legislators reporting those initial figures and which fostered the persistent underestimation of these orders' significance by historians?

At least part of the answer can be found if we revisit the campaign surrounding the Married Women's Property Bill, which was spearheaded by the Married Women's Property Committee and found an unexpected resonance with early historians of women's legal history.[1] The National Association for the Promotion of Social Science (NAPSS) which had introduced the Married Women's Property Bill in 1857 and acted as an umbrella organisation for groups including the

---

[1] The study of legislation relating to mid-Victorian women, particularly married women, has been shaped by similar forces to the study of mid-Victorian women's economic activity: those who carried out the first ground-breaking studies were academic-activists (or maybe activist-academics), and also engaged in their own political battles. Women who were not obviously subject to the negative effects of coverture and the patriarchal system in which they lived, or indeed, those who actively promoted such aspects, have tended fall outside key areas of study. See: A Vickery, 'Golden Age to Separate Spheres? A Review of the Categories and Chronology of English Women's History' (1993) *The Historical Journal* 36, 383; J Aston and C Bishop (eds), 'Discovering a Global Perspective', *Female Entrepreneurs in the*

Law Amendment Society and the Society for Promoting the Employment of Women, remained focussed on achieving their ultimate goal of extending married women's property rights, which had been thwarted by the introduction of the Matrimonial Causes Act 1857. They maintained that a root-and-branch New York-style reform of English matrimonial property law, which would leave every wife 'unmarried' with respect to property, was the way to achieve this,[2] but realised that they must present the existing system as inherently flawed if they were to have any hope of altering 'the whole law relating to marriage' and bring about a social revolution as well as access to 'civil privileges' for wives.[3] Such a 'sweeping and mischievous' measure as the one proposed by NAPSS inevitably rallied support for some less radical alternative, and many moderate reforming Liberals as well as Conservatives quickly agreed that 'much more good would be effected' by simply extending section 21 than by a drastic 'remedy (which) went beyond the disease'.[4] In April 1869, Alexander Staveley Hill told the House of Commons that,

> It would be remembered that when the Divorce Act of 1857 was passed, a clause was inserted in it which provided that a wife deserted by her husband might, on application to a magistrate, obtain an order for the protection of her past and future earnings. All that was necessary was to strike out the words relating to the desertion by the husband from that clause, and then the woman could apply to the magistrate, or, if it were thought better, to the County Court Judge, and the whole matter would be done and a proper protection afforded without the necessity for this Bill.[5]

Long Nineteenth Century (London, Palgrave Macmillan, 2020) 1–31; J Aston, H Barker, G Durepos, S Garrett-Scott, PJ Hudson, A Kwolek-Folland, DH Perriton, L Taylor S and M Yeager, 'Take Nothing For Granted: Expanding the Conversation About Business, Gender, and Feminism' (2022) 66 *Business History*.

[2] This Bill, backed by a committee of the Social Sciences Association, was modelled on the Married Women's Property Bill sponsored in 1857 by the Association's predecessor, the Law Amendment Society. One of its prime movers was Richard Pankhurst, whose somewhat extreme views on the 'emancipation' of women were sometimes challenged even by collaborators: *cf Select Committee on Married Women's Property Bill. Special Report, Proceedings, Minutes of Evidence, Appendix, Index*, HC (441) (1867–68) question 321, and 'Property of Women' *Transactions of the National Association for the Promotion of Social Sciences* (Birmingham, 1868) 279–80.

[3] 'As a rule, husbands and wives never desired any separation of their property and earnings' and 'in ninety-nine cases out of a hundred the husband and wife entirely repudiated the notion of separate interests', reported the prominent reforming solicitor and veteran of the Law Amendment Society's Committee on Married Women's Property of 1856, WS Cookson: ibid 278. This was a widespread opinion.

[4] Thus urged the Liberal common lawyer George Denman (1819–96), see the Oxford Dictionary of National Biography (ODNB), available at www.oxforddnb.com: recently Palmerston's colleague in representing Tiverton in the first parliamentary battle in this phase of the controversy, and the veteran Conservative politician JW Henley (1793–1884), see ODNB, in the second: *Hansard* HC Deb (series 3) 10 June 1868, vol 192, col 1373. Karslake as Attorney General had remarked that section 21 had had 'very beneficial consequences' and should perhaps be extended to cases of cruelty or ill-treatment, to which the sponsors of this first Married Women's Property Bill, GJS Lefevre and John Stuart Mill, retorted with their version of the 'true working' of section 21: *Hansard* ibid col 1371.

[5] AS Hill, a QC with a large probate practice, in the first sharp debate on the re-introduced Married Women's Property Bill in the very House newly elected under the 1867 Reform Act: *Hansard* HC Deb (series 3) 14 April 1869, vol 195, col 779.

He was not the only one to question why it was necessary to revolutionise the law, foist change on every family in the land and push married couples towards separate and independent interests in a way potentially disruptive of family life[6] and far in advance of public feeling, in order to 'redress the evils of a few', when a tried and tested remedy which 'worked extremely well' could easily be extended to every wife who needed it.[7]

To mid-Victorian ways of thinking, this proposal to make section 21 widely available on request had an attractive '"practical" look about it'.[8] That wives had some real legal wrongs was widely agreed; but there the consensus ended. What precisely were these real wrongs, as opposed to imaginary rights, and how could they best be remedied? More fundamentally, what were the ideals and realities of economic relationships within marriage and legislation's role in mitigating spousal ill-treatment and improving 'domestic manners'? And what were the special circumstances and needs of 'the poorer classes'? Where consensus was lacking, the usual mid-Victorian solution was permissive legislation, which allowed choice and hence the emergence of different regimes for different social or personal circumstances; and the proposal to extend section 21 was essentially such a solution to the problem of reforming married women's property law.

By 1868–69, however, advanced opinion was on the cusp of a swing towards étatiste compulsory legislation which declared and enforced a universal principle; and the determined radicals pushing for identical property rights for every citizen who unhesitatingly condemned the whole existing matrimonial property law, including section 21, as unjust in principle and an aspect of the subjugation of women.[9] Such language, however, was no way to attract the widely based support needed for parliamentary success. For this, the safest strategy was to present their drastic remodelling of the law on married women's property as a 'poor women's bill', intended to protect the earnings of industrious working-class wives and mothers 'against the rapacity of unworthy and dissolute husbands' and thus force these parasites to work.[10] To make the wife's earnings by law

---

[6] Sir Henry Taylor was not alone in thinking that 'independent rights of property … must afford additional opportunities of separation': H Taylor, 'Mr Mill on the Subjection of Women' (1870) *Fraser's Magazine* 50, 143, 154. Easier divorce was being called for, and private deeds of separation were becoming notably more common.

[7] These phrases were used by Lord Penzance, Judge Ordinary of the Divorce Court and a Liberal peer, in successive second-reading debates on the Married Women's Property Bill: *Hansard* HC Deb (series 3) 30 July 1869, vol 198, cols 979–982 and *Hansard* HC Deb (series 3) 21 June 1870, vol 202, col 605. Similar sentiments were expressed by many others.

[8] So lamented *The Spectator*: 'The House of Commons on Wives Property' *The Spectator*, 42 (17 April 1869) 471.

[9] *Select Committee on Married Women's Property Bill. Special Report, Proceedings, Minutes of Evidence, Appendix, Index*, HC 441 (1868).

[10] Allegedly, many of those who signed the petitions organised in support of the Bill in 1869 believed it to be a 'poor woman's bill' and did not understand its provisions: *Hansard* HC Deb (series 3) 17 April 1869, vol 195, col 774. Its original preamble declared both that the existing law was 'unjust in principle' and that it 'pressed with peculiar severity upon the poorer classes of the community', but the former claim was quickly deleted when the Bill came before a Select Committee in 1869: *Married Women's Property. A Bill to Amend the Law with Respect to the Property of Married Women*, HC 20 and 122 (1868–69).

'hers, and hers alone'[11] would rescue whole families from sinking into pauperised dependence, the argument ran, and thus provide the very cure for society's demoralisation then being urged by the opinion-formers anxiously setting up the Charity Organization Society.[12] By contrast, a simple extension of section 21 could never adequately safeguard poor women's earnings: experience apparently showed 'she would not give publicity to her domestic trials by applying for such an order'.[13]

For advanced radicals it was essential to convince those who mattered that however much it was extended, section 21 was incapable of delivering the protection for poor wives' earnings from their idle, drunken husbands which their own Bill would infallibly provide: the existing system was 'wholly inefficient'.[14] The Select Committee chaired by their young leader Lefevre in July 1868 accordingly guided appropriate witnesses to agree that even though the extension of the order system might be of some use, it 'would not meet the case'.[15] In Marylebone, they were told, only 14 section 21 orders had been granted in the last six months.[16] Poor women were reported to be backward in applying to magistrates for an order protecting their earnings against their brutal, drunken, idle husbands: they were too downtrodden or too shy, too forgiving or too apprehensive about the consequences, or even quite unaware that they could get such an order. This evidence, which could so easily have been refuted by examination of any Return of Judicial Statistics reports from the previous 12 years, was successfully rushed into print just before the session ended, together with a 'Special Report' to drive home the desired morals.[17]

The campaigners took care to emphasise that the Bill would not interfere with the private marriage settlements usual among the well-to-do.

[11] 'Married Women's Property', *All the Year Round* 82 (25 June 1870) 91.

[12] On the alarm of wealthy London in the 1860s at the spectre of East End pauperisation and the lead taken by professional men in combatting it by 'implanting virtue among the "demoralised" poor' by 'legislative, charitable, and visionary measures and proposals', see G Steadman Jones, *Outcast London: Study in the Relationship Between Classes in Victorian Society* (Oxford, Oxford University Press, 1984) 256, 261, 270–73. To secure evidence before the Select Committee of 1868 that the Married Women's Property Bill would be such a measure was one of Lefevre's most skilful strokes.

[13] Lefevre, *Hansard* HC Deb (series 3) 14 April 1869, vol 195, col 781.

[14] G Shaw Lefevre, an up-and-coming radical, son of the Clerk of the Parliaments and nephew of a former Speaker, and an expert manipulator of parliamentary procedure and campaigner for good causes: *Hansard* HC Deb (series 3) 10 June 1868, vol 192, col1374.

[15] Lefevre sponsored the first of this batch of Married Women's Property Bills and chaired the Select Committee upon it in July 1868. When he became Bright's secretary at the Board of Trade after the Liberal election victory in December he was replaced by Russell Gurney, and that much respected and outstandingly fair-minded senior Conservative lawyer always acknowledged that the extension of section 21 would be a 'partial remedy': *Hansard* HC (series 3) 14 April 1869, vol 195, col 766.

[16] This figure was often loosely quoted thereafter. Shaftesbury, for example, who always tended to exaggerate and rely on a few one-sided views, omitted to tell the Lords that it related only to a six-month period. With typical sentimentality, he saw protection orders as insufficient because working women were 'too forgiving': *Hansard* HC (series 3) 21 June 1870, vol 202, col 613.

[17] Evidence before the Select Committee on the Married Women's Property Bill, questions 370–71 (GW Hastings), questions 1148, 1146 (Rev Septimus Hansard of Bethnal Green), questions 1215, 1227,

The dominant narrative among this progressive group of upper-middle class legislators and activists therefore developed into a collection of pathetic anecdotes, and unenthusiastic and distorted accounts of section 21's workings,[18] the socio-economic status of the women who used it, rosy versions of New York's new matrimonial property laws,[19] and optimistic predictions that a working-class culture of self-reliance would flourish, if only humble wives' earnings became legally their own without it being 'necessary to take any public steps to secure them'. This repertoire was soon recycled throughout the media. Presentation was adapted to suit different audiences, but the message was always the same: an extension of section 21 was not the proper cure for this 'miserable state of things'.[20] Such protection would come too late, since the ruffianly husband would sweep up his wife's earnings before absconding; or it would remain unobtainable because he took care not to be absent for the supposedly required two years; or likeliest of all it would never be requested. The only solution was to give every married woman automatic absolute control over all her property and earnings. 'The wife would not apply' was thus a leitmotif of radical homilies during the political manoeuvres of 1868–1870 whose upshot settled the shape of English matrimonial property law for generations to come.

But was it true that very few women applied to magistrates for a section 21 order? This crucial question could easily have been answered at any time after 1859, for in that year the Civil Judicial Statistics published annually by the Home Office began to include returns of all the section 21 orders registered in each County Court Circuit in England and Wales. Yet these figures were never used by any of the wrangling reformers; and recent chroniclers of the campaign for married women's property law reform have for the most part, also overlooked the evidence contained within them. To this day these orders have been seen as

---

1262 (JS Mansfield, Police Magistrate, Marylebone), questions 1375–1440 (J Wybergh) (7 July 1868). Close study of the proceedings of this Committee suggests HC Lopes QC had some grounds for declaring that there was not 'a single independent or unprejudiced opinion given by any of the witnesses': *Hansard* HC Deb (series 3) 14 April 1869, vol 195, col 778.

[18] For example it was often quire wrongly asserted that two years, or 'a technical period', must elapse before a deserted wife could be given a section 21 order: eg 'Property of Married Women' (1869) *Meliora*, 12, 51, 55; FP Cobbe, 'Criminals, Idiots, Women and Minors' (December 1868) *Fraser's Magazine* 78, 777, 783. In reality, whether a wife was deserted for the purpose of section 21 was a matter of fact to be decided by the justices on the evidence before them, and one day's absence could conceivably be enough.

[19] In reality, 'substantially much of "the old Blackstone code" survived', even in New York: N Basch, *In the Eyes of the Law: Women, Marriage and Property in Nineteenth Century New York* (Ithaca and London, Cornell University Press, 1982) 222.

[20] See, eg, 'The Property of Married Women' (1 October 1868) *Westminster Review* 34, 374, 386; Cobbe (n 18) 777–84; 'Property of Married Women' (n 18) 55–56; A Hobhouse, 'On the Forfeiture of Property by Married Women' (1870) *Fortnightly Review* 7, 181, 183–84; 'Married Women's Property' (n 11) 90–91; W Collins, *Man and Wife* (New York, Harper & Brothers, 1870; published serially 1869–70) Chapter 54 s 6.

an attempt to protect the earnings of working women that was more important in principle than in practice, and these copious statistics have remained in undisturbed oblivion.[21]

According to the figures in the Civil Judicial Statistics, then, how many deserted wives were granted an economic divorce and thus became statutory *feme soles*? The overall totals for England and Wales can be quickly summarised. Between 1859 and 1870, County Court registrars recorded 7,471 orders made by magistrates under section 21, between 1871 and 1882 another 9,634 were registered, and in 1883–93, the late-Victorian twilight of these orders, a further 1,947 were registered making a total of 19,052 registrations in the whole period between 1859 to 1893. These registrars' returns, however, certainly understate the number of orders magistrates actually made. In the first place, a very sizable number were granted during 1858, before central recording of registrations began; indeed, if the relationship between the number of orders granted in 1858 and 1859 was roughly the same for magistrates as for the Divorce Court, they must have granted at least 1,000 orders in the initial rush of 1858, and quite possibly more.[22] Under-registration was also likely to be endemic, given the temptation to wives to avoid the trouble and five-shilling fee involved in actually registering their order with their local County Court registrar, especially since sight of their magistrates' 'certificate' – which could cost as little as two shillings – was usually enough to secure a policeman's action if needed.[23] Finally, around 240 orders made by the Divorce Court should be added to these totals.[24] Accordingly, at the very least 19,000 and probably over 20,000 orders for economic divorce must have been granted in the latter half of the nineteenth century.

---

[21] They were sampled in 1989 by a former student of Olive Anderson's, Tracey Medhurst, for a long essay written as part of the requirements for the BA degree in History at the University of London.

[22] In its first four months (February–May 1858), the Divorce Court received more than twice as many applications for section 21 orders as in the whole of 1859. Magistrates' registered orders may therefore have totalled well over 1,000 in 1858, given that registered orders totalled 719 in 1859.

[23] When the first order under section 21 was given at Thames Police Court, Stepney, 'Mr Pyer, the chief clerk, said that two shillings was the fee allowed to be taken for all written orders, and the same fee would be charged for an order under the new Act of Parliament': *Reynold's News* (21 February 1858) 10. At Edmonton Petty Sessions in 1879, however, the entry for Sarah Frances Allen's order notes, 'Clerk's costs, 5s.': Edmonton Petty Sessions Court Minutes, Registers and Licensing Registers, London Metropolitan Archives, PS E/E2/7, entry at the end of Register.

[24] Civil Judicial Statistics record applications for 325 orders *made* to the Court for Divorce and Matrimonial Causes, and we have calculated that at least 70% of these were successful, see Chapter Seven. Statistics showing the number of section 21 orders *granted* by the Court for Divorce and Matrimonial Causes which were successful are available only for 1 February 1858 to 31 March 1859: *Return of Persons appointed to Office in Divorce and Matrimonial Causes Court, 1858: Number of Applications, Dissolutions, and Cases Undefended or Set for Trial*, HC 269 (1859 session 1) 14: *Return of Number of Causes filed in Registry for Divorce and Matrimonial Causes* HC 99 (1862) 13–14. It should be noted that it is never possible to calculate what proportion of applications to magistrates was successful because there is no available data on the number of applications submitted.

Chart 4.1 Number of Matrimonial Orders Made 1859–1893

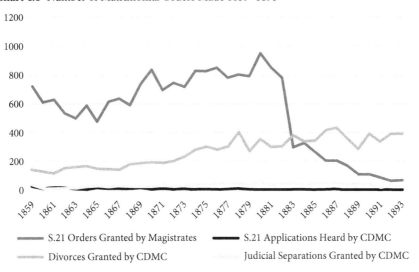

━━━ S.21 Orders Granted by Magistrates ━━━ S.21 Applications Heard by CDMC

━━━ Divorces Granted by CDMC   Judicial Separations Granted by CDMC

What of those couples whose relationship was altered by the courts? What proportion of mid-Victorian matrimonial orders and decrees were orders for economic divorce? In 1857 Parliament created a new secular legal machinery to loosen a petitioning spouse's ties to a partner found guilty of the faults declared to warrant respectively full divorce, judicial separation, or an order equivalent to a partial judicial separation (termed here economic divorce or a section 21 order),[25] and the way that this new machinery worked can be seen clearly in Chart 4.1. The central Court for Divorce and Matrimonial Causes granted an average of 264 petitions for divorce and an average of 33 Judicial Separations per year, but only heard an average of eight applications for a protection order under section 21. In contrast, justices in local petty sessions and the metropolitan police courts, granted an average of 543 section 21 orders per year. Including the small number of Restitution of Conjugal Rights and Nullity cases heard during this period (both exclusively by the Divorce Court), there were approximately 30,000 matrimonial

---

[25] The bonds of matrimony were completely broken by a decree of divorce or nullity of marriage; conjugal rights of bed and board were removed by a decree of judicial separation, which also 'unmarried' the wife with regard to all property she acquired thereafter and for the purposes of contract and suing; and thirdly (as readers of this book will be well aware), an order under section 21 of the Act 'unmarried' an unjustifiably deserted self-supporting wife in precisely the same way, with regard to property, contracts, and suing. All three alterations of the bonds on matrimony could be granted by the Court of Divorce and Matrimonial Causes; in the original legislation the second could be effected by any Judge of Assize, and the third by a metropolitan police magistrate or justices in petty sessions. For internal professional reasons no applications for judicial separation were ever heard by judges of the Assizes and their authorisation to do so was repealed in August 1858; but from the beginning magistrates equally with the Divorce Court granted section 21 orders.

orders made during the period 1858–1893. Therefore, two-thirds of the mid-Victorian spouses whose matrimonial relationship was altered by a court order or decree, was effected by an economic divorce under section 21, and moreover in 99 cases out of 100, that economic divorce was granted by magistrates and not the Divorce Court.[26]

The annual flow of registrations was not uniform however, as a glance at Chart 4.1 shows. What may have caused these fluctuations in supply and demand? The initial rush to take advantage of this new resource in January 1858 was evidently stimulated by the approving publicity given in newspapers of every kind, from *The Times* and other London dailies to the mass circulation Sunday papers and the burgeoning local press.[27] In the first few months, public awareness was fuelled by editorials and special news columns, as well as by details of applications included in the regular reports of cases in the metropolitan police courts and local petty sessions. That widely circulated Lancashire newspaper the *Preston Guardian*, for example, remarked on 16 January that 'the new Act ... has one important provision that ought to be widely known' and followed its leader on the siege of Lucknow (then absorbing the whole nation) with an enthusiastic exposition of section 21; while throughout February and March the *News of the World* reported interesting applications in a special weekly column headed 'DIVORCE BEFORE MAGISTRATES'.[28] Alert friends and advisers as well as solicitors eager to secure new business in their local magistrates' courts further encouraged women to make an application. In the early months of 1858, wives who had lived alone in legal limbo for 20 or 30 years hastened to establish their legal title to their property, get access (like Charles Kingsley's cousin) to a long-frozen legacy, secure the capacity to give or bequeath their property to their own kin, or otherwise remedy the practical financial frustrations of many years.[29]

While this backlog was still being cleared, a Treasury order ensured support from third parties who had concerns in legal and financial transactions with

---

[26] Decrees granted for divorce and judicial separation are conveniently tabulated in *Royal Commission on Divorce and Matrimonial Causes. Appendices to the minutes of evidence and report of the Royal Commission on Divorce and Matrimonial Causes*, 20 (C (1st series) 6482) (1912–13), Tables II and VI. It will be remembered that the number of orders granted by magistrates under section 21 and registered by County Court registrars is included in the County Court returns published in the annual Civil Judicial Statistics, which also provide the number of applications to the Divorce Court for orders under section 21.

[27] The Matrimonial Causes Act (MCA) 1857 came into force on 11 January 1858, the first day of the Hilary Law Term.

[28] *Preston Guardian* (16 January 1858) 4; *News of the World* 1 (28 February and 9, 14 March 1858). Even a somewhat shady advertiser touting his services 'To Embarrassed Debtors' in the downmarket halfpenny *South London Times* thought it worth his while that spring to add as a new bait, 'under the NEW DIVORCE BILL every assistance rendered': *South London Times Weekly* (20 February–17 April 1858). After their novelty had worn off, only unusual or especially interesting applications were reported in papers with little space to spare.

[29] See Chapter Two, n 46.

married women. Early in May 1858 all County Court Registrars were required to copy the entry of each section 21 order they registered to the Central Registry of County Court Judgments in Spring Gardens off Whitehall. Henceforth, any member of the public could establish cheaply and conveniently whether a particular married woman had obtained protection of her property and *feme sole* status, wherever she lived. A single name could be personally searched for at the Registry between the hours of 11am and 3pm for sixpence, or a certificate of search could be had by post for a shilling – a facility 'most important to be known to, and remembered by, every practitioner', on behalf of clients who were potential creditors, litigants, and the like.[30] Soon the value of these orders was accepted as established fact. In 1865 a Bill providing equivalent cheap local facilities for separated and deserted wives in Ireland went through on the nod, as did a Bill providing equivalent facilities in Scotland in 1874.[31] By 1868 women's rights campaigners were able to blame public smugness over the new system for Parliament's inaction over root-and-branch reform of married women's property law.[32]

Why then were there downward blips in national registration numbers in 1862–63, 1865 and 1868? Most probably these were connected with high unemployment and distress in the industrial areas where demand for economic divorce was usually highest.[33] In France, economic divorce rose 'dans le moments de crise commerciale et industrielle', since *séparation des biens* was generally used in the industrial *départements* to protect the wife's assets against the husband's creditors.[34] In England, however, where this facility was only available to wives who were self-supporting as well as deserted, the opposite was surely more likely; for although an economic slump might encourage male desertion, it also made female self-sufficiency more difficult. Still, usually a Circuit was too varied in its economic make-up and the women using section 21 socially too mixed for the impact of

---

[30] 'Protection of Married Women' (8 May 1858) 31 *Law Times* 94, commenting on the official announcement in the *London Gazette*. Forty names could be searched for within two months for 10 shillings, paid in advance, in the same way as records of County Court Judgments: eg *Law List* 1865, 755. As was shown in Chapter Two, it was a matter of the first importance for creditors and litigants to establish whether a deserted wife had an order, and if so, the date of both the order itself and her desertion as shown on the order.

[31] Married Women's Property (Ireland) Act 1865 and Conjugal Rights (Scotland) Act Amendment Act 1861. Section 21 thus became that rare thing – an element of the law of husband and wife common to all three Kingdoms. Legislation had been passed in 1861 'to give Scotland the advantages' of section 21, but this had remained 'pretty much a dead letter' because it required all wives to apply to the highest Scottish court (the Court of Session), according to G Anderson, the radical Glasgow MP who introduced the Bill: *Hansard* (series 3) HC Deb 22 April 1874, vol 218, col 978. For Ireland, see: M Luddy and M O'Dowd, *Marriage in Ireland 1600–1925* (Cambridge, Cambridge University Press, 2020) 369–70.

[32] 'The Property of Married Women' (n 20) 386.

[33] See: CH Feinstein, *Statistical Tables of National Income, Expenditure and Output of the United Kingdom, 1855–1965* (Cambridge, Cambridge University Press, 1972) Table 57.

[34] 'Report to the Emperor Napoleon III', 7 April 1855, quoted in JF Macqueen, *A Practical Treatise on Divorce and Matrimonial Jurisdiction Under the Act of 1857 and New Orders* (London, W Maxwell, 1858) 143.

local economic distress on registration levels to be clear beyond all doubt. The sharp dips in registrations in Limehouse and Southwark in 1862, for example, may perhaps reflect spasms of hardship in riverside London's decline. The cotton famine of 1862–1865 might certainly be expected to have depressed the usually high level of registrations in the Lancashire Circuits. Most cotton towns, however, either had other industries or proved able to adapt, and their Manchester metropolis always had a life of its own.[35] Registrations in the cotton districts generally fell perceptibly in 1862, but no more[36] – with one striking exception: the Circuit covering the Poor Law District most severely affected of all, Ashton-under-Lyne.[37] There, registrations dropped precipitously from 49 in 1859–61 to a mere 15 in 1863–65, clear evidence, surely, that the number of self-supporting lone wives coming forward for economic divorce was indeed reduced by widespread acute hardship in the neighbourhood, as common sense suggests. Economic divorce enjoyed its hey-day between 1869 and 1882. In 1869 more orders were registered than in any previous year, and throughout the 1870s the proportion of wives with an order rose: a record 960 orders were registered in 1880.[38] Moreover, it was claimed in 1878 that 'no complaints have ever been published' of magistrates' handling of these many applications.[39] How is this upsurge of popularity in the 1870s to be explained, especially given the apparent paradox that the first Married Women's Property Act reached the statute book in 1870?

It would be a mistake to ignore altogether the greater prosperity being experienced in the urban industrial areas where most orders were registered. Nevertheless, the upswing in section 21 orders in the 1870s probably owed less to easier economic conditions than to the terms of the first Married Women's Property legislation and the strident controversies over its passing. By 1869 few readers of the political or legal press can have been ignorant of the orders system, given the debates in both Parliament and press over whether or not a simple extension of section 21 would provide 'a reasonable protection to women who

[35] For evidence that the extent and duration of distress during the cotton famine have been exaggerated, see DA Farnie, *The English Cotton Industry and the World Market, 1815–1896* (Oxford, Oxford University Press, 1979) 156–58.

[36] In the Circuit which included Blackburn and Preston, for example, registrations fell from 55 in 1859–61 to 38 in 1862–64.

[37] See: H Southall, 'Poor Law Statistics and the Geography of Economic Distress' in J Foreman Peck (ed), *New Perspectives on the Late Victorian Economy: Essays in Quantitative Economic History, 1860–1914* (Cambridge, Cambridge University Press, 1991) 180, 203 and 211.

[38] In the 1870s the average number of orders granted annually was nearly 30% greater than in the 1860s, although the number of wives in the population was less than 13%. There were 3,488,952 wives in 1861: *Census of England and Wales 1861: General Report; Summary Tables, Abstracts of Ages, Occupations and Birthplaces of People, Division I. to Division III.* HC 3221 (1863) 19; 3,948,527 in 1871: *Census of England and Wales 1871 Volume IV. (General Report)*, HC 872-I, Table 74, 63; and 4,437,962 in 1881: *Census of England and Wales 1881 Volume III. (Ages, Condition as to Marriage, Occupations and Birthplaces)*, 80 HC c.3722, Table 3. The average number of orders granted annually by magistrates was 622.7 in 1859–70 and 802.8 in 1871–82.

[39] F Power Cobbe, 'Wife Torture in England' (April 1878) *Contemporary* Review 32, 55, 86. Cobbe argued from this that magistrates could safely be given still fuller powers.

are tyrannized over and downtrodden by those who disregarded their marriage obligations'.[40] Some justices, indeed, may thereby have come to see such orders as a useful bulwark against sweeping general legislation of the sort embodied in the Commons' original Bills, and thus regarded applications coming before them more favourably.[41]

Above all, demand for economic divorce was evidently stimulated by the limitations and ambiguities of the Married Women's Property Act itself in its confused final form. In the first place, the 1870 Act was not retroactive: any self-supporting wife who had been deserted and acquired assets before it came into operation in August 1870 therefore needed a magistrates' order as much as ever. Equally importantly, the drastic amendments which alone made the campaigners' Bill acceptable to the Lords ensured that it 'no longer provided for married women to be treated like unmarried women so far as property was concerned'.[42] Instead, a wife's own wages and earnings and certain narrowly restricted categories of property (for example, money not exceeding £200 coming to her by gift or bequest) were to be 'deemed and taken to be property held and settled to her separate use',[43] that is, her separate property during coverture in the highly technical sense these terms had acquired in the Courts of Equity.[44] Beyond these narrow limits, the rights of husbands were little changed. When the severely mutilated Bill came back to the Commons, Russell Gurney, its original sponsor, tried to sugar the pill by saying that working-class women would be given 'real though not complete relief', and this was true. Cairns, the formidable Conservative ex-Lord Chancellor who dominated the Lords, had hoisted the campaigners with their own petard, by presenting his amendments as concerned with the needs of 'women of the lower classes'.[45]

---

[40] These words are those of Lord Penzance, *Hansard* HC Deb (series 3) 20 July 1869, vol 198, col 982. It was a persistent feeling among the peers, and many others, that the law should be amended to 'protect a woman whose husband had misbehaved, but no more': *Hansard* HC Deb (series 3) 21 June 1870, vol 201, col 602–14, and *Hansard* HC Deb (series 3) 18 July 1870, vol 203, col 695.

[41] One Staffordshire Justice of the Peace, James Solly of Tipton, recommended the simple device of opening section 21 orders to all wives when root-and-branch reform was pushed again by women's rights campaigners after the Liberal election victory of April 1880: J Solly, 'Further Amendment to the Divorce Act of 20 and 21 Vict., c.85.' (Edinburgh Meeting, 1880) *Transactions* 267.

[42] So the recently ennobled Judge of the Divorce Court, Lord Penzance, assured his fellow peers: *Hansard* HC Deb (series 3) 18 July 1870, vol 230, col 395.

[43] All the clauses defining what should be deemed a wife's 'separate property' were cautious and restrictive, with the exception of those relating to property coming to her from an intestate: Married Women's Property Act 1870, s 1–8. True, by applying in writing in the manner prescribed by the Act, she could transfer into her own name as her 'separate property' money to which she was entitled that was invested in the public funds, a joint stock company or a providence society, but 10 years later Lydia Becker no doubt correctly complained that such investments were 'practically nil' and that bankers and stockbrokers 'objected to do business for married women': 'Property of Married Women: Discussion' (Edinburgh Meeting, 1880) *Transactions* 191, 194–95.

[44] This grudging, hesitating and awkward way of proceeding was 'open to obvious objections', as AV Dicey explained to the Harvard Law School in 1898: *Lectures on the Relation between Law and Public Opinion in England during the Nineteenth Century*, 2nd edn (London, Macmillan, 1914) 387–88.

[45] Gurney, *Hansard* HC Deb (series 3) 2 August 1870, vol 203, col 1488; Cairns, *Hansard* HC Deb (series 3) 21 June 1870, vol 202, cols 600–602.

To the frustration of women's rights activists, the re-drafted Act was 'professedly a poor woman's measure', but 'no longer a great measure of social reform'.[46]

The grudging terms of the Act ensured that deserted wives at every income level continued to apply for an economic divorce, and not exclusively those who were better off. A section 21 order still provided the only way in which a wife deserted before 1870 could obtain legal possession of any money or property she had earned or acquired after her desertion and before the new Act came into operation, and moreover the only way in which she could secure possession of any later gifts or bequests beyond quite narrow limits. It was also the sole route (apart from judicial separation) by which *any* wife could acquire all the economic rights and responsibilities given by *feme sole* status. It may be remembered that several of the cases singled out in previous chapters hinged on orders obtained in the 1870s by wives who needed to secure possession of either legacies from relations or their own earnings before 1870, or who wanted to obtain powers of litigation not given by the new Act.[47] These leading cases of the 1870s in turn publicised the usefulness of a section 21 order, just as a series of other cases provided vivid evidence of the limitations and inadequacies of the legislation of 1870.[48] Altogether, it is not difficult to understand why well over 10,000 deserted wives thought it worth their while to secure an economic divorce during the 12 years in which the first Married Women's Property Act was in force. Elizabeth Wolstenholme, that tireless women's rights campaigner, had been seriously premature in remarking in 1870 that at least that unsatisfactory Act had 'got rid of the absurd ineffectiveness of Protection Orders'.[49]

The number of section 21 orders granted in 1871 stands in contrast to the rest of the data presented, where Chart 4.1 shows a marked drop in the number of orders granted in 1871 (though not dropping, it should be noted, below 1868 levels). This can also be seen in Map 4.3, where only Circuit 4 (Blackburn), 11 (Bradford), and the Metropolitan Circuits, maintained a high level of uptake; virtually every other Circuit indicates a significant drop in the number of orders granted. This timing is not a coincidence. The steep climb in the number of orders granted which began

---

[46] It 'retained the old unjust principle', complained Elizabeth Wolstenholme that autumn: E Wolstenholme, 'On The Married Women's Property Act' (Newcastle Upon Tyne Meeting, 1870) *Transactions* 549, 550.

[47] See the following cases: *Re Coward and Adam's Purchase* (1875) LR 20 Eq 179; *Nicholson v Drury Buildings Estate Co* (1876) 7 Ch D 49; *Ewart v Chubb* (1875) LR 20 Eq 454; *Ramsden v Brearley* (1875) 10 QB 147; *Mahoney v McCarthy* (1892) P 21-4. In 1878 one Walworth wife pinned her faith to a section 21 order in very bizarre circumstances: *Kingsman v Kingsman* (1880) 6 QBD 122.

[48] In 1874 the Court of Probate ruled that a woman deserted in 1866 who had failed to get a protection order could only dispose by will of her savings from money she had earned *after* 1870; the rest must go to her husband, even though she had invested it as 'her separate property' under the terms of the 1870 Act: in the goods of *Pepper Re* (1874) 31 LT 274 (30 June, 7 July 1874, per Hannen J). In 1878 a particularly colourful case showed again that a married woman alone was not credit-worthy unless she had a section 21 order: *Hancocks & Co v Madame Demeric-Lablache* (1878) 3 CPD 197 (9 March 1878, per Lindley J).

[49] Wolstenholme (n 46) 550. Wolstenholme's comments suggest that she genuinely shared the persistent notion that section 21 simply protected a wife's earnings.

in the mid-1860s and continued reasonably steadily until the drop of 1871 can be seen as reflecting the increased publicity given to married women and their property from groups including NAPSS. The drop in the number of section 21 orders granted in 1871 was however, followed by a swift renewed uptake from 1872, which continued almost uninterrupted, reaching a pinnacle in 1882; indeed the number of orders granted in the decade 1872–1882 was higher than the numbers granted in the 1860s. It should be remembered that the only data relating to section 21 orders concerns the number of orders *granted* not the number of orders *applied* for, and arguably what this drop, and Map 4.2 could be showing, is a change in the behaviour of magistrates – it might well be that deserted wives were still applying for the orders, but justices were refusing to grant them.

If we view this drop in the wider context of the Married Women's Property Act 1870 and the rapid resurgence in orders granted from 1872, the data presented in Map 4.3 can perhaps be better understood as a collective pause, where women (and possibly justices too) waited with bated breath to see the effects of the Married Women's Property Act 1870. Upon realising the serious limitations of the 1870 Act, namely that it was not retroactive, it did not protect any inheritance above £200, it was still impossible for a married woman to make a last will and testament without her husband's consent, and most important of all, it did not bestow a married woman with *feme sole* status, it seems that deserted wives realised the most efficient form of economic protection remained a section 21 order. Only when the very different Married Women's Property Act of 1882 came into operation did demand suddenly plummet. Despite its incompleteness, anomalies, and obscurities,[50] the 1882 Act did substantially ensure that in future the bonds of matrimony would not include the forfeiture of the wife's property rights and legal capacities to her husband. It followed that an order which gave a wife all the property rights and capacities of a single woman could retain neither this guise of a partial divorce, nor its wide practical value. Suddenly section 21 became obsolescent. Registrations fell steeply from an annual average of 802.8 orders in 1871–1882, to one of only 177.4 in 1883–93 – less than a quarter of the previous level. (See Chart 4.1.)

Still, this is not a negligible number. Why then did some wives continue to want an economic divorce even after the new legislation came into force on 1 January 1883? Most obviously and importantly, any woman who had been married and deserted and had subsequently acquired a title to property *before* that date needed a section 21 order as much as ever, since the new Act (like the Act of 1870) had no retrospective effect. In the case of wives who were deserted *after* the Act came into operation, however, it seems at first that the new Act gave them everything they would gain from an order, and their applications were accordingly

---

[50] Authors of the first crop of handbooks dealing with the MCA 1857 frequently complained that they were obliged to offer 'argument as to what the law would probably prove to be, rather than statements of what it is': eg M Lush, *The Law of Husband and Wife Within The Jurisdiction Of The Queen's Bench And Chancery Divisions* (London, Kessinger, 1884) preface and vi–viii: R Thicknesse, *A Digest of the Law of Husband and Wife as it Affects Property* (London, 1884) vii.

not accepted by some magistrates. Nevertheless, despite a sharp drop in 1883, in 1884 registrations showed some recovery in 16 Circuits, most noticeably in the Blackburn area and south-east London, and the cotton-spinning area around Rochdale registrations always kept up remarkably well.[51] Cultural reasons were probably behind some of this persistence; but practitioners also soon realised that the 1882 Act was 'a very incomplete measure', and that orders still had their uses even for wives whose husbands had left them after the new regime began. For example, as one expert pointed out, until it was finally judicially confirmed that section 5 of the 1882 Act included property to which the wife was entitled in reversion before that Act came into operation, a wife whose husband had left her after that date still needed a section 21 order to secure such property.[52] Even where a deserted wife's title to property undoubtedly accrued after the Act came into force she could still find it worthwhile to secure an order, since only thus, it will be remembered, could she become a *feme sole* with regard to her property, contracts and civil actions, and secure unqualified contractual and testamentary capacity. In 1905 AV Dicey observed that some important points were still unsettled, and in the most funda-mental sense some remained unsettled until the reforms in the law of husband and wife of 1935–62 and beyond.[53]

Nevertheless by 1893 the worst oversights and uncertainties of the Act of 1882 had been removed by Parliament and the courts, and section 21 orders proved to be useful only in exceptional cases. In the decade 1895–1904 they were registered on average by only 26 wives a year,[54] most of them no doubt either woman for whom *feme sole* status brought particular advantages (notably the removal of a restraint on anticipation on 'separate property acquired after their desertion'),[55] or wives who had been deserted and acquired property before 1 January 1883 but had omitted previously to secure a protecting order – inevitably a diminishing band. By the turn of the century a practitioner's query on these orders in the correspond-ence columns of the *Justice of the Peace* was a rarity,[56] and the pages still devoted

---

[51] In Woolwich and Lambeth registrations slumped to six in 1883 (they had totalled 54 in 1880) but jumped back to 25 in 1884. In Circuit 5, which covered Rochdale, Oldham, Bury and Bolton, 281 orders were registered in 1883–93 – over twice as many as in any other Circuit.

[52] Thicknesse (n 50) 172.

[53] Dicey (n 44) 393, fn 1. 'In removing some old hardships (the Act) has curtained created new ones', commented a leading textbook sharply in 1896; M Lush, *The Law of Husband and Wife*, 2nd edn (London, Kessinger, 1896) vii.

[54] By 1914, when these statistics, like many others, come to an end, annual registrations had fallen to single figures.

[55] In 1887 one Mrs Hill got a section 21 order from a metropolitan police magistrate, and two years later, on the strength of the *feme sole* status she thus achieved, mortgaged the rents and profits of some leasehold property let to her 'for life for her separate use with a restraint on anticipation': See Chapter Two, nn 35 and 60.

[56] In 1902, an enquiring 'Clerk' was assured that the case of *Mahoney v McCarthy* reported in the current edition of *Stone's Justices' Manual* had no bearing on the case he outlined, which would indeed be eligible for a section 21 order: 'Husband and Wife: Protection Order' *Justice of the Peace* (5 April 1902) 223.

to them in Edwardian practitioners' handbooks can have been little scanned.[57] Long before section 21 finally disappeared from the statute book in 1964, no relic remained of the many thousands of mid-Victorian wives who had used it to escape the economic consequences of the law of husband and wife in England in their day.

No study concerned with marital experience and popular use of the law can stop here, however, for national statistics can never reveal social realities. In mid-Victorian England regional and local variations in patterns of behaviour were often massive and deep-rooted. Where was economic divorce most common, where most rare? Did its distribution change over time? Was there a tendency to convergence? What sort of communities provided the most abundant demand or generous supply of these orders? At least in broad outline, some attempt can be made to answer such questions for the years between 1859 and 1893 since in those years the number of section 21 orders registered in each County Court Circuit were separately reported in the Judicial Statistics.

Although annual Judicial Statistics for 1859–1893 give the number of section 21 orders registered in each Circuit, they do not detail its constituent districts, and Circuit populations were not included in the Census until 1901 (after a major rearrangement of boundaries). To add to the confusion, Circuits coincided with no other area. Very often they straddled several counties; and their 500-odd constituent districts, consisting of Poor Law Unions or parts of them, were noted in 1901 to be 'not in all cases co-extensive with these administrative areas or with an aggregate of entire Civil Parishes'.[58] However, the first volume of the remodelled series of Civil Judicial Statistics begun in 1895 by the barrister Alexander Pulling included careful estimates of the population of each Circuit, made on the basis of the 1891 Census and existing Circuit boundaries, and provides the constituent parts.[59] A further difficulty arises from the fact that Circuit boundaries were unstable. In a few cases population distribution or local communications changed enough for a Circuit to be absorbed altogether into its neighbours. Thus in 1872, Circuit 10 was absorbed into Circuits 4 and 5, Circuit 34 into Circuits 17, 20, and 35–37, Circuits 56 into Circuits 54–55 and 57, Circuit 46 into Circuit 47; similarly, in 1890 Circuit 39 was absorbed into Circuit 42. More frequently, constituent Districts were simply transferred from one Circuit to another; for example, in 1872 Salford was transferred from Circuit 5 to Circuit 8.[60] To mitigate these difficulties, and to allow comparisons over time, the data shown in this chapter have been calculated using the 1895 Circuit boundaries.

[57] For example W Rayden, *Practice and Law in the Divorce Division of the High Court of Justice and on Appeal Therefrom* (London, Butterworths, 1910) 102; JR Roberts (ed), *Stone's Justices' Manual*, 39th edn (London, Butterworths, 1907) 453–56.
[58] *Census of England and Wales. 1901. General Report with Appendices* HC (Cd. 2174) 108 (1904), 19.
[59] *Return of Judicial Statistics of England and Wales, 1895 (Part II. Civil Statistics)* HC (C (2nd series) 8536) 100, (1897), 16, 122 (Table 77). See Appendix III.
[60] For example, the *Law List* shows the following additions to Circuit 4 (parts of which have been particularly studied here). The period 1858–90: Haslingden and Accrington in 1867 and Bacup between 1873–75 only, from Circuit 10; Clitheroe in 1876 from Circuit 5; and Blackpool in 1882 (a new Court town). The actual change was probably a year earlier in each case.

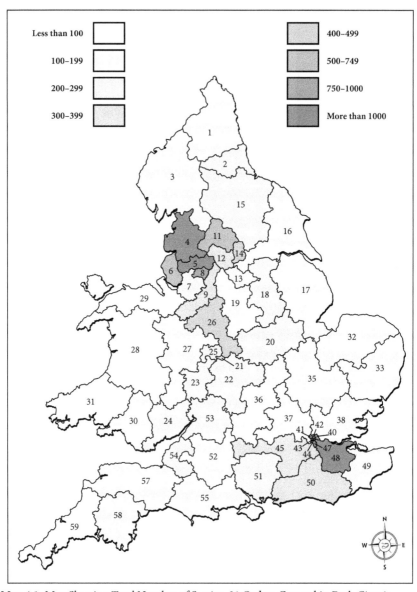

Map 4.1 Map Showing Total Number of Section 21 Orders Granted in Each Circuit 1859–1893.[61]

[61] Data drawn from annual *Return of Judicial Statistics of England and Wales* reports. See Bibliography.

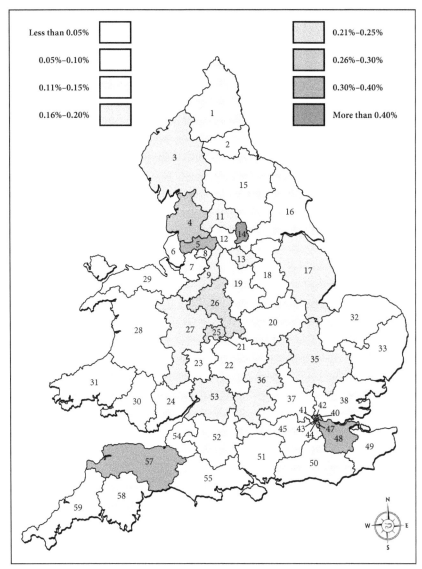

Map 4.2 Map Showing Number of Section 21 Orders Granted in Each Circuit in 1861

Map 4.1, which shows the total number of section 21 orders granted in each circuit between 1859 and 1893, reveals some striking disparities. The densely populated Metropolitan Police Court districts surrounding the City of London, together with the Lancashire cotton towns, stand in sharp contrast to the rural, agricultural, or mining areas of Wales, the south-west, the south-east and the north-east, where only a handful of women availed themselves of section 21. Nowhere though, were such women wholly absent. It was in the metropolitan district and north-east

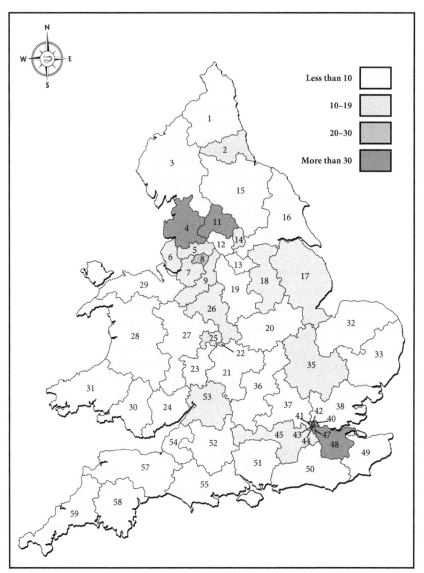

Map 4.3 Map Showing Total Number of Section 21 Orders Granted in Each Circuit 1871

Lancashire, and to some extent in the West Riding of Yorkshire and the Potteries, and a lesser extent still in the areas manufacturing glass and china, carpet and light metalwork around Kidderminster, Stourbridge, Worcester, and Bromsgrove in the West Midlands where a wife registering an economic divorce might indeed be a fairly run-of-the-mill happening.

Crucially, as Maps 4.2, 4.3, and 4.4 show, the position of the metropolitan districts and north-east Lancashire as hubs of section 21 activity did not diminish

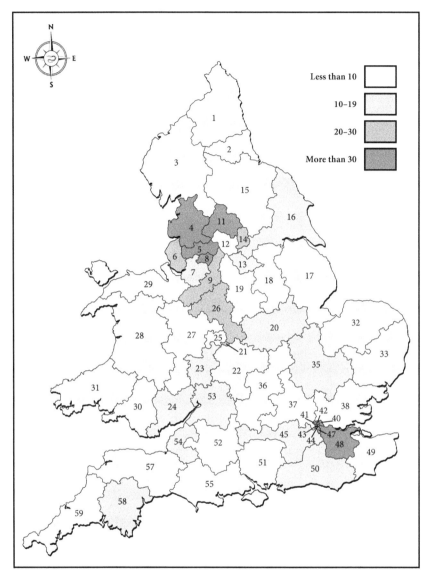

Map 4.4 Map Showing Total Number of Section 21 Orders Granted in Each Circuit 1881

between 1861 and 1881, but uptake (and likely demand too) did fluctuate across circuits. In 1861, for example, Circuit 57 which encompassed much of Devon (though notably not the most populous urban centres of Exeter, Newton Abbot, or Plymouth) and Circuit 16 which covered the East – and some of the North – Riding of Yorkshire (notably, Kingston-Upon-Hull), stand out amidst the swathe of industrial areas already mentioned. By 1871, however, section 21 orders in both these circuits had fallen, with a similar story in Circuit 22 (including Coventry,

Warwick, and Stratford-Upon-Avon) and Circuit 36 (including Northampton, Oxford, and Wellingborough). In 1871 though, there were increases in the number of orders granted in Circuit 2 (Durham, South Shields, and Sunderland), and in the adjacent Circuits 17 (much of Lincolnshire), and 18 (Nottinghamshire). As Map 4.4 shows, however, by 1881, the swathe of populous and predominantly industrial areas with higher uptake of section 21 orders that were initially seen in Map 4.2, had re-established themselves.

These sharp geographical contrasts are evidently not simply a reflection of the long recognised universal connection between large cities and high rates of divorce and judicial separation.[62] Middling-class wives living on small incomes with the security of a section 21 order might indeed be found anywhere. Such women apart, however, self-supporting wives were inevitably most common in districts with the best opportunities for married women to earn money, whether through industrial employment, a 'female' trade (dressmaking, millinery, and the like), petty entrepreneurial activity (such as dealing, or running a lodging-house, small shop, or school), or a well-paid domestic post (for example as housekeeper, cook, or monthly nurse). In mid-Victorian England large-scale demand for married female industrial labour at good wages was concentrated in a few highly localised industries – above all in the cotton towns – but also in the woollen industry of the West Riding and the earthenware and china industries of the Potteries.[63] The best opportunities for female penny-capitalists and tradeswomen always lay in these same areas of high female employment, and then in urban areas with a mobile working and lower middle class population.[64] In contrast, opportunities for women to earn a living were at their scantiest in the agrarian south and east, where women's agricultural role was dwindling and many cottage industries were declining;[65] and they could be very thin in seaports and above all in mining and heavy metal-working areas, especially in times of depression. When the Cornish mining industry collapsed after 1872, the plight of the many wives left behind when their husbands emigrated was particularly dire,[66] and it is no surprise that only 25 orders were granted in Cornwall in the years 1871–82 – the smallest

---

[62] On this connection, see Macdonell's remarks in *Return of Judicial Statistics of England and Wales, 1894 (Part II. Civil Statistics)* HC (C (2nd series) 8263) 94 (1896) 57.

[63] E Hunt, *Regional Wage Variations in Britain, 1830–1914* (Oxford, Oxford University Press, 1973) 115–27; M Hewitt, *Wives and Mothers in Victorian Industry* (London, Rockliff, 1958) 14–19, 29–30; S Horrell, J Humphries and J Weisdorf, 'Beyond the Male Breadwinner: Life-Cycle Living Standards of Intact and Disrupted English Working Families, 1260–1850' (2022) 75 *Economic History Review* 530–80; X You, 'Women's Labour Force Participation in Nineteenth-century England and Wales: Evidence from the 1881 Census Enumerators' Books' (2020) 73 *Economic History Review* 106–33.

[64] In Stockport in 1862, Ellen Barlee found that 'a very large class of women derive their maintenance entirely by providing for the wants of the (female) mill hands, earning as much, and often more, than the operatives themselves': E Barlee, *A Visit to Lancashire in December 1862* (London, 1862) 25.

[65] KDM Snell, *Annals of the Labouring Poor: Social Change and Agrarian England, 1660–1900* (Cambridge, Cambridge University Press, 1985) 317.

[66] G Burke, 'The Decline of the Independent Bal Maiden: The Impact of Change in the Cornish Mining Industry' in A John (ed), *Unequal Opportunities: Women's Employment in England, 1800–1918* (Oxford, Blackwell, 1986) 179–206.

number in any Circuit.[67] Female earning power generally, like female industrial employment, was riddled with unequal opportunities – unequal between women in one kind of place or another, as well as unequal between women and men in the same kind of place.

Inseparable from these local variations in opportunities for wives to earn their own living were local variations in cultural attitudes: in the awareness and approving responses (or otherwise) expressed in the local press and community; in wives' own readiness to apply to magistrates and thus give the husband a bad name (which might lose him his job in an occupation where respectability was all); in solicitors' encouragement of this new type of work; and above all in the local bench's laxity (or generosity) in dealing with applications.[68] Husbands who 'flitted' commonly left a trail of debts behind them, and wives everywhere might therefore be stirred to action by fear of the bailiffs or a County Court summons. In the Lancashire cotton towns, however, there swiftly emerged what can only be called a 'matrimonial orders culture'. There, independent female action was taken for granted, and not only by female factory operatives accustomed to good wages and with vigorous traditions of political radicalism and trade union activity. In these communities, exceptionally enthusiastic use of partial separation orders under section 21 between the 1860s and early 1890s[69] paved the way for exceptionally high rates of separation and maintenance orders in the early twentieth century.[70] In Blackburn, for example, as will be shown in later chapters, a network of local political, economic, and cultural factors interacted to boost demand – and also supply.

Variations in supply were indeed as endemic as variations in demand – and inevitably so, since supply was at the discretion of a multitude of lay local elites and their attorney-clerks, together with a handful of self-confident professionals accustomed to giving free rein to their own interpretation of the law in what they and everyone else regarded as *their* court. Everywhere, the habits of magistrates were a significant variable. Some were easily convinced that an application fell

---

[67] Circuit 59 covered Cornwall exclusively and completely, apart from Camelford and Launceston. Already in 1859–70, this Circuit recorded the lowest number of section 21 orders of any English Circuit. The collapse of the mining industry is thus probably not the whole explanation of these low Cornish figures.

[68] In 1869 one Jones, a manager of a City hosiery business, told the Clerkenwell police magistrate that his reason for not taking steps earlier to have his wife's section 21 order set aside was that 'it would have come to his employers' knowledge and he should have lost his situation': 'Proceedings to upset a Protection Order', 33 *Justice of the Peace* (11 December 1869) 793.

[69] In 1871–82 the four Lancashire cotton-town Circuits (namely 4, 5, 8 and 10) accounted for 19.9% of all section 21 orders registered in England and Wales, and in 1883–93 for a record 26.7%. In Circuit 5 (Bolton, Bury, Oldham, Rochdale) registrations dropped less in this twilight decade than anywhere else.

[70] Lancashire was the county with the highest but one separation order rate for 1907–1909 in the Tables submitted by Macdonell to the Royal Commission on Divorce: in *Royal Commission on Divorce and Matrimonial Causes*, Appendix 3, 33, Table XII. In a still more striking example of cultural continuity, in 1909 a higher proportion (94%) of applications for matrimonial orders under the 1895 Act succeeded in Blackburn than anywhere else: ibid, Appendix 6, 56. (Places with stipendiaries were not included in these returns.)

within section 21 if the wife's story suggested she was a deserving case; others were more mindful of the rights of husbands and creditors, and the identities of those concerned, than of the letter of the law. The uptake of economic divorces was thus very far from uniform. Nowhere was it wholly unknown, if only because it was available to wives supporting themselves from investments and any kind of property as much as to wives dependent on their own wages or earnings. Nevertheless, the concentration in certain sorts of places of acknowledged female earning power and the behavioural habits and cultural expectations that went with it, ensured that there were two nations of mid-Victorian deserted wives. On the one hand were those who lived in the few but densely populated districts which offered reasonable opportunities for lone wives to become heads of self-supporting single-parent families, whether through their own unaided efforts or with help from family and friends. In these places it was quite common for such a wife to strengthen her position still further by securing a section 21 order, thus freeing herself altogether from the claims of her absent husband or his creditors and becoming again a single woman in the eyes of the law, at least so far as all the assets acquired since her desertion and her subsequent business dealings were concerned. For a woman in circumstances like these, desertion could bring real advantages. Very different however was the position of wives who lived in the far more extensive but much less populous areas where the dice were loaded against their achieving either economic independence or its potential mid-Victorian corollary, the security of an economic divorce, and a separate legal identity. In such places, desertion was all too likely to lead not to successful self-support, autonomy, and a request to the local County Court Registrar to register a section 21 order, but to dependence, destitution, and recourse to the local Relieving Officer in search of poor relief.

Thousands of mid-Victorian wives, then, obtained an economic divorce. But how large a proportion were they of the country's total female married population, and more importantly, of the country's deserted wives? Equally, what proportion do they represent of those who obtained some kind of matrimonial order or decree? On such matters of relative incidence the statistics point to conclusions well worth examining, since they impel fresh thought on ordinary mid-Victorian women's experiences of marital breakdown, and above all on the use they made of the new machinery of matrimonial orders and decrees.

Maps 4.5 and 4.6 provide two snapshots in time, which allow some of these issues to be examined. These maps show the number of section 21 orders granted in each circuit in 1861 and 1881 as a percentage of wives recorded as 'Married with Spouse Absent' in the 1861 and 1881 census returns.[71] This measure is inevitably a gross under-representation of the number of section 21 orders granted (never

---

[71] The data used derives from an enhanced version of K Schürer and E Higgs (2014) *Integrated Census Microdata (I-CeM), 1851–1911* (data collection) UK Data Service, SN: 7481, http://dx.doi.org/10.5255/UKDA-SN-7481-1. Enhancements were made by various members of the Cambridge Group for the History of Population and Social Structure.

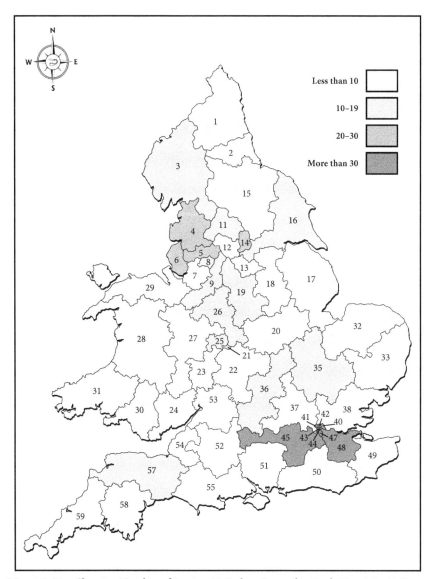

Map 4.5 Map Showing Number of Section 21 Orders Granted in Each Circuit in 1861 as a Percentage of Wives Recorded as 'Married with Spouse Absent' in the 1861 Census

mind applied for) because it cannot account for the cumulation of orders granted up to these dates, but nevertheless, it reveals important new information about both the geographical uptake of section 21 orders in relation to the numbers of married women living alone on census night, but also, and perhaps most importantly, how section 21 as a legal remedy was adopted by lone wives over the course of the mid to late nineteenth century.

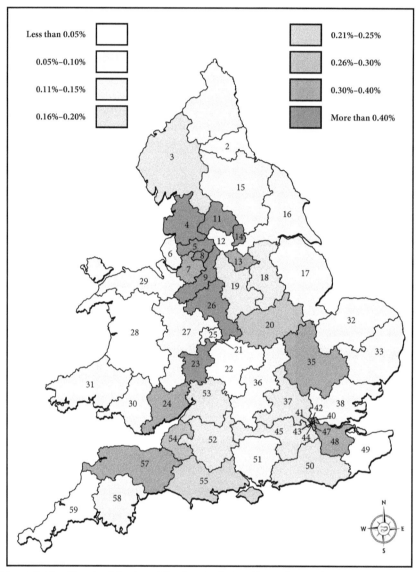

Map 4.6 Map Showing Number of Section 21 Orders Granted in Each Circuit in 1881 as a Percentage of Wives Recorded as 'Married with Spouse Absent' in the 1881 Census

Viewing the number of section 21 orders granted as a percentage of lone wives reported in the 1861 census in Map 4.5 reveals quite a different picture from both Map 4.1 and 4.2, which show the total numbers of section 21 orders granted in each circuit and the number of section 21 orders granted in 1861 respectively. Perhaps most strikingly, is the emergence of the two (very different) Circuits of

57 (Barnstaple) and 14 (Leeds), as locations where a high proportion of lone wives were applying for and being granted section 21 orders.[72] In fact, in 1861 a greater proportion of lone wives were granted section 21 orders in Circuit 14 than anywhere else, including the metropolitan circuits. The high percentage of lone wives with section 21 orders in Circuit 14 can also be seen in Map 4.6, suggesting that section 21 had been rapidly adopted by the deserted wives of Leeds and Wakefield soon after the Matrimonial Causes Act came into force in January 1858 and it remained an important legal remedy throughout the mid-nineteenth century, with numbers of orders granted only falling after the Married Women's Property Act 1882 was introduced. Circuit 57 (Barnstaple) was very different to Circuit 14 with its two extremely large urban centres of Leeds, (population c.393,000) and Wakefield (population c.100,000), and was instead populated by 13 towns all with populations of c.40,000 or less. In terms of numbers of orders granted, although Map 4.2 shows it to be a slight outlier in the south-west, by 1871 and 1881 this early enthusiastic uptake had waned with neighbouring Circuit 58 (Plymouth) overtaking it in numbers of orders granted. Yet, by examining the percentage of section 21 orders granted by the number of lone wives reported in the 1861 and 1881 census returns, the importance of these orders to deserted wives in Circuit 57 can be seen clearly, with the proportion of deserted wives there who held a section 21 order matched only by the Metropolitan Circuits (40, 41, 42, 43, 47 and 48) and Circuit 5 (Bolton) in 1861.

The new perspective offered by Maps 4.5 and 4.6 reveals several stories about section 21 orders that would otherwise remain hidden in the data. Map 4.1, showing the total number of section 21 orders granted in each Circuit between 1859 and 1893, along with Maps 4.2–4.4, all suggest that Circuits 4 (Blackburn) and 5 (Bolton), contributed relatively similar numbers of section 21 orders across the years, with the notable exception of 1871, discussed above. However, if we turn our attention to Map 4.5, it is possible to see that a larger percentage of lone wives in Circuit 5 had section 21 orders than their neighbours, Circuit 4, despite the relatively similar experience (or even dominance of Circuit 4) suggested by Maps 4.1–4.4, and contemporary opinion.[73] Similarly, Maps 4.5 and 4.6 also reveal a marked change in the use of section 21 orders in Circuit 23, which encompassed Stourbridge, Worcester and six smaller towns straddling Herefordshire, Worcestershire, and Warwickshire. In 1861, this Circuit had one of the very lowest percentages of section 21 orders by percentage of lone wives, but this situation had changed considerably by 1881, when this Circuit had become one of those with the highest percentages. Together with its adjacent circuits, Circuit 24 (Cardiff) to the south and Circuit 21 (Birmingham) to the north-east, it formed a corridor stretching from Lancashire in the north, to

---

[72] The geographic location of Circuits are identified here by their most populated District. See Appendix III for a full list of constituent Districts.
[73] 'Letter from Legality' *Blackburn Weekly Times* (14 August 1858).

Glamorganshire in the south, where deserted wives made particular use of the legal and economic relief offered under section 21.

Viewing the data in these two snapshots can also provide nuance to existing knowledge. The scarcity of cases in Circuits 29 (Wrexham, Chester, and northern Wales), Circuit 28 (Aberystwyth and central Wales), Circuit 31 (Cardigan and south-east Wales) and Circuit 30 (Swansea and the south Wales Valleys), can be seen clearly in Maps 4.1–4.4, with Map 4.1 making these Circuits appear to have particularly low uptake. If we look instead to Maps 4.5 and 4.6, we can see that actually, although orders of protection in these Circuits were relatively rare, in 1861, Circuits 31 and 30 were in fact broadly in line with many other areas of England, and by 1881, this level of usage had extended to Circuit 29 as well. Only Circuits 28, 49, and Circuit 59 (Cornwall) remained almost untouched by section 21, which is perhaps unsurprising given the highly rural nature of the constituent Districts in both.

The corridor of section 21 orders that stretched from north to south on the west of England was not replicated in the east of England, with few orders granted in the north-east, or in much of Derbyshire and Nottinghamshire. This reflects the heavy industry and widespread agriculture of these areas, which only rarely employed women, thus reducing the opportunity for them to becoming self-supporting. Curiously though, even in 1861, and certainly by 1881, the dense concentration of *feme sole* wives in Lancashire and the West Riding stubbornly skirted around the Districts of Circuit 12. This might not be noteworthy if the constituent Districts of Circuit 12 did not include Halifax, Dewsbury, and Huddersfield, all major textile manufacturing towns, with women seemingly well represented in these trades, in a similar way to Lancashire.[74] Might then the magistrates have acted differently? Other research points to women in Halifax and the surrounding area as perhaps having a complicated relationship with property ownership with examination of rate books from the town in 1851 showing that women in Halifax were less than half as likely to own property than their counterparts in Beverley or Scarborough.[75] There is much to be done on the individual workings of each Circuit and the variations highlight the importance of understanding the local context to broader, national, data. What Maps 4.5 and 4.6 demonstrate above all, however, is that the use of section 21 orders increased over time and became a key way by which deserted wives could reassert their legal independence and protect their economic future. This, together with the renewed interest in section 21 orders *following* the Married Women's Property Act 1870, should force a recalibration of the understanding of first, desertion and married women's strategies in the second half of the nineteenth century, and second, the perceived importance of the Married Women's Property Act 1870.

[74] *Census of England and Wales 1861*, Table 86, 134.
[75] J Aston, A Capern and B McDonagh, 'More Than Bricks and Mortar: Female Property Ownership as Economic Strategy in Mid-Nineteenth-Century Urban England' (2019) *Urban History* 46, 695, Table 1.1.

Calculating the true scale of desertion in the mid nineteenth century is difficult. The data available allows us to quickly discover the number of section 21
orders registered in each year but the number continuing in force at any given
time must be guesswork. Only 40 were reported as discharged in annual Civil
Judicial Statistics between 1859 and 1875, when this little used column was
dropped, but how many lapsed through resumed cohabitation? How many
through death? If every wife's order granted between 1859 and 1882 had been
maintained through her continuing survival and her continuing separation from
her husband, by 1882 at least one in every 241 wives in England and Wales would
have possessed *feme sole* status.[76] A cautiously realistic estimate, however, might
be that around half the orders granted since 1858 were still in force by 1882; and
if so, approximately one in every 500 wives then living in England and Wales was
a statutory *feme sole*, and their husbands were both expropriated and freed from
liability for their wives' debts and damages.[77]

It is impossible to assess at all accurately the aggregate net gain or loss of this
transfer of property rights and liabilities; but to place a nineteenth century value
of around £3,000,000 on the property that would otherwise have been lost to
husbands may not be too far off the mark.[78] In 1880 Lydia Becker argued that
property to the value of about £20,000,000 was lost to husbands in each year's crop
of marriages, which meant that property to the value of at least £100 was retained
by each new bride on marriage as a result of the first Married Women's Property
Act.[79] The average value of 'protected' wives' property was likely to be higher than
that of brides, since they had not only all proved that they were self-supporting
but were likely to be older and thus (among other things) would more often
inherit family legacies. Moreover, even the briefest period of economic divorce
might permanently affect the distribution of assets between the spouses. When
the wife died, the posthumous effects of her order were bound to be drastic. If she
died intestate (as did about one in three of all those who possessed property),[80] all
the assets covered by her order were distributed as though her husband was dead.
If she left a will, its provisions were valid with regard to this property, whatever
they might be. Even if her order lapsed through resumed cohabitation,[81] all the
assets it covered up to that moment were thereafter statutorily 'held to her separate use', and thus permanently 'protected'.[82] A husband who seized or continued

---

[76] See n 38.
[77] On Census night in 1881 there were 4,376,898 husbands in England and Wales (*Census of England
and Wales 1881*, v). However, a number of deserted wives' husbands were certainly overseas.
[78] The minimum equivalent of £236,300,000 today. See www.measuringworth.com.
[79] 'The Property of Married Women' (n 20) 195.
[80] As was remarked by Macdonell (n 62) 52. Wills seem to have been more common in the country,
which suggests that rather more than one in three of these wives (who were mostly town-dwellers) may
have died intestate.
[81] See Chapter Three.
[82] See Appendix I. Thus 'a prudent woman' would put any money covered by a section 21 order 'in
the savings bank or some other security, in her own name' since as to it she would always be a *feme sole*:
MacQueen (n 34) 100.

to hold a wife's protected property was always liable to criminal as well as civil action,[83] while third parties who had dealt with her in reliance on her order were statutorily indemnified against loss of any rights or remedies by its discontinuance or discharge.[84] Potentially therefore, every one of these c.20,000 mid-Victorian economic divorces had some permanent effect on the respective property rights and liabilities of the husbands and wives concerned and the third parties dealing with them, above all their creditors. Even if only one in around 500 couples had had their relationship put on a different legal footing through economic divorce, some qualification on familiar generalisations about the formal stability of patriarchal mid-Victorian matrimonial relationships thus seems called for. The marital experiences and survival strategies of these individual women deserve further investigation, and their stories are sampled in the following three chapters. These tentative figures alone, however, are enough to show that the negative resonance surrounding that emotive word 'desertion' is not always deserved.[85] Crucially, in mid-Victorian England its consequences were not always disastrous; indeed, for some women there were advantages in being left by their husbands.

To continue to focus upon the Divorce Court and its workings to study the impact of the law on that generation's marital breakdowns is thus to give central importance to what was in reality a comparatively marginal institution of change.[86] From the first mid-Victorian beginnings of a secular divorce jurisdiction, magistrates' courts were by far the most widely used channel through which the civil judicial system adapted the legal relationships of English husbands and wives to the practical realties of marriage breakdown, as they were throughout the twentieth century.[87] In 1859–78, 25 orders under section 21 were granted by magistrates for each full judicial separation by the Divorce Court; and in the 1870s, when the number of these section 21 orders granted by magistrates rose to an average of over 800 each year, applications to the Divorce Court for these same orders fell from an annual average of 14 to just nine.

---

[83] The chief villain of the propaganda of these years was the worthless husband who returned as soon as he knew his wife had acquired some assets and swept them away. The adequacy of the wife's remedies against a husband who disobeyed a magistrates' order was the only part of section 21 which provoked discussion in Parliament in 1857: *Hansard* HC Deb (series 3) 20 and 24 August 1857, vol 147, cols 1888–91, 2043. Inevitably the implementation of the law could be unpredictable. Thus in 1878 a stipendiary magistrate for Manchester refused to allow a Mrs McCarthy to prosecute her husband for having taken away certain property belonging to her under a marriage settlement under the Married Women's Property Act 1870, s 11, even though she had both a decree of judicial separation and a section 21 order, under which a wife was expressly empowered to sue her husband: *Hansard* HC Deb (series 3) 16 December 1878, vol 243, col 853.

[84] MCA 1857 s 8, 10.

[85] There were many reasons why 'splitting up' or 'leaving' might be best presented to the authorities as desertion, as Poor Law authorities were well aware.

[86] It is important to note however, that a full divorce from the Court for Divorce and Matrimonial Causes was the only matrimonial remedy to permit remarriage.

[87] The role of the social security system, alias the Poor Law, in dealing with families left destitute through marital breakdown is a distinct although not unrelated topic.

Why did mid-Victorians use magistrates' courts so much and the Divorce Court so little? Procedure was more formal in the Divorce Court and the cost of an application higher,[88] but the explanation is not simply a matter of money or social class. It had been urged in the debates of 1856–57 that 'mostly what is wanted by the injured party in cases of misconduct is not a second marriage, but relief from the pressure of the marriage law affecting property'.[89] This might have been a rhetorical device, designed to ensure that the question of married women and property would be addressed whether the Married Women's Property Bill or the Matrimonial Causes Bill triumphed. Regardless, a section 21 order from her local magistrates gave a wife that relief not only more conveniently, cheaply, and quickly than an identical order from the Divorce Court, but much more comprehensively than either a judicial separation or a divorce from that Court – since it restored her property rights from the date of her desertion, and not merely from the date of her decree.[90] Even if she contemplated a suit in the Divorce Court later, 'an interim order of protection from a magistrate will probably be found a very useful and prudent step', pointed out the *Law Times*.[91] After she had secured her order and waited for the statutory two years, however, she might very well conclude that so risky a proceeding as a petition for a judicial separation was not worth the trouble and expense,[92] at least if neither alimony payments nor child custody were at stake (for example if her husband had gone overseas or was bankrupt, or if there had been collusion).[93] Similarly, those who raise the question, 'why did so few women

---

[88] Costs ranged from 8s 6d to £2 and averaged £1: *Return of Rules and Regulations Concerning Practice and Procedure of Court for Divorce and Matrimonial Causes*, HC 106 (1859) 14–17. Despite the persistent myth to the contrary, middling and working people used the new Divorce Court for dissolution of marriage in much the same numbers as their betters.

[89] 'The Rights and Liabilities of Husband and Wife' (January 1857) *Edinburgh Review* 1010, 143, 181. Sir Erskine Perry repeated his claim that 'the main object of the innocent party is to be relieved from all pecuniary liability arising from the marriage' in introducing his Married Women Bill (sic) in the Commons: *Hansard* HC Deb (series 3) 14 May 1857, vol 145, col 268. Significantly, in the crucial debate of 7 August 1857 on the clause in the Divorce Bill providing for judicial separation by reason of desertion of husband or wife, Palmerston's Attorney General, Bethell himself opined that it was 'very rarely that the lower classes wanted … this species of judicial proceeding', although 'the wife would undoubtedly wish' for protection against the husband 'extending to her property and to her support': *Hansard* HC Deb (series 3) 7 August 1857, vol 147, col 1248. It is notable that the first decrease in the number of judicial orders, coincided with the coming into operation of the first effective Married Women's Property Act.

[90] In an undefended suit for divorce on the ground of adultery and desertion in 1869, a veteran of Doctors' Commons, Dr Thomas Spinks, asked for a section 21 order for his client before the decree *nisi* was pronounced, because 'she had recently come into property by the death of her mother; and while the decree would only date from its being made absolute, a protection order would date from the day it was issued': *Matthew v Matthew* (1869) 19 LT 662 501. In fact it would date from the day of her desertion, which much have been more than two years previously.

[91] 'The New Practice of Judicial Separation and Divorce' (20 February 1858) 30 *Law Times* 298.

[92] As competent legal advisers presumably realised, barely a third of wives who petitioned for a judicial separation were successful: *Royal Commission on Divorce and Matrimonial Causes*, Appendix III, Table VI, 30.

[93] The fact that the separation of property and full autonomy in economic matters which were often said to be all that 'the injured party' wanted from the law could be so expeditiously secured may also

choose not to take the judicial separation option?' underestimate the legal knowledge and understanding nineteenth-century women possessed about the range of options they had at their disposal.[94] As Frances Power Cobbe pointed out in 1878, section 21 orders 'practically act as Judicial Separations in all respects';[95] and SJ Lushington's remark that sections 25 and 26 (laying down the economic effects of a judicial separation) 'are in effect only an elaborate Protection Order' made the same point.[96] It should not be surprising, then, that when mid-Victorian wives turned to the law for protection and liberation from some or all of the legal bonds of a marriage, in 90 per cent of cases they had recourse to magistrates for one of these orders, and not to the Divorce Court. The applications of the small number of women who did apply to the Court for Divorce and Matrimonial Causes are examined in Chapter Seven.

In 1896 that outstandingly able and well informed jurist and statistician Sir John Macdonell warned that the English statistics for divorce and judicial separation must not be compared with those of other countries 'without taking into account the orders made by summary jurisdiction under the 1857 and 1878 Acts'.[97] His wise advice has never been heeded so far as the 1857 Act is concerned; and this has helped to keep in currency many distorted notions about that legislation and the way ordinary people used (and abused) it in dealing with their experiences of marital breakdown. It is certainly not the case, for example, that 'not many women actually derived much benefit from it' and that 'in fact the operation of the law on the whole afforded protection to more men than women'; nor is it altogether the case that it 'did nothing to relieve the plight of the brutalised, abandoned, or separated wives of the lower middle class or the poor' and 'operated to the advantage of men and the property and authority vested in them'.[98] By 1882 some 18,000 deserted but self-supporting wives knew otherwise, and so too did their husband and their husbands' creditors, sometimes to their wrath and indignation; for if section 27 embodied a double standard which favoured husbands, section 21

---

have dissuaded some mid-Victorian women entitled to petition for full divorce from doing so, when combined with the legal, cultural and financial pressures emphasised for example by G Savage, 'The Operation of the 1857 Divorce Act, 1860–1910 a Research Note' (1983) 16 *Journal of Social History* 105 and G Savage, 'Divorce and the Law in England and France Prior to the First World War' (1988) 21 *Journal of Social History*.

[94] Savage, 'The Operation of the 1857 Divorce Act, ibid 105; DC Wright, 'Untying the Knot: An Analysis of the English Divorce and Matrimonial Causes Court Records, 1858–1866' (2004) 38 *University of Richmond Law Review* 963–70.

[95] Cobbe (n 39) 84. Another reason for the failure to apply for judicial separation was surely the increasingly ready availability and validity of private deeds of separation – but that is another story.

[96] 'The Liability of a Husband' *Justice of the Peace* (1 March 1902) 131–32.

[97] *Return of Judicial Statistics of England and Wales*, 1894, Introduction, 56. Macdonell followed his own advice only with regard to orders made under the 1878 Act – logically enough, since his immediate concern was with the years 1893–94.

[98] Savage, 'The Operation of the 1857 Divorce Act' (n 93) 108; I Minor, 'Working Class Women and Matrimonial Law Reform, 1890–1914' in D Martin and D Rubinstein (eds), *Ideologies and the Labour Movement* (London, Croom Helm,1979) 103, 104; L Stone, *Road to Divorce England 1530–1987* (Oxford, Oxford University Press, 1990) 386.

embodied a different double standard which favoured wives. The mid-Victorian Divorce Act was a gendered Divorce Act – inevitably, in that society. It was an expression not so much of capitalist patriarchalism, as of the ideology of separate spheres of conjugal duty and therefore of conjugal offences and remedies. Thus, section 27 enabled a husband to secure appropriate protection against a spouse who had flouted the prime conjugal duty of a wife, namely sexual fidelity, and section 21 enabled a wife to secure appropriate protection against a spouse who had reneged on the prime conjugal duty of a husband, namely maintenance and protection.[99]

Nor was the Divorce Court given a monopoly of the power to change marital status in 1857, as is often said. On the contrary, through section 21, the very lowest tier of the judicial system was given power to require certain married women to be deemed *feme soles* in certain important respects, exactly as though they had been granted a judicial separation. Between 1858 and 1882 the first phase of the matrimonial jurisdiction of magistrates took root and flourished in symbiosis with the last phase of the patriarchal economic rights and liabilities given to husbands by coverture and the common law. From the day when the new Act came into operation, wives across a broad social spectrum took full advantage of the new machinery and made it for a generation by far the most important vehicle through which the civil judicial system adjusted the economic effects of marital breakdown. To remain ignorant of the working of section 21 is thus to remain ignorant of the working of by far the most frequently used part of mid-Victorian England's new divorce law. In understanding and appreciating this, how then, it must be asked, was economic divorce experienced?

---

[99] In one respect, and as an afterthought of Cranworth's, the definition of offence and remedy was identical for both spouses in judicial separation; this reflected the tripartite system in the Ecclesiastical Courts where husbands and wives were treated equally when seeking divorce *a mensa et thoro*.

PART III

Experiencing 'Economic Divorce'

5

Experiences of Desertion and Strategies of Independence in Mid-Nineteenth Century London and Lancashire

The history of marital breakdown as it was experienced by 'ordinary' people is still little known. The broken marriages of the rich have been examined in more detail, thanks to the documentation required in litigation involving money and property, and the ensuing press coverage of cruelty, adultery, and sexual conflicts of society figures and celebrities.[1] After 1857, the very public proceedings of the new Divorce Court aired 'juicy' details of marital misbehaviour, but a lack of understanding about the wider court has meant writers on Victorian divorce have lacked the necessary context to fully understand their own selections of spicy anecdotes.[2] Before the later twentieth century, however, marital break-up rarely ended in divorce.[3] It therefore follows that it is not divorce proceedings, but rather the *matrimonial* proceedings embarked upon by thousands

---

[1] L Stone, *Broken Lives: Separation and Divorce in England 1660–1857* (Oxford, Oxford University Press, 1993) 344.

[2] Widespread investigations of the J 77 divorce applications have been limited. Some pioneering studies include: AJ Hammerton, *Cruelty and Companionship: Conflict in Nineteenth Century Married Life* (Abingdon, Routledge, 1992); G Savage, 'They Would if They Could: Class, Gender and Popular Representation of English Divorce Litigation, 1858–1908' (2011) 36 *Journal of Family History*; G Savage, 'Divorce and the Law in England and France Prior to the First World War' (1988) 21 *Journal of Social History* 499; and G Savage, '"Intended Only for the Husband": Gender, Class, and the Provision for Divorce in England, 1858–1868' in KK Ottesen Garrigen (ed), *Victorian Scandals: Representations of Gender and Class* (Athens, OH, Ohio University Press, 1992) 11; DC Wright, 'Untying the Knot: An Analysis of the English Divorce and Matrimonial Causes Court Records, 1858–1866' (2004) 38 *University of Richmond Law Review*; DC Wright, 'Well-Behaved Women Don't Make History: Rethinking Family, Law, and History' (2004) 19 *Wisconsin Women's Law Journal*. The importance of J 77 petitions to tell the story of divorce has been highlighted in J Aston, 'Petitions to the Court for Divorce and Matrimonial Causes: A New Methodological Approach to the History of Divorce, 1857–1923' (2002) 43 *Journal of Legal History* and J Aston 'An Exceedingly Painful Case': The Aftermath of Divorce in Mid-Nineteenth Century England and Wales (2023) 26 *Family & Community History* 71–91; the lack of data will be addressed by the ongoing Economic and Social Research Council-funded project 'A New Methodological Approach to the History of Divorce 1858–1923' led by Dr Jennifer Aston, see: https://hosting.northumbria.ac.uk/divorce_history/.

[3] In 1921, when the census for the first time recorded the divorced population, only 8218 women or c.0.049% of the adult female population of England and Wales were divorced. Census 1921, General

of ordinary wives each year in magistrates' courts which offer an insight into the scale and commonplaces of later nineteenth and earlier twentieth century marriage breakdown in England and Wales.[4]

As was seen earlier, annual *Return of Judicial Statistics of England and Wales* reports revealed the circuits covering metropolitan London and the cotton towns of Lancashire in the north-west of England received the most applications from deserted wives for protection under section 21. But were their experiences of marriage, desertion, and the process of applying for an order under section 21 the same? In 1854, Mrs Gaskell gave her new novel the title of *North and South* in order to exploit the topical concern over the perceived polarity of experiences between life in Lancashire and in London. Was there a real-life gulf between 'north' and 'south' where independent lone wives and their experience of marriage breakdown in the late 1850s were concerned? In the Lancashire cotton towns, women had the reputation of being uniquely uninhibited and self-reliant, and the 'rough, but not unfriendly freedom' and 'bold fearless faces' Gaskell gave her mill-girls were exactly what her readers expected of women in the north – but not the south.[5] How different from those of their Lancashire counterparts were the experiences and strategies of London women, and particularly of wives living in that swathe of metropolitan Surrey and Kent stretching from Lambeth and Southwark to Greenwich and Woolwich where the new section 21 orders were most common? Evidence from census returns shows that female labour force participation rates were, perhaps unsurprisingly given the dominance of textiles industries, the highest in the country in the north-west, and crucially for the study of section 21 orders, this was also true for married women.[6] The rates of female labour force participation were not particularly high in London and certainly not as high as is observed in the north-west and, as Xuesheng You argues, this is likely due to the sheer numbers of women who migrated to London and a lack of capacity to occupy all of them.[7] This suggests some difference in the demographic of women applying under section 21 in north and south, however we must look to other sources to explore this further.

Understanding the experiences and strategies of the women who applied for section 21 also involves recovering intimate details of their marriages. As described above, this is a much simpler process for wealthy couples fighting over fortunes in the Divorce Court where most applications for this period survive, whereas petty

---

Tables, No XXXIV. Ages and Marital Conditions, available at www.visionofbritain.org.uk/census/EW1921GEN/6.

[4] Rachel Pimm-Smith and Rebecca Probert's investigation into the families of 100 parents living in Camberwell between 1870 and 1890 and whose children had become chargeable to the poor law authorities showed that even under these difficult circumstances, marital breakdown was relatively rare: R Pimm-Smith and R Probert, 'Evaluating Marital Stability in Late-Victorian Camberwell' (2018) 21 *Family & Community History* 38–50.

[5] E Gaskell, *North and South* (London, 1855) Chapter 8.

[6] X You, 'Women's Labour Force Participation in Nineteenth-century England and Wales: Evidence from the 1881 Census Enumerators' Books' (2020) 73 *Economic History Review*, figs 1 and 3.

[7] ibid 129.

sessions registers (which have frequently been destroyed) record little more than the applicant's name and (sometimes) address. Occasionally, subsequent litigation brought into the Law Reports themselves provide a dry and punctilious record of specific economic aspects of a 'protected' wife's marital affairs. None of these reports include the intimate domestic and sexual details given in some Divorce Court melodramas, and none provide the systematic demographic information available from poor law records for the destitute.[8] Collections of correspondence and diaries can provide a privileged and rich window into the emotional depths of individual courtships and marriages, sometimes over prolonged periods of time, and reveal much about wider life.[9] Sadly, such sources are rare and tend to survive (or exist in the first place) for the middling and upper classes, requiring a different approach to capture the experiences of marriage within the poor and working classes. Fortunately, the advent of 'Divorce Before Magistrates' in 1858 coincided with the proliferation of a cheap popular Sunday and local press whose staples included 'human interest' court cases. As a result, these new applications to magistrates were often fully reported, especially those with novelty value. What these reports offer are first person narratives of the personal experiences of marriage breakdown and its practical aftermath, given on oath by wives who were neither very rich, nor very poor.

Magistrates' matrimonial jurisdiction spanned a substantially wider social range initially than it quite quickly came to do after the passing of the Matrimonial Causes Acts Amendment Act 1878 for three primary reasons. First, because it was statutorily confined to deserted wives who were self-supporting and had property or earnings of their own; second because it was not then an appendage of a husband's conviction for aggravated marital assault (as it became after 1878); and third because comparatively little stigma was yet attached to using a police court. Reports of these first applications made to magistrates' courts thus offer a fresh perspective on mid-Victorian marriage breakdown, and the way some

---

[8] A study of the settlement of examinations of 49 destitute deserted wives in the agricultural south-east between 1835 and 1880 showed that they had been married younger and for longer than other destitute wives, more often had children, had larger families, and had been more mobile; and that Irishmen, soldiers, labourers and publicans in their mid-30s and with a large, young family to maintain were likeliest to desert, and usually did so at harvest time, and that enlisting was still the institutionally acceptable form of desertion: KDM Snell, *Annals of the Labouring Poor: Social Change and Agrarian England, 1660–1900* (Cambridge, Cambridge University Press, 1985) Table 7.8, 361; Eighteenth-century poor relief records have been used for similar studies of the parishes of St Martin's in the Fields in London and Colyton in Devon: DA Kent, '"Gone for a Soldier": Family Breakdown and the Demography Of Desertion in a London Parish, 1750–1791' (1990) 45 *Local Population Studies* 27; P Sharpe, 'Marital Separation in the Eighteenth and early Nineteenth Centuries' (1990) *Local Population Studies* 45, 66; this position has been reassessed by J Hurl-Eamon who argues that enlistment was sometimes a family *survival* strategy rather than abandonment: 'Did Soldiers Really Enlist to Desert Their Wives? Revisiting the Martial Character of Marital Desertion in Eighteenth-Century London' (2014) *Journal of British Studies* 53, 356.

[9] S King, 'Love, Religion and Power in the Making of Marriages in Early Nineteenth-Century Rural Industrial Lancashire' (2010) *Rural History* 21, 1–26; A Popp, *Entrepreneurial Families: Business, Marriage and Life in the Early Nineteenth Century*, (London, Pickering and Chatto, 2012).

wives dealt with it, at many social levels. It would be a mistake however, to take all these narratives at face value. Wildly differing kinds of marital separation were presented in court as desertion. Many applications do indeed seem to have told a straightforward story, sometimes damaging their own case in the process; but an astute or knowledgeable woman, or one primed by an experienced solicitor, could easily adapt her account (and her dress and demeanour) to improve her chances of success; and in her husband's absence her version of events was very unlikely to be challenged. More subtle distortions, moreover, are likely to have come about through the familiarity of all concerned with a melodramatic stereotype used by campaigning law reformers and the press since the mid-1850s – that of the hard-working deserted wife preyed upon by her worthless husband's relentless exploitation of his legal ownership of all she possessed.

Popular journalists have always provided what their readers expected and enjoyed, and the police court reports in the two liveliest Sunday newspapers, *Reynolds's Weekly Newspaper* and *The News of the World*, echoed the highly coloured language and narrative structure of popular plays and fiction, whether or not the sentiment and melodrama expected in the courtroom was actually forthcoming.[10] Proceedings from the Metropolitan Police Courts, including applications made for protection under section 21, were also reported widely in the mid-week papers such as *The Globe, Morning Post, Morning Advertiser*, as well as Saturday papers including the *South London Times & Lambeth Observer*, and *The Era*. Reports of cases heard by police magistrates frequently set the wicked husband – brutal, adulterous, idle (or whatever kind of blackguard best fitted the evidence given) – against his virtuous victim, the injured, industrious wife; the corroboration conveyed by dress, manner and bearing was often sketched in ('A respectably-dressed and ladylike woman applied to Mr Corrie …'); and a headline nudged the reader towards the appropriate response – usually 'poor thing!', but sometimes, 'well I never!'[11] The names of the applicants were sometimes given only in shortened form, such as 'Mrs Shepherd',[12] or were omitted altogether in favour of a physical description – 'a care-worn middle-aged woman of respectable appearance appeared on Tuesday …'.[13] Given the large population of mid-century London, reporters and editors likely recognised that it was the drama of the story that would capture the attention of readers, rather than their likely unrecognisable name.

Provincial reporters, meanwhile, employed more sober skills when covering their neighbourhood's petty sessions, whatever their particular newspaper's style

[10] A Humpherys, 'Popular Narrative and Political Discourse in *Reynold's Newspaper*' in L Brake, A Jones and L Madden (eds), *Investigating Victorian Journalism* (London, Palgrave Macmillan, 1990) 35, 38.

[11] For example, 'Worship Street. Cruel Case of Desertion' *News of the World* (11 April 1858) and 'Southwark. Singular Application under the Matrimonial Causes Act – Protecting a Milk Walk' *News of the World* (5 December 1858); or 'Marylebone. Extraordinary Application for Protection of Property' *Reynold's Newspaper* (12 December 1858).

[12] 'New Divorce Act' *The Examiner* (Saturday 30 January 1858) 12.

[13] 'The New Marriage Act' *Reynolds's Newspaper* (28 February 1858) 10.

and tone; they would mention by name every case that came up, but usually give it only a few brief and pedestrian lines. In these local papers where the actions of the readership also produced much of the content, there was genuine interest in knowing exactly who was appearing in the local magistrates' courts. They and their readers, however, were as familiar as their metropolitan counterparts with the stock figure of the working wife injured by a faulty matrimonial property law, and when the *Preston Guardian* drew attention to the new 'Protection for Injured Women' available from magistrates, it used well-worn language. Readers would remember, it was sure, 'many instances of mercenary and depraved fellows' who paid assiduous court to a woman with 'small sums in ready cash', married her, spent the money, turned to debauchery, and brutality, then desertion, but reappeared whenever she had begun to 'earn a decent livelihood or even save a few shillings weekly', and mulcted her again. 'Wretches like these are numerous in every large town', this leader-writer went on, 'and probably in every village'.[14] Whether such 'wretches' were indeed commonplace it is impossible to know but continual repetition of such scenarios had gone far to ensure all but universal approval of the protection offered to self-supporting deserted wives by section 21 of the 1857 Act.[15] Equally, however, it had provided reporters, magistrates, solicitors, and many wives themselves, with a ready-made descriptive vocabulary and interpretative framework for the personal experiences they recounted in court, and therefore any concrete, unformulaic details which emerge at these hearings carry more conviction than standard generalisations and phrases.

A particularly promising starting point for a trawl of this press evidence is offered by newspaper reports of the applications for economic divorce made during 1858 in a cluster of towns in north-east Lancashire. In 1858 the cotton towns on the northern side of the Pennines (which still combined some spinning with their many weaving enterprises), possessed not only the Conservative *Preston Chronicle* and Joseph Livesey's Liberal *Preston Guardian* (established in 1844 and providing 60 ample columns of letter-press for threepence halfpenny to a readership of 'merchants, manufacturers and the reading classes generally'), but also two Blackburn newspapers: the Conservative *Blackburn Standard*, established in 1832 and offering four pages for 3d., and the populist *Blackburn Weekly Times*, a four-page Liberal penny weekly founded in June 1855 but already claiming to be the most extensively circulated paper in Blackburn, Darwen and East Lancashire.[16] Burnley also had its penny Saturday, the 'independent' *Burnley Advertiser* founded in 1853, although this gave comparatively little space to what went on at Petty Sessions.[17] Between them, these newspapers reported

[14] 'Protection for Injured Women' *Preston Guardian* (17 January 1858).
[15] 'No one will question the equity and justice' or the 'important provision, introduced to protect wives from the rapacity of proliferate husbands': *Reynold's Newspaper* (18 January 1858) – a safe prediction, in light of the reception of section 21 in the previous months.
[16] *Mitchell's Press Dictionary for 1858* (London, 1858) 62, 102, 118.
[17] When Olive Anderson originally conducted this research, she had (sometimes incomplete) access at the Colindale Newspaper Library to the files of all these newspapers for 1858, except the *Preston*

applications by 37 local women during 1858, 14 of them living in Blackburn, and the rest in Preston (five), Burnley (five) and the neighbouring towns of Haslingden (four), Bury (three), Accrington (two), Bacup (two), Oswaldtwistle (one) and Darwen (one). In 1858, south London was not as well served by local newspapers as the cotton towns. Apart from the fourpenny *South London Journal*, it had two recently founded weeklies, the three and a halfpenny *London News* and halfpenny *South London Times*; but both were essentially advertising sheets and gave little space to Police Court news.[18] Fortunately the leading popular Sunday newspapers made a feature of reporting metropolitan court proceedings, and *Lloyd's Weekly*, *Reynold's Newspaper* and *The News of the World* all gave 'Divorce Before Magistrates' prominent coverage during its first few months. Even so, more applications went unreported here than in the Blackburn and Preston area. Only 38 press reports have been found of London hearings in 1858, with 12 cases heard at Lambeth, and the rest at Southwark (five), Clerkenwell (four), Worship Street (four), Marlborough Street (three), Wandsworth (two), Westminster (two), Woolwich (one) and Thame (one). One case was heard in the Divorce Court but reported in the local newspapers.[19] It is likely that these underrepresent the numbers of applications for section 21 orders heard as the following year (the first where data was collected), there were 45 orders granted in Circuits 4, 5 and 11 which cover the area discussed in the north-west, and 69 orders were granted in Circuits 44, 46 and 47, which covered the Metropolitan Police Courts.[20]

Although the newspapers did not report every deserted wife applying for a section 21 order, they do allow us to move beyond the broad statistics of the Judicial Returns to examine the circumstances that led to a marriage breakdown and a husband to leave in each locality. It might be argued that this is a question which can only be partially answered, since the husband's side of the story was never given and the wife was bound to assert she had been 'deserted without reasonable cause' for otherwise she would not be entitled to an order. Yet, given how frequently the reverse situation occurred, whereby a question was deemed answered with only a male perspective, this is a somewhat refreshing caveat to employ. Similarly, we might also pause to consider the rarity of a Victorian wife being not only the main character in her own story, but the narrator and director too. She is the person who, through her courtroom appearance, has constructed the narrative of her married life that we as historians are able to observe and, as Chapter Four has shown, the extremely low numbers of discharged orders suggest that they managed this process extremely effectively indeed.

Guardian, which was then classified as unfit for use and not subsequently digitised. The penny *Bury Guardian* provides full reports of applications on the other side of the Pennines.

[18] From 17 April 1858 the *South London Times* became the *Lambeth Observer and South London Times*. The *South London Journal* (published on Tuesday at fourpence and described in *Mitchell's Press Directory* as circulating among 'the principal residents, merchants, manufacturers and traders') at the British Newspaper Library at Colindale was classified as 'unfit for use'.

[19] Anderson originally identified 31 cases; this has since been expanded to 37 cases.

[20] *Return of Judicial Statistics of England and Wales, 1859* HC 2692 (1860) 133.

From the evidence heard in court, five distinct types of deserting husband emerge. Two of these: the 'Financial Failure' and the 'Addictive Wanderer' were peculiar to Lancashire, while three: the 'Calculating Quick-Buck Bridegroom'; the 'Adulterously Inclined Romeo'; and the 'Determined Emigrant', were all specific to London. The first of the Lancashire deserters were those with financial difficulties and a failed business who disappeared to escape their creditors after many years of marriage, sometimes 16 years or more. These husbands were usually small shopkeepers and artisans (for example, a tailor and draper, a shoemaker, a clothes broker, a publican). Small traders like these were always especially vulnerable to difficulties arising from debt, for their customers were usually as dependent upon credit as they were themselves. 'He said he left me because he was in difficulties and could not meet his creditors', testified Margaret Bland, the tailor and draper's wife who was the first Preston woman to be granted an order.[21] A few weeks later Blackburn magistrates heard the story of a similar 'flit' from Christiana Todd. William Todd had started life as a journeyman shoemaker in Leeds, but about three years after their marriage in 1837 Christiana inherited £160 from her father, and with this they opened a shop in North Street. Seventeen years later he did not come home one night, and when Christiana fetched a policeman to get into his workshop, she found his tools and clothes gone, the £1. 10. 0. due for their rent unpaid, and other debts of £20 and £15. His creditors applied to her for repayment, she was sold up, and their landlord took possession of the shop.[22] Occasionally the husband's failed business had been on a larger scale, and he might use correspondingly greater ingenuity in starting a new life without a wife but with some portable assets. Joseph Dall, a failed manufacturer who had owned the mill at Mellor Brook near Blackburn, reassuringly told his wife he had got a situation in Manchester of £300 a year and had taken lodgings at a guinea a week, and then persuaded her to go to Bacup for a week after first leaving 'all her wearing apparel and jewellery' for safekeeping with his brother in Manchester – which was the last she saw of either them or him.[23]

Unusually for Lancashire, another businessman used a more drastic escape route and betook himself to New Zealand. His Catholic wife, Mary Healey, told how in 23 years their upward rise had taken them from Blackburn to Fleetwood, then Preston, and finally Lytham, 'Mr Healey still carrying on a business at Preston, where he went every morning and returned every evening'. In the previous March

---

[21] 'Preston Police Intelligence' *Preston Chronicle* (13 March 1858) 5.

[22] 'Application for Protection under the Matrimonial Causes Act' *Preston Chronicle* (17 April 1858). Christiana applied to the Blackburn Petty Sessions because she had moved to live with her brother.

[23] 'Application for Protection under the Matrimonial Causes Act' *Blackburn Standard* (12 May 1858) 3. These brothers were probably two sons of John W Dall, an Amesbury manufacturer, who at the time of the Census of 1851 was still using water-power for spinning and putting out to local hand weavers, but was nevertheless able to maintain a family of five in comfort with two resident maids, until the business failed in the mid-1850s: GT Timmins, *The Last Shift: The Decline of Handloom Weaving in Nineteenth century Lancashire* (Manchester University Press, 1993) 174. His elder son, James, graduated from Trinity College Dublin in 1850.

he had disposed of his business and told her that as there was a firm giving up business in Liverpool and trade was bad in Preston, he should go to Liverpool and take that business. He left home to go to Liverpool for that purpose and said he would return in a fortnight: 'she never suspected that his intention was to leave the country'. Shortly afterwards she heard that he had gone to London and set sail to New Zealand with a family named Clarke, furniture brokers, who had sold off the stock. 'A search was made, and it was ascertained that he had taken some of his daughter's jewellery, some clothing belonging to one of his sons and six shirts, in addition to all his own clothing'. Since then she had not heard a word from him. Mr Pedder, the banker, had put in an execution under a writ of summons, and Mr Jackson, the sharebroker, had also issued an execution from the County Court, 'by which processes the household furniture was swept away'.[24] Experiences like these suggest that Bethell and some other down-to-earth Members of Parliament were not far wrong in thinking that what a deserted wife chiefly needed for her property was protection against creditors, rather than against the parasitic, vagabond husband who loomed so large in the sentimental propaganda of the time.

Yet there was a second, quite different, kind of deserter among the deserting husbands of Lancashire, and they fitted that favourite stereotype remarkably closely (at least according to their wives' stories). The 'Addictive Wanderer' did not leave to escape business failure, rather they repeatedly came and went as it suited them, selling the furniture before they went, and often going off for the first time after only a few weeks after marriage. These footloose ne'er-do-wells might indeed run up debts – Agnes Davis of Oswaldtwistle, for example, a drunken warper's wife, 'had been called upon to pay his debts and had been put into the County Court'. Moreover, she had been deserted by him on four separate occasions.[25] Unlike the first group however, these husbands were also markedly prone to drinking and brawling, womanising, and wife-beating, spells in prison and various brushes with the law. Often, they had taken up with another woman, with or without a bigamous marriage ceremony, and fathered an illegitimate child, or had been brought up in court for assault. Robert Davis, husband of Agnes above, was 'a very outward man, a great drunkard, and was always kicking and beating her'.[26] Similarly, it was a warrant that Peggy Cunliffe took out against her husband for assaulting her which had prompted the most recent disappearance of the idle, drunken Peter Cunliffe of Accrington.[27] One such husband 'never worked more than three months of the year' and had been five times imprisoned for assaults, neglect of family, and the like; and one – a Swedenborgian Richard Whalley – between his comings and goings was gaoled in Scotland for bigamy and then in Manchester for obtaining goods by false pretences.[28] Two had enlisted in the

---

[24] 'A Cruel Husband' *Blackburn Standard* (8 December 1858) 3.
[25] 'Application Under The Matrimonial Causes Act' *Preston Chronicle* (15 May 1858) 8.
[26] ibid.
[27] 'Application for Protection' *Burnley Advertiser* (18 December 1858) 3.
[28] *Preston Guardian* (6 February 1858) 7. Another convicted bigamist, who had departed after selling up all the furniture, and had been 'brought up by the relieving officer and committed for a month' was James Grierson: *Blackburn Standard* (31 March 1858) 3.

Army during the long peace and after a while deserted their regiments before making bigamous marriages (one had 'sold' his first wife to a Marine, while the other, James Breakell, changed his name).[29] A third, Luke Jackson, had taken the classic escape route offered by the Crimean War and enlisted as a single man, leaving 'large debts' behind him and writing from India in 1857 to tell his wife Nancy that 'she could get married again as he did not intend to return home'.[30] It should be remembered that despite the confusion caused by Sir Cresswell Cresswell in *Cargill v Cargill* in 1858, a wife who had secured an order only for her husband to return was not required to resume conjugal relations, the order empowered her to remain living apart and independently from him.[31]

What sort of men, then, were errant London husbands? As often as not, their occupations went unrecorded, but from the information available, they seem to have been a more varied collection than in Lancashire. Three – a tailor, a plasterer, and a shoemaker – certainly had their counterparts in the Blackburn area, where artisans and small shopkeepers predominated among absconding husbands in 1858, but not so the rest. Two were service workers (a waiter, a shopman), two were professional singers (very typical of the South Bank, always a great haunt of entertainers), three owned apparently fairly substantial businesses, one was a Marines corporal, and two (a surgeon and an employee of the General Post Office at £250 a year) were middling financial failures. Yet, on the whole, the types of deserters so common in Lancashire in 1858 were both notably rare in north and south London. No 'Financial Failures' flitting to escape creditors appear here; only one wife spoke of paying off her husband's debts (although several reported the money set aside for rent had been taken);[32] and only one wife, Susan Bragg ('a lady-like person')[33] mentioned county court proceedings (falsely, as it turned out). William Bragg was a dentist who had practised in Dalston, and his wife alleged that he had failed in business and was facing bankruptcy. The principal cause of his leaving, she asserted, was 'the embarrassed state of his affairs, the business being in a state of insolvency', and after 14 years of marriage, 'he began to get tired of me' and although her husband later acknowledged 'domestic difficulties' he insisted her statement was otherwise 'unfounded in every essential particular', and applied for her order to be rescinded.[34] Financial 'embarrassment'

---

[29] 'Bigamy at Bacup' *Blackburn Standard* (14 July 1858) 3; 'Matrimonial Causes Act 1857 in Blackburn' *Blackburn Standard* (14 July 1858) 3.

[30] 'Protection Under the Divorce Act' *Preston Chronicle* (27 February 1858) 8. A 'devastating effect in breaking up marriages' has been attributed to eighteenth-century wars: Stone (n 1) 6.

[31] Given that this scenario was not settled in the Divorce Court until 1891, we can assume that it was relatively rare. *Cargill v Cargill* (1858) 27 LJ 69, also see Chapter Two, n 23 and Chapter Three, text n 32.

[32] 'Important to Wives Requiring Protecting Orders Under the New Divorce Act' *Reynolds's Newspaper* (14 March 1858) 10.

[33] Value of the Matrimonial Causes Act, *Morning Herald (London)* (9 April 1858) 8.

[34] 'Worship Street' *The Times* (9 April 1858) 9. Her husband, who was then practising at 58 Maddox Street, Bond Street, claimed that he had himself purchased this prosperous business at a cost of £130: 'Vindication of Character' *Clerkenwell News* (24 April 1858) 2. Susan Bragg had inherited £300 from her father which her husband had thrown into his failing business, according to a friend's evidence: *The Times* (9 April 1858) 9.

did indirectly break up one of these marriages, for when he emerged from the Queen's Bench debtors prison, the surgeon Joseph Howett's aged father-in-law refused him access to his wife. This 'fashionably dressed lady', 'whose locks time had deeply silvered' (not surprisingly since she had married as long ago as 1832), 'requested he would write'; but he did not, and she had heard he was now living with another woman.[35]

Almost equally rare in this sample was the Addictive Wanderer who came and went to the accompaniment of violence, womanising, drinking and brushes with the law. Only one of these south London husbands was a chronic wanderer of this sort – and the habits of this rolling stone prompted that cautious veteran, Boyce Combe of the Southwark Police Court, to reject the application his wife made just three days after the new Act came into operation: her husband had only been gone five weeks, he told her, and might return.[36] An Islington greengrocer, Henry Lichfield, was violent enough but stayed put in his shop in Cross Street after he had turned his wife out (and dislocated her shoulder in the process).[37] Perhaps the London husband most reminiscent of this variety of deserter is the Shoreditch commercial traveller who plundered and deserted his wife three times, before finally whisking away to Scotland her jewellery and 'portables', and the female assistant she employed in her artificial flower-making business.[38] The one south London man who had 'gone for a soldier' (in the Land Transport Corps raised for Crimean service) had duly returned at the end of the war to live with his wife, Martha Bell, 'a respectable- looking female' – although at her expense.[39] There were no explicit complaints of drunkenness, and although several were said to have 'ill-used' their wives on occasion, only one, the Lambeth shoemaker Robert Geary, was alleged to have been 'always a very cruel husband'.[40]

An absconding husband in London was rarely either a harassed debtor or a roving vagabond, rather he was quite often a 'Calculating Quick-Buck Bridegroom', who used his wife as a cash-cow and left her when she had been milked. A third of these men bore out the reformers' charge that English matrimonial property law

[35] 'The Divorce and Matrimonial Causes Act' *South London Times* (13 February 1858) 3. This husband was probably the *Medical Directory*'s Joseph Howell of Southwark, *The London Medical Directory 1845*, Wellcome Trust, B24769514_i18567642 (small errors in proper names are common in Police Court reports). Mrs Howell herself was given the improbable first name of Marcino, a misspelling of Maria, see: London Church of England Parish Registers, London Metropolitan Archives, DL/T/090/019.

[36] 'Case of a Married Woman Carrying on a Business on the Old Kent Road' *Solicitors' Journal* (16 January 1859) 2, 194; This decision was instanced as incorrect in JF Macqueen, *A Practical Treatise on Divorce and Matrimonial Jurisdiction Under the Act of 1857 and New Orders* (London, W Maxwell, 1858) 98.

[37] 'Divorce and Matrimonial Causes Act: A Cruel Case' *Morning Chronicle* (29 July 1858) 8.

[38] 'Value of the Matrimonial Causes Act' *Lloyd's Weekly* (28 February 1858) 4.

[39] 'Divorce Before Magistrates' *News of the World* (28 February 1858) 7; 'The New Matrimonial Act' *Reynolds's Newspaper* (28 February 1858) 6; the 'dissipated' John Henry Bell was a currier and leather cutter (*London Post Office Directory 1851* (London, 1851) 610), which no doubt made him a welcome recruit to the Land Transport Corps.

[40] According to Caroline Geary, his wife of 30 years, the immediate cause of his leaving was 'his dread of my having him punished for throwing me downstairs, and this he did from finding fault with a breakfast I had prepared for him': *Reynolds's Newspaper* (7 February 1858) 10.

encouraged 'bad marriages' by ensuring that women tempted 'the cupidity of men' and were married only to be abandoned as soon as the plunderer had secured his spoils.[41] Pillage followed by desertion was very much the experience of Caroline Goodwin, 'a respectably dressed young woman' who owned 'a quantity of furniture and other property' when she married a waiter in Lambeth in April 1856. He immediately began selling her things; and after a few weeks 'they were all gone, including her wedding ring' – and so was he. She became housekeeper to 'a gentleman in Wandsworth Road'; but a year later her husband reappeared, and 'annoyed her until she gave him some money'.[42] The justice sitting at Wandsworth that day, Mr Dayman, immediately granted the order. A longer-term variant on this theme of marital piracy was recounted at Southwark three weeks later by a professional singer, 'a very prepossessing-looking female, dressed extremely neat': her husband had reappeared when she had secured 'an excellent engagement', and 'threatened to take her salary and the clothes which she had purchased with her own earnings'.[43] Mr Burcham, the Southwark justice, 'immediately granted the order requested'.[44] Other spongers and plunderers included the convicted embezzler who married the 'fashionably-dressed and good-looking' Walworth housekeeper, Jane Astrope, who went off with her gold watch and chain, returned, and 'ran through £245 she borrowed from her master' to set him up in business as a stationer; Sarah Lancaster's husband, who 'turned her into the street after stripping her of all her property'; and Harriet Maidwell's spouse, who 'took her bed and clothes' with him when he left.[45]

Frequently, an absconding husband left with more than just cash and household goods. The 'Adulterously Inclined Romeo' features in several cases heard before the Metropolitan Police Courts, including that of Matilda Heard, a 'highly respectable' woman who had been a Bow ratepayer for 20 years. Her husband of only three days told her he had married her 'for a lark' and decamped, taking her good bed with him.[46] Meanwhile, Mary Ann Priest, who ran a successful business off Pall Mall, within a month acquired and lost a husband who combined the features of all three varieties of deserting husband found in London. Soon after their wedding,

---

[41] This was the wrong that Harriet Martineau claimed had been reduced to 'one pillage and desertion only' by section 21 of the Matrimonial Causes Act 1857, although with typical even-handedness, she recognised that there were 'swindlers of both sexes' marrying to obtain property and then absconding: *Daily News* (28 May 1858), reprinted in *The English Woman's Journal* I (July 1858) 339–42.

[42] 'Another Case Before The New Divorce Act' *Lloyd's Weekly* (21 February 1858) 4.

[43] 'Divorce Before Magistrates' *News of the World* (14 March 1858) 7.

[44] 'The Divorce and Matrimonial Causes Act' *Marylebone Mercury* (20 March 1858) 4.

[45] 'Divorce and Matrimonial Causes Act' *South London Times* (20 March 1858) 4. Jane Astrope went on to secure a divorce in July 1859 on the grounds of adultery and desertion, although the Divorce Court initially doubted whether her husband's 'desertion' had really been a voluntary absence (despite her order from Lambeth magistrates' court): *The Times* (7 February 1859) 9; *The Times* (7 July 1859) 9. Evidently the Court was well aware that magistrates could not be relied upon to define desertion according to matrimonial law, rather than poor law. Astrope though, paid only 5s in fees, and provides a good example of the underappreciated use of the new Divorce Court by very ordinary people: *Return of Rules and Regulations*, Appendix C, 15.

[46] 'The Matrimonial Causes Act' *The Era* (21 February 1858) 14.

Sam Priest told her that he 'loved another better'. When he proposed to go to New York, she said she would sell her business first, lent him £12 from some money she had in the savings bank – and thereafter heard nothing more from him, although she 'had reason to believe he had gone off with the woman he said he loved best'.[47] The adulterous elopement of Pasquale Buonocore of Leicester Square, 'a foreign subject without letters of naturalisation', made particularly good copy, since the Orsini affair had just brought down Palmerston's Government and aliens were the topic of the moment. According to the popular press, Pasquale left his wife Sophie on Boxing Day 1857 with 'everything he could lay his hands on', including another woman, and then wrote from abroad saying he intended to marry his new partner.[48] More humdrum was the 'cruel case' of an upholsterer with an 'extensive and prosperous business in the Whitechapel Road' who went off with one of his female servants, and when upbraided on his return by his wife ('a ladylike person of care-worn aspect'), sent for a broker, sold everything in the house, and left her 'in a state of extreme privation'.[49] Interestingly, very few of the newspaper reports examined here include details to suggest a bigamous marriage had taken place. This could be a result of either the imperfect sample created by the newspaper records, or perhaps the wife's lack of knowledge about her estranged husband's activities. Alternatively, it could be that the wife consciously sought to present her case in the simplest way possible to secure an order without muddying the waters with extraneous details that might well give the legally informed police magistrate the opportunity to refer her up to the Divorce Court to petition for a full divorce.[50]

Plundering husbands were by no means peculiar to London; indeed, belief in their ubiquity was an important *raison d'etre* of section 21 of the Matrimonial Causes Act 1857. Nevertheless, a husband who married, systematically collected his spoils, and speedily departed, is a variant not encountered in the cotton towns in 1858, any more than the husband who promptly resurfaced as soon as his wife had a good salary for him to take. In this London sample there is a distinctive element of the streetwise urban spiv, matched by a gullibility on the part of some of their women not reported in Lancashire.[51] In south-east London, moreover, marital breakdown seems to have happened more quickly – not surprisingly, given the higher incidence of calculating quick-buck bridegrooms, and the rarity

---

[47] 'Protection for Women Act' *News of the World* (1 August 1858).

[48] 'Marlborough Street: Divorces' *Reynolds's Newspaper* (14 March 1858) 10.

[49] 'Cruel Case of Desertion' (Mrs Emilia Sophia Adams) *News of the World* (11 April 1858).

[50] Justices in the police courts would refer applicants to the Divorce Court in cases where they did not believe them to fulfil the criteria of section 21: 'The Ill Effects of an Elopement' *London Evening Standard* (29 November 1862) 5. 'A Forgiving Wife and her Sad Story' *Middlesex Chronicle* (19 September 1863) 7.

[51] The most striking south London marriage scam of all occurred in 1875 in New Zealand when a Lambeth widow married the 17-year-old son of her rent collector and was immediately deserted by her new husband and deprived of her rents by her agent-cum-father-in-law back in Lambeth, who knew that his infant son's agreement to assign all her property to a trustee was invalid: *Kingsman v Kingsman* (1880) LR 6 QBD 122–135.

of husbands who left for extraneous business reasons. Of those marriages whose duration is known, several had lasted only a few weeks or months, and half less than five years, while only three had lasted for more than 10.

Is there any evidence that these men were freeing themselves from the burden of a larger than average family of dependent children, as the husbands of many destitute wives in the agricultural south-east apparently did? Very little. Only six wives in either London or Lancashire emphasised at their hearing that they were or had been maintaining their children as well as themselves. A justice who heard that a wife was keeping her children as well as herself from burdening the parish could be expected to be all the readier to assist with an order and yet only three of the six wives did this. These rather small numbers are hardly surprising, since a lone wife with dependent children must plainly have been much less likely to be able to put herself in a position of economic independence to be eligible for one of the new orders. Barely half the wives in Lancashire were reported as having children, and then rarely more than one or two (small families were common in this part of the north-west);[52] and only a third seem to have had dependent young children at the time of desertion. One Lancashire couple indeed had nine children, but when they separated in 1843 after 14 years of marriage, the husband took five of them with him; children over eight could still be useful earners in these textile towns.[53] It is true that Roger Kay, a Darwen weaver who deserted his wife in 1855 after three and a half years of marriage, leaving her with four children, might well have been escaping a burdensome young family;[54] and dependent stepchildren were always easily resented. One footloose husband, the flagger and slater Noah Slater, refused almost immediately to maintain his new wife's child who was living with her and absconded shortly after he had assaulted her.[55] Agnes Davis's three young children by a previous marriage may help to explain why the drunken weaver Robert, who she married in 1853, deserted her four times in two years, if not why he was drunken and indebted.[56] Overall, however, it is notable how many of these roaming husbands left apparently childless wives and proceeded to father children with other women.

Womanising and adultery predictably figure frequently in the hearings reported in the columns of the popular press. Yet although marriages broken by the attractions of America or Australia provided less good copy than those broken by 'another woman', they must surely have been almost as commonplace in peak periods of emigration. For the 'Determined Emigrant', leaving the country was

---

[52] All women working outside the home had fewer children, and the fertility of textile workers, especially weavers, was particularly low: M Hewitt, *Wives and Mothers in Victorian Industry* (London, 1958) 87.

[53] 'Protection Under the Divorce and Matrimonial Causes Act' *Blackburn* Standard (17 March 1858) 2. Children apparently quite often stayed with the father in the past, they were useful in many occupations: KDM Snell and J Millar, 'Lone-Parent Families and the Welfare State: Past and Present' (1987) Continuity and Change 2, 387, 394.

[54] 'Protection' *Blackburn Standard* (17 November 1858) 3.

[55] 'Matrimonial Causes Act in Blackburn' *Blackburn Standard* (14 July 1858) 3.

[56] 'Application Under the Matrimonial Causes Act' *Preston Chronicle* (15 May 1858) 8.

a familiar way of escaping unwanted legal obligations of every description and Britain's nineteenth century diaspora is likely to have been quite as effective in breaking-up marriages as the eighteenth century wars with France, which have received greater attention.[57] The wife who refused outright to accompany a husband determined to go abroad, or who devised cogent health, family or business reasons to stay behind; or the husband who promised to send for his wife when he had made enough money, sailed and was heard of no more: such stories figure often enough in matrimonial proceedings, and these must be only the tip of a sizeable iceberg.[58] In a great port like London, a husband could very easily be swept into a wave of emigration by his work and companions; less so a wife. Elizabeth Smith's husband, for example, landlord of the 'Ship and Star' in Lower Shadwell on the edge of London Dock, sailed for Melbourne in 1855, leaving his wife with 'four children and £5 or £6'. He came back briefly in 1857 and 'used threats and force to induce her to leave for Australia', but she refused. This story secured an order for Elizabeth Smith, although not, it should be noted, from the first magistrate who heard it.[59]

Still, Elizabeth Smith was more fortunate than Dorothy Sewell, whose husband had been one of the 78,000 United Kingdom citizens who sailed for Australia in the boom year of 1854. Sewell applied to the Divorce Court itself (because she lived in the City, which did not have a Police Magistrate, all City residents were obliged to apply there), but was told by the Judge Ordinary that her affidavit

> omitted to state many material circumstances, for example in what capacity the husband went to Australia; whether since his departure he has failed to contribute to his wife's support; whether he has neglected to write to her, or if he has written, what was the nature of the communication.[60]

Few police magistrates, however, were so punctilious as Sir Cresswell Cresswell JO who led the Divorce Court. Mr WF Beadon of Great Marlborough Street, for one, gave an order to Susanna Moon on hearing that her husband had written to her two years before, telling her that his earnings in Australia were not enough to support them both; and RE Broughton of Marylebone similarly obliged Mrs Vesey, keeper of a small school in Camden Town, who had no better reason for believing her wood-engraver husband to be in Australia than that he had often said he would like to go there.[61]

The destination of deserting husbands was reported more rarely in London than in Lancashire, perhaps because London magistrates and newspaper readers were

---

[57] Kent (n 8); Stone (n 1) 5.

[58] During the brief post-Crimean emigration boom of 1857 some 58,000 people sailed from the United Kingdom to Australasia, the destination of deserting husbands most commonly mentioned at these hearings: BR Mitchell and P Deane, *Abstract of British Historical Statistics* (Cambridge, Cambridge University Press, 1962) 50, Table 19.

[59] See Chapter Six, page 169.

[60] 'Sewell v Sewell' *Morning Herald (London)* (6 December 1858) 7.

[61] 'The Matrimonial Causes Act' *Berkshire Chronicle* (20 November 1858) 3.

less interested than the more insular folk-communities of north-east Lancashire in learning whether absconders had left the neighbourhood. Thomas Edwin, the Leighton Buzzard grocer and Charles Cooper, the Bermondsey dairyman had both definitely been heard of in America, and Hannah Hobbs thought her husband was 'probably' in Australia.[62] George Hale, a Marines ex-corporal, had started a new life in Fareham as a policeman – with a new wife. However, this new-found domestic bliss was cut short when he was imprisoned for bigamy.[63] Jane Astrope's husband had been sentenced to four years penal servitude for repeated embezzlement and robberies, after a spell of adultery in Edmonton. Only Sarah Brown's husband was said to be living as near as Islington, just across the river, despite his talk of going abroad.[64] Perhaps, then, more of these husbands were at a safe distance than their Lancashire counterparts; certainly their wives less often pleaded fear of their imminent return. The Lancashire wives and their solicitors often tried to give their application for 'protection' an air of urgent need, and a considerable proportion of their absent husbands were indeed living near enough for their return to be genuinely feasible. Of the 19 husbands whose whereabouts were mentioned at the hearing, four were still living in the same town as their wives,[65] and eight had made no more than a local move – to Blackburn, Preston, Burnley, Bingley, or (in four cases) the Manchester area. Even those who went further afield stayed broadly within the Lancashire hinterland – Westmoreland, the Glasgow area, and the Isle of Man. Only four went overseas – Luke Jackson to the East on active services, and one apiece to Australia, America, and New Zealand.

Still, many had been absent for so long that their return could hardly have been a real risk. Here, as elsewhere in 1858, magistrates were confronted with an accumulation backlog of long-deserted wives eager to take advantage of the new legislation. A few of these Lancashire husbands had been absent for only a few weeks or months but most had been gone for between two and five years, and several for very much longer.[66] Alice Ellison, for example, had not seen her husband since he left her 15 years earlier to live with another woman in Ryton, yet decided to apply. When asked by the Blackburn justices why she wanted 'protection' in these circumstances, she simply replied that she was 'apprehensive he

---

[62] Edwin: 'Divorce and Matrimonial Clauses (sic) Act' *South-London News* (13 February 1858) 3; Cooper: 'Police Intelligence' *Morning Post* (1 December 1858) 7; Hobbs, 'Lambeth' *Express (London)* (27 October 1858) 4.

[63] Hale: 'A Singular Application' *South London Times and Lambeth Observer* (24 July 1858) 3.

[64] Astrope: 'Divorce and Matrimonial Causes Act' *Marylebone Mercury* (20 March 1858) 4; Brown: 'The Divorce and Matrimonial Causes Act' *Morning Advertiser* (27 May 1858) 7.

[65] Such husbands could be held to have deserted their wives within the meaning of section 21, though in Liverpool a few years later this was not considered to be the case: *Select Committee on Married Women's Property Bill. Special Report, Proceedings, Minutes of Evidence, Appendix, Index,* HC (441) (1867–68) 72.

[66] Mary Pearson, for example, successfully applied five weeks after her husband went, assuring the Justices at Bacup Petty Sessions that he had said he was leaving her altogether: 'Application Under The Divorce Act' *Bury Times* (9 October 1858) 3.

might come back and break up her house', and she got what she wanted.[67] Even when the husband had not been seen for even longer than this, or was safely locked up in gaol, an order might still be asked for – and given. Alice Whalley of Accrington's desire to take precautions against the imminent release from prison of her fraudster husband is understandable, but the usual plea was simply apprehension of being 'sold up' by their husbands.[68] Nine claimed to have already suffered this, just before or just after they were deserted, and far more feared this fate – very plausibly, since clothes and furniture were easily sold and absconding husbands always needed cash.[69]

Just as much as there were common 'types' of absconding husbands, so too there seem to have been three types of women who sought an economic divorce. The first wanted an order simply to secure the personal and household effects they claimed to have acquired by their own 'unwearied industry', or very occasionally with the aid of a small unearned income, against threats which do not seem to amount to a great deal. The *reductio ad absurdum* of such applications was that women such as Mary Marshall, formerly of the Hare and Hounds Inn near Haslingden, applied for (and was incorrectly refused) protection of one table and an old chair against her husband, 'a person of weak intellect, formerly in a lunatic asylum ... accustomed to go off now and then'.[70] Among such women something of a bandwagon effect may well have been at work. Certainly, the continual publicity given to the plight of the industrious wife living in dread of her worthless husband coming back to 'sweep away' her earnings, can only have encouraged such fears, and sometimes emphasising them (or perhaps their invention) was a sure route to success at a hearing.

The second type of applicant, almost equally common, had a more specific objective: to secure their business interests or the tools of their trade, not just against their husband but also against third parties. One of the very first applicants in the north-west was a Blackburn milliner who explained that she had been frequently summoned to the County Court for her husband's debts, and that to avoid his creditors, 'she had had to carry on her business in her father's name, in whose house she lived'.[71] Four more had settled all their husbands' debts and believed them safely on the other side of the globe, but wanted to put themselves into the stronger business position given by the status of *feme sole*, which would allow them to legally contract, sue and raise credit in their own name. Another wife needed that status in order to get access to a small legacy which the executors

[67] 'Application Under The New Divorce Act' *Preston Chronicle* (13 March 1858) 6.
[68] 'The New Divorce Act at Accrington' *Blackburn Standard* (10 February 1858) 3.
[69] Mrs Margaret (Peggy) Cunliffe of Accrington, for example, had 'property in her own right' which brought in 11s a week, and said she wanted protection against her violent, drunken husband returning and selling her household goods yet again: *Preston Guardian* (11 Dec 1858). On this application, see above, text at n 27.
[70] *Preston Guardian* (6 November 1858). Earlier in 1858, Mary and husband William had been brought before the magistrates on charges of selling spirits and tobacco without licenses. Mary was discharged but William was convicted: 'Excise Conviction' *Preston Chronicle* (27 March 1858) 5.
[71] Boardman: *Blackburn Standard* (17 February 1858) 3.

were refusing to pay her (correctly, since a married woman's signature alone could not constitute a valid receipt).[72] With regard to wives as well as husbands, therefore, the experiences recounted at the hearings in these Lancashire cotton towns in 1858 justified both the parliamentary lawyers' hard-headed concern with safeguarding the financial interests of third parties and of both spouses, and the propagandists' sentimental domestic scenario of the hard working wife preyed on by a vagabond husband.

Only a handful of wives in either location attributed a significant role to help from kin, usually in the form of housing, although family support may well have been underplayed, since the Act required justices to be satisfied that the wife was self-supporting. Perhaps surprisingly in the heartland of the married female millworker, only two of the 19 women in Lancashire whose way of making a living was reported, were described as working in a mill.[73] Agnes Davis, the Oswaldtwistle woman with three children from a previous marriage mentioned earlier, was one of these. She explained to the County justices that when the spasmodic absences of the drunken warper she had married in 1853 culminated in his permanently going off to Manchester leaving her with a County Court summons to pay his debts, 'she was obliged to begin to work, to keep her children', and therefore 'went to the mill and learned to wind'. Her sister took a house for her, and by 1858 two of her children were also working, and the future (which she wanted to protect) belonged to her.[74] A similar strategy had served the turn of a life-long Blackburn weaver, Matilda Warburton. After the fellow weaver whom she had married in 1851 brought in the bailiffs to take all their furniture to be sold by auction at the Grapes Inn in 1855 and deserted her for the third time, she went to live with her mother and carried on weaving. By 1858 she had 'saved a little money' (weavers were well paid) and was 'anxious to leave the mill' and 'open a small shop'; that, she explained, was why she wanted a magistrates' order.[75] Warburton's story not only illustrates the comparatively good earnings of Lancashire women power-loom weavers,[76] for they could save as well as support

---

[72] 'Matrimonial Causes Act in Blackburn' *Blackburn Standard* (14 July 1858) 3.

[73] Perhaps some of the remaining 17 were doing so. In any case, this is less surprising that it seems at first sight since although the cotton industry indirectly provided employment to most of the local population, it nowhere employed directly more than about a third: DA Farnie, *The English Cotton Industry and World Market, 1815–96* (Oxford, Oxford University Press, 1979) 76.

[74] See text at n 25. Winding was quieter and easier work than weaving, though rather less well paid and less abundant: J Liddington and J Norris, *One Hand Tied behind Us: The Rise of the Women's Suffrage Movement* (London, Virago Press, 1978) 91–94.

[75] She had traced her husband in Manchester with a young woman, who had had one child; but she had not seen or heard from him for the last two years: 'Application for Protection Under The Matrimonial Causes And Divorce Act' *Preston Chronicle* (12 June 1858) 5.

[76] About 12s. a week in Blackburn in 1860: GH Wood, 'The Statistics of Wages in the Nineteenth Century. Part XIX.--The Cotton Industry' (1910) *Journal of the Royal Statistical Society* 73 585, 587. At the beginning of the cotton famine, one woman investigator reported that since the masters preferred female labour, 'it is quite true that many women do keep their husbands and families; the men merely doing such jobbing work as they can pick up': E Barlee, *A Visit to Lancashire in December 1862* (London, 1863) 31–32.

themselves, but also bears out a Scots lawyer's observation in 1857 that women operatives 'who wanted something better, left the mill and opened a shop or the like' (as indeed men did too).[77]

'Opening a shop or the like' was the most frequent strategy of all the Lancashire wives. Cap-making, dress-making, trading as a milliner and draper, clothes-dealing, food-making and selling, running an inn, a temperance hotel or a brothel, providing board and lodging, or keeping house for working children: these were the enterprises which were most often reported to have enabled deserted wives in the north-west to be self-supporting – not waged employment, still less an income from rents.[78] All were the recognised resorts of widows, and equally the natural resorts of deserted wives, provided they could overcome their legal handicaps as married women. Such ventures could usually be run from home and started with very little capital. To acquire the stock-in-trade and effects of an inn, as did Susannah Barnes of The Wellington in Burnley, was indeed no small matter; but this scale of venture was an exception rather than a rule.[79] Food shops were especially cheap to start.[80] Elizabeth Moulden, for example, decided to apply for an order and 'open a little shop' after she lost her situation in Darwen.[81] If heavier initial expenditure was necessary, a relative or friends might help. Christiana Todd, who it may be remembered had been running a shop in Leeds with her shoemaker husband when he left her in 1855, spent time in Constantinople in service with a merchant's family and held another position as cook in a Birkenhead boarding school, before moving to Blackburn in 1858 because her brother lived there and 'wished her to commence business there'.[82] In these enterprises, what was chiefly needed was personal input: long hours, reliability, effort to please, the right sort of personality, and an eye for a local niche for a personal service.[83] All these a deserted wife – especially one without infant

---

[77] Milne claimed this was because women were never promoted to be overseers: JD Milne, *Industrial and Social Position of Women in the Middle and Lower Ranks* (London, 1857) 227, but 'desire to get away from factory work' was not peculiar to women and had deeper roots than this. In 1868 the editor of the *Blackburn Times* explained that 'the enterprising operative betakes himself to peddling and small trading': WA Abram, 'The Social Position and Political Prospects of the Lancashire Workman' (1868) *Fortnightly Review* 4, 426, 432. Farnie (n 73) 76, 190.

[78] The Irish woman, Sarah Conway, secured an order to protect 'her property and the wages of her children': 'Protection Under The Matrimonial Causes Act' *Blackburn Standard* (11 August 1858) 3. Work on the 1851 census has shown that in Lancashire, Irish women heading households were particularly likely to be housekeeping for their working children, and not otherwise employed: WJ Lowe, *The Irish in Mid-Victorian Lancashire: The Shaping of a Working-Class Community* (New York, Peter Lang, 1989) 85, 91.

[79] 'Applications Under The New Divorce Act' *Burnley Advertiser* (27 February 1858) 4.

[80] J Benson, *The Petty Capitalists: A Study of Nineteenth-Century Working Class Entrepreneurs* (London, Gill & Company, 1983) 116.

[81] 'Application for Protection Under The Matrimonial Causes and Divorce Acts (sic)' *Preston Chronicle* (3 April 1858) 8.

[82] 'Application for Protection Under The Matrimonial Causes Act' *Preston Chronicle* (17 April 1858) 8.

[83] Ellen Barlee heard in 1862 that a great many women in mill towns earned as much or more than the millhands by child-minding (at 3s. per week for each infant under four), preparing their tea-breaks (at 4d. each per week for some 200 hands) and otherwise providing for their daily wants: Barlee (n 76) 27, 128–29.

children – could often provide in abundance. Moreover, buying and selling could give community status as well as earnings, and meet social as well as economic needs. In the 'quasi-peasant society' of north-east Lancashire's 'overgrown villages', where people were doggedly industrious, shrewdly money-conscious, and respected personal relations and material independence, a small shop as a way of making a living was second only to hill-farming in esteem.[84]

A wife engaged in buying or selling had good reason to apply for a section 21 order, even if her husband was on the other side of the globe and his creditors had all been paid. Such an order, and only such an order, would suspend her *coverture* and thus remove the many legal obstacles to turning her own exertions to account faced by every wife, whether deserted or not. Female 'subordination and dependency' was by no means always 'intrinsic to the legislative intent of the state at the time', nor was the purpose of protective legislation always 'the erasure of women's rights to contract'.[85] On the contrary, section 21 of the Matrimonial Causes Act 1857 is proof that protective legislation could sometimes explicitly and deliberately equip women with full rights of contract. Parliament thereby enabled lone wives who were independent in practice to become independent in law and rid themselves of the hindrances to their economic viability fabricated by coverture, while simultaneously equipping themselves to maximise the fruits of their industry, benefit from any windfall they might inherit, and generally exercise their civil rights for themselves. Legislative opinion, after all, was increasingly coming to regard a husband who intentionally deprived his wife of his support and protection as thereby depriving himself of his rights over her financial affairs. He had deliberately put her in the practical position of a widow; it seemed only just, therefore, that the law should put her in the legal position of a widow and give her the rights as well as the burdens of a woman without coverture. Credit was vital for small traders and expected by most of their customers, yet as the sympathetic Scottish lawyer JD Milne pointed out, it was impossible for a wife to 'obtain pecuniary credit, since no one will lend on an obligation that is legally worthless; and her debtors may defy her, for she cannot sue them at law'.[86] An economic divorce immediately removed these legal handicaps, as well as safeguarding her against the seizure by her husband's creditors of her takings or the tools of her trade – a landlady's furniture, for example, or a clothes dealer's stock.[87] There has been very limited research into the bankruptcies of women, particularly women in business outside of London, but evidence suggests that in small firms,

---

[84] Farnie (n 73) 71, 190, 290, 324.

[85] In 1861 in legislating with regard to the irremovable poor, Parliament accepted without discussion the treatment of long-deserted wives as widows: 'if she resides for three years in such a manner as would if she were a widow render her exempt from Removal, she shall not be liable to be removed from the parish wherein she is resident, unless her husband returns to cohabitation', Poor Removal Act 1861, s 3.

[86] Milne (n 77) 294.

[87] In the revised edition of this work, JD Milne acknowledged this: *Industrial Employment of Women* (London, 1870) 295.

men and women traded in very similar ways in terms of business size, strategy, and success.[88] With women accounting for 30 per cent of all business owners in mid-to-late nineteenth century Britain and business ownership offering the potential for social and economic advancement for men and women, establishing oneself in trade, even if just in a very small way, gave deserted wives a very real opportunity to not only survive their husband's desertion, but also to thrive.[89]

Although two of the London wives were housekeepers, and one was engaged as a vocalist, here, even more than in Lancashire, they were predominantly free-lance buyers and sellers – whether of personal services, goods, or accommodation. A dancing teacher, a greengrocer, dairy-keeper, and the owner of an unspecified 'business in the Old Kent Road' all figure here,[90] as well as the usual female cast of a wardrobe dealer, three dress-makers and two landladies.[91] This mix is not surprising and reflects the surrounding population. According to the census of 1871, the proportion of occupied females who were professional entertainers in Lambeth was above average, while in St Saviour's Southwark the proportion engaged in buying and selling was two and a half times greater than the national average.[92] South London's music-hall singer and dancing teacher may thus be seen as counterparts of the Lancashire sample's winder and weaver – women who were earning a living through exploiting opportunities distinctive of their area, rather than through the universal female enterprises connected with dress and lodging which were expanding everywhere.

The third type of wife seeking protection can be found when we start to compare how lone wives in London were supporting themselves and achieving the financial independence which entitled them to seek an economic divorce. In Lancashire, only one wife wanted an order to get access to a legacy; in London two-thirds of applications for which a reason was reported were made in connection with an inheritance – past, present, or prospective. Some of these small-scale heir-esses had been left £50 or £200 by a parent, uncle, or father-in-law (as happened to the long-deserted wife of the Leighton Buzzard grocer who had absconded to New Orleans); others had unspecified 'expectations' from parents, or in the case of the housekeeper Jane Astrope, from her 83-year-old 'gentleman'; and one,

[88] J Aston and P Di Martino, 'Risk, Success, and Failure: Female Entrepreneurship in late Victorian and Edwardian England' (2017) *Economic History Review* 70, 837–58.

[89] C van Lieshout, H Smith and RJ Bennett, 'Female Entrepreneurship: Business, Marriage And Motherhood In England and Wales, 1851–1911' (2019) 44 *Social History*; J Aston, *Female Entrepreneurship in Nineteenth-Century England: Engagement in the Urban Economy* (London, Palgrave Macmillan, 2016).

[90] Respectively, Roxby: 'Southwark' *Globe* (26 January 1858) 4; Beale: 'The Divorce and Matrimonial Causes Act' *South London Times and Lambeth Observer* (13 February 1858) 3; Cooper (n 62); Anon: 2 *Solicitors' Journal* 194 (16 January 1858) and *The Times* (15 January 1858) 9.

[91] Respectively, Freeman: see Introduction n1; Hobbs: 'Protection Under The Matrimonial Causes Bill' *Morning Herald (London)* (27 October 1858) 8; Phelps: 'Divorce Before Magistrates' *South-London News* (27 February 1858) 6; Anon: *South London Times* (16 January 1858); Lancaster: 'Lodging House Keeper' *South London Times* (20 February 1858).

[92] Census 1871, vol 3, Table 13, 22–23.

Martha Bell, wanted to protect an annual income of £100 from house property left by her father.[93] Only one applicant lived entirely on unearned income: the 'fashionably attired' wife of the barrister HC Sirr (recently British Vice-Consul at Hong Kong and Queen's Advocate for the southern circuit of Ceylon), who took a cab to Hammersmith police court and told its dignified magistrate, James Ingham, that she had been deserted at Ostend the previous November and wanted to have protected 'what little property there had been left, such as what a gentlewoman might possess in wearing apparel, jewellery, etc'.[94] This pronounced difference in motivation to seek an order, combined with the differing types of husband who necessitated the application in the first place, suggests that Gaskill's divergence between north and south might have stretched to the magistrates' courts.

Exactly what kind of 'industry' had enabled other applicants to acquire the 'property' they wanted to protect is often not clear. Two women certainly let furnished apartments, one relied on friends and 'my needle', one kept a small school, one was monthly nurse, one was the housekeeper and barwoman of a pub, and a Shoreditch commercial traveller's wife turned to embroidery and artificial flower-making. Otherwise, these reports simply refer to a 'business' – probably a small shop or lodging house, both standard ways for wives and widows to make a living. Susan Bragg, the dentist's wife, for example, told CT D'Eyncourt that after she had been left destitute by her husband in August 1857 with 'only one bed and the refuse of their (her friend) well-furnished house', she borrowed money from her friends 'and set up in a small way of business, which has fortunately prospered', and by April 1858 had 'amassed £50 worth of property, earned by my own industry'.[95]

A fair number of wives applied for an order because of some sort of inheritance. The 'careworn, ladylike' Emilia Adams, for example, after suffering 'extreme privation'; had suddenly inherited 'a considerable amount of property that she wished to protect'.[96] While Mrs Lowry (or Louisa) Litchfield, a 'very respectably dressed and ladylike female', who 'had been supported partly by friends and partly by her needle' after being abandoned to the Islington workhouse by her grocer

---

[93] This property was 'secured to her by trustees, but her husband had threatened her if she did not hand him the proceeds, to spend in dissipation'. Evidently, she thought one of the new orders would be a more effective protection. For Burcham's refusal of this application see: Chapter Six, page 173.

[94] On Sirr (1807–72) and Ingham (1805–90), later Chief Magistrate, see Oxford Dictionary of National Biography (ODBN), available at www.oxforddnb.com. Presumably she was living on the property 'settled upon her trustees' and was trying to damage Sirr's reputation by this application. That a wife might exploit against her husband laws passed for her protection was a common enough theme of anti-sentimentalists: eg a bill against wife-beating prompted the warning that the wife might plot to be beaten in order to bring her husband into court, rid herself of him for a number of years, and disgrace him: *Hansard* HC Deb (series 3) 2 May 1860, vol 158, col 524–25. Mrs Sirr did not know why he deserted her, she told Ingham, except that 'he complained of her being fidgety and irritable' – probably justifiably, since she went on to get her cab driver fined for not giving her a receipt: 'A Singular Affair' *Reynolds's Newspaper* (23 May 1858) 10.

[95] *Morning Herald (London)* (9 April 1858) 8.

[96] 'Worship-Street' *Magnet (London)* (12 April 1858) 7.

husband in 1855, had 'acquired some little property' and was 'expecting some more in a short time from the death of a relative'.[97] Similarly, Susanna Moon of Titchborne Street had 'got some property left her by her mother', although she had also managed to pay off the debts left by her husband when he went to Australia and 'acquire some little property' by her own industry.[98] All these hard-working, small-time heiresses were easily outclassed, however, by Mrs Robert Beauchamp on Westminster, 'an exceedingly well dressed and respectable-looking woman', who had supported her family by her industry for nine years, and wanted to secure an order to not only protect her furniture (presumably she let furnished apart-ments), but also so she could force a Chancery order to pay her £50 from the interest accruing from her uncle Mr Philip Noel's bequest of some money which was to come to her in ten years' time and which her husband 'had talked of coming to London to claim'.[99]

Almost as notable is how often women in London explained that they were applying at the insistence of others, namely friends and relatives who were intend-ing benefactors, as well as executors (who would otherwise be unable legally to discharge their responsibilities). Jane Astrope's employer, for example, was 'anxious to leave her something' but 'wanted to have it placed beyond the control of her husband by obtaining protection under the Act'; similarly, the father of Mary Ann Phelps, a middle-aged dress-maker in Clapham, 'wished her to obtain the order to prevent her husband having future claim upon her'.[100] Other rela-tions or friends had made it a condition of providing 'assistance' in setting up a business that a property protection order was first secured.[101] Only two women, Hannah Hobbs a Waterloo dress-maker and Clarissa Roxby the dancing teacher, seem to have considered an order a necessary part of their business plans entirely on their own initiative. Otherwise, that air of self-reliance and decisiveness so strong in Lancashire wives is much less in evidence. Equally absent is the sense of urgent need to ward off a threatening husband or his creditors.[102] These women, or quite often their friends and relations on their behalf, seem rather to have been looking ahead and applying for an order as a kind of insurance policy in light of their current expected legacies – thus implying their awareness both of the risks of petty entrepreneurship, and the usefulness of one of the new orders to a wife who ran those risks.

[97] 'Clerkenwell' *Kentish Mercury* (31 July 1858) 7.
[98] 'Protection Act' *Morning Chronicle* (28 April 1858) 8.
[99] This bequest, she explained, was then in Chancery: 'The New Divorce Act' *Lloyd's Weekly* (14 February 1858) 4.
[100] For Astrope see n 45; for Phelps, see n 91.
[101] This had prompted the application of Martha Bell, see n 39 and text to n 93, and of the unnamed married woman carrying on a business on the Old Kent Road, see n 36.
[102] The notable fact that over three-quarters of the applications reported in south London in 1858 were made within nine weeks of section 21's coming into operation compared with less than a quarter in north-east Lancashire, probably does not indicate either that Londoners' need for the new facil-ity was more urgent, or that they were swifter to make use of it, but simply that the national popular press (the chief source of reports of Londoners' applications), unlike local newspapers, found these applications less newsworthy after the first few weeks.

Was it also particularly easy there for women purposely to play up to the paternal ideology of protection, and exploit it to their own advantage?[103] Did an order quickly become a way not only of strengthening their hands as earners and providers, but of getting the better of an abusive, inadequate, or irksome husband? Lancashire working women were accustomed not only to looking after themselves, but to speaking up for themselves as well.[104] It would be strange if they did not use all the verbal and histrionic skill at their disposal in order to ensure that they got what they wanted from the two or three relaxed and expansive worthies in the courtroom, all anxious to maintain their social and political capital.[105] After all, no witnesses had to be produced, and no attempt to notify the husband of an application was required, nor indeed was there any prior publicity at all, so it must have seemed an easy matter to get accepted at face value whatever evidence she chose to give, at least by the notably accommodating Blackburn justices.

Despite the different types of absconding husbands that could be found in London and Lancashire, and the increased likelihood of women in London to receive legacies, in both locations the lone wife's usual route to economic independence emerges as petty trading, whether of goods or services. In the cotton towns, where married women had long had easy access to well-paid industrial employment and there was a distinctive culture of self-reliant working wives, this penny capitalism has the air of an independent choice and possibly social and economic advancement; in London however a wife was apparently often guided by the advice or financial help of friends and relations. England's first independent wives in both north and south thus seem very often to have been *tres petites bourgeoises*, getting their living from a combination of their own labour and a very little capital of their own, and with styles of living which were often not necessarily working class. No doubt lone wives often followed this particular survival strategy precisely because it was so well tried and obvious, as well as so adaptable to domestic life. Even in places where industrial employment at good wages was readily available, mid-Victorian married women who needed to make their own living usually turned for preference to some kind of petty entrepreneurialism in which they could use their particular skills – skills of housekeeping, purchasing food and household goods, valuing as well as making and maintaining apparel, and supplying personal needs and likings.

---

[103] For an example of a woman's exploitation of this idea in court in a very different context, see J Fulcher, 'Gender, Politics and Class in the Early Nineteenth Century English Reform Movement' (1994) *Historical Research* 67, 57, 65. A century later the first woman magistrate to sit in the Manchester City Court found herself 'quite often whole-heartedly on the man's side, being rather quicker as seeing through the "helpless little woman" than some of my male colleagues, who were apt to come down heavily on their own sex': G Mitchell (ed), *The Hard Way Up: The Autobiography of Hannah Mitchell, Suffragette and Rebel* (London, Faber and Faber, 1968) 235.

[104] H Benenson, 'Patriarchal Constraints on Women Workers' Mobilization: The Lancashire Female Cotton Operatives 1842–1919' (1993) *The British Journal of Sociology* 44, 613, 617.

[105] For a study of the way in which women successfully used the courts to their advantage in breach of promise cases, see G Frost, '"I shall not sit down and crie": Women, Class, and Breach of Promise of Marriage Plaintiffs in England, 1850–1900' (1994) *Gender and History* 6, 224–45.

None of this is surprising; for although it was well recognised that innumerable women 'made a living by keeping small shops or taking in lodgers',[106] only now is the scale and scope of female owned enterprise in the nineteenth century becoming apparent.[107] The neglect of the history of the barely visible but nevertheless economically productive small-time entrepreneur, together with a disproportionate focus on unoccupied middle-class women, has thus contributed to the belied belief that in the second half of the nineteenth century, with the establishment of the male family wage, 'there was virtually no way that a woman, who normally earned less than half a man's wage, could support herself and children without resorting to private or public charity'.[108] Not only has research into women's waged labour shown that the notion of a family (male earned) wage is seriously flawed,[109] but the evidence given by thousands of lone wives in mid-Victorian magistrates courts demonstrates that there *was* a way for women to be self-supporting; but that way was very often not a wage-earning one at all. Although research from the past two decades has begun to demonstrate the important role women played in the world of business in Britain, further research is required in light of this study to specifically examine the relationship between women – unmarried, lone married, married, and widowed – and formal credit in the mid to late nineteenth century.

The marital experiences and strategies discussed in the newspapers – and subsequently here – are inevitably both one-sided and selective. They reveal very little of the husband's side of the story, and nothing of the experiences of deserted wives too poor, too timid, or too closely enmeshed with kin to claim to be self-supporting in a magistrates court. The samples used are small but they provoke some fresh thought on the splitting up of mid-Victorian couples, and even more on the supposed vulnerability, ignorance, and powerlessness of mid-Victorian women in the face of the need to make a living and an intimidatory, male-dominated legal process. For the women studied, severe poverty had not usually been the cause of their husband's leaving, and it was certainly not its consequence, but this is likely a result of the qualifying criteria set out in the Act; women who did face destitution were in the workhouse, or worse. In London and other centres, as well as in the northern strongholds of female self-confidence and independence, thousands of mid-Victorian wives proved able to declare on oath, like Southwark plasterer's wife Mary Huken in 1858, that 'I gain my own livelihood, and do not require any assistance from my husband towards my maintenance'.[110] These wives supported themselves (and sometimes their children too), usually by their own enterprise, but sometimes by paid employment, and occasionally by a small investment income or inheritance. Some of these women, like some

---

[106] JR Gillis, *For Better, for Worse: British Marriages, 1600 to the Present* (Oxford, Oxford University Press, 1985) 246.

[107] See Introduction, n 31 for a brief but by no means exhaustive description of this literature.

[108] Gillis (n 106) 246.

[109] See Introduction, nn 55 and 57.

[110] 'Divorce Before Magistrates' *Morning Chronicle* (11 March 1858) 7.

men, were helped by networks of friends and kind with commercial advice and credit or help in kind; and when they achieved self-sufficiency, they safeguarded their independence by taking advantage of the facility available from 1858 to any self-supporting deserted wife to regain the legal autonomy enjoyed by unmarried woman and men.

As the following chapter will show, what happened in the courtrooms of London, and above all Blackburn, was not necessarily either intimidatory or distressing to women. Many alert and energetic women successfully turned section 21 of the Matrimonial Causes Act 1857 to their own advantage, sometimes making very creative use of a court appearance. Gendered laws and cultural norms always had to be put into practice not only by chance combinations of personalities, but within a prescribed institutional framework operating in a particular local environment. The court a wife applied to was dependent on where she lived: geographic location dictated whether she made her application to a metropolitan police magistrate, a petty sessional division of a county Bench, or two or three borough justices, with the only alternative being the central Court for Divorce and Matrimonial Causes which sat in London under the Judge Ordinary.[111] The way these very different agents of social administration handled such applications in different places could vary as widely as the manifold local institutions of mid-Victorian England handled any other task.[112] Still, the fact that demand for these orders persisted in Lancashire longer than anywhere else,[113] and well after the Married Women's Property Act of 1882 had ended their usefulness to most women, suggests that they had established themselves firmly in local culture as something an independent married woman living apart from her husband would do well to obtain. Still, as will be seen in the following chapter, to a wife who genuinely needed and deserved protection, a big-city stipendiary could be helpful and obliging, whether from conscientious philanthropy, casual kindness, or sheer haste; and so too could county magistrates or a pair of Borough justices, whether from habitual paternalism or expansive clientelism. Above all, whatever the kind of tribunal she was obliged to use, whatever the geography of power in her neighbourhood, a resourceful wife could always increase her chances of getting what she wanted from the gendered content of the law, by exploiting the equally gendered code of chivalrously supportive behaviour likely to be the public response of an

---

[111] See Chapter Seven.

[112] For an examination of the complex geography of local administrative power in nineteenth century Britain, see M Ogbom, 'Local Power and State Regulation in Late Nineteenth Century Bristol' (1992) *Transactions* 17, 215–26; C O'Reilly, 'Creating A Critical Civic Consciousness' (2020) *Media History* 26, 249; P Jones, S King and K Thompson, 'Clothing the New Poor Law Workhouse in the Nineteenth Century' (2021) *Rural History* 32, 127.

[113] The County Court Circuit covering the area under discussion in this chapter, Circuit 4, was the only circuit in which the number of orders registered was still in double figures in 1893. In 1883–93 the three 'Cottonia Circuits' (Circuits 4, 5 and 8) for the first time accounted for a higher proportion than the metropolitan area of the total number of orders registered in England and Wales, namely 26.7%, as against 23% in the metropolis, most of them in Circuit 47 (Lambeth, Woolwich and Greenwich). See Chapter Four.

all-male court to a plausible appeal by an injured woman for protection against her scoundrelly husband.[114] 'A mischievous and ill-tempered woman could very easily impose on a magistrate' remarked one Home Office under-secretary in 1860.[115] A quick witted woman could play up to the paternalism of either the dignified or the soft-hearted variety as easily as she could to easy-going informality or heavy humour; and however stiff the Bench, she would never have had to handle the battery of formal questions, requirements of corroborative evidence, and long procedural delays common in the Divorce Court.[116]

In 1858 Harriet Martineau may have been too optimistic when she predicted in her column in the *Daily News* that the workings of the new legal resource available to self-supporting deserted wives would help to secure a long-overdue 'full, practical recognition of women as breadwinners'.[117] Still, married women's standing in their community, as well as their personal self-confidence, can only have been strengthened as increasing numbers of middling and working-class wives were able to show not only that they were supporting themselves, but that they possessed all the legal rights and responsibilities of men with regard to property, contracts and suing and being sued. What is certain is that in 1858, English wives in broken marriages acquired a new resource with far-reaching possibilities, and one through which even women in the cotton towns far from London never ran any risk of being overlooked. The fearlessness, self-confidence and independence of Lancashire working women so notable in the suffrage movement between 1884 and 1914, owed much to local traditions of female activity in trade unionism and political radicalism stretching back to Peterloo.[118] Equally, it owed much to a culture where married women were used to going out to work and valued their independence; and in light of this study of economic divorce, it can be added that it owed something to a culture where lone, self-supporting wives had long been accustomed to use their local magistrates' court to secure for themselves the full legal rights and liabilities of a man with regard to property, contracts, and litigation.

---

[114] See Astrope (n 45).

[115] *Hansard* HC Deb (series 3) 2 May 1860, vol 158, col 519–36, debate on an Aggravated Assault Act Bill.

[116] S Horrell and J Humphries, 'Women's Labour Force Participation and the Transition to the Male Breadwinner Family, 1790–1865' (1992) 48 *Economic History Review* 90 and 113.

[117] According to S Bamford, Edwin Waugh (1817–90) (see ODNB) wrote this dialect in 1856 while his wife and children were in the Marland Workhouse and he was living with another woman in Strangeways. Among many parodies was Ben Brierly's 'Go Tar, the Ragged children and Flit': M Vinicius, *Industrial Muse: Study of Nineteenth Century British Working-class Literature* (London, Barnes and Noble, 1974) 212, 235 and fn 27.

[118] Lancashire women were 'the vanguard of British working women': J Liddington and J Norris, *One Hand Tied Behind Us: The Rise of the Women's Suffrage Movement* (London, Virago, 1978) 263.

6

Experiences of Applying for 'Economic Divorce' in Mid-Nineteenth Century London and Lancashire

As Chapter Three has shown, the machinery adopted for implementing section 21 of the new divorce legislation created a dichotomy between those wives who lived in a place with a professional magistrate, and therefore had to apply to him for an order, and the many more who did not. Similarly, Chapter Five has suggested that the reasons why wives were deserted, and their motivations to apply for an order under section 21 differed between north and south. How then, did these two factors converge? Did this much matter? How different were a London wife's experiences in a metropolitan police court, say, from a Lancashire wife's experiences in the courtroom of Blackburn's new Town Hall? This chapter will explore what happened to women as they appeared before the stipendiary magistrates of the metropolitan police courts in London and the lay magistrates in the north west circuits, highlighting the impact that the existing legal mechanisms might have had on the implementation of section 21.

There is certainly evidence to suggest that contemporaries viewed implementation of section 21 as being uneven. In August 1858, the *Blackburn Weekly Times* published a letter from a disgruntled husband – whose gripes (and identity) are explored further below – under the pseudonym 'Legality'. He argued,

> No one will deny for a single moment that (the Divorce Act's section 21) is a useful and valuable measure, and it may be safely said that there is not a town in England where more married women have availed themselves of its protection than Blackburn ... but still there is something very defective in its mode of administration by the local magistracy.[1]

This letter from 'Legality' protested not at what section 21 did, or even at what the Matrimonial Causes Act 1857 did, but at what he perceived to be the 'defective' way that local magistrates were administering the Act. The author identifies two separate issues: first, that the women of Blackburn were using the legislation more frequently when compared to the women of other towns, and second, that the magistrates in Blackburn were also behaving out of the ordinary. This contemporary opinion reflects what has been shown in previous chapters;

---

[1] 'Letter from Legality' *Blackburn Weekly Times* (14 August 1858).

that married women in the north experienced desertion in different ways to their sisters in the south, primarily, it seems, as a result of fewer opportunities for northern husbands to abscond overseas, an increased chance that the women would be relatively well-paid, and a decreased likelihood that they would stand to inherit from family members. These factors combined to create a situation where deserted wives in Blackburn were largely responsible for their own economic security, and they were able to capitalise on the local tradition of female political activism to harness the full potential of section 21 and its protections. 'Legality's' second point – that the Blackburn magistrates were themselves acting outside normal conventions – requires a closer examination of the legal structures in action in each locality, including exactly what went on within the courtroom when these applications were being made and considered.

Crucially, 'Legality' points to Blackburn as a specific example of 'defective' practice, not the other towns in surrounding circuits which Chapter Four has shown also granted high numbers of section 21 orders. Does what happened in neighbouring towns suggest that section 21 was indeed more freely used but less correctly implemented in Blackburn? Blackburn County Court was in County Court Circuit 4, where an average of 18 section 21 orders were registered each year in 1859–61; in 1858 the number was probably higher everywhere (as has already been argued) as courts dealt with the backlog of women who had not previously had access to any legal remedy. County Court circuit returns, however, amalgamated the returns from all courts in that circuit; and those for Circuit 4 thus represent the orders registered at Preston, Chorley, Garstang, Kirkham and Poulton, as well as Blackburn.[2] Figures to compare individual towns or Benches must therefore be sought elsewhere and with no suitable governmental reports available, we must return to newspaper reports.

Of course, figures like these can never establish the exact number of applications heard or granted by any individual Bench, given the uneven coverage of petty sessions proceedings and the potentially erratic coverage of the newspapers. Still, the fact that press reports have been found for 20 section 21 orders granted within Circuit 4 in 1858,[3] two more than the average recorded there in 1859–61, suggests that in this instance, press coverage of cases in that area can be taken to be reasonably complete and accurate.[4] Moreover, from the data presented in Table 6.1, it does appear that Blackburn wives were making a disproportionately high number of applications.

---

[2] In 1858, Blackburn's Circuit 4 adjoined Circuit 10 (Bacup, Bury, Haslingden and Accrington, Leigh, Wigan) and Circuit 11 (Burlet, Clitheroe, Colne, Bradford, Keighley, Otley, Skipton). The annual average number of section 21 orders registered in 1859–61 was 20 in Circuit 10 and 15 in Circuit 11. See Chapter Four for further details of the Court Circuits.

[3] Reports have been found of 14 successful applications in Blackburn, five in Preston (with one further hearing postponed and not further reported), and one in Lancaster (Mary Hothersall, the deserted wife of a former keeper at Lancaster Asylum: *Preston Guardian* (11 September 1858).

[4] See Chapter Four for further discussion of the national uptake of section 21.

Table 6.1 Section 21 applications (With Outcomes) Detailed in Newspaper Reports in Circuits 4 and 10 in 1858

Town	Successful	Unsuccessful
Accrington	1	1
Bacup	1	1
Blackburn	13	1
Burnley	4	1
Bury	3	0
Darwen	1	0
Haslingden	2	1
Lancaster	1	0
Oswaldtwistle	1	0
Preston	4	1

Although London experienced rapid change and population growth in the nineteenth century, its system of magistrates courts had been well established since the late eighteenth century with stipendiary (paid) and legally trained magistrates at the helm.[5] In contrast, the 1850s was a decade of institutional mushroom growth in Blackburn, prompted by the boom in its economy and population in the 1830s and 1840s. In 1851 it had become an incorporated borough, and in 1852 the Conservative Home Secretary, Spencer Walpole, had agreed to give Blackburn its own Commission of the Peace of up to 12 justices.[6] In 1858, two different Petty Sessions were held in Blackburn each week: one for the Municipal Borough itself, when the Borough justices sat, and the other for the outskirts, when County justices sat – although some justices were on both Benches.[7] The busiest of the two was always the Borough Petty Sessions, held on Thursdays in the large courtroom on the ground floor of Blackburn's new Italianate Town Hall,[8] and most of the

---

[5] The Middlesex Justices Act of 1792 established 'seven several Publick Offices to be established in or near the following Places; namely, the Parishes of Saint Margaret, Westminster; Saint James, Westminster; Saint James, Clerkenwell; Saint Leonard, Shoreditch; Saint Mary, Whitechapel; and Saint Paul, Shadwell, in the County of Middlesex, and at or near Saint Margaret's Hill, in the Borough of Southwark, in the County of Surrey, and at each of the said Publick Offices to appoint three fit and able Persons, being Justices of the Peace for the said County of Middlesex, and County of Surrey respectively, to execute the Office of a Justice of the Peace, together with such other Justices of the Peace for the said Counties respectively, as may think proper to attend'.

[6] PA Whittle, *Blackburn As It Is: A Topographical, Statistical, and Historical Account* (Blackburn, 1852) 138.

[7] William Pilkington, Daniel Thwaites, and William Hoole, for example, were both County and Borough justices, and heard section 21 applications at both County and Borough Sessions.

[8] WA Abram, *A History of Blackburn, Town and Parish* (Blackburn, 1877) 377, 386. This massive compilation by the then editor of the *Blackburn Times* is the source of many scraps of information used here.

applications for section 21 orders reported in the local press were made to this Bench; only a few were heard at the County Petty Sessions held on Wednesdays in the Town Hall's smaller courtroom.[9]

THE NEW TOWNHALL, BLACKBURN.

Figure 6.1 The New Town Hall, Blackburn
© Illustrated London News LTD/Mary Evans.

Three distinctive features of the stipendiary magistracy: their professional legal training, their lack of connection to the area where they sat, and their willingness to offer free legal advice to the community, all ensured that what went on at one of their hearings was unlikely to replicate what went on at Blackburn's weekly Petty Sessions. Most immediately apparent was their greater legal awareness in implementing their powers, and their ready resort to practises they had learnt at the Bar. All these metropolitan magistrates were experienced counsel with some years of judicial service, often as a Recorder as well as a police magistrate; and some were writers on legal issues or involved on the fringes of official business. The men who served as Borough justices in the provinces had a markedly

---

[9] Fewer still were heard at Blackburn, Haslingden, Accrington and Over Darwen Petty Sessions. These four places, together with Walton le Dale, made up the Petty Sessional Division of Lower Blackburn in the County of Lancaster: see the map in 'The County of Blackburn' Victoria County History, *County of Lancaster* VI (London, 1911) 236 and *Return of Number of Justices of Peace for each County in England and Wales, 1852–54* HC 110 (1856) 134.

different profile. They were drawn from the local elite, from established members of the landed gentry and from the ranks of the newly risen industrialist mill-owners, whose economic exploits were chiefly responsible for the recent boom in legal and public infrastructure in the area. Not surprisingly, those with formal legal training often paid strict attention to the exact terms of section 21, were inclined to interpret them in the light of their legal context (especially matrimonial property law and the Divorce Court's decisions on matrimonial desertion), and readily examined and cross-examined applicants. There were 21 stipendiary magistrates serving seven police courts in London, who would sit alone to hear cases. Although legislation allowed for 12 magistrates in Blackburn, the great majority of the work in 1858 was dealt with by just two workhorses: the Tory stalwart, Thomas Hart, and the town's leading Liberal and the then current Mayor, William Pilkington, an ex-office chairman of the Borough Bench until his term of office ended in November 1858.

William Pilkington was part of the Liberal-Nonconformist Pilkington clan and even the Tory *Standard* regarded him as a model mayor, for this Liberal Congregationalist and brother of James Pilkington, MP, devoted his leisure and wealth to the welfare of the town, ensuring it possessed schools, chapels, an infirmary – and ornamental fountains in the new Corporation Park. The Pilkington's were matched position by position by the Tory-Anglican Hornby clan, headed up by William Henry Hornby, who had been Blackburn's first mayor in 1851. Both clan-leaders were large mill-owners, paternalist employers and benefactors of the town, and co-existed with little apparent tension, either with their workers or each other: a Hornby and a Pilkington shared unchallenged the presentation in Parliament of this two-Member constituency in 1857 and again in 1859, and Blackburn's leading Liberals were often best labelled 'Lib-Con'.[10] The Hornby man on the bench was Thomas Hart who, by contrast, was never in the limelight, and held none of the town's honorific appointments. He had been returned in the first crop of Councillors elected in November 1851 for the solidly Hornby-Tory-Anglican Ward of St John's and seems to have been a useful Tory dogsbody with the 'mundane humanity' typical of the Hornby style, who could be relied upon to hold a watching brief for Hornby-Tory interests.[11] In 1858 he was present without fail for every hearing by the Borough Bench of an application for a section 21 order, whereas even the assiduous Pilkington was absent on two such occasions. Only one other Justice heard more than one of these applications: Alderman William Hoole, a Liberal veteran of municipal politics and administration who was the

---

[10] The analysis of Blackburn politics and society offered in P Joyce, *Work, Society and Politics: The Culture of the Factory in Later Victorian England* (Harvester Press, Brighton, 1980) was the starting point for much of the analysis here. The usual connections flourished between brewers, publicans, Anglicans, and Tories, and between craftsmen, retailers, dealers, Nonconformists and Liberals, and also between beerhouses, trade unionists., secularists and radicals: ibid 293. The stiff property qualifications kept radical artisans off the Town Council.

[11] Abram (n 8) 376. On the Hornby style, see Joyce (n 10) 187.

proprietary and energetic headmaster of a renowned Nonconformist Academy in King Street which had just launched the young John Morley on his upward climb. Whenever there was 'a hunt for magistrates', a messenger would be despatched to King Street, and Hoole would leave his pupils and 'take the place of the default-ers' on the Bench.[12] If Hart and Pilkington were men who in their different ways cultivated human sympathies, Hoole was a more bracing and astringent charac-ter, renowned for 'accurate teaching and severe exactitude in general habits'.[13] The invariable presence of Hart and Pilkington to counterbalance each other is signifi-cant and sets Blackburn apart from metropolitan London where one man alone made decisions about the cases before him.

This troika of Pilkington, Hart, and Hoole in effect implemented section 21 in Blackburn. Three other justices were each reported as sitting alongside Hart on a single occasion: the big Tory brewer, Daniel Thwaites; Thomas Dugdale, a 'town improver' with high-spending ideas matching his railway and banking interests; and (after he had succeeded Pilkington as Mayor) John Baynes, a Liberal Anglican mill-owner who was a product of Rugby and Oxford. Only once did five Borough magistrates sit instead of the usual two or three, when Hart, Pilkington and Hoole were joined by Robert Hopwood, a former Conservative Mayor (owner of the great Nova Scotia mills and father of the sitting MP for Clitheroe) and another Tory, Dr Richard Martland (the town's veteran medical man). This was surely no accident, for the wife whose application was heard that day had just taken her husband before the County Petty Sessions, and the case had all the makings of a well-published conflict between the two Benches as well as the two spouses.[14] It is surely not an accident that two Liberals are never reported as sitting alone, and only once, the two Conservatives. Blackburn's Borough Bench, although not socially impressive by County standards, reflected accurately the networks of business, political, socio-religious and family relationships between the town's notables, and the equipoise which kept their conflicts low-key; and so too, evidently, did the counterpoised combination of justices who sat to hear applications for economic divorce. All this makes very believable the longer story told by 'Legality' in the *Blackburn Weekly Times*: that Blackburn justices were administering section 21 based on their intrinsic understanding of the socio-economic demands of the locality, rather than with proper regard for the exact wording of the legislation. It follows that Blackburn's recently acquired Borough Bench was chiefly responsible for its reputation as a place where section 21 orders were readily available.

---

[12] *Blackburn Standard* (6 October 1858). Hoole had been Chairman of the Improvement Commissioners until their duties were taken over by the Council in 1854 (and thus responsible for the newly built Market Place and Market House), and Mayor in 1855–56.

[13] J Morley, *Recollections* (London, Macmillan, 1917) vol I, 6 and FW Hirst, *Early Life and Letters of John Morley* (London, Macmillan, 1927) 9–10.

[14] Application of Elizabeth Moulden, *Preston Guardian* (3 April 1858) and *Blackburn Standard* (7 April 1858) and see below, page 173.

THOMAS HART, J.P., 1799-1861.

From an Oil Painting

Figure 6.2 Thomas Hart
© Blackburn with Darwen Library and Information Service.

In stark contrast, the most distinctive feature of the metropolitan police courts, however, was neither the personal dominance of one man at each of their sittings, nor their lack of intimate connection with their jurisdiction, but rather, their role as an informal Citizen's Advice Bureau – a role which demanded that they have an accurate and comprehensive grasp of the law. Married women in the poorer districts of east and south east London especially, had long been in the habit of regarding their local police magistrate as a freely accessible, fair, and sensible adviser, who would bring the law miraculously to bear upon their family troubles. The emotive and easily misunderstood name given to the new magistrates' orders available from 1858, ensured that 'protection order' took lasting pride of place in London working women's confused expectations of help from their police court. (The mistaken popular belief that the new Divorce Act empowered magistrates to end an abusive marriage altogether has already been noted.)[15] 'For the thousandth time I explained there was no such thing as a protection order', groaned a newly-appointed and ill-informed magistrate on a typical morning in August 1890 in his east end court;[16] but a generation earlier even the newest police magistrate would readily have explained to each woman that he could give a protection order for a wife's property but not her person,[17] and offered her personal guidance on its appropriateness.

In south-east London it was certainly quite common in 1858 for a deserted wife to go direct to the magistrate before he took his seat on the bench, explain her circumstances, and seek his advice on how best to make use of the new Act. Two days after it came into force, for example, a 'respectable-looking female' who let lodgings, came to Mr Boyce Combe at Southwark police court and asked him to divorce her from the husband who had deserted her three years before. Combe explained that he had no power to do this but could give her 'protection' if she had any property of her own or was earning her own livelihood, although he observed that her husband could come and claim the furniture which was her means of support, as he supposed he had left her in possession of it. When she replied that her first husband had left her and her daughter about £200 worth of furniture, 'therefore her present husband could have no claim on that', Combe said 'he should like to see the will before he gave any further advice' (wisely, since if the legacy had not been left to her for her separate use, it would have passed automatically to her second husband), but volunteered that if she was in any business where she was earning her own livelihood he could protect her and her property. The applicant thanked his worship for his advice and left the court promising to bring the will on a future day, when she hoped to obtain a divorce from her 'brute of a husband'.[18]

The case of the 'respectable looking female' who let rooms, and whose case was heard by Boyce Combe, illustrates not only London wives' ready access to free legal advice, but also the invincible popular conviction that section 21 enabled a magistrate to grant 'a divorce'. Three weeks later another 'decent-looking

---

[15] See Chapter One.

[16] An hour or so later he told a very old woman, 'I think the best thing for me to do will be to put a large notice on the door of the Court to the effect that there is no such thing as a protection order': M Williams, *Later Leaves: Being The Further Reminiscences Of Montagu Williams* (Macmillan & Co, London, 1891) 308, 316. Williams was a successful Old Bailey counsel who had been invalided out to the police courts. His misapprehensions are followed by J Davis, 'A Poor Man's System of Justice: the London Police Courts in the Second Half of the Nineteenth Century' (1984) 27 *Historical Journal* 302.

[17] Magistrates commonly bound over violent husbands to keep the peace even for relatively minor offences and were willing to imprison those who did not comply. See: J Hurl-Eamon, 'Domestic Violence Prosecuted: Women Binding over Their Husbands for Assault at Westminster Quarter Sessions, 1685–1720' (2001) *Journal of Family History* 26, 435, 437, 449.

[18] 'Southwark': *Globe* (14 January 1858) 4.

middle-aged female', Priscilla Pearce, applied to George Norton at Lambeth 'for advice and assistance' because her father's executors refused (quite properly) to pay the legacy he had left her until she obtained the sanction and signature of her husband. Norton told her that if she wished he could give her a certificate under the new Act which would protect from her husband and his creditors any property she might have acquired since she and her husband separated (an offer she immediately accepted), but that 'he could not arm her with any authority to compel the executors to pay the money', which was sound enough at the time, for it was not until May that the Master of the Rolls established that an order enabled a wife to compel the executors of a will to pay her a legacy without her husband's signature.[19] There is undeniably a certain piquancy about Norton's volunteering to protect this wife's property by means of the very legislation commonly attributed to his estranged wife's eloquent denunciation of his own interference with her earnings and inherited property.[20]

In the neighbouring district of Wandsworth, JT Ingham volunteered even more detailed advice to a Clapham dress-maker, Mary Phelps, explaining that she could make it quite certain that her husband could touch neither her property she currently held nor the inheritance she expected from her father, either by persuading her father to give her immediately what he intended her to get after his death and then applying for an order, or by leaving the property to trustees for her life. When she replied that her father had already done this, Ingham said he would grant an order to protect her earnings and the property acquired since her desertion three years ago.[21] The more 'the wife's protecting order' became a 'household word',[22] the more magistrates were called on to give advice upon its uses. Mr Paynter of Westminster, for example, had to assure a woman whose husband had absconded in order to escape affiliation payments that she did not need to get an order to protect her 'little things' from being seized to pay the arrears now due to his illegitimate child's mother: her husband would first have to be captured upon a warrant, and since he was taking good care to prevent that, 'her furniture was perfectly safe', though one imagines this was of little comfort to the wife.[23] The readiness with which deserted wives came to consult a particular magistrate in this way provides a fair guide to his local reputation and the perception that he would 'see them right'.

In London then, the way section 21 worked depended not only on the informal advice a magistrate gave on the usefulness of an order in a wife's own personal circumstances, but also on his sole judicial decision; and this ready availability of

[19] 'Lambeth: Relief Under the Divorce and Matrimonial Causes Act' (5 February 1858) 7. See Chapter Two.
[20] M Poovey, 'Covered but Not Bound: Caroline Norton and the 1857 Matrimonial Causes Act' (1988) *Feminist Studies* 14, 467.
[21] 'Wandsworth: Important To Wives Requiring Protection Orders Under The New Divorce Act' *Morning Herald (London)* (10 March 1858) 8.
[22] This was the state it had achieved by 1860, in the no doubt partial opinion of JF Macqueen, *A Practical Treatise on Divorce and Matrimonial Jurisdiction Under the Act of 1857 and New Orders* (London, W Maxwell, 1858) 379.
[23] 'Protection from a Vagabond' *Lloyd's Weekly Newspaper* (23 May 1858) 4.

authoritative advice probably partly explains deserted wives' markedly less frequent use of solicitors in London than in Blackburn. In Southwark and Lambeth, for example, a solicitor was present in 1858 at barely over half the reported hearings, whereas in Blackburn, virtually every wife was accompanied in court by a 'legal adviser'. This could have been due to the fact that in Blackburn, where justices who were already busy men of affairs and not born to the Bench, they had neither the time nor the legal ability to provide the free advice seen in the London police courts. The Borough justices' gentlemanly Tory Clerk, for example, a Mr Henry Hoyle of Little Harwood Hall, was conspicuous for neither zeal nor assertiveness.[24]

Figure 6.3 John Pickop
© Blackburn with Darwen Library and Information Service.

[24] In 1856 Hoyle failed to send a return of the Justices of the Peace sitting for the Borough: Return of Number of Justices of Peace for each County in England and Wales, 1852–54 HC 110 (1856) 134. He plumped for Hornby in the contested election of 1852: *Blackburn Standard* (23 June 1852) and in 1853 was appointed Clerk, an appointment he retained for 20 years: Abram (n 8) 560.

Figure 6.4 Thomas Ainsworth
© Blackburn with Darwen Library and Information Service.

Each of the Blackburn wives except one (an Irish immigrant), was 'supported' by a solicitor;[25] and that solicitor was virtually always either the Tory, John Pickop, or the Liberal, Thomas Clough. Since Blackburn had no shortage of solicitors (some 45 were then practising in the town),[26] it is clear that these two men had quickly established themselves as the town's 'divorce' specialists, whether intentionally, in order to exploit a promising source of income and professional reputation, or simply as the result of becoming known for handling these novel applications successfully. The two could hardly have been more different; and this is surely another manifestation of that Tory-Anglican, Liberal-Nonconformist dualism which pervaded the town's life. The 25-year-old Pickop, whose yeoman ancestors had lived in the

---

[25] Sarah Conway's application was only very briefly reported. She had pursued her husband from Sligo to Blackburn and was given an order protecting 'her property and the wages of her children': *Blackburn Standard* (11 August 1858) 3.

[26] The *Law List* shows 27 solicitors in Blackburn with practising certificates, and it was estimated in 1853 that two-fifths of the profession did not take out certificates: H Kirk, *Portrait of a Profession: A History of the Solicitor's Profession, 1100 to the Present Day* (Oyez Publishing, London, 1976) 114.

area for generations, was the self-confident only son of a mother widowed when he was two and had just joined his uncle in the practice of the law. Barely a fortnight before he appeared in the Borough courtroom on 11 February in support of one of the first two wives to apply there for a section 21 order, Pickop had audaciously pointed out that the very well-connected and long-serving Town Clerk, Thomas Ainsworth,[27] had 'got up his case in a very unsatisfactory manner' in a municipal *cause celebre* ('I have taken every pains', spluttered Ainsworth, 'but a boy like this …'), and then told the Bench that they had misunderstood the new Summary Proceedings Act.[28] This irrepressible young man's client was heard second on 11 February, as was only proper, for the other wife's solicitor was one of the town's hereditary elite, Henry Brock-Hollinshead, a partner in a long-established family firm specialising in local government work (Ainsworth, Hargreaves and Kay) who had only just ceased to be Borough Treasurer, and was a Clerk to the County magistrates and Clerk to Darwen Local Board of Health, as well as churchwarden of Holy Trinity church and a mason.[29] Fortunately for this part of Pickop's practice, however, 24 hours before the third application to the Borough Bench was heard, Brock-Hollinshead died suddenly, and that application as handled by his partner Kay; thereafter this elite firm seems to have withdrawn from such cases. Pickop's only competitor in Blackburn for 'divorce' work became Thomas Clough, a man altogether outside Blackburn's network of hereditary social leaders. Clough had been elected a Councillor for St Mary's Ward in the Liberal electoral triumph of November 1852. Thereafter he sedulously campaigned for a Public Free Library in the town,[30] but never rose higher than the Vice-Chairmanship of the Blackburn Board of Guardians, that bottom rung of borough politics and 'bastion of petty authority'.[31] For the rest of 1858 these two men virtually monopolised 'divorce' work in Blackburn. One wife alone turned elsewhere; and as it happened, hers was the only application that failed.[32]

---

[27] Ainsworth was also a Clerk to the County magistrates, Clerk to the burial board, and the like, and connected with the Preston legal clan of that name.

[28] Pickop was defending a cottage-owner who had been summoned for non-payment of charges for the Corporation's lavish recent improvements. He cleverly took 'every possible technical objection', finally telling the Bench that they must abandon their notion of submitting the case to the Queen's Bench under Summary Jurisdiction Act 1857 s 2, since what was as issue was fact, not law: *Blackburn Standard* (3 February 1858) 2. Not surprisingly, Pickop soon developed a successful practice. In 1873 he became a Borough Justice and Mayor: Abram (n 8) 582.

[29] 'Death of Henry Brock-Hollinshead' *Blackburn Standard* (17 March 1858) 3. Brock-Hollinshead's mother-in-law was a Hargreaves and his grandmother an Ainsworth.

[30] As it happened, when at last the Public Free Library moved into its magnificent permanent building in June 1874 it was opened by none other than John Pickop, then Mayor; Clough had to be content with one of the places on its management committee reserved for non-members of the Town Council: Abram (n 8) 378–79.

[31] The phrase is that of Joyce (n 10) 151.

[32] Isabella Slater's solicitor was the uncertificated 'Mr H Backhouse', presumably a scion of TJ Backhouse, the Burnley and Blackburn attorney and the same 'Mr Backhouse' who had acted for the first Burnley applicant for a section 21 order *Burnley Advertiser* (27 February 1858) 4, which again suggests that these women chose a lawyer known locally to specialise in handling such cases. Slater failed because the Borough police pointed out that she 'kept a private brothel': *Preston Guardian* (10 July 1858) and see below, page 183.

More hearings were reported in south London than anywhere else by the London press,[33] and in that area a solicitor specialising in 'divorce before magistrates' emerged even more quickly than in Blackburn. The first woman in the country to secure an order, it will be remembered, was a client of Joseph Solomon, of the firm of J and S Solomon in Finsbury Square and Borough Road; and within a month at least five more of his clients had also secured orders from the Lambeth, Southwark, and Wandsworth courts. No doubt the press publicity given to Solomon's early successes helped to bring him more local business of the same court; equally, the early failures of the other leading practitioner in the Southwark court, William Edwin, must have lost him such clients.[34] Every police court, however, had a few attorneys who regularly practiced there, often from offices located next door to the courtroom, where they were well-placed to pick up work; and attorneys like these were adept at exploiting the system to a client's (or their own) advantage. George Fletcher, for example, a specialist in sea-wages and shipping cases whose offices were next door to the Thames police court in Arbour Square, off Commercial Road in Stepney, knew precisely what to do when his client Mrs Smith's application for an order was firmly turned down by the sitting magistrate there, Edward Yardley: he took her instead to John Hammill at the Worship Street court in nearby Shoreditch, telling him she lived in the Worship Street district. (In fact her pub, 'The Dolphin', was on the border of the two districts.) 'Mrs Smith repeated the statement she had made to Mr Yardley and Mr Hammill immediately granted the order.[35] In better-off areas like Marylebone and Westminster, however, applications were likely to use a firm with a general practice in the neighbourhood rather than a specialist in police court work, although such a firm would usually send to the hearing only an articled clerk, or at best its managing clerk, an uncertificated practitioner[36] or a junior partner.[37]

The processes observed in the London magistrates' courts then seems quite different from those of Blackburn in 1858, where four or five men settled the way the new practical separation orders operated. The Tory Thomas Hart and a Liberal

[33] This was probably not the result of over-reporting, but a reflection of the social and economic nature of the district. A later police magistrate commented that Lambeth had more than its share of matrimonial disputes at the turn of the century: C Chapman, *The Poor Man's Court of Justice: Twenty-Five Years as a Metropolitan Magistrate* (London, Hodder and Stoughton, 1925) 98.

[34] 'The New Divorce Act' *London Evening Standard* (15 January 1858) 8. Mr Edwin tried hard to persuade Boyce Combe to grant his client an order but was unsuccessful as Combe decided that an absence of five weeks did not equal a desertion.

[35] 'Thame': *Morning Herald (London)* (12 October 1858) 8. Yardley's reaction had been to refuse to grant an order before it was actually needed, Hammill's was to give one without ado to a legally eligible application.

[36] One such produced 'documentary evidence' and won congratulations from WF Beadon of Great Marlborough Street on having 'got up the case very well': 'Marlborough': *London Evening Standard* (11 March 1858) 8.

[37] Quite soon after he joined his father's firm in Holborn, George Lewis (1833–1911) (see Oxford Dictionary of National Biography (ODBN), available at www.oxforddnb.com) – later Society divorce lawyer *par excellence*, intimate of Edward VII, a knight, and finally a baronet – appeared at Marylebone police court for one of the first applicants dealt with there by the ageing RE Broughton, Mrs Vesey, a wood-engravers deserted wife who kept a small school in Camden Town.

justice (most likely the cordial Pilkington) heard each wife's application, which was usually supported in the courtroom by Pickop or Clough, depending on whether the wife's connections were in the Tory-Anglican or Liberal-Nonconformist camp. Pickop (or Clough) gave the date and place of his client's marriage, submitting her marriage certificate as evidence; then he described the absent husband's bad behaviour and any previous desertions, giving details of any appearances before the Bench for assault or 'neglecting his family'; and finally he called the wife, who then confirmed his statements on oath – whereupon Pilkington (or in his absence the senior justice present) usually 'at once', 'immediately' or 'without hesitation' told her the order she required was granted, often adding 'with great pleasure' or 'very willingly' – phrases not reported to have been used at other Petty Sessions in the area.

Was the almost invariable success of Blackburn wives' applications the result of Blackburn justices' laxity, or was it simply the result of employing the right lawyer? In semi-rural Accrington, Haslingden, Bacup, and Darwen, where solicitors were rare, only one out of eight applications was handled by a lawyer; whereas in urban Blackburn (and Preston), where they abounded, virtually every wife was 'supported' by a solicitor. This is easy to understand. Not only were there more practising lawyers per head of the population in the 1850s than today, but they had not yet been made inaccessible to ordinary people by professionalisation, higher fees and status, and increased formality in legal life. Defendants before early Victorian lay justices were said to 'raise a guinea at any sacrifice' in order to secure a lawyer's presence[38] and familiarity with this attitude to a court appearance may have led these wives too to believe that they would be more likely to succeed if they took a solicitor with them, particularly one with a well-publicised tally of successes. Were they right? Blackburn's 'divorce' specialists were certainly worth their fee (probably a moderate 6s. 8d.), if success is the yardstick, although success seems to have been easily come by. Each made it his business not only to prove all the facts required in the Act, but to deflect any probing into those facts by making much of the husband's general neglect of his 'duties' and of any convictions he might have had, while picturing the wife as a hard-working victim and ignoring anything to her discredit. More important still, surely, each was well known to the Bench through regular appearances before them, and above all, through personal links with the network of political, social, and family connections between the town's leaders. Young John Pickop (that future mayor) was already prominent in the town's most contentious affairs; Brock-Hollinshead and his partner John Hargreaves Kay were at the head of its legal elite, and members of the Bench frequently sat on multiple, over-lapping committees that governed the local civic community. Having the right lawyers cannot be the whole explanation of Blackburn wives' success, although no doubt it helped. Only one of the six unsuccessful wives from the other towns in this sample had no lawyer at all; and although one of these unsuccessful

---

[38] Sir G Stephenson, *Magisterial Reform Suggested in a Letter to Viscount Palmerston* (London, 1854) 8.

legal advisers was uncertified, and another merely a lawyer's clerk, two were leading Preston solicitors. In the fifth case, at Accrington, the effect of her lawyer's
successful presentation of Peggy Cunliffe's husband as a drunken, idle parasite
was destroyed a week later at the adjourned hearing (required only because her
marriage certificate was carelessly not brought to the first hearing), when in her
solicitor's absence, she let slip that she had left her husband, and not vice versa.[39] It
is difficult to attribute other refusals outside Blackburn to the absence, negligence
or other shortcomings of the wife's legal man.

The Matrimonial Causes Act of 1857, with its poorly defined clauses and
inadvertent loopholes, led some magistrates in London to feel their way in the
first few weeks more cautiously than others. One such magistrate was William
Corrie of Clerkenwell.[40] Corrie's first applicant under section 21 was a 'respectably dressed and ladylike woman' who was planning 'to improve her means' by
letting out furnished apartments. He questioned her very closely about her property, and then told her it seemed to him her application was made too early. The
Act allowed the magistrate to give a 'protecting order' only for earnings and
property acquired since desertion, he explained, and it seemed she had none; but
if she went and purchased furniture, he would give her an order for that. When
she replied that if her husband heard she had purchased anything, 'he would
most assuredly return and take it', Corrie told her that another question arose
before he made an order, namely, whether the husband should not be present;
and asked if she knew where he was and would like him to be served with a
summons to be present when an order was made, so that he might be able to
offer any objections he had. On hearing that she knew where he was but would
not like him to be present, he first said that he should not like to make an order
unless he was there, but then had some sensible second thoughts. Perhaps he
speculated (quite correctly) the intention for the order to be made first and then
for the husband to appeal if he thought proper. Could she produce any witnesses
to give evidence of her husband's desertion? When she said she could, Corrie
told her she had better bring them, and then he would see about the order. She
'thanked him for his attention and said she would most assuredly bring them
forward her witness'. Throughout these exchanges, Corrie was evidently grop-
ing for a practical procedure in implementing section 21 of the new Act which
could reconcile the realities of a deserted wife's situation with his professional

[39] On learning this, the two justices concerned, G Walmsley and the recently appointed J Grimshaw,
ordered the husband instead to find surety to keep the peace, or in default serve 21 days; *Preston
Guardian* (11 December 1858) and *Burnley Advertiser* (18 December 1858) 3. The *Advertiser* perhaps
chose to depart from its usual practice of not reporting such cases because these justices had emphasised that their new power was limited to the desertion of *husbands* and had returned to the traditional
way of dealing with marital misbehaviour.

[40] Corrie had briefly practised as a solicitor before moving to the Bar and had been a police magistrate since 1851. He moved to Bow Street in 1860, and then in 1864 became City Remembrancer:
F Boase, *Modern English Biography* (Truro, Netherton and Worth, 1892) vol I, A–H, 723.

instinct to hear the other side and get evidence of the material facts from reliable witnesses, particularly when interfering with property rights.[41]

Corrie was unfortunate in having a first application which was both a border-line case, and one in which the evidence had not been pre-digested and neatly presented by a solicitor. Across the river in Lambeth, GP Elliott was able to grant the country's first 'protecting order' to Lucy Freeman (who we met in the Introduction) without ado in January 1858. The customary courtroom procedure (precisely like that followed in Blackburn) worked smoothly at this hearing in Kennington Lane. First, the wife's solicitor, Joseph Solomon, narrated the circumstances which he claimed established his client's eligibility for an order; then the wife herself was sworn, and corroborated his statement on oath, adding a few details; finally Elliott, the sitting magistrate, having on this first occasion 'read through the clause' (that is section 21), 'without hesitation' granted an order.[42] That was the end of the matter so far as the magistrate was concerned. All that remained was for the clerk to fill in one of the certificates from the ready printed supply he soon kept on his table and handed it to the wife in exchange for a fee of two shillings.[43] It was left to her responsibility to register it at the nearest County Court.

Lucy Freeman's application would probably have been successful in any court-room in the land, for Solomon had shown not only that she was a deserted wife maintaining herself by her own industry, but also that her husband had previ-ously been imprisoned on a charge of desertion in that same courtroom. Elliott's next hearing was also plain sailing, for the same reason.[44] His habits and skills as a barrister were only called into play at his third hearing, when he quickly dealt with a long story told by a shoe-maker's wife who had no solicitor by asking a few pertinent questions: why did he leave? Do you know where he is? Have you acquired any property since he left? Upon hearing her answers he promptly replied 'Well, you may have an order'.[45] Perhaps in the absence of pre-existing social, political, and economic ties to the area, the barrister-magistrates in London often took some pains to establish the circumstances of an applicant, particularly whether the already possessed property came within the terms of the Act, rehearsing the law of matrimonial property as they did so. Corrie's early wariness of granting an order to protect merely expected or intended acquisi-tions, proved typical of the metropolitan magistracy, although some were more

[41] 'Clerkenwell: Protection of a Deserted Wife's Property' *Lloyd's Weekly* (24 January 1858); 'Applications Under The New Divorce Act' *Solicitor's Journal*, II (6 February 1858) 275–76. Perhaps Corrie's request for witnesses was a way of postponing a decision while he considered his course of action; certainly later they were not usually required. Not until early March did he grant an applica-tion as a matter of routine, simply explaining to the wife that she must now go to the County Court and register her order: 'Divorce before Magistrates: The New Divorce Act' *News of the World* (7 March 1858).

[42] 'Police Intelligence' *Sun* (London, 20 January 1858) 4.

[43] 'Marrying for a Lark' *Reynold's Newspaper* (21 February 1858) 10.

[44] Mary Ann Brown, whose husband had been summoned in 1854 for neglecting his wife and children, *South London News* (30 January 1858).

[45] C Geary, 'The New Divorce Act' *South London News* (6 February 1858).

relaxed in their questioning than others. A particular stickler was TB Burcham of Southwark. Mrs Martha Bell was given an outline of matrimonial property law in the course of his interrogation in February 1858, as he first elicited that her house property was 'secured to her by trustees', and therefore she did not need an order for that, and then that her furniture had been in her house before her desertion, and therefore belonged to her husband. He was 'extremely sorry' for Mrs Bell, he concluded, but he could not grant her the required order at present.[46] Similarly, Burcham first investigated whether the Bermondsey dairy-keeper Elizabeth Cooper's husband had left her any cows when he absconded to America seven years earlier (if he had, she would not have been deserted in law, since she would have been left the means of supporting herself);[47] next, told her that the furniture he had left behind 'decidedly belongs to him'; and finally (and surely mistakenly) refused her application, because 'the Act could not protect earnings from a milk walk'.[48] Indeed, that busy man of affairs, Henry Selfe of the Thames Court, apparently remembered his matrimonial property law better than he did section 21, for he asked the first wife who applied to him 'if the property was acquired before marriage, or after?', although all that mattered at such a hearing was whether it had been acquired before or after *desertion*.[49]

Questions from the Bench in Lancashire concerning any aspects of the case were rare. One wife, Elizabeth Moulden née Duckworth, was 'examined at length', and moreover by a full Bench of five – but very understandably, for when this woman had brought her husband before the Court of Petty Sessions for assault the previous week, he had claimed that she was living with another man and was disowned by all her friends, and asserted as proof of this that he was now living with her mother. When she appeared to apply for an order under section 21, the Borough magistrates accordingly asked her where her husband was living. She replied that her husband was living with her mother, yet the magistrates did not pursue this line of questioning and declared that they 'had great pleasure in granting the application'. They had accepted her story, for reasons which can only be surmised (indeed, some of them may have been sitting on both occasions). There is no indication in the press report that the magistrates made any attempt to investigate whether she had indeed given her husband 'reasonable cause' to leave her, nor that anyone in the courtroom appreciated that her black eyes were irrelevant in establishing her eligibility for a section 21 order, however important they had been in substantiating her charge of assault the week before.[50]

---

[46] 'Divorce before Magistrates' *News of the World* (28 February 1858) 7.

[47] See Chapter Two, page 86.

[48] *Reynold's Newspaper* (5 December 1858); *cf* also Burcham's questioning of Mary Huken, 'Divorce Before Magistrates' *Morning Chronicle* (11 March 1858) 7.

[49] Since this particular wife had been deserted only three days after her marriage, Selfe's confusion of the two is perhaps excusable: 'Divorce before Magistrates' *News of the World* (21 February 1858) 7. Selfe was London agent for Canterbury, New Zealand and sat on the Weedon commission to investigate contractors' supply of clothing to the troops in the Crimea.

[50] On this case see n 14.

Apart from Moulden, the only other applicant questioned was seemingly the wife of a failed Preston businessman who had absconded to New Zealand, and whose creditors included 'Mr Pedder the banker' and 'Mr Jackson the share broker', two prominent Preston figures with links to the Blackburn cottonocracy. This is no doubt why Pilkington asked whether there was any property which could be said to belong to her husband's creditors before he (and Hart) agreed to grant her section 21 order.[51] Witnesses, moreover, were never called – although at one Wednesday hearing, Clough's involvement in poor law administration was rewarded when the Guardian and rate collector for his client's township of Great Harwood (who were both in the courtroom), confirmed his damning account of a Mrs Bradshaw's husband. He was 'one of the worst characters in the country', they declared, and at this, the Bench 'without the slighted hesitation', granted her order.[52] With questioning from the Bench being such a minor and unusual event in proceedings, the onus really was on deserted wives to present their information in the best light possible, appealing particularly to the local knowledge of the Bench, and wait for their order to be granted. In this respect, employing a solicitor to direct their testimony (and prompt them when to keep quiet as much as when to speak) was perhaps money well spent by an applicant, regardless of any potential laxity on the part of the magistrates.

Another difference in the way that section 21 was implemented in Blackburn and London was through their respective positions on granting an order as an insurance policy to safeguard future acquisitions and earnings, rather than those already acquired. Blackburn justices were willing to grant orders based on the desire of a deserted wife to go into business in the future, a position that was absolutely not shared by the London magistrates, who had been known to refuse an order even if the applicant was already supporting herself, but whose penny-capitalist enterprise was not deemed to be a true business by the upper-middle class male magistrates.[53] Greater familiarity with matrimonial property law and awareness of the criticisms of section 21's loose draftsmanship current in London legal circles may possibly have made them more alert to the risk of wrongly depriving the husband's creditors of assets which properly belonged to them. Moreover, until the amending legislation of August 1858 was passed, there was some doubt whether an order would cover property not already in the wife's possession on the date when it was made,[54] so the insistence that the wife must already have acquired the property she wanted to protect might reflect not only a strict reading of the statute, but concern for the wife's own interests. Still, this cannot be the only

---

[51] *Preston Guardian* (4 December 1858).

[52] Clough had stated that the husband, William Bradshaw, had been imprisoned five times for assault and neglect of family: 'Application for Protection' *Blackburn Standard* (13 October 1858) 3.

[53] See Elizabeth Sophia Cooper's inability to secure an order for her business of a milk run: *Morning Post* (1 December 1858) and above, page 173.

[54] JT Ingham of Wandsworth helpfully explained this point to a wife seeking to safeguard the 'provision' her father intended to make for her: *Reynold's Newspaper* (14 March 1858). Ingham was Chief Metropolitan Magistrate, 1876–90.

explanation of this attitude, for even after legislation had clarified this position, some magistrates still refused to grant an order not immediately needed. Edward Yardley of the Thames Court, for example, told Mrs Eliza Smith that since her husband was in Australia and his creditors had all been paid, there 'would be time enough to apply if he returned and molested her': in his eyes, section 21 should be a *reactive* piece of legislation, rather than the *proactive* as seen in the north.[55]

The barrister-magistrates, then, were more likely to cross-examine a wife on the legally relevant issues than Blackburn's lay justices, and less likely to be content with a victim-centred narrative of a husband's ill-treatment and misbehaviour. Nevertheless, London hearings were not necessarily unsympathetic legalistic ordeals. What mattered more was who heard an application, for a second distinctive feature of a police court was its unique responsiveness to the judicial style of one man – the sitting magistrate of the day. A metropolitan magistrate's social as well as professional and official rank and prestige created a gulf between himself and the attendant clerks and practitioners and ensured that his personal temperament set the court's tone. He might not preside over the same court for long, for there was a clear professional career ladder, ascending from Thames and Worship Street in the east end to the far more desirable courts within easy reach of clubland and residential west London, and most metropolitan magistrates climbed its rungs as swiftly as vacancies, seniority and influence as the Home Office allowed; only a few stayed among the poor for the whole of their working lives.[56] While he was in post, however, his worship's distinctive habits in dispensing law, advice and charitable aid powerfully affected the readiness of local people to come to his court, and what happened when they got there.

Sometimes it happened that a single court was manned by two magistrates whose personal styles differed widely, and in such a district the knowledgeable soon discovered which of the two would be likelier to prove obliging, on which days he sat and made their applications accordingly. Similarly, those who lived on the border between two heavily built-up districts might be able to exploit the opportunities this gave them, for although sometimes a magistrate would say firmly that an address was not within his court's district and send the wife packing to a neighbouring court,[57] sometimes he would accept her solicitor's assertion that the address given was in his side of the boundary and hear the application. A knowledgeable or well-advised woman could thus sometimes get from one magistrate the order just refused by another, as in the case of Eliza Smith.[58]

---

[55] 'A Protecting Order Refused' *Morning Chronicle* (9 October 1858) 6. See above, page 173.

[56] Marylebone, Great Marlborough Street, Westminster and Bow Street were the preferred courts, unless a magistrate had a taste for life in the raw or a sense of social mission.

[57] In the first week of the Matrimonial Causes Act 1857's operation, for example, Norton of Lambeth told a 'well-dressed young woman' resident in Southwark that she must apply to that court; and a fortnight later Burcham of Southwark asked Solomon where his client's business was, and on hearing that it was near Astley's Theatre, Lambeth, told him she must apply to Lambeth police court: *Lloyd's Weekly* (16 January 1858) and *News of the World* (31 January 1858).

[58] See n 55.

This is in marked contrast to the model seen outside of the police courts, where local political factions and individual personalities were tempered somewhat by the presence of fellow members drawn from other sections of the community and the balance of power was finely tuned.

Eighteen metropolitan magistrates figure in the reports of the popular Sunday press on 'divorce before magistrates' in 1858, a few of them often enough for an impression to emerge of personal style at a hearing, though any failings are usually hidden within the lines. A magistrate might (or might not) be reported as spoken of in the neighbourhood 'with gratitude and respect', as was James Traill of the Woolwich and Greenwich court, even 20 years after his death.[59] LC Tennyson D'Eyncourt (son of the Whig politician who had been MP for Lambeth 1832–52 and cousin of the poet), ended his long police court career with a well-established reputation for gentlemanliness and consideration,[60] and was indeed notably patient and sympathetic in handling applications at his east end court of Worship Street. In February 1858 he gradually drew out a 'most painful' story from 'a care-worn middle-aged woman' unable to speak for some time from 'agitation and nervous excitement', and two months later treated courteously two other 'lady-like' persons with 'care-worn aspects' and sad stories.[61] His colleague, the Lancashire man and former Commissioner of Bankruptcy in Liverpool, John Hammill, unlike Edward Yardley of Thames, was ready to give an eligible wife what she asked for, without any paternalist investigation of whether she needed it at that moment.[62] That man of precision, TB Burcham, a Fellow of Trinity College Cambridge and straight from the Recordership of Bedford, acted as an energetic new broom at Southwark, and dealt with many applications – unlike his colleague Boyce Combe, a hardened old police-court hand, whose sittings may have been avoided because of two refusals of an order when they first became available.[63]

In the neighbouring district of Lambeth the two magistrates were the Hon George Norton, the heir presumptive to a barony and George Percy Elliott, the scholarly son of a Devon clergyman. They were the same age and had been at school together (Winchester), were members of the same Inn (Middle Temple), went to Lambeth in the same year (1845) and stayed there together for nearly 25 years. Elliott, who dealt with more reported applications than any other single magistrate in 1858, emerges as calmly efficient, always punctilious in his questioning and Norton, handled nearly as many cases, and somewhat remarkably given his personal history, was exceptionally obliging and accommodating in implementing this legislation. His 'constant anxiety for and sympathy with

---

[59] J Traill (1794–1873) (see ODNB) 'lived at Blackheath among his people', in this 'most wretched' waterside district, Williams (n 16) 234.

[60] 'Death of Mr D'Eyncourt' *St James's Gazette* (14 December 1896) 7.

[61] 'The New Marriage Act' *Lloyd's Weekly* (28 February 1858) 10; 'Police' *The Times* (9 April 1858) 11; *News of the World* (11 April 1858).

[62] 'Worship Street: A Protecting Order' *Globe* (12 October 1858) 4.

[63] 'Southwark' *Globe* (14 January 1858) 4; 'Southwark: The New Divorce Act' *Morning Herald (London)* (15 January 1858) 7.

the poor made him very popular', said an old colleague in his courtroom at his death; and in 1858 he was the only magistrate reported to have enquired, 'What has become of the children?' – a question wholly in character, for he was notably fond of children and animals.[64] The kind and considerate treatment by George Norton in the courtroom, and his reputation for 'meeting the difficulties of a case with good temper', is at odds with his reputation as a cruel and violent husband, described as a 'Tory aristocratic younger son whose slenderness of means was rivalled only by his physical and emotional brutality'.[65] One cannot help but wonder if George saw himself reflected in any of the applications presented before him.

Given their wide statutory powers and local influence, magistrates' personalities could noticeably accentuate the differences between proceedings in different courtrooms which inevitably sprang from the sharp social and economic contrasts between different parts of London. Where their new duties under the Matrimonial Causes Act 1857 were concerned, their professional attention could veer towards easy-going readiness to accommodate a woman's request for help, or conscious remedying of the law's perceived wrongs to deserted wives, as well as towards briskness, searching interrogation, and sceptical caution over tales of part abuse and present fears. Nor should this be surprising. Even the most upwardly mobile magistrate might spend five or six years in a district, and could stay far longer, particularly if they developed a sense of belonging with 'their' poor.[66] Yet they never had that intimate familiarity with their neighbourhood's social and economic currents and crosscurrents possessed by lay justices brought to the local bench. That said, the sheer number of cases coming before these busy professionals from the same district, day in and day out, must have bred confidence in their own ability to appraise the trustworthiness of a story and settle the best way to deal with its teller, just as those who lived in the district must soon have picked up a shrewd idea of their local magistrates' habits and prejudices, and the best way to play upon them. In a London courtroom, a wife's experiences thus depended quite significantly on which one of the 23 metropolitan police magistrates heard her application; and that in turn depended on where she lived and, in most cases, on the day of the week on which her application was considered. Some magistrates 'could not truthfully be praised' in 1858, any more than

---

[64] *The Times* (26 February 1875) 12; *Lloyd's Weekly* (28 November 1858) 4. Caroline Norton herself acknowledged his 'kindness to the poor' as a magistrate, as well as his 'very great love' for his own children: JG Perkins, *The Life of Mrs Norton* (London, 1910) 10, 171 and 178. Due to academic and popular focus on the personal affairs of George and Caroline Norton, George's work as a magistrate has been virtually ignored, and the piquant situation just outlined never noted.

[65] Poovey (n 20) 469. See also Perkins (n 64) 250; D Atkinson, *The Criminal Conversation of Mrs Norton* (London, Preface Publishing, 2012); and A Fraser, *The Case of the Married Woman: Caroline Norton: A 19th Century Heroine Who Wanted Justice for Women* (London, W&N, 2021).

[66] A magistrate might be a 'soft touch' over alms from his court's poor box and take the part of 'his' poor against the local poor law authorities and sometimes the police, as did both Selfe and Yardley: Davis (n 16) 327–28.

50 years later; but many were the sort of upper middle-class gentlemen a later police court clerk remembered as

> turned out in numbers in the Victorian period. Not greatly distinguished, not marvellously equipped with natural gifts, but sane and sensible, firm, kind, chivalrous ... dignified, but never pompous or vain ... not a profound lawyer, but with a sufficient knowledge of law for his work.[67]

Far more cogent reasons than these, however, make it altogether likely that applications for economic divorce were genuinely more frequent in Blackburn than the surrounding area. Blackburn was more dependent on the cotton industry than anywhere else in the country and married women had long played an unusually prominent role in its economy. More than half its cotton operatives were female, and a higher proportion of these were married than in any other town.[68] Piecerates were the same for men and women; and in 1853 female and male weavers had acted together in the Blackburn Association of Cotton Weavers to negotiate the first district price list for weaving. Indirectly, moreover, the mills provided various sources of income for many other married women, who moved in and out of economic activity to suit their personal circumstances. Altogether the town was well accustomed to active, independent wives and it is entirely probable, therefore, that demand for economic divorce was indeed unusually high in Blackburn.

Were there any financial inducements which might explain the readiness of Blackburn justices to grant orders? Their Clerk, Henry Hoyle, certainly had no personal interest in multiplying his Bench's section 21 orders, since he was one of the few clerks remunerated by a fixed annual salary instead of fees.[69] The Borough's coffers would indeed benefit, but at most by five shillings from each order. It is true that the clerks to the County justices at Blackburn (and Haslingden), John Bolton and his partner (and uncle), Henry Hargreaves, were paid by fees, and moreover that in September 1858 Bolton became Registrar of Blackburn County Court. Thereafter, John Bolton stood to gain from every order granted in Blackburn sessions, with the five-shilling registrar's fee as well as the clerk's fee of two or three shillings. Bolton, however, was a man of 'sterling integrity'; and moreover to this, highly respected, substantial, and gentlemanly firm, sums like this can surely have had little significance.[70] Altogether, the fees brought in by a section 21 order can

---

[67] 'They might blunder through narrow sympathies, but constantly made good by fine character': A Lieck, *Bow Street World* (London, Robert Hale, 1938) 38–39. Lieck began his career as a police court clerk in the 1890s.

[68] In 1851, 24.14% of women cotton operatives in Blackburn were married, as against 17.89% in Burnley: M Hewitt, *Wives and Mothers in Victorian Industry* (London, Rockliff, 1958) 14. In Blackburn in 1861, 68% of working women over the age of 20 worked in cotton manufacture, compared to 60% in Burnley: *Census of England and Wales 1861: Population Tables Volume II*, HC 3221 (1863) 643–47.

[69] By paying Hoyle a salary of £200, the Borough saved £350 in 1857–58: *Return of Stipendiary Magistrates in England and Wales 1855*, HC 50 371 (1856) 1–6.

[70] Abram (n 8) 395; *Law List*, 1858; *Blackburn Standard* (8 September 1858) 3. Henry Hargreaves had been Blackburn's first Town Clerk, 1851–54.

hardly have done more than ensure that the Blackburn clerks had no personal financial incentive to hinder an applicant's success.

Nevertheless, here as elsewhere the town's justices could have a *corporate* financial interest in giving a deserted wife an order, whenever this seemed likely to prevent her and such dependent children as she might have from burdening the rates. Quite often, as will be shown later, the property a wife wanted to protect was property through which she was earning a living. Indeed, in November 1859 Clough (who was still Vice-Chairman of the Blackburn Board of Guardians) told the Borough justices very explicitly that his client, Mary Jordan, who had been deserted by her husband (the unusually-monikered River Jordan), had been threatened with proceedings for her husband's debts. If these proceedings were instituted against her, she and her five children aged between 11 and two 'would have to become chargeable to the township' – at which 'the magistrates said they had great pleasure in granting the order'.[71] By granting an application, then, justices could be protecting their rate-payers' pockets as well as the resources of a deserted wife.

Corporate and community interests together are surely the key to these proceedings in Blackburn's courtroom. Work, society, and politics came together as much in the operation of this new branch of matrimonial property law, as they usually did in magistrates' operation of the criminal law. The ready demand and equally ready supply of section 21 orders seemingly both alike reflect Blackburn's distinctive culture – a culture produced by its mushroom growth around its great cotton mills in the previous 30 years, and the migration there of a weaving peasantry from the rural upland townships round about.[72] In Blackburn, vertical social relationships combined industrial paternalism with popular independence; and significantly, females had a prominent place in both. 'Ready to respect where respect on any good ground was due, ready too with a blunt pride that is no bad form of self-respect; independent, shrewd, quick, keen-bitten', was John Morley's memory of Blackburn folk he had known in the 1840s and 1850s.[73] Social relations in Blackburn were neither cringing and apathetic on the one side, nor high-handed and dictatorial on the other. It is no surprise that at the first onset of the cotton famine its hitherto prosperous operatives themselves convened a meeting at the Town Hall, summoned the mayor, and demanded assistance, in a way outsiders considered premature.[74] Tory Anglicanism was dominant in the town, but Liberal Congregationalism provided a vigorous undertow, there was also space for dissenting groups such as the Swedenborgians, who built a substantial

---

[71] 'Application for Protection' *Blackburn Weekly Times* (26 November 1859) 6.

[72] Abram (n 8) 230.

[73] J Morley, *Recollections* (London, Macmillan, 1917) 5. Morley's father had migrated there from near Halifax, to build up a practice as one of the town's medical men and evolving in the process from a Wesleyan to a Church goer.

[74] E Barlee, *A Visit to Lancashire in December 1862* (London, 1863) 107.

church in Accrington.[75] Above all, Blackburn wives were unrivalled in their earning power and recognised value as workers, and in their political and industrial
self-confidence. It has been argued that as women entered powerloom weaving
(which was increasingly Blackburn's specialty), they became 'more fully conscious
of their rights'.[76] Certainly, it appears that Blackburn women were fully conscious
of their rights under the new Matrimonial Causes Act, and energetic in securing
them at their Town Hall.

But if the local culture of female economic participation and assertiveness was
the fundamental source of the lively demand for orders, the fundamental source of
the readiness with which this demand was met was surely the equally strong culture
of factory paternalism and civic concern among the local notables. Outstanding
here was a phalanx of Tory Anglican employers, whose attitudes and connections
reflected their roots as members of the landed gentry; but in their more improving way, the Liberal mill-owners led by the Congregationalist Pilkington, could
not be outdone in proprietary concern for their people's welfare.[77] 'The protection of injured women' was something on which paternalists of every style could
agree, and not only the heirs of the Tory-Radical campaigners for the Factory Acts.
Such protection had always been seen as the *raison d'etre* of section 21. There
should be nothing surprising, then, about the readiness to grant these new orders
shown in 1858 by Blackburn's Bench of local notables, chaired by the philanthropic
Pilkington and John Baynes.

Above all, when the woman concerned came within the personal fiefdom of
a sitting magistrate, the cohesion of the sub-communities within the town was
very real. How often was the Town Hall courtroom the scene of a hearing like that
of 12 June 1858, when Daniel Thwaites, the town's biggest Tory brewer, sat with
fellow-Tory Thomas Hart of St John's Ward, that stronghold of the town's Tory
magnates, the Hornbys, with their great mill, Brookhouse, at its centre, to hear the
application of Matilda Warburton, a weaver at that same mill, for an order protecting her property against her husband, a former Brookhouse weaver who had gone
to Stalybridge and 'picked up a young woman there'?[78] That Matilda Warburton
should get her order must surely have been a foregone conclusion to all concerned,
for St John's Ward was 'a citadel of cotton paternalism',[79] and Hart and Thwaites
can only have seen this Brookhouse weaver as one of 'their' people, who had been

[75] In 1851, Blackburn was predominately Anglican, though there were small but well-established
Congregationalist, Baptist, Wesleyan and Roman Catholic communities: *Census of Great Britain 1851:
Religious Worship (England and Wales): Report and Tables* HC 1690 (1853) 96–97. Accrington's first
Swedenborgian 'New Jerusalem' church was built in 1805: *Victoria County History, County of Lancaster*
VI (London, 1911) 427.
[76] C Morgan, 'Women, Work and Work Consciousness in the Mid-Nineteenth Century English
Cotton Industry' (1992) *Social History* 17, 23, 41.
[77] Joyce (n 10) 188–90.
[78] 'Application for Protection Under The Matrimonial Causes Act' *Preston Chronicle* (12 June 1858) 5.
[79] Joyce (n 10) 207. Unfortunately the addresses of Blackburn applicants, unlike those elsewhere, are
not usually reported.

badly treated by another. Given the strength of cohesion within the community, it cannot be surprising that caution, corroborative evidence, safeguards against a wife's suppression of important facts or perjury, or even strict compliance with the terms of the statute are all absent from Blackburn hearings. 'Protection' was what this new piece of legislation was recognised to be about; and open-handed protection was what Blackburn employers had long been accustomed to providing – and Blackburn workers to expect – as their due.

The columns of the local press itself offer one or two clues as to why wives in Blackburn responded to this new legislation compared to their counterparts in nearby towns. Positive editorial comment and regular reporting of applications imply a favourable local climate of opinion, and both were conspicuously present in the local newspaper read in Blackburn – and conspicuously absent in the local newspaper of neighbouring Burnley, a town about three-quarters of the size of Blackburn, but where the number of applications reported was only a quarter of that town's. In 1858, four newspapers were regarded as Blackburn's local newspapers by its mayor, and by the local press itself: the *Blackburn Standard* and *Blackburn Weekly Times*, and the *Preston Guardian* and *Preston Chronicle*.[80] Publicity and support for the new 'protection for injured women' was given promptly and at length by the long established and well-respected three-penny *Preston Guardian*. On 16 January, after doing justice to the siege of Lucknow, its editor dedicated his second leader to emphasising that 'the new Act relating to matrimony and divorce has one important provision that ought to be widely known', namely section 21 – which was printed in full. Thanks to this clause, readers were informed, a deserted wife

> although she may not re-marry, can exercise the same control over her own cash and estate as a single woman, or *feme sole* as the lawyers would say … if she will only appeal to the magistrates for an order, in accordance with the new Act.[81]

Thereafter, this newspaper, the *Blackburn Weekly Times* and *Blackburn Standard* (which had already reprinted the paragraph on orders in *A Handy Book of Property Law*),[82] all covered applications under the new Act as part of their regular reporting of proceedings at petty sessions held in their neighbourhood; and since applications were usually successful, this coverage can only have encouraged further applications.[83]

---

[80] 'The Mayor and the Press', first leader, *Blackburn Standard* (3 November 1858) 2.

[81] *Preston Guardian* (16 January 1858) 2.

[82] *Blackburn Standard* (13 January 1858) 4: 'A Deserted Wife's Earnings' extract from Lord St Leonards, *A Handy Book of Property Law in a Series of Letters* (London, William Blackwood & Sons, 1858) 77. St Leonards was an ex-Conservative Lord Chancellor and a puff piece for his work was natural in the Tory *Standard*, but in any case, this was a remarkably successful series. This particular *Handy Book* went through six editions in 1858, and a Canadian edition appeared as late as 1917.

[83] *The Guardian* seems to have borrowed its reports of what went on at Blackburn Petty Sessions from *The Standard*; the penny *Times* evidently had its own reporter.

Burnley, however, was outside their regular reporting area; and Burnley's only 'independent' penny weekly, the *Burnley Advertiser*, had a perceptibly different editorial line and distribution of column inches. There, 'Police News' took second place to 'Parliamentary Intelligence' and reports of Chartist doings and although three applications under section 21 at the Burnley courthouse were duly reported on 27 February, a lengthy disquisition was added to 'correct an erroneous impression which prevails as to this Act. Many people believe that if an order is granted by the magistrate it operates as a Divorce. This is not so.' An order simply protected the earnings and property of a wife after desertion by the husband, readers were informed. The paper then processed to plagiarise selectively, and without acknowledgement, an article in the previous week's *Law Times*, reproducing its remarks on the limitations and drawbacks of an order but omitting those on its many advantages.[84] Whether coincidentally or not, only one further application in Burnley was reported in the course of the year.[85] Such differences in the tone and extent of press comment, make it not implausible that a real difference may have arisen in local use.

Only one of the 15 reported Blackburn applicants was refused an order, and this was because of police evidence that she kept a brothel;[86] whereas at five of the 17 hearings reported in Burnley, Accrington, Haslingden, Darwen, Bacup and Preston, the Bench was not satisfied that a proper case had been made. These neighbouring justices postponed an order when the marriage certificate was not produced, or because they required 'explicit legal proof of the desertion';[87] and they refused one altogether when questioning revealed that the wife had left the husband and not vice versa,[88] or had acquired no property since his departure,[89] or she was still gaining her living from the stock in trade he had left behind – or even, in echoes of Elizabeth Sophia Cooper's milk-walk, when they considered her property too scant to be worth protecting.[90] Across the Pennines in Bury, too, justices turned away their first applicant on the grounds that her husband had

---

[84] 'Applications Under The New Divorce Act' *Burnley Advertiser* (27 February 1858) 4; 'The New Practice of Judicial Separation and Divorce' *Law Times* (20 February 1858) 298. This critical tone tends to support what is suggested by the politics of section 21: that mainstream Liberal-Conservative opinion favoured the new orders, while radicals and extreme Tories belittled these.

[85] 'Police Intelligence' *Burnley Advertiser* (20 March 1858) 3.

[86] 'Matrimonial Causes Act In Blackburn' *Blackburn Standard* (14 July 1858) 3.

[87] 'Accrington' *Preston Guardian* (11 December 1858); 'Preston' *Preston Guardian* (7 August 1858). When Mrs Mercer declared that her husband had eloped to America four years before with another man's wife, the Preston Bench asked for more corroborating evidence and if the man should be called who 'saw the guilty pair in Liverpool'. They then postponed the case *again* when it emerged that her husband had been communicating with her for a few months: see O Anderson, 'Emigration and Marriage Break-up in Mid-Victorian England' (1997) 163 *Economic History Review* 106. In this last case, the wife had only an old table and chair and the husband was a former inmate of a lunatic asylum who might merely have wandered off for a few weeks.

[88] 'Accrington' *Burnley Advertiser* (18 December 1858) 3.

[89] 'Application for Protection Under The Divorce and Matrimonial Causes Act' *Preston Chronicle* (31 July 1858) 5.

[90] See the case of Mary Marshall in Chapter Five, page 146.

been absent for only a week and there was no proof that she had earned anything from their beerhouse in that time.[91] Objections like these were never voiced in Blackburn – although it should be said that all but three Blackburn applicants had been deserted for nine months or longer, and thus might well seem less likely to be benefitting from stock left behind by the husband, and more likely to have acquired some property of their own since his departure.[92] Moreover, when personal violence was the wife's chief complaint, Blackburn justices did not refuse an order and tell her to have her husband bound over instead – as happened in Burnley and elsewhere, including London.[93]

Are there any indications that some of this particular group of Lancashire wives gave misleading or false information in support of their application, or suppressed relevant but damaging facts, as some wives elsewhere certainly did? Peggy Cunliffe of Accrington, it may be remembered, when she brought her marriage certificate to an adjourned hearing, let slip to the County justices concerned that she had left her husband, and not he her – something not revealed at her successful first hearing – and thus did not get her order after all.[94] In Blackburn, Isabella Slater's involved description of her short married life to her allegedly violent second husband Noah accidently revealed that they had agreed to live separately (no doubt she did not realise that in matrimonial law this meant she was not deserted), and that she had moved into lodgings, where he had once come and assaulted her. This appeared in a very different light when four borough policemen gave evidence that 'she kept a private brothel in King's Entry'. Slater's application was refused – although this could as well have been because the local inhabitants were just then complaining loudly to the police and Town Council about the notorious brothel-beerhouses in King Street – as because of any of the three grounds on which she was in law disqualified, none of which were actually taken up by the Bench. First, she was supporting herself by immoral earnings; second, she had given her husband reasonable cause to desert her; and third, she was voluntarily living apart from him.[95] No other applicant failed to get what she wanted from the Blackburn justices in 1858 – not even Elizabeth Moulden, although they were certainly aware that her husband had told a County Bench the week before that it was because she was living with another man that he had used 'threatening language' towards her – something which if confirmed would have

---

[91] 'Application for Protection Under The New Divorce Act' *Bury Guardian* (20 February 1858) 2.

[92] Mary Healey, though, might very well have been refused an order elsewhere, since she only *intended* to borrow money to buy furniture to set up a lodging house: *Preston Guardian* (4 December 1858).

[93] 'Applications Under The New Divorce Act' *Burnley Advertiser* (27 February 1858) 4; and 'Accrington' *Burnley Advertiser* (18 December 1858) 3.

[94] 'Accrington' *Burnley Advertiser* (18 December 1858) 3.

[95] *Blackburn Weekly Times* (10 July 1858); *Blackburn Standard* (17 August 1858). Blackburn had been singled out by the widely respected chaplain of Preston gaol, John Clay, to illustrate the connection between beerhouses and prostitution: 'Crime, Its Causes and Its Cure' *Blackburn Standard* (17 March 1858) 2.

given him 'reasonable cause' for his desertion and thus disentitled her to an order, and which she took care not to mention in the long description of her husband's violence she gave at her hearing.[96]

The most strikingly successful creative evidence was that given by Harriet Bennett, who is the most likely candidate to be the wife of 'Legality', whose letter to the *Blackburn Weekly Times* first highlighted the unusual circumstances surrounding the implementation of section 21 in Blackburn.[97] According to 'Legality's' version of this marriage, the husband was a young spinner of good character, a 'Sunday School teacher', who had married a young woman of 'exceptional beauty' whose parents went to occupy a 'notorious beerhouse' soon after their marriage (by implication, one of the town's many brothel-beerhouses). When his new wife spent time there, in spite of her new husband's protests, they separated; but 'he left her in possession of everything, even his own clothes', and 'she sent the child after him, which he maintained, almost naked'. When he next heard of her, she had got protection from the magistrates, although he had witnesses that 'the statements she made, as reported in the newspapers, were incorrect'. He applied for his clothes and belongings (she was living with her parents) but 'she told him they were hers, as she had got Protection', even though he had had 'no intimation' of her application, and the Act confined protection to 'property acquired by her own lawful industry'.[98]

The version of married life given by Harriet Bennett was altogether different. Her husband beat her several times, she told the Bench, and 'her screams brought the neighbours in crowds'. She 'took out a summons, but he induced her to settle it' (this was a common claim). Three weeks later he beat the elder of the two children at one in the morning, and she 'ran to a neighbour for protection'. They then lived separately for eight or nine months. When he came back 'and promised to do better', her mother 'put them into a house'; but he soon 'broke out again and punched her'. He was then bound over for 12 months and left her. (The Blackburn Borough justices would not necessarily have known whether this was true, since the Bennetts were then living in Oswaldtwistle, which had its own Petty Sessions.) She lived with her parents during the intervals when he had 'deserted' her, as she did now, she said; and he next came to see her on Whit Saturday, he beat her, and her father and mother, and 'said he had 3s. to draw of his wages, but he would draw it and spend it; and he did so', thus blatantly flouting his duty to maintain her. The Monday following, he returned and took away the eldest child; and she did not see him again till the previous Saturday, when he came to her, and she would

---

[96] *Preston Guardian* (3 April 1858); *Blackburn Standard* (7 April 1858); and see Chapter Three.

[97] Bennett's is the only application for an order that fits 'Legality's' account of the husband's occupation, time of their marriage, number of children, the wife going to live with her parents and his having the elder child.

[98] 'Legality' *Blackburn Weekly Times* (14 August 1858); this newspaper was then edited by the 'ultra-radical' Ernest King, who was no doubt glad enough to print this attack on the local elite's use of power: Joyce (n 10) 317. For Harriet Bennett's story, see 'Matrimonial Causes Act in Blackburn' *Blackburn Standard* (14 July 1858) 3.

not speak to him. 'For the last fourteen months he had not contributed a farthing towards her maintenance' – a favourite and damning final punchline since failure to maintain was the popular definition of desertion.[99]

If Harriet Bennett was indeed 'Legality's' wife, all of this makes it easy to understand his indignation that he was given 'no intimation of her intention to apply', as well as his emphatic reminder that the statute gave protection only to 'property acquired by the wife's *own lawful industry*' and his pointed remark that it was 'to the credit of the magistrates that in one case they have refused Protection where it was proved that the applicant either lived at or kept a house of ill fame'. Equally, even if 'Legality's' version of events is true, it is difficult not to be impressed by Harriet's intuitive chutzpah, as well as her fluency in telling a detailed story whose twists were evidently not too highly coloured for these accommodating Blackburn justices, Messers Pilkington, Hart and Hoole. How she would have dealt with the kind of searching questions the County magistrates or the Preston Bench were apt to ask is another matter entirely. There was certainly a strong incentive to mislead the magistrate, both in order to get the practical advantages of an economic divorce (so much more widely publicised than the drawbacks), and to hit back against the husband who had left her by branding him as a man who left his family destitute, a wife-beater, business failure, philanderer or whatever else she chose to weave into her story, and thus ruining his reputation among the respectable.[100] Loss of reputation and consequently income, and perhaps employment, awaited any respectable man known to have deliberately left his wife destitute – even more surely than they awaited a husband known for 'wife-beating', and far more surely than they awaited a man who simply lived separately from his wife.

In the south London press reports, however, nothing more emerges beyond unrealistic and ill-informed generalisations and expectations of what could be delivered by this easily accessible and much-publicised new legal remedy.[101] It is possible that the formidable powers and reputation of the metropolitan police magistrates deterred malicious or imaginative applications, but whatever the reason, only four refusals were reported, an even smaller proportion than in Lancashire, and three of them were given with expressions of regret, on the ground that the application was premature. True, in 1859, GP Elliott of Lambeth discharged the order he had given to Elizabeth Rudge in 1858, when her husband satisfied him that he had not deserted her 17 years before, as she had alleged. In this case George Rudge was evidently quite as alert to profit from section 21 as his wife, for he only resurfaced when Elizabeth – in her new capacity as a *feme*

---

[99] 'Matrimonial Causes Act in Blackburn', ibid.

[100] 'Police' *The Times* (9 April 1858) 9; *Clerkenwell News* (24 April 1858) 2. *The Times*'s criticism of the drafting of section 21 as 'a rather hopeless remedy for a penniless woman whose husband cannot be found' was quickly reproduced in the *English Woman's Journal* 1 (May 1858) 187.

[101] In the fourth case, Burcham refused Elizabeth Cooper's request for protection for the profits of her milk walk with 'I don't think the Act of Parliament can protect a milk-walk': 'Southwark – Singular Application Under The Matrimonial Causes Act – Protecting A Milk Walk' *Morning Post* (1 December

sole – began a suit as a residuary legatee.[102] A Southwark order, too, had to be discharged in 1859. In practice though, a weak case must often have escaped challenge. It may be remembered that magistrates were advised to accept the wife's evidence when in doubt and leave it to the husband to show that her order should be discharged; yet an order was very rarely discharged.[103] When the Bolton magistrates did rescind one of their orders at the end of September 1858, they were hailed by the *Preston Guardian* as the first Bench in the country to use this power.[104] As has been explored in Chapter Four, discharging an order was as straightforward as applying to have one granted in the first place. A husband who believed his wife was not entitled to the economic divorce afforded by a section 21 order could apply to the magistrate for its discharge and, provided that he could show that he had not deserted his wife and that he had provided for her, the magistrate could rescind the order and the *feme sole* status acquired by the wife would be immediately dissolved and she would once again be subject to *coverture*. With the usual caveats concerning the dangers of relying on Judicial Statistics Reports aside, the reported numbers returned show that there were never any more than seven section 21 orders discharged by magistrates in one year, and indeed in 1878 the Government stopped requesting information on discharges, presumably because the numbers were so small and the space was needed to report ever more detailed bankruptcy proceedings.[105] Yet there is no denying that the process to have an order discharged was less publicised than applying for one, and it is perhaps no surprise that a husband, presumably previously confident in his position of utmost legal dominance over his wife, might feel aggrieved.

The question 'what should he do?' at the end of 'Legality's' story of a virtuous husband deprived of his clothes and belongings by his rackety wife's protection order is a reminder that the ordinary run of husbands and small creditors might well be at a loss to know how to fight back by getting a re-hearing. This was a new proceeding still too rare to have been made familiar by newspaper reports and one on which the Matrimonial Causes Act 1857 itself was notably uninformative. In any case, very many absent husbands must simply not have known of their wife's changed legal status; and those who did no doubt often accepted the view that what they gained by escaping liability for her debts more than made up for the

1858) 7. There was laughter in court, but surely Cooper's earnings from her milk walk were surely as eligible for protection as those from any other little business.

[102] *Rudge v Weedon* (1859) 28 LJ Ch 889. Unfortunately no press report of Mrs Rudge's application order in 1858 has been traced.

[103] For further discussion of discharged orders, see Chapter Four and Seven.

[104] Probably mistakenly, for an indignant Liverpool husband had tried to get his wife's order rescinded several weeks before: see Chapter Three, page 83. The Bolton magistrates heard from the husband of Mrs Esther Haslam, 'who appeared a quiet and respectable man', that he had always treated his wife well, was shocked when *she left his house*, and had been half a dozen times to induce her to return to him, but her relations would not allow her to speak with him. He produced a neighbour as a character witness, and 'as Mrs Haslam did not make her appearance in court, the magistrates rescinded the order': *Preston Guardian* (2 October 1858).

[105] *Return Of Judicial Statistics Of England And Wales, 1865* HC 3726 (1866) 11. Applications for section 21 orders to be rescinded could also be made to the Court for Divorce and Matrimonial Causes: see Chapter Seven.

loss of the little she was likely to acquire on her own account.[106] Only when a wife unexpectedly prospered in her business or inherited a legacy was her husband likely to take action to try to get her order discharged by proving that she had given false information or supressed relevant facts.[107] Susan Bragg, whose application was examined in the previous chapter, did just this; but unfortunately for her, a report of her court hearing was taken up by *The Times* as a peg for criticising legislative draftsmanship, and thus received such wide publicity that her dentist husband was provoked into defending his 'professional interest and character'.[108] It was quite true, his solicitor said, that he had left her upon more than one occasion in consequence of domestic differences; but 'so far from leaving her destitute, he allowed her to retain the greater portion of the goods, together with the profits of a prosperous business, which he himself had purchased at a cost of £120'.[109]

A little earlier, on 5 March 1858, a Westminster wife, Mrs Thomas, secured an order from the Bow Street magistrate David Jardine by telling him that her husband had deserted her 18 months before when in reality it was she who had left her husband and gone to live with another man. This fictionalised narrative (which was surely not unique) was intended to protect her savings out of her earnings for looking after a shop for her husband, which she claimed to have deposited for safe keeping with another shopkeeper, described only as 'Head'. Securing an order proved to be a shrewd move, for when Head denied her story in 1860, Mrs Thomas's *feme sole* status enabled her to become the first wife to maintain an action for savings out of her earnings.[110] A resourceful wife could nevertheless push her skill in exploiting the law too far. Sarah Rashleigh of Marylebone had secured outdoor relief of 6s. 6d a week while her husband was in prison for failing to maintain her and his child, despite the relieving officer's suspicions that she did not need it; but then rashly instructed a solicitor to apply to the magistrates' court for an order to protect the property she claimed to have acquired 'independent of her husband and the parish'.[111] When the application came up, the relieving officer passed the magistrate, George Long, a copy of the Poor Law Amendment Act 1849, s 16, with the result that far from being protected, he ruled that her property must be appropriated by the Guardians to reimburse them for all their expenditure on

---

[106] The economic effects of a section 21 order were identical with those of a sentence of judicial separation, and on those a lawyer predicted, 'probably the chief profit will be by the husband … especially in the case of the middle or lower classes': 'The New Practice of Judicial Separation and Divorce' *Law Times* (20 February 1858) 298.

[107] 'Re, Jones: Proceedings to upset a Protection order' 33 *Justice of the Peace* 793 (11 December 1869).

[108] See Chapter Five, page 139.

[109] Her husband had never tried to get Jardine's order rescinded and the clues to her false evidence were not picked up during the trial. However, the jury evidently did not entirely believe her account, for they gave her a verdict for only £5 of the £40 she claimed to have deposited: *Thomas v Head* (1860) 175 ER 971-2 (coram Hill, J).

[110] The aged Long (1780-1868) (see ODNB) had published 'Observations' on some proposed poor law changes in 1820 but was apparently not *au fait* with this legislation of 1849. Remarkably, even this case went unreported in the *Marylebone Mercury*, which filled its pages with the affairs of the Guardians, the Vestry and the like and ignored all applications under section 21 in 1858 – apart for that of Jane Astrope, on which see Chapter Five.

[111] 'Extraordinary Application For Protection Of Property' *Globe* (8 December 1858) 4.

her relief during the previous 12 months. Apparently Sarah Rashleigh was one of those capable lone wives who did a good deal better for themselves than their husbands ever did.

It was not London's sheer size and socio-economic make-up alone which ensured that over a quarter of all the country's cases of 'divorce by magistrates' in the next 10 years were given there; it was also the ingrained readiness of even the most respectable mid-Victorian Londoners to make use of their local police court for help and advice, and the willingness of many metropolitan magistrates to meet their neighbourhood's needs. The mid-Victorian police courts were well used to tackling issues which might be seen as petty or trifling to more senior Benches, such as drunken and disorderly behaviour, assaults, support of both legitimate and illegitimate children, and disagreements between apprentices and masters, but cumulatively, it was this work which maintained the fabric of the local community. The new powers given to magistrates under section 21 of the Matrimonial Causes Act 1857 also reflects the ethos of both the contractual rule that those who renege on an obligation must lose the corresponding benefit, and the social philosophy that the strong should protect the weak. The assumptions underpinning the workings of the machinery of 'divorce before magistrates' in London and in Blackburn therefore were thus no more identical than the way the justices of each location chose to enact it. In the London police courts, protection was seen on both sides as a generalised right or duty expressing the role of the law as every man and woman's protector against abuse of authority, whether by poor law officials, police constables, or husbands. In Blackburn, on the other hand, protection was rather part of a network of personalised paternalism better described as clientelism – the 'grace and favour' due from an individual employer or leading denizen of a particular neighbourhood towards his community. In such a courtroom what counted most were the ties which grew from local habits and values, and above all from family, business, religious and political interests and alliances, ties which might dispose a given pair of justices to brand a particular man as a bad husband, or to give a particular woman what she asked for, without asking many questions. To a metropolitan police magistrate, however, the basic issue was rather whether the legal rights of the husband had been cancelled out by the wrongs done to the wife – both of whom were probably personally unknown to him. He was performing his function of dispensing ad hoc justice to the people, within his interpretation of the law and of the story he had heard; whereas the Blackburn justices were 'with pleasure' protecting injured women of their borough against being ill-used by 'idle wretches'. The difference was an important one for the conduct of hearings, as well as their outcome.

That a deserted wife should be able to apply to her local magistrate or justices and immediately secure all her self-acquired property against the inroads of a 'rascally spouse' and his creditors went very much with the mid-Victorian cultural grain – above all with its gender culture, but also with its evangelical zeal to combine punishment for evil-doers with care for their victims, its encouragement of economic 'self-help', and its preference for individual choice and local self-government. Not surprisingly, by 1868 the new system was winning praise as eminently 'practical' (always a sign that contemporary shibboleths have not been disturbed), and thousands of orders had been granted. Section 21 was never intended to help destitute wives and families and was bound to seem of little use to charity workers, just as it was bound to be obnoxious to a doctrinaire feminist or a believer in universal rules as a framework for all relationships. The secret of its viability, however, was precisely the feature all these condemned – that its working was left to the whim of a Bow Street magistrate or even worse, a pair of Country justices, and to the initiative of wives. In the heterogeneous society that made up mid-Victorian England, with its intensely decentralised politics, administration, and legal system, only a machinery which allowed the operation of local person-alities and circumstances and gave some freedom of personal choice was likely to win acceptance.

'Divorce before magistrates' thus proved workable, not only because of its prac-tical usefulness and moral attractiveness, but also because of its mixed machinery and open procedure. In one respect at least, this new social legislation was no different from most other locally administered social legislation whether by elected persons or otherwise: in different sorts of places, its significance assumed different guises. How this was implemented was left in the biggest cities to the discretion of a handful of barrister-professionals, and everywhere else to a legion of social leaders. What went on in Blackburn in 1858 illustrates suggestively the links between demand and supply in 'divorce before magistrates', and the realities and relationships of local work, society, and urban institutions, when the magis-trates concerned were lay justices in petty sessions. Equally, when it was used at all, it depended on the individual initiative of the wives themselves, and it succeeded because hundreds of women each year chose to use it to look after their own inter-ests and get their own back on an absent husband, not only by depriving him of his marital property rights, but by giving him a bad name for 'failure to provide', often backed up by descriptions of ill-treatment, cruelty and womanising which necessarily lost nothing in the telling.[112] Astute choice of the right lawyer, manipu-lation of the prejudices and sympathies of the bench, economy with the truth in the witness box, and occasionally downright perjury were all common enough in these wives' repertoire. Nor is this surprising, given that (as has been well said), 'subversion and resistance were part of the accepted reality of marital relations'.[113] Women married to a man who they or their families resented or despised, as well as women married to a man who was a bad provider, brutal, a blatant womaniser, or simply footloose, now had another means of looking after their own (and some-times their children's) interests. In the courtroom, rather than through physical flight or resistance, they could use these skills on the local great and good and dispensers of philanthropy or poor relief.

---

[112] It should be noted, however, that attitudes to desertion were class and culture related. A Lancashire millworker would hardly have claimed, as did the manager of a leading hosiery house in St Paul's Churchyard, that he would have lost his situation if his employers had heard that his wife had secured a section 21 order to protect her property against him: 'Proceedings to Upset a Protection Order' (1869) *Justice of the Peace* 33, 793.

[113] J Bourke, 'Housewifery in Working-Class England, 1860–1914' (1994) *Past & Present* 143, 167, 189.

7

Traversing 'This Dangerous Ground': Deserted Wives and the Court for Divorce and Matrimonial Causes

Previous chapters have outlined the experiences of deserted wives who applied to their local magistrates or police court for an order of protection under section 21 of the Matrimonial Causes Act 1857. This provision, which allowed deserted wives to access legal and financial emancipation for just a few shillings so close to home, was perhaps the most radical element of the entire matrimonial legislation of 1857, but it was not the only way for wives to secure an order of protection. Section 21 also provided an alternative route for applications via the Court for Divorce and Matrimonial Causes, which had been established by the 1857 Act and sat only in London. It was presided over by the Judge Ordinary (JO), and applications for a section 21 order were therefore heard alongside petitions for judicial separation, and the restitution of conjugal rights, as well as those for full divorce. The intended users of the Court for Divorce and Matrimonial Causes were women living in the City of London, which was not served by a separate magistrates' or police court, however the wording of the legislation also meant that it was possible for wives from anywhere in England and Wales to make their application there. Unlike cases heard in metropolitan police courts, or provincial petty sessions, the newspapers only rarely reported on applications made under section 21 to the Divorce Court but also unlike cases heard in those locations, the actual applications submitted to the Divorce Court for protection under section 21 survive. This chapter will therefore offer a different, comparative, perspective of applications made under section 21 by using applications made to the Court for Divorce and Matrimonial Causes to provide the first insight into the applications as they were presented to the Court, rather than how they were reported in newspapers.

The surviving applications to the Court for Divorce and Matrimonial Causes are worthy of detailed examination for several reasons. First, they are the only substantial surviving cache of section 21 applications and they exist only because they were swept up in the archives of the more numerous petitions for full divorce; they are also the only documents which allow the actual application made by a wife to be examined, rather than relying on newspaper accounts to learn the alleged facts and outcome of a case. Second, analysis of these original records generates important new information about the otherwise invisible processes of the Court and its interpretation of the law which, when compared with the decisions made by magistrates around the country, also reveals how those decisions were (or were not) cascaded through the court structure. Finally, these documents act as a rare window to the most intimate of relationships. Although it might be argued that all applications or petitions made to a court are legal constructs and the opportunity to hear the authentic voice of the wife is therefore limited, it is argued here that applicants deliberately engaged with the court-prescribed method of storytelling precisely to share and amplify their experiences and seek not just economic protection, but also some form of restorative justice. Rather than the application process being a shameful one, it could act as an opportunity for women to share their stories and have their experiences acknowledged in a public arena. Examining details of the 187 surviving cases heard before the Court for Divorce and Matrimonial Causes against the backdrop of those made to provincial magistrates' courts therefore allows key questions to be asked and answered about legal process, and the way deserted wives were able to – and chose to – access the nineteenth century legal system to be understood. Perhaps most importantly for our understanding of mid-nineteenth century matrimonial law, scrutinising data from these applications provides some explanation as to why some deserted wives consciously rejected the low-cost and easily accessible option made available to them under the 1857 legislation, and which the evidence of the previous chapters suggest could have offered the most likely chance of success.

A deserted wife who was considering applying to the Court for Divorce and Matrimonial Causes for a section 21 order of protection had some important issues to consider. By eschewing her local magistrates' court, she was committing to either travelling to London to make her application in person or instructing a London-based solicitor (most likely through an existing connection with a local firm) to act on her behalf: even in this latter scenario, there was a chance that she would be asked to appear in person before the Court. Either option would generate substantially higher costs than applying locally. In the case of women who lived outside of London, an applicant would also have been moving away from a venue where their case would be heard by two or three local men with no formal legal training but who were personally invested in maintaining the social and economic equilibrium of the local area, to one where they would have to plead their case before one of the most senior members of the English judiciary. This perhaps explains why, as earlier chapters have shown, only very few women used the Court for Divorce and Matrimonial Causes to apply for a section 21 order. The exact numbers are – as with so many of the official records relating to mid-nineteenth century matrimonial law – unclear.

Chart 7.1 Number of J 77 Digitised Files v Number of Reported Section 21 Applications Made to the Court for Divorce and Matrimonial Causes (1858–1899)

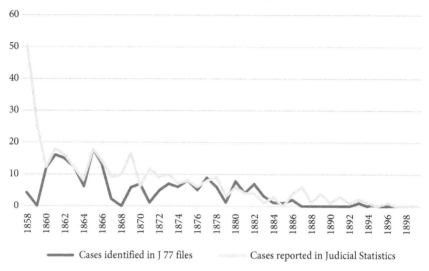

Cases identified in J 77 files   Cases reported in Judicial Statistics

The annual *Return of Judicial Statistics of England And Wales* reports suggest that there were 327 applications for a section 21 order of protection made to the Divorce Court between 1858 and 1914, however it is only possible to identify the details of 216 surviving case files using the index to petitions made to the Court (held under J 78 at The National Archives).[1] Of these 216 index entries, only 187 can be confirmed to be section 21 applications. A small number of the cases have been recorded as 'file missing' (and so though they have a file number, they do not exist), others have been misrecorded as applications for protection under section 21 when they were actually petitions for judicial separation, but the majority of the additional 140 cases identified by the annual *Return of Judicial Statistics of England and Wales* reports simply do not exist in either the J 78 index, or the J 77 case files. There is seemingly no pattern to either the survival rate, or the accuracy of reporting. In 1860, 1863, 1865, 1875 and 1881, the number of reported cases tallies exactly with the number of surviving case files, while in 1877, 1870, 1880, 1882 and 1883 too many actual case files exist compared to the numbers reported in the Judicial Statistics. All remaining years between 1858 (when the Court sat for the first time) and 1914 (the year the final section 21 applications were made) have fewer case files than there should be, according to the numbers reported in the

---

[1] All surviving applications and petitions made to the Court for Divorce and Matrimonial Causes are held at The National Archives under J 77. The index to these documents is held under J 78. The individual case files have been heavily edited by various groups over the years, and since 1923, only a sample of records were kept. Records in J 77 may be subject to a 100-year rolling embargo. All J 77 files referred to in this book are held by The National Archives, Kew and have also been digitised at www.ancestry.co.uk/search/collections/2465/.

annual statistics. Yet despite these inconsistencies, these are the best records available. If we take the officially reported statistics of cases as a rough base line, then approximately 1.7 per cent of all section 21 applications were made to the Court for Divorce and Matrimonial Causes.[2] This chapter will examine all the surviving section 21 applications identified in the J 78 index, allowing change over time to be observed and direct comparisons with findings from the magistrates' courts to be made.

As has been shown in previous chapters, the success of applications made to the magistrates' and police courts of the provinces and metropolitan London could be varied, with any calculation of definitive success rates proving impossible in the absence of data reporting number of applications made and outcome. However, matching the outcomes of case files in J 78 with the numbers reported gives a (very) tentative indication of the success rate of applications made to the Court for Divorce and Matrimonial Causes. These are not conclusive figures as, frustratingly, many of the applications heard in the first four years of the Court's existence do not explicitly record the outcome of the case.[3] Yet despite these caveats, analysis suggests that at least 70 per cent of all section 21 applications made to the Court for Divorce and Matrimonial Causes were successful, putting it broadly in line with the wider London courts, but likely less generous than provincial magistrates' courts. This adds support to the argument made in previous chapters that applications made to judiciary with formal legal training were more likely to be scrutinised and subsequently found not to meet the criteria of the Matrimonial Causes Act 1857.

Although the intended demographic of the Court for Divorce and Matrimonial Causes – so far as section 21 was concerned, at least – was women living within the City of London, evidence from the surviving files shows that the reality was very different. The annual Judicial Statistics suggest that only 8.6 per cent of cases heard before the Court for Divorce and Matrimonial Causes between 1858 and 1914 were made by deserted wives living in the City, which raises the question: who was applying to the Divorce Court and where did they live? The simple answer to this question is that the majority of applicants, some 58 per cent, were made by women who lived in the Home Counties of Berkshire, Essex, Hertfordshire, Kent, and Middlesex, with Middlesex alone accounting for over half of all these cases.[4]

---

[2] Statistics taken from annual *Return Of Judicial Statistics of England and Wales* (Part II. Civil Statistics) 1858–1896.

[3] Although the case files do not consistently record the outcome of the application, the number of awarded section 21 orders declared in the annual Judicial Statistics indicate that the majority of these cases with unknown outcomes were successful. Given the lack of clarity over which case files were preserved and why, the analysis here continues to treat them as 'unknown' rather than successful cases. All percentages calculated here therefore use (known successful cases/total number of J 78 cases examined*100) to give the most accurate (but lowest) possible success rate. Of the cases where outcome is recorded on the J 77 case file, 86% were successful and 14% unsuccessful.

[4] These figures seem broadly in line with Gail Savage's research on *in forma pauperis* divorce petitions which suggests 55% of cases came from the area surrounding London: G Savage, 'They Would

When this figure is combined with those women in the City of London, it suggests that approximately 67 per cent of all section 21 applications made to the central Divorce Court came from an area within easy travel of London. This still leaves a sizeable minority however, who lived further afield, and of these, the two areas with the highest number of applicants were the North-West and Yorkshire and the Humber. Previous chapters have shown that the circuits covering Lancashire, along with those of Greater London, received the most applications from deserted wives seeking a section 21 order, however, the region with the next highest demand was Yorkshire. These findings suggest that women were not applying to the Divorce Court because they did not have access to provision under their local magistrate, because we can see many other women in their local area applied for – and were granted – orders in precisely this way, but for some other reason. Sadly, the motivation for applications to the Court for Divorce and Matrimonial Causes over a local magistrates or police court is not something explicitly stated in the applications and the JO was never recorded as querying their choice. With these caveats, analysis of the case files can still give some indication as to the myriad reasons why a small proportion of deserted wives opted to pursue this seemingly more difficult route toward economic divorce.

The explanation could, of course, rest with the applications themselves: was there something intrinsically different about applications under section 21 of the Divorce and Matrimonial Causes Act 1857 made to magistrates across England and Wales, and those made to the JO in the Court for Divorce and Matrimonial Causes? It might be that the applicants felt their story to be too complicated for a provincial court. Certainly there were at least two cases heard before the JO that were related to other ongoing cases being heard in Chancery. One of these women, Mary Penton, lived in the City of London and could therefore only apply to the Court for Divorce and Matrimonial Causes. The other, Sarah Dunsmere, lived in Kirkdale, Lancashire and so her decision to apply to the central divorce court was a conscious choice. Her application explained that she married James Dunsmere on 31 December 1849 in Greenock in 'Northern Britain' (Scotland), and they lived together for three years there and in Leith, and had two children, one of whom died.[5] James had left the marital home once and then returned, but in April 1853 he left again, and Sarah later discovered that he had sailed from Glasgow to Australia in September of that year. Perhaps driven by the necessity to house herself and her remaining child, Sarah took a job as a nurse at an industrial school in Kirkdale in Lancashire. In addition to her income from this employment, she became entitled to a sum of £400 from a chancery case and it was this that she sought to protect. A marriage made in Scotland, her English domicile, a husband who had disappeared to Australia, plus the added complication of the chancery

---

if They Could: Class, Gender and Popular Representation of English Divorce Litigation, 1858–1908' (2011) 36 *Journal of Family History* 64.

[5] Application of Sarah Dunsmere, J 77/14/D58.

case: it seems entirely plausible that Sarah – or someone with legal training – thought the JO sitting in the Court for Divorce and Matrimonial Causes might be better suited to consider the application. Unfortunately, with no central registry of cases made to magistrates, it is not possible to see if Sarah applied to the Liverpool magistrates first and was advised that she should take her case to London, or if she went there directly.

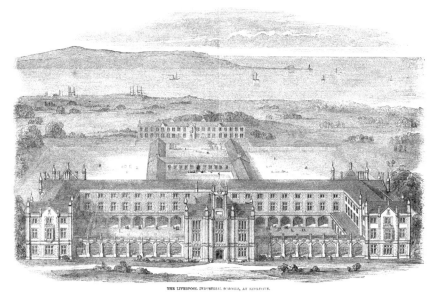

Figure 7.1 The Liverpool Industrial Schools at Kirkdale 1850
© Illustrated London News/Mary Evans

The international nature of many of the marriages contained within the applications, and a lack of understanding about the full workings of the legislation, may also have contributed to an assumption that the Court for Divorce and Matrimonial Causes was the correct place to make an application for protection under section 21.[6] Marriages made by British nationals living abroad, or between British and foreign nationals were not unusual, especially in the mid-nineteenth century with its large-scale emigration. Just over 30 per cent of the applications made by women living outside of the City of London make mention of one or both parties being domiciled outside of the United Kingdom at some point during the marriage. For some women, their marriage took place abroad and they later returned to England where they then attempted to access the support of the English legal

---

[6] For further discussion of international, specifically interracial, marriages, see G Frost, 'Vindictiveness on Account of Colour'?: Race, Gender, and Class at the English Divorce Court, 1872–1939' (2020) *Genealogy* 4, 82.

system. In 1838, for example, Jane Mahon married Henry Ricketts (at the time a member of the 16th Regiment of Lancers) in Meerut, Bengal, India, only to discover just three years later, when his regiment was shipped back to England, that he was 'engaging in adulterous intercourse with certain women whose names are unknown to me'.[7] She initially remained in India where she was employed as a servant for families who were travelling between England and India, amassing savings of £600, which she was 'apprehensive the said Henry Ricketts may obtain possession of and appropriate to his own purposes unless prevented by an Order of Prevention by this Court'.[8]

Access to the Court for Divorce and Matrimonial Causes (for any purpose) was based on having a legal domicile in England or Wales, regardless of where the marriage ceremony itself took place, though this position took several decades to be settled. The issue of domicile was generally only raised if a petition for divorce was challenged,[9] but it could cause problems even without a disgruntled respondent, as Letitia Newport Seiller, who applied to the Divorce Court for a section 21 order on 14 May 1874, was soon to discover.[10] She married the French merchant Octave Henri Seiller in Brittany on New Years Eve 1856.[11] In the 12 years of their marriage (only six of which were spent cohabiting), Letitia and Octave lived in Paris and Versailles, France and Brussels, Belgium, and had three children, two of whom were still alive when Octave deserted his family on 18 July 1868 and likely returned to France. Letitia had been motivated to seek the protection of the law six years after her desertion following the death of her brother, a late Captain in the army, who had died unmarried and intestate, which meant she stood to inherit one-third of his estate under English law.[12] She explained that following Octave's desertion, it was her brother who had given her 'some assistance', which had allowed her to establish herself in business. The application itself does not specify her trade, but the 1871 census records Letitia as living in England and working as a needlewoman.[13]

The 1871 census also records Letitia as being a widow and born in Paris, France: both of these statements were incorrect. Letitia's husband was very much alive and well, and she had in fact been born Letitia Newport Tinley in Ireland,

---

[7] Application of Jane Ricketts, J 77/45/R53. The outcome of this case is unknown, but it was unlikely to be straightforward because it could well be argued that Jane had in fact deserted her husband, thus making her ineligible for a section 21 order.

[8] ibid.

[9] *Yelverton v Yelverton* (1859) 164 ER 866; *Briggs v Briggs* (1880) 5 PD 163; *Scott v Att. Gen* (1886) 11 PD 128; *Le Mesurier v Le Mesurier* (1895) AC 517.

[10] The spelling 'Loetitia' is used in the J 78 Index but this is a mistranscription and therefore the spelling 'Letitia' is adopted in this chapter.

[11] Application of Letitia Newport Seiller, J 77/146/3276.

[12] ibid.

[13] 1871 England Census, RG10/1162/7/7/827796.

the daughter of Gervase Tinley, also a Captain in the Army.[14] Crucially though, the column heading in the census return states 'Where Born', but the question that Letitia answered was 'what is your nationality'. Until the British Nationality Act was passed in 1948, if a British woman married a foreign national then she assumed his nationality. Therefore, in the eyes of the law, Letitia was indeed a French citizen. There was a great fashion for French dressmakers and milliners in the nineteenth century, and it is possible that Letitia initially found this persona a helpful way of marking her business as distinctive from her 'domestic' competition. Unfortunately though, her foreign nationality undermined her application for a section 21 order. A pencilled note in the file states, '(there is) nothing to show that the wife is domesticated in England', and Letitia's statement indicated the desertion (like the marriage) actually occurred in France. These cumulative circumstances caused the JO to examine Letitia's case extremely closely before concluding that – as an ostensibly French national who married another French national in France, even though she was Irish born with an established business in England – it was not within the jurisdiction of the Court for Divorce and Matrimonial Causes. There is no final outcome recorded on the application (an unusual situation for cases heard in the 1870s), but as it was deemed to be outside the jurisdiction of the Court, it could not have been successful.[15] Letitia's file does not tell us what happened next: did Octave return and seize the fruits of her industry and the inheritance due from her brother? We do not know, but at 4.30pm on Sunday 16 May 1875 (one year and two days after her first application to the Court for Divorce and Matrimonial Causes) Letitia was admitted to the Whitechapel Union Workhouse with her six-year-old son, Frederick, due to their destitution. She was then admitted a second time on Tuesday 10 August 1875.[16] Their first stay lasted a fortnight and their second only a few days, but it does not appear that Letitia's financial circumstances improved, as she died in March 1879 at Westminster Hospital and was buried in a common grave at St Margaret's Church.[17]

Letitia was, however, unlucky. The question over the appropriate geographical jurisdictional basis for the Divorce Court was only settled at the turn of the century and had she been able to prove some other connection to England, it is likely that she would have been successful. Some of the wives who appealed to the Court for Divorce and Matrimonial Causes for help had also married a foreign national abroad, such as Mary Ann Frances Rosetta Oliveira, who married her husband Francis Oliveira on the island of Madeira on 13 July 1853 before returning

---

[14] 'Exeter' *Exeter Flying Post* (22 September 1803) 4; *Westminster Church of England Parish Registers*, City of Westminster Archives Centre, STM/PR/6/39.
[15] I am grateful to Dr Maebh Harding for her guidance on domicile and the Divorce Court. These issues are explored in her forthcoming book, *From Catholic Outlook to Modern State Regulation: Developing Understandings of Marriage in Ireland* (Cambridge, Intersentia, 2025).
[16] *Workhouse Admission and Discharge Records, 1764–1921*, London Metropolitan Archives, STBG/WH/123/011 and 012.
[17] *Brompton Cemetery Records*, Ref:97/135.

to England in 1858. She was a British citizen by birth but (improbably) claimed to be unaware of the nationality of her husband, which she would have assumed automatically upon marriage. The couple lived between Madeira and London for six years but the marriage broke down when Francis ran away with a woman who had accompanied them on their voyage, and who he had claimed was the sister of a clergyman he had promised to escort to England.[18] Although Mary Ann and her husband had married in Madeira and spent most of their short marriage living there, she stated in her application that when they returned to live at 221 Euston Road, London in 1858, it was 'with the intention of making England our home'. Her desertion, therefore, happened on English, and not foreign soil, and moreover, Francis was also living in England when he left her without 'any reasonable cause', which was enough to establish her domicile and grant access to the protection of the Court for Divorce and Matrimonial Causes.

Other couples in the case files were both born British citizens and had married in the United Kingdom before travelling abroad, with wives tending to return after the breakdown of the marriage and the husbands remaining abroad. In some cases, the return to England was not entirely through choice. We might spare a thought for Emma Hughes, who followed her husband Isaiah to New York with their young children in 1845, only to find that although he had established a shoe shop, he had not yet secured living accommodation. This did not bode well. During the following nine tumultuous years Emma established a successful boarding house so that she and her three children (plus one more who was born in the United States) had somewhere to live, while Isaiah managed to fail in several different businesses. Believing that he and his family would have more luck in Australia, he instructed Emma and their only surviving child to return to England while he travelled to Australia, after which they would all reunite, presumably with Isaiah's new-found fortune, in New York. In 1853, Emma and her child duly set off for England only to find that nearly all contact with Isaiah ceased and, with the exception of £2 that was sent in 1854, so did any financial support. It turned out that Isaiah had never actually left the United States of America, and Emma never heard from him again.[19]

Far more common than any of these scenarios was for a husband to disappear across the horizon to far flung reaches of the globe, seemingly in an effort to outrun their domestic responsibilities.[20] These husbands share a profile with their 'Determined Emigrant' counterparts in the London Police Courts, with many of the desertions suggesting that the husband had been tempted by wider employment prospects and relatively cheap international travel options that presented themselves. One such husband was mining engineer Joseph Harris Smallman, who married Sophia at the Wesleyan Chapel in Wednesbury, Staffordshire on

---

[18] Application of Mary Ann Frances Rosetta Oliveira, J 77/40/O11.

[19] Application of Emma Hughes, J 77/90/1045.

[20] O Anderson, 'Emigration and Marriage Break-up in Mid-Victorian England' (1997) 163 *Economic History Review* 109.

26 November 1862.[21] They lived together for nearly two years in Wednesbury, and had one son, Herbert, who was born in September 1863.[22] Nine months later, Joseph left Wednesbury for Aotearoa New Zealand, where he was planning to establish a gold mine. He promised Sophia that when the mine was operational, he would return to England to collect her and Herbert and bring them to their new life. Things did not progress as quickly as Sophia might have expected, and six years later, in 1870, Joseph wrote to her to tell her that he was very ill, but also that he had a good interest in a gold mine. Then, to Sophia's concern, all communication ceased. In October 1875 (some 11 years after Joseph had left England), Sophia confirmed through the Agent General of New Zealand that Joseph was in fact alive, well, and living in Aotearoa New Zealand. This news was exacerbated when an unnamed cousin of Sophia's (who had emigrated to Aotearoa New Zealand and settled in the Hauraki district where Joseph was living) wrote to Sophia telling her that Joseph was not only alive, but was also living 'in the Bush' with the daughter of a Pakeha Māori Chief, Harete Charlotte (with whom he had gone through a form of marriage ceremony) and their three children.[23] Local records suggest Joseph and Harete were 'married' in the late-1860s, with their children born between 1869 and 1873.[24] Sophia reported that Joseph had written to her cousin, 'in which he complained of her having given me the information she had done', but he made no effort to write to his wife back in Wednesbury. Sophia's order was granted on 8 April 1880.[25]

While adultery and subsequent cohabitation was a common feature of the applications, bigamous husbands were relatively rare, with only five deserted wives claiming their husband had made a bigamous marriage. Moreover, bigamy tended to be mentioned as an additional example of their husband's poor character, rather than as a motivator for requesting the protection order.[26] This could well be due to the fact that adultery with the additional offence of bigamy would have provided a wife with grounds to apply for a full divorce, so perhaps more women with bigamous husbands chose to sever all legal ties. In 1871, Sarah Butcher from High Street, Peckham, applied unsuccessfully to the Court for Divorce and Matrimonial Causes under section 21.[27] She explained that she and her husband Joseph had been married in 1828 and had lived together until 1844, when he left the family home with 'no reasonable cause'. According to her application, the next Sarah heard of her husband was in 1851, when he was convicted of bigamy and imprisoned

---

[21] Application of Sophia Smallman, J 77/241/6833.

[22] *FreeBMD, England & Wales, Civil Registration Birth Index, 1837–1915*, Oct-Nov-Dec 1863.

[23] Application of Sophia Smallman, J 77/241/6833. The union between Joseph and Harete would not have been recognised as legally binding, see: *Armitage v Armitage* (1866) LR 3 Eq 343, but seems to have been accepted in the local community.

[24] P Hart, 'Joseph Harris Smallman' (2016) *Te Aroha Mining District Working Papers, The University of Waikato*, 25, 1, 15–16.

[25] Application of Sophia Smallman, J 77/241/6833.

[26] Many more men were accused of adultery and cohabitating with other women, but relatively few of actual bigamy.

[27] Application of Sarah Butcher, J 77/111/1889.

for 12 months, having married a woman (confusingly but perhaps conveniently for him) also called Sarah, while still being legally married to the first Sarah. Yet Sarah's application does not tell the full story. In 1844, the *Bury and Norwich Post* reported how a happily honeymooning couple (Joseph and the second Sarah) were staying at the George Hotel in Colchester when they were disturbed by 'a lady from Leicester-square, coming down by railway … (who) burst into their apartment, and claimed the gentleman as her liege lord'.[28] Joseph denied he had ever been married to (the first) Sarah, but their marriage had been reported in the same paper almost exactly 16 years earlier.[29] Joseph was eventually convicted of bigamy and sentenced to one year in prison, but not until 1851, which when we stop to consider that Sarah did not apply for a section 21 order until 1871, raises more questions than it answers.[30]

One of the first cases heard in the Court for Divorce and Matrimonial Causes was that of Elizabeth Brown. She was already in possession of a divorce a *mensa et thoro* from her husband John, which had been granted in 1851 on the basis of his adultery, but she was now gravely ill with cancer and wished to apply for a protection order, presumably so that she could make a last will and testament and ensure that her estranged husband did not return to seize her possessions.[31] She explained that John had 'remarried' in 1848, but there is no evidence from the case file or newspapers that any further action was taken against him with regard to the charge of bigamy. Similarly, Eliza Osborne accused her husband William of making a bigamous marriage with Agnes Fitzherbert Lewsey, but although there is a record of the marriage happening in 1859 (where William claimed to be a widower), there are no records to suggest it was considered a crime, or punished.[32] Of course, not all wives knew about their spouse's subsequent relationships. Emily Clementina Cooper and Eleanor Quarrell's husbands both moved to the United States of America after they deserted and went on to remarry there.[33] The geographical distance between estranged couples, for example Emily in Regent's Park, London and her husband Bridge Frodsham Cooper in New York, and Eleanor Quarrell in Chelsea and her husband George in Texas, meant that it is only with the advent of genealogical databases that many cases of bigamy are discovered.[34]

Of course, women could be bigamists too. Rhoda Bertram applied for an order of protection from her husband George Bertram, a farmer of 23 acres who she

[28] 'Charge of Bigamy' *Bury and Norwich Post* (12 June 1844) 2.

[29] 'Cambridge: Married' *Bury and Norwich Post* (16 July 1828) 2.

[30] 'Bigamy' *Bury and Norwich Post* (9 April 1851) 4.

[31] Application of Elizabeth Brown, J 77/2/B20.

[32] Application of Eliza Osborne, J 77/40/O9; London Church of England Parish Registers, London Metropolitan Archives, P84/JN/015.

[33] Marriage of Bridge Frodsham Cooper to Mary Ellen Sequin, *Michigan, U.S., County Marriage Records, 1822–1940* (30 January 1862); Application of Emily Clementina Cooper, J 77/10/C88; Naturalisation Papers of George Quarrell, *Soundex Index to Petitions For Naturalizations Filed in Federal, State, and Local Courts in New York City, 1792–1906*, The National Archives in Washington DC, M1674/216/1880/880/217C/286; Application of Eleanor Quarrell, J 77/44/Q1.

[34] R Probert, 'Escaping Detection: Illegal Second Marriages and the Crime of Bigamy' (2022) *Journal of Genealogy and Family History* 6, 27–33. This innovative project crowd-sourced details of bigamy cases from family historians before going on to investigate and verify the marriages.

had married in 1842.[35] She said that George had been a heavy drinker and in 1856 he had disappeared with no warning or just cause, and she had not heard from him since. The 1861 census shows Rhoda living with her children as a servant in the household of the recently widowed Hugh Lawrence in the same village of Southwold, Suffolk, where she had lived with George.[36] On 18 April 1867, Rhoda – allegedly believing George to be dead – made a second marriage with Hugh Lawrence. Rhoda's application did not explain why she believed George to be dead and the pair (perhaps wisely) married at St Stephen's Church in Norwich, some 30 miles from their home in Southwold. She recorded herself as a 'spinster' and married under her maiden name of Butler, rather than her married name of Bertram and he used the name Joseph Laurence, rather than Hugh Lawrence.[37] Rhoda and Hugh appear to have lived happily together until Hugh's death in 1877 and in his last will and testament, Hugh appointed Rhoda to be an executor of his will and a legatee.[38] Unfortunately for Rhoda, this coincided with her son-in-law Albert Sharpe revealing that he had in fact seen her first husband George Bertram in the last 12 months and that he was alive and well.[39] One can only wonder at the family dynamics that led the husband of Rhoda and George's daughter Maria, to reveal this information, or to share it so publicly that Rhoda could not ignore it, but it is worth noting that Maria secured a divorce from Albert two years later on account of his adultery and cruelty.[40]

Newspaper calls giving notice to creditors to claim under Hugh's estate give the name 'Rhoda Bertram'. Similarly, the entry for Hugh Lawrence's last will and testament in the National Probate Calendar describes Rhoda as 'Rhoda Bertram (wife of George Bertram) of Lowestoft, so it was recognised that her second marriage was not legally valid. It seems likely that Rhoda was relying on the wording of the Offences Against the Person Act 1861 which set out that:

> Nothing in this section contained shall extend to any second marriage contracted else-where than in England and Ireland by any other than a subject of Her Majesty, or to any person marrying a second time whose husband or wife shall have been continually absent from such person for the space of seven years then last past, and shall not have been known by such person to be living within that time.[41]

Eleven years had passed between George's desertion and Rhoda's remarriage, and if she genuinely did not know if he was living, then no offence had been committed.

---

[35] Application of Rhoda Bertram, J 77/198/5257; 1851 Census, HO107/1803/803/7/207453-207454.

[36] 1851 Census England and Wales, HO107/1803/803/7/207453-207454; 1861 Census England and Wales, RG 9/1183/50/4/542770.

[37] *Norfolk Church of England Registers*, Norfolk Record Office, PD 484/18.

[38] Last Will and Testament of Hugh Lawrence, *England & Wales, National Probate Calendar (Index of Wills and Administrations), 1858-1995*, proved at the Principal Registry, 14 November 1877.

[39] Application of Rhoda Bertram, J 77/198/5257. The marriage certificate of Albert and Maria from 1866 records George as being alive and a publican, see: *London Church of England Parish Registers*, London Metropolitan Archives, P83/PHE/005.

[40] Maria Sharpe, Petition for Divorce, J 77/232/6506.

[41] Offences Against the Person Act 1861, s 57.

When Rhoda died in 1888, she made her own will under the name of Rhoda Lawrence and she described herself as a widow.[42] The discretion with which this case appears to have been handled – for unlike the local applications, there were no reports in the press – suggests that some women may have seen the extra cost and potential inconvenience involved in applying to the Court for Divorce and Matrimonial Causes as a price worth paying for the anonymity it offered, especially in small communities such as Southwold, where Rhoda and Hugh lived.[43]

While some deserting husbands, like Joseph Harris Smallman, appeared to (at least initially) thrive in the 'new world' when they were free of their wives and domestic binds, for others the grass did not turn out to be greener. On 14 May 1865, Thomas Steele Mathwin, believing himself to be close to death, wrote a morose letter from America to his three now adult children, Henry, Mary, and John, sending it care of Henry, who had graduated university and become a schoolmaster.[44] Thomas had not seen his children, nor had any contact with them, since he left the family home nearly 20 years earlier, in December 1845.[45] The date that he sailed for America is unknown, however in his letter of 1865, which was affixed to Jane's section 21 application, it is clear that Thomas had been deeply embroiled in the fighting of the American Civil War. He wrote, 'we are all fighting one against the other. I have lost all I gained since being here' and detailed his many injuries, including the loss of all toes on his left foot, and 26 stitches across his face; significant injuries for any man, let alone one who was in his sixties.[46] Faced with an uncertain future, Thomas's actions of 1845 were clearly playing on his mind, and his postscript stated 'I want tell you to forgive me, that I may know that before I die'. Yet any growing fear over his imminent demise and his desire to repair the relationship with his estranged children did not dominate his thoughts enough to stop him throwing a parting shot at Jane, stating that 'I would never have done what I did if your mother had not asked me what I wanted when I came to bid you goodbye. I could not stand that'.[47] Jane's response to the letter was to apply for an order of protection.

Like the Police Courts, in addition to the 'Determined Emigrant', the applications made to the Court of Divorce and Matrimonial Causes also detail cases where the husband deserted his wife by 'going for a soldier' and enlisting in the armed forces. When Elizabeth Price discovered her husband's dire financial difficulties

---

[42] Last Will and Testament of Rhoda Lawrence, *England & Wales, National Probate Calendar (Index of Wills and Administrations), 1858–1995*, proved at the Principal Registry, 8 May 1888.

[43] As Rebecca Probert has argued, this is not a question of tolerance in the community, in many cases people in the community did not know that the marriage was bigamous: R Probert, 'Escaping Detection: Illegal Second Marriages and the Crime of Bigamy' (2022) 6 *Journal of Genealogy and Family History* 32.

[44] 1861 Census of England, RG 9/2759/52/9/543024.

[45] Application of Jane Maria Mathwin, J 77/38/M144.

[46] ibid; England, Birth of Thomas Steel Mathwin (1 January 1802) *England, Select Births and Christenings, 1538–1975*, 1068907/5.

[47] Application of Jane Maria Mathwin, J 77/38/M144.

and extramarital affairs, he 'enlisted in the Turkish Contingent for the Crimea' and, with the exception of a few weeks when the war finished, he remained apart from his wife from that point on.[48] Similarly, in 1863 Arthur Herman Faulkner had already been bought out of the army and set up in business as a tobacconist by his parents so that he might live with his new wife Jessie. This state of affairs lasted for just over a year, when they had a terrible fight during which Jessie accused Arthur of 'treating me with great violence, striking me and threatening my life'. Following this, Arthur closed the business, sold their furniture, and re-enlisted in the Royal Artillery: he was last heard of in Ahmednagar, India.[49] Some nine years earlier, Amy Wootton had experienced a very similar set of circumstances. Her husband, Fuller Harvey Wootton, sold the furniture she had bought for their home with her money when he could not pay that quarter's rent. On the day of the sale, Fuller grabbed Amy by the throat and attempted to strangle her saying, 'I have not done with you. I will do for you yet', at which point she managed to run to a neighbour's house for safety. Following the altercation, Fuller disappeared and eventually Amy heard that he had 'enlisted for a soldier and was then on his way to the Crimea'.[50]

The experiences of these three women highlights a difference in the level of physical violence described in newspaper reports, and the detail in applications made to the Court for Divorce and Matrimonial Causes. Although some of the newspaper reports examined in previous chapters included mention of physical abuse, deserted wives applying to the Divorce Court frequently described severe 'ill-treatment', including Sarah Mack, whose application of 1870 details how her husband struck her 'a violent blow'.[51] Five years previous, Hannah Castle had told the Court of her ordeal at the hands of her husband, Thomas, who 'beat me with his fists, also with a stick and on several other occasions beat me and ill-used me without any cause whatever'.[52] Eliza Hicks, a milliner and dress-maker whose address on Lower Seymour Street, London, put her in the jurisdiction of the Marylebone police court, applied to the Divorce Court for protection from her husband Robert. Prior to deserting her and their four daughters in 1845, Robert had spent over £1,000 of Eliza's money on drink and beaten her repeatedly.[53] As a result of this treatment, which took place over a period of eight years and spanned the pregnancies of all four children, Eliza suffered 'severely from tremors and numerous dropsy' in her left side that required operations.[54] Other wives also detailed abuse that had taken place during their pregnancies. In 1874 Mary Ann Adams described the 'misconduct and irregular habits of (her) husband',

---

[48] Application of Elizabeth Price, J 77/134/2785.
[49] Application of Jessie Faulkener, J 77/142/3130.
[50] Application of Amy Wootton, J 77/62/W195.
[51] Application of Sarah Mack, J 77/100/1420.
[52] Application of Hannah Castle, J 77/12/C176.
[53] Application of Eliza Hicks, J 77/98/1374.
[54] In this period such an operation would likely be the 'mechanical removal of body fluids (bleeding, leeching, lancing)', G Eknoyan, 'A History of Edema and its Management' (1997) *Kidney International* 59, 118–26.

John Joseph Adams, who had, on one occasion, locked her 'in a room for a whole day in the early part of the year 1864 (where she) was prematurely confined of a male child which survived only 3 hours'.[55] The previous year, Nancy Rogers had explained to the Court how her husband, John, had treated her 'very cruelly and nastily', and just before the youngest of their five children was born, 'gave me a black eye'.[56] This is a common theme throughout the 56-year run of applications examined, indicating that the inclusion of such information was not in response to section 4 of the Matrimonial Causes Act 1878, which gave wives of husbands convicted under the Offences Against the Person Act 1861 the right to maintenance payments and the custody of all children under the age of 10.[57] Rather, this was an opportunity for wives who had been maltreated to have these (moral if not criminal) offences recognised as such in a formal arena.

Physical injury was not limited to blows. Several more women revealed in their application that their husbands had given them sexually transmitted diseases. Eliza Hutchinson Freeman's husband beat her with his fists but also committed adultery with someone from whom he contracted 'syphilitic disease' which he then passed on to Elizabeth. As a consequence of that infection, she had to be admitted to the Lying-In Hospital on the York Road, Lambeth for treatment.[58] Amy Harriet Liggins detailed a variety of abuse, identifying different levels of physical violence: he 'assaulted and struck' her, but then also 'violently assaulted' her and beat her with his watch chain, then on one occasion, he nearly strangled her.[59] In addition to this however, like John Rogers, he committed adultery, contracted a 'venereal disease' which he then promptly transmitted to Amy. In a time before antibiotics and antivirals, the effects of such diseases could be devastating. In 1884, Jane Champion came before the Court seeking an order of protection from her husband, Charles. She set out a story of true marital woe of exactly the kind imagined by the popular press, which began with Charles' repeated but short-lived desertions after just two years of marriage (while she was confined with their second child), and then escalated to physical violence. In addition to this, Jane believed that Charles had squandered £1,550 in 'dissipation', and as a direct consequence had 'twice communicated to (her) a loathsome disease', which she in turn had given to three of their four children. Tragically, as a result of this illness (likely syphilis), Jane's two youngest children were both dead before the age of 15 months.[60]

These descriptions of physical violence and medical harm could be further evidenced here multiple times over, a situation which is emphatically different to the description of the applications made to magistrates and police courts in the press. Now, this could reflect a bias in the reporting of the applications heard in London and Lancashire; perhaps they were reluctant to share the level

[55] Application of Mary Ann Adams, J 77/161/3865.
[56] Application of Nancy Rogers, J 77/134/2786.
[57] Matrimonial Causes Acts Amendment Act 1878.
[58] Application of Eliza Hutchinson Freeman, J 77/152/3542.
[59] Application of Amy Harriet Liggins, J 77/373/1285.
[60] Application of Jane Champion, J 77/313/9343.

of unpleasant detail heard in such cases, but other stories in the same papers would suggest that this was not the case. For example, in January 1858, there was extensive coverage of the murder of Robert Kershaw who lived in Over Darwen, Lancashire[61] and the *Blackburn Standard* also covered multiple trials for assault of wives, infanticides, and horrific deaths of children.[62] Similar tales can be found in the local London papers. Reading the pages where details of section 21 applications were reported reveals stories including 'Attempt to Strangle a Wife' and 'A Forgiving Wife'.[63] In this latter case Margaret Cleave appeared before the Aldermen at the Guildhall following – as the paper reported – a 'most brutal and savage assault' by her husband, who had struck her about the head with his fists, causing a severe cut to her nose, black eyes and 'the most frightful contusions'. Put bluntly, it seems highly likely – given the voracious public appetite for lurid detail from the courtrooms and the widespread impression that section 21 would protect honourable women from feckless husbands – that had the cases presented to the lower courts included details of extensive physical harm, they would have been reported.

The inclusion of information about the physical and mental maltreatment of many of the deserted wives in the applications heard before the Divorce Court emphasises the fact that blame for the desertion lay purely at the feet (or fists) of the husband. Establishing the fault of a party was absolutely crucial in the applications for divorce that were heard more frequently in the Court for Divorce and Matrimonial Causes, where the success of the case relied on proving not only that one party was guilty but that the other was innocent.[64] Applications for section 21 orders were, however, slightly different, in that the two essential criteria to be proved were that (i) the husband had deserted and (ii) that the wife was self-supporting: the desertion proved the guilt. Yet although the legislation was only available to wives whose husbands had deserted them, and the fact that it was specifically designed to protect women who were legally hamstrung by their legal status as married women, there was still an explicit requirement in the Matrimonial Causes Act 1857 that if desertion had occurred, it must have occurred 'without reasonable cause'.[65] If the wife had in anyway created circumstances that made it intolerable for a husband to live with her, then his removing himself from the family home was not desertion in the legal sense. It might be

---

[61] 'Shocking Murder At Over Darwen' *Blackburn Standard* (20 January 1858) 2.

[62] 'The Preston Infanticide Case' *Blackburn Standard* (24 March 1858) 3; 'Deaths From Burning' *Blackburn Standard* (3 March 1858) 3.

[63] 'Attempt To Strangle A Wife' *Globe* (29 September 1858) 3; 'A Forgiving Wife' *Globe* (18 May 1858) 3.

[64] Strict rules concerning condonation and connivance, plus the requirement for the petitioning party to be 'innocent' of matrimonial offences (such as adultery) themselves, required the assignation of guilt and innocence. The Queens Proctor investigated cases where they suspected couples had been less than honest with the Court and could block or reverse divorce petitions. See: J Aston, 'Petitions to the Court for Divorce and Matrimonial Causes: A New Methodological Approach to the History of Divorce, 1857–1923' (2022) 43 *Journal of Legal History* 16–17, and WE Schneider, *Engines of Truth: Producing Veracity in the Victorian Courtroom*, (New Haven, Yale University Press, 2016) Chapter 4.

[65] Matrimonial Causes Act (MCA) 1857, s 21.

remembered from Chapter Six, that the Blackburn magistrates deliberately chose not to question Elizabeth Moulden's version of the events that led to her husband leaving their home and going to live with her mother, but this laxity would almost certainly not have happened in either the London Police Courts, or the Court for Divorce and Matrimonial Causes.[66] In 1863, the JO, Sir James Plaisted Wilde (later Lord Penzance), rejected the application of Annie Wild of Gravelly Bank, Staffordshire, because although her husband had emigrated to Australia and 'stated that he would never come to England again', he had also 'expressed a wish that I should follow him to Australia': ergo, this was not a desertion at all, but a husband seeking to provide for his family abroad after his farm in England failed. The fact that no further information about his location, or financial support that would enable Annie to travel to Australia, had been forthcoming in the intervening decade was, according to the JO, neither here nor there.[67] Similarly, Selina Maria Laws had her application to the Court for Divorce and Matrimonial Causes rejected four years later because 'the circumstances under which the husband left the petitioner (need) to be more fully set out' and the Judge was not convinced that her husband had left without due cause.[68]

Chart 7.2 Average Length of Time Between Marriage and Desertion[69]

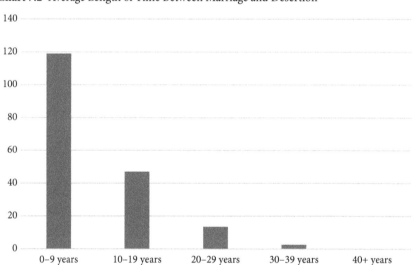

This decision might seem draconian, but the threshold to prove desertion under section 21 of the Matrimonial Causes Act 1857 was actually far lower than the level which had to be met in cases of judicial separation or divorce. In those cases, a petitioner was required to prove 'desertion without cause for two years and

[66] See Chapter 6, page 173.
[67] Application of Annie Ward, J 77/61/W142.
[68] Application of Selina Maria Laws, J 77/73/373.
[69] There were 181 cases in the sample.

upwards', thus the clock was reset every time the wandering husband returned to his wife.[70] With no minimum term of desertion set out in section 21, wives who believed (rightly or wrongly) that they had been permanently deserted were able to apply for protection as soon as they were confident that they could meet the legal requirements of supporting themselves through their own industry.[71] Chart 7.2 shows the length of time between the date of marriage and the date that the applicant alleged desertion occurred.[72] It is immediately apparent that the desertion occurred most frequently within the first 10 years of the relationship, with nearly two-thirds of desertions occurring within that period. This suggests that the majority of desertions took place in a response to the domestic incompatibility of the couple, and possibly also the pressures of family life. Some cases demonstrate this very clearly: Elizabeth Griffiths married her husband John Griffiths in August 1866, and by October of the same year, he had begun to 'abuse, ill-treat and assault' her.[73] Following a particularly violent episode between the couple, Elizabeth was forced to flee the marital home for her safety, and eventually took up residence with her father, where she assisted him in running his draper's shop. They had cohabited for less than seven weeks.[74] Other women also experienced difficult circumstances very soon after their marriage. Elizabeth, a servant, married baker Charles Barwick in St Leonard's Church, Shoreditch on 25 October 1852.[75] Roughly three weeks after their marriage, a woman came into the couple's shop carrying a baby, claiming that Charles was the father. He admitted paternity and it emerged that he had already been before the magistrate where he had been ordered to pay two shillings and six pence per week in financial support. In her application, Elizabeth explained that this discovery had caused 'a significant quarrel' during which Charles had struck her and 'used very abusive language'.[76] On 15 December 1852, just 51 days after their marriage, Charles sold their shop and business without discussing it with Elizabeth (though, of course, as a married woman she had no rights of ownership anyway), and left, giving her no details of his whereabouts, nor any financial support. Elizabeth went on to work as a domestic servant, and later as a barmaid in a public house. Charles, meanwhile, over the subsequent decade was declared insolvent, lived with another woman, fathered at least one more illegitimate child, and later spent time in prison where Elizabeth visited in order to identify him, though she did not speak to him directly.[77]

---

[70] MCA 1857, s 21. It is worth noting that the Matrimonial Causes Act 1884 made a refusal to comply with an order for the restitution of conjugal rights statutory desertion, even if it had not lasted two years: Matrimonial Causes Act 1884, s 5.

[71] Of course, whether the judge also believed that their husband was gone for good is another story, see Elizabeth Smith: Chapter 6, page 175.

[72] It was possible to determine these dates for 181 section 21 applications made to the Court for Divorce and Matrimonial Causes between 1858 and 1914.

[73] Application of Elizabeth Griffiths, J 77/189/4923.

[74] ibid.

[75] London Church of England Parish Registers, P91/LEN/A/01/MS 7498/65.

[76] Application of Elizabeth Barwick, J 77/130/2633.

[77] ibid.

Remarkably, despite the dramatic and seemingly permanent difficulties that were almost instantly apparent within some marriages, most women did not apply for protection under section 21 as soon as they were able to. This would have been immediately in the case of Elizabeth Griffiths who was deserted in 1866, and from 1 January 1858 in the case of Elizabeth Barwick who had been deserted in 1852. Rather, Griffiths applied for her protection order 11 years after her husband deserted her, and Barwick applied 21 years after she was deserted. They were not unusual: the average amount of time that elapsed between desertion and submission of an application for a protection order by women who had been deserted after less than a year of marriage was nearly 16 years. Part of this can be explained by the fact that some women had been deserted prior to the Matrimonial Causes Act 1857 becoming law and so they did not have that recourse open to them, but previous chapters have shown how eagerly anticipated the provision was, and yet those women with short-lived marriages deserted prior to 1858 did not apply for protection until the mid to late 1860s, or even 1870s.

Chart 7.3 Average Length of Time Between Desertion and Applying for Protection[78]

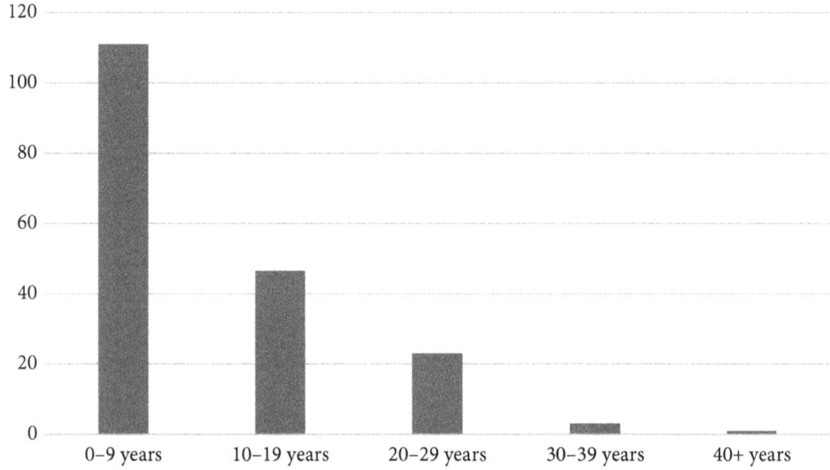

The average length of time between desertion and an application under section 21 being made was approximately nine years, but the longest time elapsing between the alleged date of desertion and date of application can be found in the case of Sarah Benson, an orphaned milliner from the small village of Bishopthorpe near York. Her husband William deserted her one week after their marriage in 1818 (which had taken place at his father's public house and without the consent or knowledge of her grandfather), after he discovered that the said grandfather would not be providing Sarah with a marriage settlement. She alleged that William struck her and 'drove (her) out of the house', at which point she moved to Leeds where

---

[78] There were 184 cases in the sample.

she had lived ever since.[79] Her order, made 48 years later in 1866, was refused, most likely because her argument that he had deserted her was weak, but maybe also due to her failure to fully set out how she had supported herself. It is clear that Sarah was not in any imminent danger of William returning to claim any of her assets – if he had not come to pillage within the first four decades, it is unlikely that he would do in the fifth – rather, the shaky and unsteady spider crawl of a signature that Sarah made to confirm her affidavit indicates that her motivation was much more likely to be ensuring her ability to make a legal last will and testament.

The lack of urgency seen in applying for an order of protection under section 21 at the Divorce Court suggests that (contrary to findings from the north-west) some deserted married women felt confident that they could function within society and maintain themselves and their children despite the legal barriers which, in theory at least, might be in their way.[80] Moreover, it also suggests that it was often external events – above and beyond a desire to be able to protect earnings or assets – that triggered a deserted wife to make her application. Thirty-seven per cent of the applications submitted to the Court for Divorce and Matrimonial Causes make an explicit reference to the applicant becoming entitled to an inheritance from a friend or relative and it was this that caused them to initiate proceedings: this reflects observations made in the London Police Courts in previous chapters. Some of these sums were relatively small, for example in 1877, Jane Norton applied for a protection order so that she could sell a property that she was entitled to under her late first husband's estate. She wrote in her application that 'if she obtain a protection order she could realise about £50 which to her is a great object she being seventy-seven years old'.[81] Other inheritances were far more substantial. In 1865, Selina Edwardes found herself in the enviable position of being entitled to a 50 per cent share of £8,620 8s 8d under the terms of her grandfather's will.[82] Her husband, a registered medical practitioner, was however in 'embarrassed circumstances' and had deserted her in June 1864, travelling abroad in an attempt to escape his debts. Selina sought to secure a protection order before Charles could return to claim her inheritance and it appears that she was successful; when she died in 1898, she left an estate valued at £8,907 3s 2d.[83]

Only 11 per cent of the cases that included details of inheritances were refused, indicating that the Divorce Court viewed financial investment as a qualifying means of self-support. There is an important distinction to address here: as discussed in Chapter Six, magistrates in the metropolitan police courts determined that property (whether it be tangible objects or financial gains) be in hand before an order could be granted. This was in stark contrast to the lay magistrates

---

[79] Application of Sarah Benson, J 77/7/B265.

[80] This fits with ideas of a 'permissive marketplace' whereby men and women worked alongside each other in the commercial world and trust and creditworthiness were built on personal relationships and networks and relied heavily on local introductions.

[81] Application of Jane Norton, J 77/212/5766A.

[82] Application of Selina Edwardes, J 77/17/E54.

[83] Selina Edwardes, *England & Wales, National Probate Calendar (Index of Wills and Administrations), 1858–1995* (1898) 15.

in the north-west, who were happy to grant a section 21 order on the speculation that the applicant would go onto establish herself in business. In the cases where an inheritance was mentioned in applications to the Court for Divorce and Matrimonial Causes, the women were either already in receipt of the bequest, or trustees and executors were demanding that a protection order be acquired before the bequest be made. Indeed, evidence suggests that although these applications were ostensibly made by the deserted wife herself, and couched in the terms of her personal story, at least some of the applications made to the central Divorce Court were made by solicitors not acting solely on the instructions of a deserted wife, but as part of a much bigger probate process.

On 4 May 1877, an unnamed representative of Hawkes and Co, a firm of solicitors located at 101 Borough High Street, Southwark, entered an *ex parte* application for the protection of Mrs Rosa Elizabeth Hart's property. It explained that she had married Thomas Ingleman Hart at St Mary's Church, Kensington, on 17 October 1843, and lived with him until 1 June 1852, during which time they had four children.[84] Theirs had not been a happy marriage. Thomas, according to the application made to the Court, 'gave way to intemperate habits and was frequently very violent in his conduct … and has gone so far as to threaten her (Rosa's) life'. The couple had briefly separated when she had sought 'the protection of her father's roof', but she had returned to the marital home and remained there despite Thomas's increasingly intemperate and violent behaviour. On or about the 1 June 1852 he, 'of his own accord', left for Australia, alone. Rosa's application reveals a great deal about her financial affairs. She was the recipient of an indenture of £1,500 made by Thomas Ingleman Hart on 18 December 1850; a settlement of £2,500 from her father, John Cass, under his last will and testament of 1853; and £250 per annum under the last will and testament of her aunt, Ann Elizabeth Moon Chuck, who died 14 January 1860. Rosa's entitlement to each of these incomes was protected by law even before her desertion as they had all been settled for her 'sole and personal use', so although she did not have access to the capital, neither did her husband.

The catalyst for Rosa's application for protection under section 21 in May 1877 came not as a real or imagined threat from Thomas, but rather upon the death of her mother, Sophia Cass, on 29 January 1877. Under her own marriage settlement made on 24 June 1812, Sophia had enjoyed the income generated by a £2,000 investment and, according to the terms of the settlement, upon her death the remaining sum should be converted to cash and divided between any living children who reached the age of 21. By May 1877 this process had taken place and Rosa was entitled to one-seventh of £1,809 10s 0d; nearly £260. This inheritance was different to those Rosa had received under her marriage settlement and the wills of her father and her aunt because it was not an investment but a lump sum. The terms of the bequest were not that it was bequeathed in a trust for 'her sole and separate use', which would have protected it (even if only in theory) from the hands of her husband, but that it be paid in cash. Furthermore, the Married

84 Application of Rosa Elizabeth Hart, J 77/191/4990.

Women's Property Act 1870 only allowed for married women to inherit sums of up to £200 in their own right.[85] Rosa's solicitor therefore stated that she was 'desirous of being able to give a valid receipt to the trustees of said indenture for my share of the said trust money', hence her application for protection under section 21 which would allow her to revert to *feme sole* status, inherit any sum in her own name, and prevent her estranged husband accessing it.

In contrast to many of the other applications heard in the Court for Divorce and Matrimonial Causes and reports of applications made in both the north-west and metropolitan police courts, Rosa acknowledged that she had communicated with Thomas since he fled to Australia. Her solicitor stated carefully that she had 'not *seen* the said Thomas Hart since the said 1 June 1852'. This was perhaps a risk: certainly the common perception from the metropolitan police courts seemed to be that it was far wiser to have as much literal and figurative space between the applicant and the deserted husband as possible; something that was not always possible (or expected) in the more closely knit communities of Lancashire. It was, however, a clever ploy by Rosa's solicitor, for she was a woman of substantial means and one of her sources of income was the £1,500 indenture created by Thomas for her in December 1850. The income from this investment was for her sole and separate use during her lifetime and upon her death would be divided between her surviving children, technically meaning that although Thomas had left the marital home and gone to Australia, he had not deserted Rosa in the sense of leaving her destitute and reliant on her own means. Although this had not been held as a defining feature of desertion since 1868, Rosa's solicitor still addressed this issue directly, stating that although Thomas had indeed created an income for his wife and their four children, Rosa, having come to a situation following the death of her aunt in 1860 whereby she could 'maintain myself and my family by my separate property and independently of the income arising' from Thomas's settlement did so. Moreover, she,

> knowing that Thomas Ingleman Hart was in needy circumstances in Australia have from time to time remitted to him sums of money which amount in the whole to more than the income which I have received under the said indenture since the decease of the said Ann Elizabeth Moon Chuck.[86]

This clever move meant that Rosa had technically been supporting herself and her children since 1860 and was in fact also at least partially supporting her absent husband. To emphasise Thomas's deliberate desertion, the application closed with the statement that despite these communications and Rosa's gifts of money, Thomas had not, in the 25 years since he had left for Australia, 'expressed … any wish or intention to return to me nor asked me to go to out to him'.

---

[85] 'Where any woman married after the passing of this Act shall during her marriage become entitled to any personal property as next of kin or one of the next of kin of an intestate, or to any sum of money not exceeding two hundred pounds under any deed or will, such property shall, subject and without prejudice to the trusts of any settlement affecting the same, belong to the woman for her separate use, and her receipts alone shall be a good discharge for the same': Married Women's Property Act 1870, s 7.

[86] Application of Rosa Elizabeth Hart, J 77/191/4990.

Unlike in the newspaper reports of applications under section 21 heard before magistrates, with scarce newspaper coverage and heavily pruned case files, we have no sense of the process that the JO, Sir James Hannen, followed as he made his decision, or the comments he made in Court when he granted Rosa's application. The next file on his docket was another *ex parte* application, also submitted by an unnamed solicitor from the firm Hawks, Willmott and Stokes of Southwark, this time on behalf of their client Susanna Matilda Francis.[87] Susanna had married William Francis on 21 September 1843 at St Mary's Church, Ware, Hertfordshire, and over the following seven years they had four children together, three of whom were still living in 1877 when the section 21 application was made. Susanna's solicitor explained that in July 1850, when she was around five months pregnant with their fourth child and away from home visiting her father's house, William 'suddenly of his own accord without any notice and without any reasonable cause left his home deserting me and leaving our children destitute and entirely dependent on my said Father'. Although she had not seen him since that month, Susanna apparently had reason to believe that he had travelled to the United States of America. This is not such an exceptional story in itself; indeed it is reminiscent of some of the husbands described in the London Police Courts, but what makes Susanna's story interesting is that she was the sister of Rosa Elizabeth Hart and also stood to inherit under the same marriage settlement of her late parents. Like Rosa, she was also the recipient of a trust of £2,500 inherited following the death of their father in 1853 and a £250 per annum income from an indenture created following the death of their aunt Ann Elizabeth Moon Chuck. Both these incomes were (as in the case of Rosa) already protected from William's interference because the capital was held in trust and the income from interest paid quarterly but again, the possibility of what an absent husband might mean on the death of her mother Sophia and subsequent dissolution of her marriage settlement and its conversion to cash had not been anticipated when it was written in 1812. Despite this oversight, Susanna's father, John Cass, seems to have been well aware of his son-in-law William's character flaws. In John's last will and testament he bequeathed a debt of £1,000 owed to him by William and its bond to his two executors with the instruction that they should retrieve the debt and invest the sum into annuities for his daughter, Susanna.[88] Like Rosa, Susanna was 'desirous of being able to give a valid receipt to the trustees distributing the remainder of her mother's marriage settlement and, also like Rosa, Susanna's application was successful.

The applications of Rosa Hart and Susanna Francis point to section 21 being used in a strategic way, as part of a much broader legal process, and perhaps at the insistence of a solicitor. Further evidence for this argument can be found in the applications of distant cousins Jane Steele and Caroline Maginnes.[89]

---

[87] Application of Susanna Matilda Francis, J 77/191/4991.

[88] Last will and testament of John Cass, *Records of the Prerogative Court of Canterbury*, The National Archives, Kew; PROB 11/2175.

[89] Application of Jane Steele, J 77/194/5080; Application of Caroline Maginnes, J 77/194/5081.

Like Rosa and Susanna, Jane and Caroline were both represented by the same solicitor and the decision to make the application at the Court for Divorce and Matrimonial Causes seems likely to have been the decision of the solicitor's firm who were handling the probate of Richard Clemson Barnett's estate. In October 1871, after nine years of marriage and four children, William Steele had 'without any reasonable cause' deserted his wife Jane, who lived in Shoreham, Sussex. She and the children managed to survive for a short time, but they entered the Steyning Union Workhouse in August 1872 and were still inmates nearly five years later when her application for protection was submitted on 7 July 1877.[90] Jane alleged that William had been in regular employment throughout their time in the workhouse, and despite most of his family living within the vicinity of Shoreham Union Workhouse and knowing she and their children were inmates there, no one intervened. Jane's health was reported to be too delicate to support her family.[91] The requirement for a deserted wife seeking a protection order to be self-supporting was designed to ensure that any woman living outside of the support of her husband through no fault of her own, was not forced to become dependent on the parish. Jane could have, and it is highly likely that the Parish did, pursue William through the local magistrate court to secure an order that would compel him to properly maintain his family. According to Jane, however, William had taken employment on various boats and paddle steamers and was last heard of sailing for Odessa, well clear of the jurisdiction of the English legal system.

In what must have felt like a miracle, Jane discovered that she was entitled to a share in the estate of a distant relative, Richard Clemson Barnett, which was worth an estimated £700.[92] This would, however, only be payable upon the death of Richard's wife, Elizabeth, who had thus far outlived him by 20 years.[93] A further complicating factor came from the way the bequest had been written in the original will. The money that Jane stood to receive was part of a bequest made by Richard to a number of his nephews and as several of these nephews had predeceased Richard and/or Elizabeth, Jane became a beneficiary. Unfortunately, the clause to dictate what happened after the deaths of the nephews did not consider that the recipient might be a married woman, therefore it did not contain the invaluable phrase 'for her sole and separate use'.[94] This was a crucially important omission for Jane as it meant that any money over £200 that she received as inheritance would automatically fall under the control of her husband, William.

---

[90] Application of Jane Steele, J 77/194/5080.

[91] ibid.

[92] The equivalent of £572,800 today, a life changing amount for a long-term workhouse inmate.

[93] Last will and testament of Richard Clemson Barnett, *England & Wales, National Probate Calendar (Index of Wills and Administrations), 1858–1995*, died 7 May 1858, probate granted 26 May 1880.

[94] ibid. See also: see E Spring, *Law, Land and Family: Aristocratic Inheritance in England, 1300 to 1800* (Chapel Hill, University of North Carolina Press, 1993) and A Erikson, *Women and Property in Early Modern England* (Abingdon, Routledge, 1993).

Although it might not have seemed it during her five years in the workhouse, from a legal perspective it was fortunate that William had so conclusively deserted Jane and her children as it made a section 21 protection order available to her. There had been earlier debate as to whether being an inmate of a workhouse could be considered to be self-supporting, and there had been an established reluctance in the Police Courts to grant a protection order before the property was in hand, or the transfer at least imminent. It appears however, that Sir James Hannen JO – perhaps recognising that as William was somewhere in the Black Sea and far from the reach of the Court – thought it pragmatic to grant prospective protection which would ensure Jane and her family would eventually stop burdening the State. In this respect, the Court for Divorce and Matrimonial Causes therefore mirrored the holistic approach of the Blackburn magistrates, rather than the close reading of the law favoured by the legally educated police magistrates. Jane's application was granted on 11 July 1877.[95] Richard Clemson Barnett's widow, Elizabeth, died on 14 December 1879 and probate on Richard's estate was complete on 26 May 1880.[96] Subsequent census records show Jane occupying a whole house with her children in Hove, Sussex until her death in 1917.[97]

On the same day that Jane Steele's application was submitted, Caroline Maginnes' solicitor, also applied to the Court for Divorce and Matrimonial Causes for protection under section 21. Her application is almost a verbatim copy of Jane Steele's: both were entitled to a share of Richard Clemson Barnett's estate worth approximately £700, and both had been deserted by their husbands. Caroline had married Henry Maginnes on 2 September 1845 and had lived with him for 'various periods during' the next 23 years. On 29 May 1869, he 'without any reasonable cause' deserted Caroline and had remained living apart from her ever since. Unlike Jane's husband William, who had left Sussex for life on the high seas, Henry had taken to moving around that same county and seemingly deliberately spending his winters in the workhouse. Caroline, meanwhile, had managed to establish her own home and maintain herself and her child through her own work, first as a domestic servant and then later as a dress-maker, thus making her application more straightforward than Jane's.[98] Like Jane, Caroline's application was granted on 11 July 1877, and she lived with her children in Brighton, Sussex until her death in 1916.[99]

---

[95] Application of Jane Steele, J 77/194/5080.

[96] Last will and testament of Elizabeth Barnett, *England & Wales, National Probate Calendar (Index of Wills and Administrations), 1858–1995*, died 14 December 1879, probate granted 14 January 1880; Last will and testament of Richard Clemson Barnett (n 93).

[97] 1881 England Census, RG11/1098/105/4/1341259; 1891 England Census, RG12/819/56/2/6095929; 1901 England Census, RG13/938/19/30; 1911 England Census, RG14/5196/104; Jane Steele, *England & Wales, Civil Registration Death Index, 1916–2007* (January 1917) 2b, 495.

[98] Application of Caroline Maginnes, J 77/194/5081.

[99] ibid; 1881 England Census, RG11/75/118/15/1341017; 1891 England Census, RG12/811/35/12/6095921; 1901 England Census, RG13/938/5/1; Caroline Maginnes, *England & Wales, Civil Registration Death Index, 1916–2007* (October 1916) 2b, 385.

Figure 7.2 Caroline Maginnes
Reproduced with permission from a private Wilcox family collection.

Figure 7.3 Henry Maginnes
Reproduced with permission from a private Wilcox family collection.

Court records reveal that although Jane and Caroline each had their applications for protection under section 21 heard and awarded within five days in July 1877, both women already had active cases working their way through the Divorce Court. They (or rather, their shared representative, Mr Ballard), had already entered a petition for divorce on behalf of Jane on 18 April 1877, and a petition for judicial separation on behalf of Caroline on 25 April 1877. Unlike applications under section 21, both these proceedings took time, and the court documents reflect this. Jane's application – though straightforward because William did not contest her accusations of adultery coupled with desertion – was not heard until 29 May 1877, at which point Sir James Hannen JO said that the case should be heard by oral evidence and set the date of 22 November 1877 for witnesses to appear. William chose not to attend and defend the suit, but Jane presented evidence, as did a woman named Eva Parker, who 'spoke of being reacquainted with the respondent, who presented himself as a single man'.[100] The *decree nisi* was granted that day, and the *decree absolute* was granted following the standard six-month interval on 16 July 1878.[101]

Court records show that several stages of Jane and Caroline's cases were considered in the same sittings of the Divorce Court and, as in Jane's case, on 29 May 1877, Sir James Hannen JO ruled that Caroline's application for judicial separation should also 'be heard by oral evidence before the Court itself' on 22 November 1877.[102] Caroline gave testimony to support her application for judicial separation on the grounds of Henry's cruelty and desertion (she was missing the crucial ingredient of adultery necessary to petition for a full divorce), explaining to the Court that prior to his desertion on 29 May 1869, Henry had been of 'intemperate and indolent habits' and had beaten her so badly that on 13 September 1859 he had been sent to Lewes Prison for three months.[103] Although no newspaper report of this offence can be found, it is easy to believe given Henry's appearance before the Lewes magistrates on 4 August 1855. On that occasion he was ordered to pay a fine of five shillings, plus five shillings costs after the police were called first to his house where he had been drunk and 'beating his child', and then to the Primitive Chapel on Fisher Lane, Lewes, where he had entered the Friday evening service drunk and proceeded to swing his hat 'about him in an exceedingly reckless way', before then setting about 'addressing the congregation in a very unintelligible and abusive manner'. The report went on to note that he 'leads a very disreputable life'.[104] Caroline's judicial separation was granted by Sir James Hannen JO the same day.

Despite Jane's status as an inmate of the workhouse and Caroline's presumably limited income gathered from her work as a domestic servant and then

---

[100] 'A Hull Divorce Suit' *York Herald* (23 November 1877) 7.
[101] Jane Steele, Petition for Divorce, J 77/190/4937.
[102] Caroline Maginnes, Petition for Judicial Separation, J 77/190/4950.
[103] ibid.
[104] 'Magisterial Business' *Sussex Advertiser* (7 August 1855) 5.

dress-maker, neither of these applications were heard *in pauperis*. Costs were eventually charged to William Steele and Henry Maginnes respectively as the 'guilty' parties, but these circumstances, plus the fact that both women were involved in a complicated (and high value) probate process, and were represented by the same solicitor, suggest that their cases were pursued due to the strong likelihood they would be successful, and on the promise of their inheritance. It seems likely that the applications for protection under section 21 were made as a temporary 'stop-gap' measure, in case Elizabeth, widow of Richard Clemson Barnett, was to die while the petitions for divorce and judicial separation were still being considered. Both section 21 applications stated that 'the said tenant for life (Elizabeth) is about 85 years and in bad health'.[105] As it turned out, Elizabeth did not die until 14 December 1879 when both Jane and Caroline were legally divorced and separated from their respective husbands, but the speed and ease by which they had been able to secure *feme sole* status for themselves under section 21 (a process that might well have been even quicker if they had applied to their local petty sessions), shows the importance of this particular legal remedy. It is not known whether Jane and Caroline had a personal relationship but it is not difficult to imagine the two women marvelling at the good fortune of their inheritance and conferring anxiously with Mr Ballard before they entered the Divorce Court at Westminster Hall on that damp November day in 1877.

The way newspaper reports describe the applications for section 21 orders made to the magistrates and police courts bestows a significant amount of agency on the part of applicant, making is seem very much as though the deserted wife was driving the process. Indeed, this is how the application form was framed and how the courtroom process naturally developed, with the female applicant appealing to the male-populated bench to help her. The cases examined above – particularly those of Rosa Elizabeth Hart and Jane Steele, whose applications might easily have been challenged on technical points of law – suggest that having the correct legal guidance might, as in Blackburn and London, have greatly improved a wife's chance of success. The different ways deserted wives accessed this legal advice in London and Lancashire has been explored in previous chapters and although the courtroom discussions of the applications made to the Court for Divorce and Matrimonial Causes are not available to dissect, the case files themselves reveal clues of the processes that occurred and ways women navigated the system. One of the most striking differences between the cases heard in the police courts of wider London and the magistrates' courts of the north-west was the number of women who made their applications using the services of a solicitor rather than self-representing, with the vast majority of Lancashire women employing professional advice compared to around half of those in the London courts.[106] Perhaps

---

[105] Jane Steele, Petition for Divorce, J 77/190/4937; Caroline Maginnes, Petition for Judicial Separation, J 77/190/4950.
[106] See Chapters Five and Six.

unsurprisingly, given the gravity of appearing before the JO in the highest family court compared to appearing before a volunteer magistrate with no formal legal training, fewer than four per cent of wives chose to make their application to the Court for Divorce and Matrimonial Causes without legal representation, and one of that number later employed a solicitor.

Yet, echoes of the role of police magistrates as a source of legal advice in the community can also be seen in the Court for Divorce and Matrimonial Causes. When Emma Beesley, wife of carpenter George Watkinson Beesley, filed her own application on 22 October 1883, it was so sparse that the JO requested further information.[107] This was not in itself unusual, the vast majority of applicants were required to submit further information to the Court but what was remarkable was the detailed annotation on the cover of the application. There, Clerk to Sir James Hannen JO wrote:

> The president does not consider there is sufficient information as to how the husband left the wife, on what terms they were living and whether he only left in search of work and whether she has had any communication with him since.

Then a different hand has also added that that applicant has 'to state whether she knows where her husband is and has any communication with him'. These annotations are significantly longer and more detailed than in any other cases and whereas the explicit reason that an application was denied is rarely given – a line or two merely states that 'the Judge Ordinary having read the Application and Affidavit … made no order', or even simply, 'refused' – here Emma has been given a blueprint to her follow-up affidavit. She took this advice, providing these details in her subsequent affidavit of 12 December 1883, and she was granted her protection order accordingly. The success (or failure) of a case did not necessarily rest on using a solicitor, but deserted wives clearly recognised that legal representation improved their chances of success or might at least make the experience more tolerable. Future research will show if the solicitors undertaking this work were specialists in the family court system established by the Divorce and Matrimonial Causes Act 1857, but evidence from these petitions suggests that this was not the case.[108] Of the 180 applications for protection made to the Court for Divorce and Matrimonial Causes by legal representatives, 170 different firms or individual solicitors were employed, indicating that in contrast to the dominance of John Pickop and Thomas Clough in Blackburn, any clustering by specialism had yet to take place.

Deserted wives outside London nearly always made their application for protection under section 21 to the Court for Divorce and Matrimonial Causes *ex parte*, completing the paperwork in their home town before sending it to a London-based firm who would present it to the Court. This process seems to

---

[107] Application of Emma Beesley, J 77/306/9121.
[108] ESRC New Investigator Grant, ES/X014169/1, *A New Methodological Approach to the History of Divorce 1858–1923*, https://hosting.northumbria.ac.uk/divorce_history/.

have been well established, despite the relative newness of the legislation. In 1861, for example, Eliza Hunt, a weaver from Macclesfield, made her affidavit before John May, a well-known local solicitor, before her application was then sent to Lewis and Son in London.[109] Her decision to apply to London cannot have been due to concern about the legal skills of her solicitor: John May had been in practice for over 20 years, and was a 'venerated townsman' renowned for his 'wise counsel'.[110] Furthermore, he was deeply concerned with the lives of the poor in the town, acting as a Poor Law Guardian from 1838, and had given evidence to Home Select Committees on the Poor Law several times, which suggests he would have been well aware of how section 21 might help deserted wives.[111] Furthermore, the annual *Return of Judicial Statistics* report Circuit 9 (of which Macclesfield was part) granted 19 section 21 orders in 1859,[112] compared to the 17 in Circuit 4 (which included Blackburn), so magistrates in Macclesfield were granting orders, and in reasonably high numbers. Despite this however, the local newspaper, the *Macclesfield Courier and Herald* only reported one application made to the Macclesfield magistrates, though they regularly reported on divorce petitions heard in the Court for Divorce and Matrimonial Causes. The sole section 21 case which was reported in the *Macclesfield Courier and Herald* did not give any details of the applicant or her circumstances, and the purpose of the story was actually to detail a disagreement between the magistrates and Town Clerk about section 21. In the hearing one magistrate had interpreted the legislation of section 21 to mean that property could be protected from whenever the date of desertion might have occurred, but the Town Clerk – Mr Thomas Parrott, a man 'whose legal opinion is of great weight anywhere' – disagreed, arguing (incorrectly) that property could only be protected from January 1858 when the Divorce and Matrimonial Causes Act came into law.[113] As well as being Macclesfield's Town Clerk, Thomas Parrott was a partner in the firm of Parrott, Colville and May, and given the early date of Eliza Hunt's application – only two years after the Act came into law – it could be that the firm deliberately submitted it to the Court for Divorce and Matrimonial Causes to see what the JO Sir Cresswell Cresswell, would rule, rather than directing it to the untrained Macclesfield magistrates.

The extent to which the strategy of these applications were driven by legal representatives rather than by the deserted wives themselves can be difficult to establish, but the application of Ellen Crompton sheds some light on this. Ellen lived in Over Darwen, Lancashire and could therefore have applied to the lenient and understanding Blackburn magistrates. Despite this however, her application was filed at the Court for Divorce and Matrimonial Causes on 15 December 1873 after she had made her affidavit before experienced Blackburn solicitor John Bolton.[114]

---

[109] Application of Eliza Hunt, J 77/24/H95.
[110] 'After Forty Years' *Macclesfield Courier and Herald* (6 May 1911) 4.
[111] 'Death of John May MP' *Blackpool Times* (30 November 1904) 5.
[112] 1859 is the first year the Annual Judicial Statistics were returned.
[113] 'Macclesfield' *Macclesfield Courier and Herald* (23 January 1858) 4.
[114] Application of Eliza Hunt, J 77/140/3036.

Ellen's circumstances were not auspicious. She was illiterate and since the desertion of her husband the previous month she had managed to acquire a 'small stock of fish' so that she could work as a fishmonger. Ellen said that although she had made extensive enquiries about the whereabouts of her husband James Crompton, she could not locate him and thought that he had 'either left this country altogether or gone to some distant part of it'. She had three children to support and explained that before he left, James had been 'dissolute' in his habits, very violent and had also taken with him all the money in the house including that week's income from fish sales. Her family and friends were willing to help establish her in a 'small business' but only if her earnings would be protected. Ellen's application was granted two days later. The contents of the case file itself does not give any indication as to why it was not held in front of the Blackburn magistrates who would likely have been only too eager to grant Ellen her order.

A newspaper report from the following year, however, does shed light on the situation. It details a bigamous marriage made by John Wilkinson and Ellen Crompton in February 1874, just two months after Ellen was granted an order of protection. The majority of reports from the Lancaster Spring Assizes only described John Wilkinson marrying a woman named Ellen Crompton when his own wife, Jane, was still alive.[115] The *Preston Herald*, however, gave details of both parties, explaining to readers that the said John Wilkinson had already been committed to 12 months penal servitude with hard labour the previous week but that Ellen had also set out to deceive, making the marriage using the name Ellen Errington and claiming to be a widow.[116] When Ellen, 'formerly fishmonger and greengrocer' came before the Darwen Police Court the following week, she 'stood in the dock as composed as if she were not at all implicated in marrying a second husband and while the first was living' and the court heard that Ellen was well aware that John was already married.[117] Furthermore, witness evidence revealed that far from Ellen's first husband James going abroad or to a far-flung end of Britain, he was in fact, still living in Over Darwen. Ellen was also sentenced to 12 months imprisonment.[118]

This ill-advised bigamous marriage raises a number of possibilities: did Ellen make the same mistake as scores of women and mistakenly believe that a protection order meant she was fully divorced, especially as her order had been issued by the Court for Divorce and Matrimonial Causes? If she did, then she made no mention of it to try and mitigate the bigamy offence during her trial and one cannot help but wonder what she told John Bolton during her appointment to produce the affidavit for her application. Alternatively, was she attempting to have her cake and eat it too, by using section 21 to protect her assets (as she saw them)

[115] 'Bigamy By A Preston Man At Over Darwen' *Lancaster Gazette* (14 March 1874) 10.
[116] *Lancashire, England, Church of England Marriages and Banns, 1754–1936*, Lower Darwen (1874) 83.
[117] 'The Darwen Female Bigamist' *Preston Herald* (18 March 1874).
[118] Ellen Crompton, *England & Wales, Criminal Registers, 1791–1892*, HO 27/168/28.

from her first union but seeking such protection far from home so as to avoid the inevitable scrutiny that would have accompanied an application to the Blackburn magistrates' court? Given that a section 21 order would stand until a husband made an application to have it discharged and even then, his application might not be successful, Ellen could be reasonably assured that James would be unsuccessful if he attempted to overturn the order, but public knowledge of their relationship status might well jeopardise her 'marriage' to John Wilkinson. There is nothing to suggest that the Assize court was ever made aware of Ellen's protection order, or indeed that it was ever formally discharged. Following her imprisonment, somewhat surprisingly, Ellen returned to live with her first husband James, and census records show they went on to have two further children.[119] By resuming their marriage 'by mutual consent and renewed cohabitation', Ellen's protection order ceased to be in effect, although it did continue to protect (in theory) the property she had acquired during their separation.[120]

The discharge of the section 21 order by mutual consent also happened in the case of Sophia Smallman, who the 1891 census shows to be living in Wednesbury, Staffordshire, with Joseph Harris Smallman – the husband who had deserted her in 1864, told her he was gravely ill, made a bigamous second marriage, and had three further children.[121] He returned from Aotearoa New Zealand sometime after 1886, possibly following the breakdown of his relationship with Harete Charlotte, who appears to have had a child with another man that year.[122] The 1911 census shows the couple visiting their son Herbert Spencer Smallman at his home in Stratford-Upon-Avon, suggesting that they had some form of relationship, though how Joseph explained his 20-year absence is anyone's guess.[123] The *Return of Judicial Statistics* reports show a total of 40 protection orders discharged between 1859 and 1876, therefore anyone who was successful in receiving an order had a very good chance of keeping it indefinitely.[124]

Only five records of applications for the formal discharge of section 21 orders remain in the J 77 files. Two of the five cases had originally been heard at the Court for Divorce and Matrimonial Causes, one at Westminster Police Court, one at Dover petty sessions, and one at Southampton petty sessions. All five applications for discharge were at least partially successful, and the wives lost the protection that they had applied for. Yet the small number of applications for discharge suggests that the JO did not routinely overturn decisions made in the

---

[119] 1891 Census, RG12/3413/122/7/6098523. Some 20% of those accused of bigamy returned to their first spouses, see R Probert, *Double Trouble: The Rise and Fall of the Crime of Bigamy*, Selden Society Lecture Delivered in the Old Hall of Lincoln's Inn,(8 July 2013).

[120] MCA 1857, s 25. In Ellen's case it is highly unlikely any court would have enforced her order given the adultery and then bigamy she had committed during the period the order was theoretically in place.

[121] 1891 Census, RG12/2261/39/22/6097371.

[122] Hart (n 24) 28.

[123] 1885–1886 Tauranga Electoral Roll, *New Zealand Electoral Rolls, 1853–1981*, 25.

[124] Numbers of discharged orders were not reported after this date, presumably because so few were reported and space was required to report the increasingly numerous and complex bankruptcy procedures.

lower courts and the Court for Divorce and Matrimonial Causes did not routinely act as an appeals court in section 21 applications.[125] Despite their relative rarity, the circumstances of the applications that were discharged by the Divorce Court highlights the danger that even wives with orders of protection could experience when confronted with a determined husband. Jane Jones had been awarded a protection order by magistrates in Southampton in 1873.[126] Jane's case had depended on the argument that Arthur had left her with no good reason, in fact, their daughter, Annie, testified that Arthur had not only deserted them, but also insisted that they welcome his long-term paramour, Mrs Mary Ann Ward, into their home. When he learned that Jane was due to inherit the interest from £800 following the death of her sister (the motivating factor for Jane's application), he applied for her order to be discharged, producing letters suggesting that the couple had been negotiating a separation if he would pay her a sum of £250. Arthur's solicitor argued that they had therefore separated by mutual consent, and unfortunately for Jane, Sir James Hannen JO agreed and discharged her order on 12 December 1876. This left Arthur free to claim Jane's inheritance 'to which I am by law entitled in right of my said wife'.[127] Fortunately, Jane was able to seek further legal advice and, based on the grounds of Arthur's adultery with Mary Ann Ward, applied to the Court for Divorce and Matrimonial Causes for a judicial separation in February 1877. Having read the application, Sir James Hannen JO decided that both parties should appear before the Court, which they did on 9 November 1877, and after hearing evidence, he granted the judicial separation.[128] It is not known how much of the £800 remained.

Husbands could also seek to have orders discharged after the death of their wives. Shenck Mackleh Abrahams[129] had applied for and been granted a section 21 order by the Dover Borough magistrates on 29 May 1876 on the grounds that her husband, Myers, had deserted her and travelled to California.[130] On 5 July 1876 Shenck used her new-found status as a *feme sole* to write a last will and testament bequeathing stock-in-trade and other assets; somewhat fortuitously as she died in childbirth on 7 September 1876.[131] When Myers returned from California later that month, he discovered that his wife had died, that she had taken out a protection order, and that her executor – a neighbour of theirs called George Carrier – had

---

[125] It is possible that not all applications for discharge survive, but the extremely small numbers of discharges reported in the *Return of Judicial Statistics* reports, together with the evidence showing how much of section 21 business was conducted outside of the Court for Divorce and Matrimonial Causes, it seems likely that there were simply very few applications for discharge heard by the JO.

[126] Application of Jane Jones, J 77/183/4709.

[127] ibid.

[128] ibid.

[129] Shenck was also known as 'Martha Abrahams'.

[130] Application of Myers Abrahams for the discharge of Shenck Mackleh Abrahams' protection order, J 77/187/4851.

[131] Last Will and Testament of Shenck Mackleh Abrahams, *England & Wales, National Probate Calendar (Index of Wills and Administrations), 1858–1995*, proved at the Principal Registry on 30 May 1877.

taken possession of property and stock-in-trade that Myers believed to be his. Myers argued that he had letters in his possession from Shenck 'written in a friendly strain' received while he was in California – the exact period she was applying for her order of protection and that he had gone to California with her express permission and blessing. These letters were, he admitted, written in the hand of his daughter, because Shenck could not write, and the overall tone of his application is one of total shock and confusion as to why his wife had done such a thing.[132]

Newspaper records, however, paint a very different picture of the Abrahams' marriage, Shenck's business activities, and the couple's pre-existing relationship with the Dover magistrates. First, Shenck Abrahams placed regular advertisements in the *Dover Chronicle* between 1871 and 1874, advertising her business as a new and second-hand furniture dealer, all of which name her as proprietor of her own business and not merely a caretaker of the family firm while Myers was away. It was also in her capacity as a business owner that she was brought before Dover Police Court in July 1870 and fined 10 shillings for refusing to move a bedstead and chairs that were blocking the footway outside her shop. She apparently told the policeman who asked her to move them that she would 'if he paid her rates and taxes' and then 'sat in a chair opposite her door watching them'.[133] The following year Shenck appeared as a witness in a case of a private in the 67th Regiment which was stationed at Dover and were accused of committing criminal damage. Several men observed Private John Sanderson jumping over roofs to move between properties and when Police Constable Geddes caught up with him at Mrs Abraham's yard, Shenck was 'holding him by the collar' and the prisoner was taken into custody.[134]

There was also a pre-existing relationship between Shenck's executor George Carrier and her estranged husband, Myers Abrahams. On Friday 10 July 1874, George Carrier had been summoned to Dover Police Court for assaulting Myers.[135] During the hearing, the two magistrates, R Rees and RH Jones Esqs, heard that 'for a long time, complainant (Abrahams) had been in bad odour in the neighbourhood in which he lived for many reasons'.[136] Myers accused George Carrier of pushing him into bankruptcy multiple times and Mrs Carrier of interfering in his marriage. He said that he had shouted at Mrs Carrier to leave them alone, at which point George had become involved and Myers was punched to the ground. All remaining semblance of usual legal proceedings dissolved as Myers repeatedly refuted the allegation that he had ever physically assaulted his wife and George Carrier's solicitor, a Mr Mowle, described the case as the 'most impudent and preposterous case that had ever been brought into that court', and exclaimed that

---

[132] Application of Myers Abrahams, J 77/187/4851.
[133] 'Robbing A Comrade' *Dover Chronicle* (2 July 1870) 6.
[134] 'Eluding the Piquets' *Dover Chronicle* (31 March 1871) 6.
[135] 'Strife Among the Israelites' *Dover Chronicle* (10 July 1874) 6.
[136] ibid.

'as their worships knew, (Myers) had been there in that Court time after time for illtreating his wife, and the neighbours often had to interfere to protect her from his violence'.[137] Indeed, some eight years previous, Myers had been summoned to Dover Borough petty sessions after a policeman had attended the Abrahams' home following reports that a woman had been screaming 'murder' from the house.[138] During the hearing it transpired that Shenck had also attended the police station the previous Thursday to complain about Myers' poor behaviour towards her.[139]

Curiously, although Myers's application for the discharge of Shenck's order of protection only mentioned an order granted in May 1876, newspaper reports show that she had also applied (under the name of Martha Abrahams), to the Dover magistrates under section 21 in August 1869, stating that she believed her husband had gone abroad.[140] Certainly this timeline fits more closely with the newspaper coverage of Myers's regular appearances before the magistrates in Dover. His continued drunkenness and frequent fighting regularly intertwined with his life as a small business owner in a busy port town, but newspaper reports of his exploits where he appeared in person, including multiple bankruptcies, ceased in 1868 when he successfully applied for the discharge of his bankruptcy[141] and then recommenced in 1874 when he brawled in the street with George Carrier.[142] In the hearing for this latter case he stated 'these last five or six years since I went abroad, when my business was in ruin, I did the best I could, and my wife too'.[143] It seems likely that he was abroad from 1868 to summer 1874, which also coincided with the period where Shenck was carrying on and advertising the business under her own name. By recommencing life together as husband and wife, Shenck effectively ended her protection order in 1874 but she retained protection for the period the order was in place. It seems that she then applied for a second order under section 21 after he left again for California in 1875/76, and this was the order that Myers had applied to have discharged. Despite his best efforts though, Shenck's last will and testament bequeathing £600 to her children, was proven at the Principal Registry by George Carrier on 30 May 1877, under 'certain limitations', namely that her assets were only gathered during the periods her protection order was in place.[144]

Just as in the local courts, proving that an applicant met the two crucial criteria of being deserted without due cause and being self-supporting was an essential part of applying for a section 21 order in the Divorce Court. Wives (and solicitors)

---

[137] ibid.

[138] 'Disturbing a Neighbourhood' *Dover Telegraph and Cinque Ports General Advertiser* (4 August 1866) 5.

[139] ibid.

[140] 'Protection of Married Women's Property' *Dover Chronicle* (7 August 1869) 5.

[141] 'Bankrupts' *Dover Chronicle* (20 June 1868) 6.

[142] 'Strife Among the Israelites' (n 135)) 6.

[143] ibid.

[144] Shenck Mackleh Abrahams, *National Probate Calendar (Index of Wills and Administrations), 1858–1995* (1877) 8.

recognised this and 51 per cent of all applicants to the Court for Divorce and Matrimonial Causes attempted to fulfil the second criteria of section 21 of 'maintaining herself by her own industry or property', by stating that she was involved in a specific business, employment, or means of generating an income.[145] The types of work that the women engaged in varied enormously and gives some indication of the socio-economic status of women who were accessing the Divorce Court. Only eight of those who specified economic activity were making what Davidoff and Hall famously termed 'hidden investments', whereby the money rather than the woman herself was generating the income.[146] These women generated money from annuities, property portfolios, being the part owner of a ship, and money lending. Far more women were engaged in actively generating an income through business; with occupations listed including typical occupations for nineteenth century working-class women, such as milliners, dress-makers, laundresses, drapers, shopkeepers, provision dealers and hoteliers. There were several barmaids and pub landladies who would have had extra reason to seek a return of their legal status to that of a *feme sole*: married women could not hold a licence in their own name before the Married Women's Property Acts were passed. One such woman was Barbara Aitken, whose husband of 20 years deserted her and their six children in January 1871.[147] The family had lived for some time at The Bird Cage public house in Bethnal Green where William had been the landlord, and after he left – allegedly to the United States of America – the brewery agreed that Barbara could take over as the licensee so long as she could get a protection order. She submitted her application on 28 February 1872 and it was granted two days later. On 25 May 1872, the *East London Observer* reported an application made to the Tower Hamlets Licensing Transfers Committee for a transfer of the licence of The Bird Cage from the existing tenant to Mrs Barbara Aitken.[148] It was observed that

> the only difficulty arose from the fact that she was a married woman ... (but) ... she had procured an order from Lord Penzance, which declared that in reference to property she should be in the position of *feme sole*. The Bench held this to be sufficient and granted the application.[149]

The range of occupations – and the high number of relatively humble occupations – within the surviving case files, combined with the broad geographic spread of applicants, indicates that the access to the Court for Divorce and Matrimonial Causes was not restricted to wealthy elites, chiming with research into couples who petitioned the same Court for full divorce.[150] Unlike the petitions for divorce, none of the applications for a section 21 protection order were marked as being heard

---

[145] MCA 1857, s 21.

[146] L Davidoff and C Hall, *Family Fortunes: Men and Women of the English Middle Class 1780–1850*, 3rd edn (Abingdon, Routledge, 2019) Chapter 6.

[147] Application of Barbara Aitken, J 77/121/2269.

[148] 'Tower Hamlets Licensing Transfers' *East London Observer* (25 May 1872) 7.

[149] ibid.

[150] Savage (n 4).

in pauperis, suggesting that the court fee for this remedy was accessible even for the poorest women, as was the intention of legislators.[151] Several women worked as domestic servants, including Emma Keys, who was the servant of George Cary Elwes.[152] Her husband had also been a servant and the two of them lived in different households for a number of years, until in 1843 when he quit his position to move to the country but then effectively disappeared. Emma maintained herself and her two children through her work as a domestic servant, most recently as a nursemaid for the children of George Cary Elwes and his wife Isabella.[153] Emma made her application in 1863 following a bequest that George Cary Elwes had left her in his last will and testament. According to a codicil made shortly before his death, he left Emma the interest from £400 for her lifetime and then the sum to her children following her death.[154]

Some women's applications indicate that they were exceptionally financially vulnerable, with three of the women – Mary Ann Ryland, Rhoda Bertram, and Hannah Gidney – working as wet nurses to provide for themselves and their families, primarily because they lacked the resources to do anything else. Mary Ann Cobb married George Ryland at St Martin's-in-the-Field on 22 December 1839.[155] Her family were farm labourers from Diss, Norfolk, and before her marriage she had been employed as a housekeeper to a family living in Chelsea. George was a cordwainer, a trade that could be extremely lucrative, however when Mary Ann applied for a protection order in 1866, she reported that he was 'lazy, indolent and dirty', and failed to fulfil his potential.[156] She took to binding shoes and making children's clothes to make ends meet. In 1840, Mary Ann had their first child, who lived about a year. Mary Ann became pregnant again in 1842, and shortly before her due date, George left the house after breakfast and did not return; his apprentice believed he had travelled abroad. Mary Ann gave birth to a little girl three weeks later, but the baby only lived for a week. In her application for a protection order, Mary Ann stated that she 'was in the greatest distress and was obliged to go out as a wet nurse'.[157] Mary Ann went first to work for the Nately family who lived on Queen's Row, Chelsea. Their baby was 'sinking' but thankfully Mary Ann managed to nurse it back to health. She then went to work as a wet nurse for the newborn girl-boy twins of 'the eminent artist' Joseph Severn, who doctors feared were dying. Again, Mary Ann was able to restore the two babies to health and, perhaps overcome with gratitude, the Severns embraced Mary Ann into their family as a close confident and friend. Nursing the Severn twins was the last time Mary Ann acted as a wet nurse, for she was then appointed as an attendant at

[151] See Chapter One.
[152] Application of Emma Keys, J 77/31/K26.
[153] 1851 Census, HO107/1478/151/20/87801.
[154] 'Wills And Bequests', *Illustrated London News* (18 June 1859) 7. This newspaper report states that Emma had been left the interest of £400 in addition to a pre-existing bequest of £200.
[155] Westminster Church of England Parish Registers, STM/PR/6/34.
[156] Application of Mary Ann Ryland, J 77/47/R126.
[157] ibid.

Dr Sutherland's Establishment for Insane Ladies, perhaps through the influence of the Severn family, and she was soon promoted to the role of Superintendent Under Commissioner in Lunacy.[158] Mary Ann's unexpected career proved to be a financially lucrative one. The 1881 census shows her living in Pembroke Square, Chelsea, with a companion and a live-in servant, and her probate records reveal that she left a fortune of £9,392 14s 5d.[159] Joseph Arthur Palliser Severn, one of the babies she had saved in 1842 – by then a grown man and successful artist in his own right – served as her executor.[160]

In contrast to many of the reports of cases heard before the Lancashire magistrates' and the London police courts, children – and the ability to care for them and support them financially – were at the heart of many applications for protection made to the Court for Divorce and Matrimonial Causes, with 57 per cent of applicants describing themselves as having living children, though they were not always dependents.[161] For women who reported having surviving and dependent children, the family size varies from 11 children to one, with the average being 2.87. For some women, like Mary Ann Ryland, Rhoda Bertram, and Hannah Gidney, above, motherhood, desertion, and their ability to meet the criteria for a section 21 order were inextricably linked.[162] The most common occupation for deserted wives who had responsibility for children was a trade connected to keeping house, for example letting rooms, running a lodging house, acting as a housekeeper, running an inn or public house, or acting as a domestic servant. Occupations connected to the textile trades were also well represented with laundry work, dress-making and millinery all featuring prominently. Unlike the application of Sarah Conway in Blackburn, there is little mention of any income generated by children, however this might well be to avoid complicating the narrative that the applicant was self-supporting.[163] The common thread through all these typically feminine occupations is the ease with which they could be taken up with little or no formal training, that the trade provided shelter as well as an income, and the work was self-employed and therefore able to be picked up around other responsibilities, or a combination of all three. In contrast, deserted women who did not have children tended to be engaged in retail-based trades or teaching.

Of course, the relationship between these trades and the double-bind faced by so many women whereby they had to simultaneously generate an income while providing care for children (and other family members) is as old as time itself.

[158] 1861 England Census, RG 9/16/21/3/542557.
[159] 1881 England Census, RG11/23/90/37/1431005.
[160] Mary Ann Ryland, England & Wales, *National Probate Calendar (Index of Wills and Administrations), 1858–1995* (1885) 342.
[161] This figure rises to over 60% when women who were mothers but had no surviving children are included.
[162] These women had all been abandoned while either pregnant or nursing very young children and therefore wet nursing provided an immediate source of income. In many cases, lactation continues as long as a child is feeding and therefore this could be an extended source of employment.
[163] See Chapter Six, n 25.

What was different following the introduction of section 21 orders, was that the law now made it necessary for women who wanted protection to pull together what employment or self-employment she could in a more organised way. The danger of failing to do business 'properly', it will be remembered, was seen in the Southwark Police Court in 1858, when magistrate Mr Burcham refused to protect the property of Elizabeth Sophia Cooper because he deemed her dairy and accompanying milk walk as too trifling to be protected by the 1857 Divorce Act.[164] The criteria of section 21 may well therefore have had the effect of pushing more women into formal paid employment or organised business ownership at precisely the time popular rhetoric suggested women were retreating to the home.[165] With tens of thousands of orders granted, and an unknown higher number applied for, the requirement of a deserted wife to prove she was supporting herself and her family, made formal economic activity essential. The process of finding employment, or establishing a business, was sometimes a gradual one and this might explain why there was often such a long delay between the husband's desertion and the wife's application to the Court.[166] For example, when Hannah Castle's husband of 12 years deserted her in 1856, she moved from their home in London and took the children to live with her mother in Oxford. She then worked for five and a half years as a housekeeper, first for a Mr Bolton at Priors Harwick, Warwick, and then for a Mrs Campbell at 20 Brompton Square, London. The 1861 census shows that Hannah's daughter Charlotte was employed as her assistant.[167] In March 1863, Hannah had saved enough money to rent and furnish a house at 120 Stanley Street, Pimlico, and 'she took the said children home' to begin generating an independent income by 'letting furnished rooms to single gentlemen'. She successfully applied for her order of protection in 1865.[168]

Whether through their own determination, or the disinterest of the deserting husbands, most women did manage to retain custody of their children, even if that meant all went to the workhouse, as was seen in the case of Jane Steele. Similarly, following the desertion of her husband in 1865, Rachel Elizabeth Massey was 'compelled to ask relief of the authorities of the parish of Aston ... and was with my said three children taken in as indoor paupers at the Erdington Workhouse'. They remained there for 'some time' and had it 'not been for the kindness of some friends who offered to assist me in obtaining work to support myself and children (we) should be there now'.[169] Others were not so fortunate. Letitia Newport Seiller, who we met earlier as she failed to prove that she was domiciled in England and

---

[164] 'Protecting a Milk Walk' *Morning Post* (1 December 1858) 7.

[165] Although this notion, popularly described as the 'Separate Spheres Theory' has been widely challenged in the past two decades, particularly by historians of women in business, the idea that women's lives post-1830 became increasingly restricted to domestic duties pervades, particularly in popular narratives.

[166] See Chart 7.3.

[167] 1861 Census, RG 9/55/32/14/542565.

[168] Application of Hannah Castle, J 77/12/C176.

[169] Application of Rachel Elizabeth Massey, J 77/348/491.

therefore entitled to access the English legal system, also had to contend with her husband, Octave, taking their eldest child with him when he deserted her. She explained in her application that on the

> 18th day of July 1868 to the best of my recollection and belief he went out of the house … taking with him our eldest child as I thought on business or for a walk but he did not return or communicate with me in any way and although I made every possible enquiry I entirely failed to trace what had become of my husband or my child.[170]

The sex of the child is not given but given that they were the eldest and (based on the ages of their younger siblings) around 10 years of age at the time of the desertion, it is possible that they had value to Octave as a wage earner, whereas their siblings, Helene and Frederick, would have been aged six and one in 1868 and a financial burden – as Letitia was to experience. Although the law surrounding child custody under the Matrimonial Causes Act 1857 did recognise the importance of maintaining a relationship between the child and both parents, it remained weighted heavily in favour of the father's common law right to custody of his children. Even if Letitia had been able to track down Octave and her child, she would have been required to prove 'some further misconduct' to give the Court reason to intervene, especially as the child was over seven.[171] There is nothing in the case file or other archival documents to suggest that she was reunited with her eldest child before her death in 1879.

While Letitia's case lacks a satisfying resolution, for many of the women who applied to the Court for Divorce and Matrimonial Causes for protection under section 21, the granting of such an order represented a new start. It gave deserted wives a privileged legal status, instilling them with the confidence to build a future away from husbands who, if we believe the experiences described in the applications, were frequently drunk, frequently violent, and frequently caused significant difficulties for their wives, often over prolonged periods of time. For some women, the protection order was sufficient, while for others it was part of a much longer process of matrimonial litigation. At least 10 of the 187 petitioners identified in this study had either applied for divorce *a menso et thoro* under the old pre-1857 tripartite system or applied to the Court for Divorce and Matrimonial Causes for a judicial separation, or a full divorce. This could be a relatively swift process, such as in the case of Anne Elizabeth King, who was granted a section 21 order in 1881 and then petitioned for full divorce in 1882, which was granted in 1885.[172] Alternatively, it could take much longer, as Adelaide Victoria Dane discovered

---

[170] Application of Letitia Newport Seiller, J 77/146/3276.

[171] MCA 1857, s 6. For paternity rights in nineteenth-century England and Wales, see: B Griffin, 'Paternal Rights, Child Welfare and The Law in Nineteenth Century Britain and Ireland' (2020) *Past & Present*, 246, 109–47.

[172] Application of Anne Elizabeth King, J 77/255/7363; Anne Elizabeth King, Petition for Divorce, J 77/287/8474.

when she finally secured a full divorce 11 years after she had been awarded a section 21 order.[173]

For the vast majority of the deserted wives whose applications for protection came before the JO however, having the legal recognition that restored them to *feme sole* status, and the confidence that this gave creditors and trustees, was enough. Examination of the applications made to the Divorce Court provides a new perspective to the newspaper coverage of applications made to metropolitan and provincial courts, revealing levels of agency – and details of often heartbreaking abuse – that are not detectable in press reports. The decisions made in the Divorce Court do also reflect some of the pragmatism of the Blackburn lay magistrates and the advisory role played by the stipendiary magistrates in the London police courts. This suggests that, in many ways, although being able to have their application heard before a lay magistrate may have given deserted wives a greater chance of success, appearing before any of the courts which heard section 21 applications represented an important and affordable way for deserted wives to protect their assets and reinstate their legal identity, in some cases decades before any other piece of legislation granted even some of those powers.

---

[173] Application of Adelaide Victoria Dane, J 77/15/D111; Adelaide Victoria Dane, Petition for Divorce, J 77/129/2595.

Afterword

In 1899, Lady Violet Beauchamp wrote an article for *The Humanitarian* titled 'The Woman's Century'. In it, she declared,

> It is, I fear, no new remark if I state that the century now so rapidly drawing to its close is 'The Woman's Century'. I am sure that the four or five hundred years that preceded the now dying century did far less for the cause of womanhood than has been done in our own times.[1]

This certainly chimes with the traditional narrative of women's rights in the nineteenth century as a period where the gross inequities women faced were slowly but steadily eroded, with tireless campaign groups such as the Langham Place Ladies building the foundations that would eventually lead to women's social, political, legal, and economic emancipation in the twentieth century. Most of the key players in this narrative were, like Lady Violet Beauchamp, privileged. This privilege was not necessarily experienced in the same way by each woman; some had the privilege of money, others of access to education, or of being the daughter or wife of a man who believed that they were capable of more than producing children or running a home, but all shared the privilege of having enough time to contribute to the remarkable (and underestimated) efforts of feminist campaigning seen in the mid-to-late nineteenth century. Their victories: the Infant Custody Acts, Married Women's Property Acts, the repeal of the Contagious Diseases Acts, and eventually, the Representation of the People Act, are all (rightly) celebrated as landmarks in the civil rights of women and stand as testament to the power of female-led campaigns.

In contrast, however, section 21 of the Matrimonial Causes Act 1857 has, until now, been consigned to obscurity. The tens of thousands of women who utilised the remedy were, for the most part, neither very rich, nor very poor, in fact, they were so 'ordinary' that their records were not considered important enough to preserve. The majority do not seem to have been protected by the existing safety nets of marriage settlements enjoyed by aristocratic and upper middle-class women, rather, they were well used to contributing towards a family economy, rather than relying on their husband's ability to earn a family wage, and the cases explored in this book demonstrate how quickly they could turn their hand to self-employment when required. These women were not radicals themselves but the legislation they utilised was. Section 21 revolutionised the relationship between women, property,

---

[1] V Beauchamp, 'The Woman's Century' (1899) *The Humanitarian* 15, 271–72.

and the law, pushing women into formal economic activity at precisely the time popular rhetoric dictated they should be retreating to the home. The introduction and uptake of section 21 challenges the notion that legal protections were only exploited by the Victorian intelligentsia, and moreover, the case studies examined here, for example the illiterate bigamist fishmonger from Lancashire, Ellen Crompton, suggests women from these lower ranks were not only well informed about legal developments and the introduction of potentially useful legal measures such as section 21, but they also knew how to exploit such provisions to their maximum benefit – even when this took them outside of the law.

For Wives Alone is a story about rediscovery: the rediscovery of source material; the rediscovery of the tens of thousands of women who managed to get economic and legal security for themselves and their children; and, of course, it is the rediscovery of Olive Anderson's typescript, which, like the section 21 applications in the newspapers and J 77 archives, was momentarily lost from sight. The applications heard under section 21 that have been considered here, and our wider analysis of the legal-political context of the time, renders much of the discussion surrounding the Married Women's Property Acts, and the widely accepted timeline of 'progress' of women's rights in the nineteenth century, imprecise and incomplete. The basic 'facts' of social, political, economic and legal history of women in nineteenth century England and Wales have appeared settled for so long but are now disturbed and I hope that the new knowledge and perspectives offered in *Deserted Wives and Economic Divorce in Nineteenth Century England and Wales: 'For Wives Alone'*, will act as a call to historians and legal scholars alike to challenge what is known. To return to the statutes, the newspapers, the parliamentary debates, the diaries, the memoirs, and the case files to see what other long-held assumptions should also be reconsidered.

This is a call not just in the pursuit of scholarly knowledge, though that is of course important, but because of the more pressing fact that even though section 21 was a provision that changed the lives of tens of thousands of women between 1858 and the 1890s, it did so *through the gift of men*. The provision was designed by men, passed into law by men, enacted by men, and – crucially – it could also be removed by men. Moreover, this piece of legislation was only necessary because the majority of male legislators (and those male voters who elected them) were unwilling to yield their economic dominance and allow married women to retain their legal personhood and own property in the same way as their unmarried or widowed counterparts and men of any marital status. Understanding the structural inequalities of the law, as well as the conscious and unconscious cultural, economic, political, and social effects of these inequalities, many of which persist today, is absolutely central to creating a genuinely equal society, where everyone has the opportunity to access and experience justice.

APPENDIX I
MATRIMONIAL CAUSES
ACT 1857 S 21 AND S 25

XXI: A wife deserted by her husband may at any time after such desertion, if resident within the metropolitan district, apply to a police magistrate, or, if resident in the country, to justices in petty sessions, or in either case to the court, for an order to protect any money or property she may acquire by her own lawful industry, and property which she may become possessed of after such desertion, against her husband or his creditors or any person claiming under him; and such magistrate or justices or court if satisfied of the fact of such desertion, and that the same was without reasonable cause, and that the wife is maintaining herself by her own industry or property, may make and give to the wife an order protecting her earnings and property acquired since the commencement of such desertion, from her husband and all creditors and persons claiming under him, and such earnings and property shall belong to the wife as if she were a *feme sole*: Provided always, that every such order, if made by a police magistrate or justices at petty sessions, shall, within ten days after the making thereof, be entered with the registrar of the county court within whose jurisdiction the wife is resident; and that it shall be lawful for the husband and any creditor or other person claiming under him to apply to the court, or to the magistrate or justices by whom such an order was made, for the discharge thereof: Provided also, that if the husband or any creditor of or person claiming under the husband, shall seize or continue to hold any property of the wife after notice of any such order, he shall be liable at the suit of the wife, which she is hereby empowered to bring, to restore the specific property, and also for a sum equal to double the value of the property so seized or held after such notice as aforesaid: If any such order of protection be made, the wife shall during the continuance thereof be and be deemed to have been, during such desertion of her, in the like position in all respects with regard to property and contracts, and suing and being sued, as she would under this Act if she obtained a decree of judicial separation.

XXV: In every case of a judicial separation the wife shall from the date of the sentence, and whilst the separation shall continue, be considered as a *feme sole* with respect to property of every description which she may acquire or which may come to or devolve upon her; and such property may be disposed of by her in all respects as a *feme sole*, and on her decease the same shall, in case she shall die intestate, go as the same would have gone if her husband had been then dead; provided that if any such wife should again cohabit with her husband, all such property as she may be entitled to when such cohabitation shall take place shall be held to her separate use, subject however to any agreement in writing, made between herself and her husband when separate.

APPENDIX II
TEMPLATES FOR AN APPLICATION
UNDER SECTION 21 AND A PETITION
FOR REVERSAL OF A DECREE[1]

Figure A.1 Form of Application under Section 21. Image courtesy of UK Parliamentary Archives

No. 13.—*Form of Application under Sect.* 21.

To the Judge Ordinary of the Court for Divorce and Matrimonial Causes.

The application of *C. B.*, of   , the lawful wife of *A. B.*, showeth,—
That on the   day of   she was lawfully married to *A. B.* at   ;
That she lived and cohabited with the said *A. B.* for   years at   , and also
at   , and hath had   children, issue of her said marriage, of
whom   are now living with the applicant, and wholly dependent upon her
earnings ;
That on or about   the said *A. B.*, without any reasonable cause,
deserted this applicant, and hath ever since remained separate and apart from her ;
That since the desertion of her said husband this applicant hath maintained herself by
her own industry [*or* on her own property, *as the case may be*], and hath thereby and
otherwise acquired certain property, consisting of [*here state generally the nature of
the property*].
Wherefore she prays an order for the protection of her earnings and property acquired
since the said   day of   , from the said *A. B.*, and from all creditors and
persons claiming under him.

---

[1] Court for Divorce and Matrimonial Causes, Return of all Rules and Regulations 1859, HC 22 (106) 8–9.

Figure A.2 Petition for Reversal of Decree. Image courtesy of UK Parliamentary Archives

No. 14.—*Petition for Reversal of Decree.*

To the Judge Ordinary of Her Majesty's Court for Divorce and Matrimonial Causes.

The   day of   18 .

The petition of *A. B.*, of   , showeth,—

1. That your petitioner was on the   day of   lawfully married to   :

2. That on the   day of   your Lordship, at the petition of   , pronounced a decree affecting this petitioner, to the effect following ; to wit :

[*Here set out the Decree.*]

3. That such decree was obtained in the absence of your petitioner, who was then residing at

[*State facts tending to show that the petitioner did not know of the proceedings ; and further, that had he known he might have offered a sufficient defence.*]

or,

That there was reasonable ground for your petitioner leaving his said wife, for that his said wife

[*Here state any legal grounds justifying the petitioner's separation from his wife.*]

Your petitioner therefore humbly prays,—

That your Lordship will be pleased to reverse the said decree.

And your petitioner will ever pray, &c.

APPENDIX III
LIST OF CIRCUITS WITH
CONSTITUENT DISTRICTS

Circuit 1	Circuit 2	Circuit 3
Alnwick	Bishop Auckland	Alston
Berwick	Consett	Ambleside
Gateshead	Durham	Appleby
Hexham	Hartlepool	Brampton
Morpeth	Seaham Harbour	Carlisle
Newcastle-upon-Tyne	South Shields	Cockermouth and Workington
Rothbury	Sunderland	Haltwhistle
North Shields	Wolsingham	Kendal
Wooler		Keswick
		Kirkby Lonsdale
		Penrith
		Settle
		Ulverston and Barrow in Furness
		Whitehaven
		Wigton
Circuit 4	**Circuit 5**	**Circuit 6**
Bacup	Bolton	Liverpool
Blackburn	Bury	Ormskirk and Southport
Blackpool	Oldham	St. Helens and Widnes
Chorley	Rochdale	
Clitheroe	Wigan	
Garstang		
Haslingden and Accrington		
Kirkham		
Lancaster		
Preston		

(continued)

(Continued)

Circuit 7	Circuit 8	Circuit 9
Altrincham	Manchester	Ashton-under-Lyne and
Birkenhead	Salford	Stalybridge
Leigh		Congleton and Sandbach
Northwich and Winsford		Hyde
Runcorn		Macclesfield
Warrington		Nantwich and Crewe
		Stockport
		Whitechurch
Circuit 11	**Circuit 12**	**Circuit 13**
Bradford	Dewsbury	Glossop
Burnley	Halifax	Rotherham
Colne	Holmfirth	Sheffield
Keighley	Huddersfield	
Otley	Saddleworth	
Skipton	Todmorden	
Circuit 14	**Circuit 15**	**Circuit 16**
Leeds	Barnard Castle	Barnsley
Wakefield	Darlington	Beverley
	Easingwold	Goole
	Helmsley	Great Driffield
	Knaresborough	Hedon
	Leyburn	Howden
	Northallerton	Kingston-on-Hull
	Richmond	New Malton
	Ripon	Pocklington
	Stockton-on-Tees and	Scarborough
	Middlesbrough	Selby
	Stokesley and	Whitby
	Guisborough	
	Tadcaster	
	Thirsk	
	York	

(continued)

(Continued)

Circuit 17	Circuit 18	Circuit 19
Barton-on-Humber	Bugham	Alfreton
Boston	Doncaster	Ashbourne
Brigg	East Retford	Bakewell
Caistor	Mansfield	Belper and Ilkeston
Gainsborough	Newark	Burton-on-Trent
Great Grimsby	Nottingham	Buxton, Chapel-en-le Frith and
Holbeach	Thorne	New Mills
Horncastle	Worksop	Chesterfield
Lincoln		Derby
Louth		Wirksworth and Matlock
Market Rasen		
Sleaford		
Spalding		
Spilsby		

Circuit 20	Circuit 21	Circuit 22
Ashby-de-la-Zouch	Birmingham	Alcester
Bourne		Bromsgrove
Grantham		Chipping Norton
Hinkley		Coventry
Leicester		Daventry
Loughborough		Evesham
Lutterworth		Pershore
Market Bosworth		Redditch
Market Harborough		Rugby
Melton Mowbray		Shipston-on-Stour
Nuneaton		
Oakham		
Stamford		
Uppingham		

Circuit 23	Circuit 24	Circuit 25
Bromyard	Abergavenny	Dudley
Droitwich	Cardiff	Walsall
Great Malvern	Chepstow	West Bromwich
Kidderminster	Crickhowell	Wolverhampton
Ledbury	Monmouth	
Stourbridge	Newport	
Tenbury	Pontypool	
Worcestershire	Ross	
	Tredegar	
	Usk	

(continued)

(Continued)

Circuit 26	Circuit 27	Circuit 28
Atherstone	Bishops Castle	Aberystwyth
Burslem	Bridgnorth	Baln
Cheadle	Cleobury Mortimer	Builth
Hanley	Hereford	Corwen
Leek	Leominster	Dolgelly
Lichfield	Ludlow	Hay
Market Drayton	Madeley	Kington
Newcastle-under-Lyme	Newport	Knighton
Rugeley	Oswestry	Llanfyllin
Stafford	Shrewsbury	Llanidloes
Stoke-upon-Trent and Longton	Wellington	Machynlleth
Stone	Wem	Newtown
Tamworth		Portmadoe and Blacnan Festiniog
Tunstall		Presteign
Uttoxeter		Pwllheli
		Rhayader
		Welshpool
Circuit 29	**Circuit 30**	**Circuit 32**
Bangor	Aberayron	Attleborough and Watton
Carnarvon	Cardigan	Aylsham
Chester	Carmarthen	Downham Market
Conway and Llandudno	Haverfordwest	East Dereham
Denbigh	Lampeter	Ely
Holywell	Llandilo Fawr	Holt
Llangefni, Holyhead and Menai Bridge	Llandovery	Kings Lynn
Llanrwst	Llanelly	Little Walsingham and Fakenham
Mold and Flint	Narberth	March
Ruthin	Neath	North Walsingham
St. Asaph and Rhyl	Newcastle-in-Emlyn	Norwich
Wrexham and Llangollen	Pembroke Docks	Soham
		Swaffham
		Thetford
		Wisbech
		Wymondham

(continued)

(Continued)

Circuit 33	Circuit 35	Circuit 36
Beccles and Bungay	Ampthill	Abingdon
Bury St. Edmunds	Bedford	Banbury
Diss and Eyo	Biggleswade	Bicester
Framlington and	Bishop Stortford	Brackley
Saxmundham	Cambridge	Buckingham
Great Yarmouth	Haverhill	Farringdon
Hadleigh	Hitchin	Kettering
Halesworth	Huntingdon	Northampton
Harleston	Newmarket	Oxford
Ipswich	Oundle	Thame
Lowestoft	Peterborough	Towcester
Mildenhall	Royston	Wantage
Stowmarket	Saffron Walden	Wellingborough
Sudbury	St. Neots	Witney
Woodbridge	Thrapston	Woodstock
Circuit 37	**Circuit 38**	**Circuit 40**
Aylesbury	Braintree	Bow
Barnet	Brentwood	Shoreditch
Chesham	Chelmsford	
Henley-on-Thames	Colchester	
High Wycombe	Dunmow	
Leighton Buzzard	Edmonton	
Luton	Halstead	
Newport Pagnell	Harwich	
St. Albans	Hertford	
Uxbridge	Maldon	
Wallingford	Romford	
Watford	Southend	
Windsor	Waltham Abbey	
Circuit 41	**Circuit 42**	**Circuit 43**
Clerkenwell	Bloomsbury	Brentford
	Whitechapel	Brompton
		Marylebone

(continued)

(Continued)

Circuit 44	Circuit 45	Circuit 47
Westminster	Chertsey	Greenwich
	Croydon	Southwark
	Epsom	Woolwich
	Farnham and Aldershot	
	Guildford and Godalming	
	Hungerford	
	Kingston-on-Thames	
	Newbury	
	Reading	
	Wandsworth	
Circuit 48	**Circuit 49**	**Circuit 50**
Bromley	Ashford	Arundel
Dartford	Canterbury	Brighton
Gravesend	Deal and Sandwich	Chichester
Lambeth	Dover	Dorking
Maidstone	Faversham	East Grinstead
Sevenoaks	Folkestone	Hastings
Tonbridge	Hythe	Haywards Heath
Tunbridge Wells	Margate	Horsham
	Ramsgate	Lewes and Eastbourne
	Rochester	Midhurst
	Romney	Petworth
	Sheerness	Redhill
	Sittingbourne	Rye
	Tenterden and Cranbrook	Worthing
Circuit 51	**Circuit 52**	**Circuit 53**
Alton	Bradford and Trowbridge	Cheltenham
Andover	Calne	Cirencester
Basingstoke	Chippenham	Dursley
Bishops Waltham	Chipping Sodbury	Gloucester
Newport and Ryde	Devizes	Malmsbury
Petersfield	Frome	Newent
Portsmouth	Marlborough	Newnham
Romsey	Bath	Northleach
Southampton	Melksham	Stroud
Winchester	Swindon	Tewkesbury
	Temple Cloud	Thornbury
	Warminster	Winchcombe
	Westbury	

(continued)

(Continued)

Circuit 54	Circuit 55	Circuit 57
Axbridge	Blandford	Axminster
Bristol	Bridport	Barnstaple
Wells	Christchurch and	Bideford
Weston-Super-Mare	Bournemouth	Bridgwater
	Crewkerne	Chard
	Dorchester	Honiton
	Fordingbridge and	Langport
	Ringwood	South Molton
	Lymington	Taunton
	Poole	Tiverton
	Salisbury	Torrington
	Shaftesbury	Wellington
	Wareham	Williton
	Weymouth	
	Wimborne Minster	
	Wincanton	
	Yeovil	
Circuit 58	**Circuit 59**	
Crediton	Bodmin	
Exeter	Camelford	
Kingsbridge	Falmouth	
Newton Abbot and	Helston	
Torquay	Holsworthy	
Okehampton	Launceston	
Plymouth and East	Liskeard	
Stonehouse	Penzance	
Tavistock	Redruth	
Totnes and Churston	St. Austell	
Ferrers	St. Colomb Major	
	Truro	

BIBLIOGRAPHY

Archival Sources

Archive of AJ Bethell, Bodleian Libraries, University of Oxford.

Brompton Cemetery Records.

Brougham Papers, University College London Special Collections.

Court for Divorce and Matrimonial Causes, later Supreme Court of Judicature: Divorce and Matrimonial Causes Files, J 77 (1858–1923).

Diaries and correspondence of JC Hobhouse, Lord Broughton, British Library.

Edmonton Petty Sessions Court Minutes, Registers and Licensing Registers, London Metropolitan Archives.

England & Wales, Civil Registration Death Index, 1916–2007.

England & Wales, Criminal Registers, 1791–1892.

England & Wales, National Probate Calendar (Index of Wills and Administrations), 1858–1995.

England, Select Births and Christenings, 1538–1975.

FreeBMD, England & Wales, Civil Registration Birth Index, 1837–1915.

Hansard (series 3).

Lancashire, England, Church of England Marriages and Banns, 1754–1936.

London Church of England Parish Registers, London Metropolitan Archives.

Michigan, US, County Marriage Records, 1822–1940.

New Zealand Electoral Rolls, 1853–1981.

Norfolk Church of England Registers, Norfolk Record Office.

Palmerston Papers, MS62/PP/GC, Broadlands Archive, University of Southampton.

Records of the Prerogative Court of Canterbury.

Soundex Index to Petitions For Naturalizations Filed in Federal, State, and Local Courts in New York City, 1792–1906, The National Archives in Washington DC.

Westminster Church of England Parish Registers, City of Westminster Archives Centre.

Workhouse Admission and Discharge Records, 1764–1921 (1857) London Metropolitan Archives; CABG/173/3.

Workhouse Admission and Discharge Records, 1764–1921, London Metropolitan Archives.

Family Papers

Typescript of '*For Wives Alone: Economic Divorce*', held by the estate of Olive Anderson.

Judicial Statistics

Return of Judicial Statistics of England and Wales, 1859, 64 HC 2692 (1860).

Return of Judicial Statistics of England and Wales, 1860, 60 HC 2860 (1861).

Return of Judicial Statistics of England and Wales, 1861, 56 HC 3025 (1862).

Return of Judicial Statistics of England and Wales, 1862, 65 HC 3181 (1863).

Return of Judicial Statistics of England and Wales, 1863, 57 HC 3370 (1864).
Return of Judicial Statistics of England and Wales, 1864, 52 HC 3534 (1865).
Return of Judicial Statistics of England and Wales, 1865, 68 HC 3726 (1866).
Return of Judicial Statistics of England and Wales, 1866, 66 HC 3919 (1867).
Return of Judicial Statistics of England and Wales, 1867, 67 HC 4062 (1868).
Return of Judicial Statistics of England and Wales, 1868, 58 HC 4196 (1869).
Return of Judicial Statistics of England and Wales, 1869, 63 HC C.195 (1870).
Return of Judicial Statistics of England and Wales, 1870, 64 HC C.442 (1871).
Return of Judicial Statistics of England and Wales, 1871, 65 HC C.600 (1872).
Return of Judicial Statistics of England and Wales, 1872, 70 HC C.871 (1873).
Return of Judicial Statistics of England and Wales, 1873, 71 HC C.1055 (1874).
Return of Judicial Statistics of England and Wales, 1874, 81 HC C.1351 (1875).
Return of Judicial Statistics of England and Wales, 1875, 79 HC C.1595 (1876).
Return of Judicial Statistics of England and Wales, 1876, 86 HC C.1871 (1877).
Return of Judicial Statistics of England and Wales, 1877, 79 HC C2154 (1878).
Return of Judicial Statistics of England and Wales, 1878, 76 HC C.2418 (1879).
Return of Judicial Statistics of England and Wales, 1879, 77 HC C.2726 (1880).
Return of Judicial Statistics of England and Wales, 1880, 95 HC C.3088 (1881).
Return of Judicial Statistics of England and Wales, 1881, 75, HC C.3333 (1882).
Return of Judicial Statistics of England and Wales, 1882, 77 HC C.3763 (1883).
Return of Judicial Statistics of England and Wales, 1883, 86 HC C.4170 (1884).
Return of Judicial Statistics of England and Wales, 1884, 86 HC C.4518 (1884–85).
Return of Judicial Statistics of England and Wales, 1885, 72 HC C.4808 (1886).
Return of Judicial Statistics of England and Wales, 1886, 90 HC C.5155 (1887).
Return of Judicial Statistics of England and Wales, 1887, 108 HC C.5553 (1888).
Return of Judicial Statistics of England and Wales, 1888, 85 HC C.5882 (1889).
Return of Judicial Statistics of England and Wales, 1889, 80 HC C.6164 (1890).
Return of Judicial Statistics of England and Wales, 1890, 93 HC C.6443 (1891).
Return of Judicial Statistics of England and Wales, 1891, 89 HC C.6734 (1892).
Return of Judicial Statistics of England and Wales, 1892, 103 HC C.7168 (1893).
Return of Judicial Statistics of England and Wales, 1893 (Part II. Common Law and Equity; Civil and Canon Law), 95 HC C.7510 (1894).
Return of Judicial Statistics of England and Wales, 1894 (Part II. Civil Statistics) 94 HC C8263 (1896).
Return of Judicial Statistics of England and Wales, 1895 (Part II. Civil Statistics) 100 HC C.8536 (1897).
Return of Judicial Statistics of England and Wales 1896 (Part II. Civil Statistics) 104 HC C.8838 (1898).

Government Reports

Return of Number of Causes Filed in Registry for Divorce and Matrimonial Causes, 44 HC 99 (1862).
Return of Number of Justices' Clerks Paid by Salary instead of Fees in England and Wales, 58 HC 276 (1866).
Return of Number of Justices of Peace for each County in England and Wales, 1852–54, 50 HC 110 (1856).
Return of Number of Police Force employed in Metropolitan District, and City of London, 1841, 1851, 1861 and 1866, 57 HC 89-1 (1867–68).
Return of Persons appointed to Office in Divorce and Matrimonial Causes Court, 1858: Number of Applications, Dissolutions, and Cases Undefended or Set for Trial, 22 HC 269 (1859 session 1).
Return of Rules and Regulations concerning Practice and Procedure of Court for Divorce and Matrimonial Causes, 22 HC 106 (1859 Session 1).
Return of Sessions at which Clerks to Justices are paid by Salaries, 22 HC 24 (1859 Session 1).

Return of Stipendiary Magistrates in England and Wales, 50 HC 371 (1856).
Special Report From The Select Committee On Married Women's Property Bill; Together with the
    Proceedings of the Committee, Minutes of Evidence, Appendix, and Index, 7 HC 441 (1867–68).

Newspapers and Journals

All the Year Round
Blackburn Standard
Blackburn Weekly Times
Burnley Advertiser
Bury and Norwich Post
Bury Times
Dover Chronicle
Dover Telegraph and Cinque Ports General Advertiser
Edinburgh Law Review
Edinburgh Review
English Woman's Journal
Exeter Flying Post
Express (London)
Globe
Illustrated London News
Journal of Jurisprudence and Scottish Law Magazine
Justice of the Peace
Kentish Mercury
Lancaster Gazette
Law Magazine and Review
Law Times
Leeds Evening Express
Leeds Mercury
Lloyd's Weekly
London Evening Standard
Macclesfield Courier and Herald
Macmillan's Magazine
Magnet
Marylebone Mercury
Meliora
Morning Advertiser
Morning Chronicle
Morning Herald (London)
Morning Post
News of the World
Preston Chronicle
Preston Guardian
Punch
Reynold's Newspaper
Saturday Review
Sheffield Independent
Solicitor's Journal
South London Times
South-London News

Sun
The Annual Register
The Era
The Examiner
The Guardian
The Humanitarian
The People
The Spectator
The Times
Transactions of The National Association for the Promotion of Social Science (1879)
York Herald

Websites

British Newspaper Archive at www.britishnewspaperarchive.co.uk/.
Cambridge University Alumni, 1261–1900 at www.ancestry.co.uk/search/collections/3997/.
England & Wales, Civil Divorce Records, 1858–1918 at www.ancestry.co.uk/search/collections/2465/.
ESRC project ES/X014169/1, 'A New Methodological Approach to the History of Divorce' at https://hosting.northumbria.ac.uk/divorce_history/.
Integrated Census Microdata (I-CeM), 1851–1911 [data collection] K Schürer and E Higgs (2014) UK Data Service, SN: 7481 at http://dx.doi.org/10.5255/UKDA-SN-7481-1.
Office for National Statistics 'Divorces in England and Wales' dataset (2022 edition) at www.ons.gov.uk/peoplepopulationandcommunity/birthsdeathsandmarriages/divorce/datasets/divorcesinengland andwales.
Oxford Dictionary of National Biography at www.oxforddnb.com.
Measuring Worth Calculator at www.measuringworth.com/calculators/ukcompare/relativevalue.php.

Books

Abram, WA (1877) *A History of Blackburn, Town and Parish* (Blackburn).
Aston, J (2016) *Female Entrepreneurship in Nineteenth-Century England: Engagement in the Urban Economy* (London, Palgrave Macmillan).
Aston, J and Bishop, C (eds) (2020) *Female Entrepreneurs in the Long Nineteenth Century: A Global Perspective* (London, Palgrave Macmillan).
Atkinson, D (2012) *The Criminal Conversation of Mrs Norton* (London, Preface Publishing).
Atlay, JB (1906) *The Victorian Chancellors* (London, Smith, Elder & Co).
Barker, H (2006) *The Business of Women* (Oxford University Press).
Barlee, E (1863) *A Visit to Lancashire in December 1862* (London).
Basch, N (1982) *In the Eyes of the Law: Women, Marriage and Property in Nineteenth Century New York* (Ithaca and London, Cornell University Press).
Bellamy, C (1988) *Administering Central-Local Relations, 1871–1919* (New York, Manchester University Press).
Benson, J (1983) *The Petty Capitalists: A Study of Nineteenth-Century Working Class Entrepreneurs* (London, Gill & Company).
Blackstone, W (1765) *Commentaries on the Laws of England*, Vol 1 (Oxford).
Boase, F (1892) *Modern English Biography*, Vol I, A–H (Truro, Netherton and Worth).
Browne, GA (1876) *A Treatise on the Principles and Practice of the Court for Divorce and Matrimonial Causes*, 3rd edn (London).

Burn, R (1837) *The Justice of the Peace and Parish Officer*, 28th edn 6 vols (London).

Chapman, C (1925) *The Poor Man's Court of Justice: Twenty-Five Years as a Metropolitan Magistrate* (London, Hodder and Stoughton).

Coleridge, EH (1904) *Life and Correspondence of John Duke Lord Coleridge, Lord Chief Justice of England* (London).

Collins, W (1870) *Man and Wife* (New York, Harper & Brothers).

Colloms, B (1975) *Charles Kingsley: The Lion of Eversley* (London, Constable).

Conley, C (1991) *The Unwritten law, Criminal Justice in Victorian Kent* (Oxford, Oxford University Press).

Cretney, SM (2003) *Family Law in the Twentieth Century: A History* (Oxford, Oxford University Press).

Deane, P (1962) *Abstract of British Historical Statistics* (Cambridge, Cambridge University Press).

Demolombe, C (1854) *Du Mariage et de la Separation de Corps* (Paris).

Dicey, AV (1914) *Lectures on the Relation between Law and Public Opinion in England during the Nineteenth Century*, 2nd edn (London, Macmillan).

Doggett, ME (1993) *Marriage, Wife-Beating and the Law in Victorian England* (South Carolina University Press).

Ellis, SM (1931) *Henry Kingsley 1830–1876: Towards a Vindication* (London).

Erikson, A (1993) *Women and Property in Early Modern England* (Abingdon, Routledge).

Eversley, WP (1885) *The Law of Domestic Relations* (London).

Farnie, DA (1979) *The English Cotton Industry and the World Market, 1815–1896* (Oxford, Oxford University Press).

Feinstein, CH (1972) *Statistical Tables of National Income, Expenditure and Output of the United Kingdom, 1855–1965* (Cambridge, Cambridge University Press).

Foyster, E (2005) *Marital Violence: An English Family History, 1660–1857* (Cambridge, Cambridge University Press).

Fraser, A (2022) *The Case of the Married Woman: Caroline Norton and Her Fight for Women's Justice* (London, Pegasus Books).

Fraser, D (1976) *Urban Politics in Victorian England* (Leicester, Leicester University Press).

—— (1979) *Power and Authority in the Victorian City* (Oxford, Blackwell).

Friedman, W (ed) (1955) *Matrimonial Property Law* II (London, Stevens).

Fry, E (1858) *Treatise on the Specific Performance of Contracts* (London).

Gaskell, E (1885) *North and South* (London).

Gillis, JR (1985) *For Better, for Worse: British Marriages, 1600 to the Present* (Oxford, Oxford University Press).

Graveson, RH and Crane, FR (eds) (1957) *A Century of Family Law, 1857–1957* (London, Sweet and Maxwell).

Hammerton, AJ (1992) *Cruelty and Companionship: Conflict in Nineteenth Century Married Life* (Abingdon, Routledge).

Harding, M (2025) *From Catholic Outlook to Modern State Regulation: Developing Understandings of Marriage in Ireland* (Cambridge, Intersentia).

Heuston, RVF (1987) *Lives of the Lord Chancellors, 1940–1970* (Oxford, Clarendon Press).

Hewitt, M (1958) *Wives and Mothers in Victorian Industry* (London, Rockliff).

Hirst, FW (1927) *Early Life and Letters of John Morley* (London, Macmillan).

Hoggett, B and Pearl, D (1991) *The Family, Law and Society: Cases and Materials*, 3rd edn (London, Butterworths).

Holcombe, L (1983) *Wives and Property: Reform of Married Women's Property Law in Nineteenth Century England* (Oxford, University of Toronto Press).

Hollams, J (1906) *Jottings of an Old Solicitor* (London).

Hunt, E (1973) *Regional Wage Variations in Britain, 1830–1914* (Oxford, Oxford University Press).

Joyce, P (1980) *Work, Society and Politics: the Culture of the Factory in Later Victorian England* (Harvester Press, Brighton).

Kay, AC (2009) *The Foundations of Female Entrepreneurship: Enterprise, Home and Household in London, c. 1800–1870* (Abingdon, Routledge).

Kha, H (2021) *A History of Divorce Law: Reform in England from the Victorian to Interwar Years* (Abingdon, Routledge).

Kirk, H (1976) *Portrait of a Profession: A History of the Solicitor's Profession, 1100 to the Present Day* (London, Oyez Publishing).

Liddell, AGC (1911) *Notes from the Life of an Ordinary Mortal* (London).

Lieck, A (1938) *Bow Street World* (London, Robert Hale).

Lowe, WJ (1989) *The Irish in Mid-Victorian Lancashire: The Shaping of a Working-class Community* (New York, Peter Lang).

Luddy, M and O'Dowd, M (2020) *Marriage in Ireland 1600–1925* (Cambridge, Cambridge University Press).

Lush, M (1884) *The Law of Husband and Wife Within the Jurisdiction of the Queen's Bench And Chancery Divisions* (London, Kessinger).

Macqueen, JF (1858) *A Practical Treatise on Divorce and Matrimonial Jurisdiction Under the Act of 1857 and New Orders* (London, W Maxwell).

—— (1848) *The Rights and Liabilities of Husband and Wife at Law and in Equity* (London).

Miles J, Monk, D and Probert, R (eds) (2019) *Fifty Years of the Divorce Reform Act 1969* (Oxford, Hart Publishing).

Milne, JD (1857) *Industrial and Social Position of Women in the Middle and Lower Ranks* (London).

—— (1870) *Industrial Employment of Women* (London).

Mitchell, G (ed) (1968) *The Hard Way Up: The Autobiography of Hannah Mitchell, Suffragette and Rebel* (London, Faber and Faber).

Morley, J (1917) *Recollections* (London, Macmillan).

Nash, TA (1888) *The Life of Richard Lord Westbury* (London).

Oke, GC (1868) *The Magisterial Formulist: Being a Complete Collection of Forms and Precedents for Practical Use by Magistrates, their Clerks, Attorneys and Constables* (London).

—— (1893) *Oke's Magisterial Synopsis*, 14th edn (edited by SH Lushington) (London, Butterworths).

Perkins, JG (1910) *The Life of Mrs Norton* (London).

Phillips, N (2006) *Women in Business, 1700–1850* (Woodbridge, Boydell and Brewer).

Poovey, M (1988) *Uneven Developments: The Ideological Work of Gender in Mid-Victorian England* (University of Chicago Press).

Popp, A (2012) *Entrepreneurial Families: Business, Marriage and Life in the Early Nineteenth Century* (London, Pickering and Chatto).

Rayden, W (1910) *Practice and Law in the Divorce Division of the High Court of Justice and on Appeal Therefrom* (London, Butterworth).

Reeve, H (ed) (1911) *The Greville Memoirs* (8 vols) (London).

Roberts, JR (ed) (1907) *Stone's Justices' Manual*, 39th edn (London, Butterworths).

Rolt, Sir J (1939) *Memoirs of the Right Hon. Sir John Rolt* (privately printed).

Saunders, TW (1858) *The Practice of Magistrates' Courts*, 2nd edn (London).

Schneider, WE (2016) *Engines of Truth: Producing Veracity in the Victorian Courtroom*, (New Haven, Yale University Press).

Shanley, ML (1989) *Feminism, Marriage and the Law in Victorian England* (Princeton University Press).

Simpson, AWB (1984) *A Biographical Dictionary of Common Law* (London, Butterworths).

Smith, BLB (1854) *A Brief Summary in Plain Language of the Most Important Laws Concerning Women; Together with a Few Observations Thereon* (London).

Snell, KDM (1985) *Annals of the Labouring Poor: Social Change and Agrarian England, 1660–1900* (Cambridge University Press).

Spring, E (1993) *Law, Land and Family: Aristocratic Inheritance in England, 1300 to 1800* (Chapel Hill, University of North Carolina Press).

St Leonards, E (1858) *A Handy Book Of Property Law in a Series of Letters* (London, William Blackwood & Sons).

Steadman Jones, G (1984 edn) *Outcast London: Study in the Relationship Between Classes in Victorian Society* (Oxford, Oxford University Press).

Stebbings, C (2002) *The Private Trustee in Victorian England* (Cambridge, Cambridge University Press).

Stephenson, Sir G (1854) *Magisterial Reform suggested in a Letter to Viscount Palmerston* (London).

Stone, L (1990) *Road to Divorce England 1530-1987* (Oxford, Oxford University Press).

—— (1993) *Broken Lives: Separation and Divorce in England 1660-1857* (Oxford, Oxford University Press).

Strahan, JA (1919) *The Bench and Bar of England* (Edinburgh).

Thicknesse, R (1884) *A Digest of the Law of Husband and Wife as it Affects Property* (London).

Timmins, GT (1993) *The Last Shift: The Decline of Handloom Weaving in Nineteenth Century Lancashire* (Manchester, Manchester University Press).

Wakelam, A (2020) *Credit and Debt in Eighteenth-Century England: An Economic History of Debtors' Prisons* (Abingdon, Routledge).

White, W (1898) *The Inner Life of the House of Commons* (London).

Whittle, PA (1852) *Blackburn As It Is: A Topographical, Statistical, and Historical Account* (Blackburn).

Williams, M (1894) *Later Leaves: Being the Further Reminiscences of Montagu Williams, Q.C.* (London).

Wood, JC (2004) *Violence and Crime in Nineteenth Century England: The Shadow of our Refinement* (Abingdon, Routledge).

Chapters in Edited Volumes

Aston, J and Bishop, C (2020) 'Discovering a Global Perspective' in Aston, J and Bishop, C (eds) *Female Entrepreneurs in the Long Nineteenth Century* (London, Palgrave Macmillan) 1–31.

Burke, G (1986) 'The Decline of the Independent Bal Maiden: The Impact of Change in the Cornish Mining Industry' in John, A (ed), *Unequal Opportunities: Women's Employment in England, 1800-1918* (Oxford, Blackwell) 179–206.

Conaghan, J (2018) 'A Brief Summary of the Most Important Laws Concerning Women by Barbara Leigh Smith Bodichon, 1854' in Rackley, E and Auchmuty, R (eds) *Women's Legal Landmarks: Celebrating the History of Women and Law in the UK and Ireland* (London, Bloomsbury Publishing) 55–61.

Heggie, J (2019) 'Women's Involvement in Property in the North Riding of Yorkshire in the Eighteenth and Nineteenth Centuries' in Capern A, McDonagh, B and Aston, J (eds) *Women and the Land 1500-1900* (Woodbridge, Boydell and Brewer) 201–25.

Humpherys, A (1990) 'Popular Narrative and Political Discourse in Reynold's Newspaper' in Brake, L, Jones, A and Madden, L (eds) *Investigating Victorian Journalism* (London, Palgrave Macmillan).

Minor, I (1979) 'Working Class Women and Matrimonial Law Reform, 1890-1914' in Martin, D and Rubinstein, D (eds), *Ideologies and the Labour Movement* (London, Croom Helm) 103–24.

Ross, E (1989) '"Fierce Questions and Taunts" Married Life in Working-Class London, 1870-1914' in Feldman, D and Stedman Jones, G (eds) *Metropolis: London, Histories and Representations since 1800* (London, Routledge) 219–44.

Savage, G (1992) '"Intended Only for the Husband": Gender, Class, and the Provision for Divorce in England, 1858-1868' in Ottesen Garrigen, K (ed) *Victorian Scandals: Representations of Gender and Class* (Athens, OH, Ohio University Press) 11–42.

Southall, H (1991) 'Poor Law Statistics and the Geography of Economic Distress' in Foreman Peck, J (ed) *New Perspectives on the Late Victorian Economy: Essays in Quantitative Economic History, 1860-1914* (Cambridge, Cambridge University Press) 180–217.

Journal Articles

Abram, WA (1868) 'The Social Position and Political Prospects of the Lancashire Workman' 4 *Fortnightly Review* 426–41.

Anderson, O (1997) 'Emigration and Marriage Break-up in Mid-Victorian England' 163 *Economic History Review* 104–109.

—— (1997) 'Hansard's Hazard's' 112 *Economic History Review* 1202–15.

—— (1999) 'State, Civil Society and Separation in Victorian Marriage' 163 *Past & Present* 161–201.

Anonymous (1868) 'The Property of Married Women', 34 *Westminster Review*, 374–99.

Anonymous (1869) 'Property of Married Women' 12 *Meliora*, 51–60.

Anonymous (1883) 'Recollections of Lord Westbury' *Macmillan's Magazine* 47, 469–81.

Aston, J (2022) 'Petitions to the Court for Divorce and Matrimonial Causes: A New Methodological Approach to the History of Divorce, 1857–1923' 43 *Journal of Legal History* 161–86.

—— (2023) '"An Exceedingly Painful Case": The Aftermath of Divorce in Mid-Nineteenth Century England and Wales' 26 *Family & Community History* 71–91.

Aston, J and Di Martino, P (2017) 'Risk, Success, and Failure: Female Entrepreneurship in Late Victorian and Edwardian England' 70 *Economic History Review* 837–58.

Aston, J, Capern, A and McDonagh, B (2019) 'More Than Bricks and Mortar: Female Property Owner-ship as Economic Strategy in Mid-Nineteenth-Century Urban England' 46 *Urban History* 695–721.

Aston, J et al (2022) 'Take Nothing For Granted: Expanding the Conversation About Business, Gender, and Feminism' 66 *Business History* 93–106.

Beauchamp, V (1899) 'The Woman's Century' 15 *The Humanitarian* 271–72.

Becker, L (1879) 'On the Progress of the Movement for the Enfranchisement of Women' (Manchester Meeting) *Transactions of the National Association for the Promotion of Social Sciences* 215–18.

—— (1880) 'Property of Married Women: Discussion' (Edinburgh Meeting) *Transactions of the National Association for the Promotion of Social Sciences* 191–205.

Begiato, J (2018) 'Beyond the Rule of Thumb' 15 *Cultural and Social History* 39–59.

—— (2023) 'A "Master-Mistress": Revisiting the History of Eighteenth-Century Wives' (2023) 32 *Women's History Review* 1–20.

Benenson, H (1993) 'Patriarchal Constraints on Women Workers' Mobilization: The Lancashire Female Cotton Operatives 1842–1919' 44 *The British Journal of Sociology*, 613–33.

Bourke, J (1994) 'Housewifery in Working-Class England, 1860–1914' 143 *Past & Present* 167–97.

Cobbe, FP (1868) 'Criminals, Idiots, Women and Minors' 78 *Fraser's Magazine* 777–94.

Davis, J (1984) 'A Poor Man's System of Justice: the London Police Courts in the Second Half of the Nineteenth Century' 27 *Historical Journal* 309–35.

Eknoyan, G (1997) 'A History of Edema and its Management' 59 *Kidney International* 118–26.

Frost, G (1994) '"I Shall Not Sit Down and Crie": Women, Class, and Breach of Promise of Marriage Plaintiffs in England, 1850–1900' 6 *Gender and History* 224–45.

—— (2020) 'Vindictiveness on Account of Colour'?: Race, Gender, and Class at the English Divorce Court, 1872–1939' 4 *Genealogy* 82–99.

Fulcher, J (1994) 'Gender, Politics and Class in the Early Nineteenth Century English Reform Move-ment' 67 *Historical Research* 57.

Griffin, B (2020) 'Paternal Rights, Child Welfare and The Law in Nineteenth Century Britain and Ireland' 246 *Past & Present* 109–47.

Hobhouse, A (1870) 'On the Forfeiture of Property by Married Women 7 *Fortnightly Review* 181–86.

Horrell, S and Humphries, J (1992) 'Women's Labour Force Participation and the Transition to the Male Breadwinner Family, 1790–1865' 48 *Economic History Review* 89–117.

—— (1997) 'The Origins and Expansion of the Male Breadwinner Family: the Case of Nineteenth Century Britain' 42 (supplement 5) *International Review of Social History* 25–64.

Horrell, S, Humphries, J and Weisdorf, J (2021) 'Family Standards of Living Over the Long-Run, England 1280–1850' (2021) 87 *Past and Present* 87–134.

—— (2022) 'Beyond the Male Breadwinner: Life-Cycle Living Standards of Intact and Disrupted English Working Families, 1260–1850' 75 *Economic History Review* 530–80.

Hughes, A (2010) 'The 'Non-Criminal Class: Wife-Beating in Scotland (c.1800–1949) 14 *Crime, Histoire & Sociétés / Crime, History & Societies* 31–53.

Humphries, J (2013) The Lure of Aggregates and the Pitfalls of the Patriarchal Perspective: A Critique of the High Wage Economy Interpretation of the British Industrial Revolution 66 *Economic History Review* 693–714.

Hurl-Eamon, J (2001) 'Domestic Violence Prosecuted: Women Binding over Their Husbands for Assault at Westminster Quarter Sessions, 1685–1720' 26 *Journal of Family History* 435–54.

—— (2014) 'Did Soldiers Really Enlist to Desert Their Wives? Revisiting the Martial Character of Marital Desertion in Eighteenth-Century London' 53 *Journal of British Studies* 35–77.

Johnson, GJ and Cookson, WS (1868) 'Property of Women' *Transactions of the National Association for the Promotion of Social Sciences* 275–81.

Jones, P, King, S and Thompson, K (2021) 'Clothing the New Poor Law Workhouse in the Nineteenth Century' 32 *Rural History* 127–48.

Kahn-Freund, O (1952) 'Inconsistencies and Injustices in the Law of Husband and Wife' (1952) *MLR* 15, 133–54.

—— (1970) 'Recent Legislation on Matrimonial Property' 33 *MLR* 601–31.

Kaye, JW (1857) 'The Marriage and Divorce Bill' 27 *North British Review* 164–67.

Kent, DA (1990) '"Gone for a Soldier": Family Breakdown and the Demography of Desertion in a London Parish, 1750–1791' 45 *Local Population Studies* 27–40.

King, S (2010) 'Love, Religion and Power in the Making of Marriages in Early Nineteenth-Century Rural Industrial Lancashire' 21 *Rural History* 1–26.

Macmillan, C (2005) 'Rogues, Swindlers and Cheats: The Development of Mistake of Identity in English Contract Law' 64 *Cambridge Law Journal* 711–44.

Morgan, C (1992) 'Women, Work and Work Consciousness in the Mid-Nineteenth Century English Cotton Industry' 17 *Social History* 23–41.

O'Reilly, C (2020) 'Creating A Critical Civic Consciousness' 26 *Media History* 249–62.

Ogbom, M (1992) 'Local Power and State Regulation in Late Nineteenth Century Bristol' 17 *Transactions* 215–26.

Philips, D (1975) 'The Black Country Magistracy, 1835–60' 3 *Midland History* 161–90.

Pimm-Smith, R and Probert, R (2018) 'Evaluating Marital Stability in Late-Victorian Camberwell' 21 *Family & Community History* 38–50.

Poovey, M (1988) 'Covered but Not Bound: Caroline Norton and the 1857 Matrimonial Causes Act' 14 *Feminist Studies* 467–85.

Power Cobbe, F (April 1878) 'Wife Torture in England' 32 *Contemporary Review* 55–87.

Probert, R (2022) 'Escaping Detection: Illegal Second Marriages and the Crime of Bigamy' 6 *Journal of Genealogy and Family History* 27–33.

Rosser, AS (2013) 'Businessmen in the Parliament of 1852–7: Players or Spectators?' 32 *Parliamentary History* 477–505.

Savage, G (1983) 'The Operation of the 1857 Divorce Act, 1860–1910 a Research Note' 16 *Journal of Social History* 103–10.

—— (1988) 'Divorce and the Law in England and France Prior to the First World War' 21 *Journal of Social History* 499–513.

—— (2011) 'They Would if They Could: Class, Gender and Popular Representation of English Divorce Litigation, 1858–1908' 36 *Journal of Family History* 173–90.

Sharpe, P (1990) 'Marital Separation in the Eighteenth and early Nineteenth Centuries' 45 *Local Population Studies* 66–70.

Shepard, A and Stretton, T (2019) 'Women Negotiating the Boundaries of Justice in Britain, 1300–1700: An Introduction' 58 *Journal of British Studies* 677–83.

Snell, KDM and Millar, J (1987) 'Lone-Parent Families and the Welfare State: Past and Present' 2 *Continuity and Change* 387–422.

Solly, J (1880) 'Further Amendment to the Divorce Act of 20 and 21 Vict., c.85' (Edinburgh Meeting) *Transactions of the National Association for the Promotion of Social Sciences* 267–68.

Taylor, H (1870) 'Mr Mill on the Subjection of Women' 50 *Fraser's Magazine* 143–65.

van Lieshout, C, Smith, H and Bennett, RJ (2019) 'Female Entrepreneurship: Business, Marriage and Motherhood In England and Wales, 1851–1911' 44 *Social History* 440–68.

Vickery, A (1993) 'Golden Age to Separate Spheres? A Review of the Categories and Chronology of English Women's History' 36 *The Historical Journal* 383–414.

Williams, G (1947) 'The Legal Unity of Husband and Wife' 10 *MLR* 16–31.

Wolfram, S (1985) 'Divorce in England 1700–1857' 5 *OJLS* 55–186.

Wolstenholme, E (1870) 'On The Married Women's Property Act' (Newcastle Upon Tyne Meeting) *Transactions of the National Association for the Promotion of Social Sciences* 549–51.

Wood, GH (1910) 'The Statistics of Wages in the Nineteenth Century. Part XIX.--The Cotton Industry' 73 *Journal of the Royal Statistical Society* 585–66.

Wright, DC (2002) 'The Crisis of Child Custody: A History of the Birth of Family Law in England' 11 *Journal of Gender and Law* 175–270.

—— (2004) 'Untying the Knot: An Analysis of the English Divorce and Matrimonial Causes Court Records, 1858-1866' 38 *University of Richmond Law Review* 903–1010.

—— (2004) 'Well-Behaved Women Don't Make History: Rethinking Family, Law, and History' 19 *Wisconsin Women's Law Journal* 212–315.

You, X (2020) 'Women's Labour Force Participation in Nineteenth-century England and Wales: Evidence from the 1881 Census Enumerators' Books' 73 *Economic History Review* 106–33.

Other

Dictionnaire de Biographie Française (1965).

Fryar, GJ (2022) *Suffering or Fallen Angels? Wife-Beating in Victorian Liverpool 1850–1889: Class, Cause and Community Response* (The Open University, Unpublished MA Thesis).

Hart, P (2016) 'Joseph Harris Smallman' 25 *Te Aroha Mining District Working Papers, The University of Waikato*, 1–34.

Norton, CS (1854) *English Laws for Women in the Nineteenth Century* (London).

—— (1855) *A Letter to the Queen on Lord Chancellor Cranworth's Marriage and Divorce Bill* (London, Longman, Brown, Green and Longmans).

Probert, R (2013) 'Double Trouble: The Rise and Fall of the Crime of Bigamy', Selden Society Lecture Delivered in the Old Hall of Lincoln's Inn (8 July).

Ranyard, D (2019) *'Decree Nisi with Costs, My Lord?': A Study of Divorce in England and Wales, 1909-37* (University of Lincoln, unpublished PhD thesis).

Simon, J (1964) 'With All My Worldly Goods', paper given to the Holdsworth Club of the University of Birmingham.

The London Medical Directory 1845.

The London Post Office Directory 1851.

Victoria County History, *County of Lancaster VI* (London, 1911).

INDEX